MW00615944

THE
INCORRUPTIBLES

ALSO BY DAN SLATER

Love in the Time of Algorithms

Wolf Boys

THE
INCORRUPTIBLES

A TRUE STORY OF KINGPINS,
CRIME BUSTERS, AND THE BIRTH
OF THE AMERICAN UNDERWORLD

DAN SLATER

LITTLE, BROWN AND COMPANY
New York Boston London

Little, Brown and Company
Hachette Book Group
1290 Avenue of the Americas, New York, NY 10104
littlebrown.com

First Edition: July 2024

Little, Brown and Company is a division of Hachette Book Group, Inc. The Little, Brown name and logo are trademarks of Hachette Book Group, Inc.

The publisher is not responsible for websites (or their content) that are not owned by the publisher.

The Hachette Speakers Bureau provides a wide range of authors for speaking events. To find out more, go to hachettespeakersbureau.com or email hachettespeakers@hbgusa.com.

Little, Brown and Company books may be purchased in bulk for business, educational, or promotional use. For information, please contact your local bookseller or the Hachette Book Group Special Markets Department at special.markets@hbgusa.com.

ISBN 9780316427715
LCCN 2023951854

Printing 1, 2024

LSC-C

Printed in the United States of America

For Silas & Felix

In those days there was no king in Israel;
everyone did what was right in his own eyes.

—Judges 21:25

Table of Contents

Table of Contents

Author's Note

Scenes and dialogue in this book are drawn from a constellation of sources. While some materials, such as archived documents and trial transcripts, were created more or less contemporaneously with the events they describe, other accounts, including memoirs and oral histories, were rendered years or decades after the fact, and are thus based on faded memory. When such narratives contain an abundance of detail, it's reasonable to assume that they may have been styled or modified by their authors for effect. I've just quoted what I found.

THE INCORRUPTIBLES

Prologue

After midnight on July 16, 1912, a gambler and casino owner named Herman Rosenthal ate dinner alone in the Metropole Hotel in Times Square. Rosenthal, a dapper man with dark wavy hair and a strong jawline, wore the self-assured grin of someone who could handle himself on the streets of prewar New York. Suit coat off, shirt unbuttoned at the collar, he swabbed his face with a silk handkerchief. Fans had been running all day in the hotel lobby but the air was still oppressive, the summer of 1912 being the hottest on record. He finished his steak, walked to the entrance, and bought several newspapers. Back at his table, he read the *World* headline and smiled: GAMBLER CHARGES POLICE LIEUTENANT WAS HIS PARTNER.

The piano player belted out another ragtime hit, singing, "Oh, you beautiful doll, you great big beautiful doll..."

As Rosenthal scanned the *World* piece, admiring his handiwork, a fellow gambler entered the restaurant and told Rosenthal that someone wanted to see him outside. As if this was the summons he'd been waiting for, he dabbed the corners of his mouth and slapped a dollar on the table to cover the eighty-cent bill. On the Metropole steps, beneath the lights of Broadway, he clutched a cigar in one hand, newspapers in the other, and waited, unaware that he'd set in motion the end of a criminal era.

A gray Packard screeched to a halt, four gunmen emerged, and pistol shots hit Rosenthal in the neck and head. As the Packard charged away, the gambler who had summoned Rosenthal bent at the waist, hands in pockets. "Hello, Herman," he said, then straightened up. "Goodbye, Herman."

In the New York City of 1912, murders occurred daily. The day after Rosenthal's murder, two men went into a barbershop on East Tenth Street and shot a customer. A few hours later, a craps-game proprietor was shot ten times on Second Avenue. In only one-third of such murders was anyone arrested. Of those arrested, only 10 percent were convicted. Many homicides didn't even make the newspapers.

But if these gamblers thought that killing Herman Rosenthal would solve their problems, they were mistaken. The unique circumstances surrounding the murder—namely, the alleged involvement of a cop; an ambitious district attorney; and the fact that Rosenthal had given a confession to that district attorney regarding that cop hours before he was killed—caused the case to become a global sensation. It received more attention than any crime ever had in the city, staying on front pages of papers for the next three years.

In the end, though, the Rosenthal case would be more relevant for what it incited than for how the case itself was resolved. In its shadow, a more important story played out, one that was largely hidden from view when it happened, and later buried by history.

Part One

Nobility in Dollar Land

1

Between Worlds

A S A BOY, ARNOLD ROTHSTEIN DIDN'T LIKE SCHOOL, because the teachers thought they knew more than he did. Arnold spent his time devising schemes to offset that superiority, such as teaching fellow students dice games and amazing them with calculations of odds in a flash. Math was the only subject that interested Arnold.

New York in the 1890s was a place where a boy with a brain for numbers could put that talent to use on the streets. The city was "wide open," largely unregulated, and gambling was everywhere. The Rothsteins moved often, living all over Manhattan. From home bases on Henry Street and Mercer, in Gramercy Park and Harlem, on West End Avenue and Lexington, Arnold would roam the city, impulsively gathering the rules and schemes for every game he came across: the slight edge of betting against the dice roller; the odds of a hard four. By fifth grade he was two years behind in school, and soon his younger brother caught up with him.

But it was Arnold's older brother, Bertie, who inspired his resentment. A devoted student and Talmud scholar, Bertie was a near-perfect

7

clone of their perfect father, Abraham Rothstein, the pious owner of A. E. Rothstein, a cotton-goods wholesaler that supplied garment manufacturers. Abraham Rothstein was known as Abe the Just for his philanthropy, his regard for labor unions, and his ability to mediate industrial disputes. Annually he gave away between one-fourth and three-fourths of his earnings, and he sat on the board of Beth Israel Hospital, which treated immigrants and the poor for free. Years later, when a skeptical journalist wondered about the veracity of such a sainted reputation and decided to interview people who knew the man, the journalist reported, "The reaction was always the same: A. E. Rothstein was a splendid character." A splendid character to friends and colleagues, and a difficult act to follow for the second son.

"Why not be more like your brother?" Abe the Just often asked Arnold, reiterating that gambling was a sin. "You should be proud of being a Jew."

"Who cares about that stuff?" Arnold said. "I'm an American. Let Bertie be a Jew."

A natural leader, outgoing and upbeat, Bertie was a boy of easy laughter in a way that Arnold could never be, at least not genuinely. Arnold didn't like his own appearance. He was a pudgy child. His chalky cheeks never took on color, and he had a soft row of upper teeth that chipped easily. And yet when he gambled, none of that mattered.

Arnold, born in 1882, gravitated to his downtown birthplace, the Lower East Side ghetto, known simply as the East Side, where he played dice and poker with young strays, the children of immigrants. Like many of these kids, Arnold came from Russian-Jewish ancestry, but his was a rare circumstance. His Russian grandfather, Harris Rothstein, emigrated to America in the 1840s, during the era of the German-Jewish immigration, and built a legacy garment business that he left to his sons, Arnold's father and uncles. In the 1860s and '70s, when Abe the Just was growing up, there were only a handful of Jews in New York and they stuck together. The father's house, the mother's table — that, and the community around them — was their little world.

When Abe the Just started his adult life, with an arranged marriage to the daughter of an Orthodox family from San Francisco, he tried to pass those values on, but discovered that his father had been able to exert more influence on him than Abe the Just was able to exert on his own children in the late 1800s, as the city modernized and the pace of life sped up. The Rothsteins moved out of the East Side at the same time that new waves of Eastern European Jewish refugees began to arrive. By the 1890s, the garment industry in New York became the domain of these refugees, and the word "sweatshop" came into use on the East Side.

Now, the parents of Arnold's East Side friends were these new immigrants, bewildered men and women who worked sixteen-hour days in unventilated spaces, where they tried not to contract tuberculosis or go blind from staring at needlework in the dark. They'd made it to America, but they remained stranded between worlds: between the largest ghetto in history — the Pale of Settlement, those provinces along Russia's western border where Jews were slaughtered in pogroms, or massacres — and what would soon become the most crowded ghetto in history, the East Side of New York. Their children, born either in Eastern Europe or on the East Side, were hard-eyed and rough, estranged from their Yiddish-speaking parents. In these families, the children formed a kind of advance guard: They were the first to learn English, the first to abandon old-world practices and embrace the commercialized ideal of modern American life, even if that life felt impossibly distant for poor strangers who were derided as coming from inferior stock. A common result of this chasm was a feeling of shame and anger, and it was on this ground that Arnold, despite his air of entitlement, related to the ghetto crowd.

He befriended an older boy named Herman Rosenthal. Born in Odessa, a rough port city on the Black Sea, located at the southern end of the Pale of Settlement, Herman was fast on his feet and took care of bullies. On the East Side, Herman was part of a group of young Jewish gamblers. He introduced Arnold to these people, the first generation of Jewish criminals in New York, and to a powerful Tammany Hall politician named Tim Sullivan.

Like many Tammany Hall honchos of his vintage, "Big Tim" Sullivan started out as a gang leader, then became a saloon owner who accrued power by gathering votes for Tammany, and finally a state senator at age twenty-nine. Big Tim's face was well known to New Yorkers. A lithograph of that face — red-cheeked, blue-eyed, smiling — adorned coffee houses and saloons and hung over the mantels of tenement flats like a reigning sovereign. His name was plastered everywhere, on advertisements and political posters and tour boats that carried constituents to free parties, picnics, and barbecues.

Big Tim's Tammany Hall subsumed the Democratic Party in New York, the country's most populous Democratic state. For decades Tammany had ruled the city, empowered not by any political agenda — it had none — but by a base of immigrants whom Tammany served with patronage jobs, impunity for crime, and day-to-day welfare needs not yet provided by formal government, such as shoes and coal, beer and meals. Immigrants, in turn, guaranteed the survival of Tammany on election day, through voter fraud and intimidation. In the 1890s, Tammany was losing its old voter base of Irish and German immigrants, but Big Tim was adept at capturing the votes of the new immigrants. He attended bar mitzvahs and provided food for Passover feasts. Big Tim could get your kid out of jail and into college and law school, then bring him back to the East Side to function as a cog in a graft system designed to keep criminals on the street, earning money.

When it came to crime, Big Tim Sullivan knew talent when he saw it. He was charmed by the speed and elegance of the craps game Arnold and Herman ran, in which money might change hands six times in a minute. Their sidewalk action helped bring business into Big Tim's "poolroom," a place where lottery tickets were sold and off-track betting was offered.

"You're smart Jew boys," he told Arnold and Herman, "and you'll make out as gamblers. That business takes brains."

Arnold fed off these words. He loved to shine, and he delighted in defying the law in order to do so. His chalky cheeks and soft teeth stuck with him, but he grew into a slim and handsome teenager who, at five foot seven, moved with what one observer called "pantherish quickness" and "catlike suavity."

At fifteen, he went on the road as a salesman for his father's company, but it didn't always go well. In Chicago he lost his expense money in a high-stakes game of pinochle. And then tragedy struck. He was in Erie when he got the news that his older brother, Bertie, had died of pneumonia. Arnold thought of the times he'd wished Bertie dead, and wondered if all that wishing had at last killed him. This guilt forced a resolution: Arnold would return home, go to synagogue, and work for his father full time. He decided to leave the underworld behind and *become* Bertie, replacing his brother in his parents' affections. But it wasn't so easy. Six years earlier, the Rothsteins had lost one of Arnold's sisters, also to pneumonia, at age four. The death of Bertie, their oldest child and family pride, tipped them into a remote, all-consuming grief.

That Arnold loved his parents dearly, and on some level desperately wanted Abe the Just's approval, only stoked his resentment. Their rejection of him, whether perceived or real, unleashed sensitive anger and hypervigilant energy, creating a part of Arnold that would do anything to make the winning mark his father made, even if it meant mixing generosity with avarice, and compassion with coldhearted selfishness. After a month of being ignored, Arnold packed his bags and vowed never to live at home again. He did take something with him, though: Bertie's famous laugh.

For Arnold, the Bertie laugh came off as a surface demonstration, a movement of facial muscles synchronized with a sound, but he'd work on the laugh, and each year it would become more convincing.

He moved into the Broadway Central Hotel, a popular lodging spot for indigent gamblers and grifters, and got a job selling cigars at hotels and saloons. He was wide-eyed and genial. He could smile broadly and chat amiably about unimportant things. His habit of listening closely to people's stories made him an effective salesman, and he averaged $100 a week. He added to his bankroll by taking up billiards. With his skillful hands and quick movements, Arnold was a natural, and this new endeavor brought him into contact with famous athletes, such as ballplayers, horse jockeys, and boxing champs. The emerging celebrity culture of Broadway, a culture that would eventually coalesce around a new place called Times Square, paid special tribute to such people: the *best* jockey, the *best* writer, the *best* producer. Arnold wanted to secure himself a place in this hierarchy, and felt he could do so by becoming the best gambler.

In the summer of 1898, when Arnold was sixteen, he stood on the corner of Fifth Avenue and Forty-Fourth Street, where his idol, Richard Canfield, the country's leading gambler, was spending an unheard-of half-million dollars to renovate a brownstone for a new casino. For Canfield, an art collector and bibliophile, 4 East Forty-Fourth Street was to be his grandest gambling palace yet. There would be Whistler paintings and rare Chinese porcelains. Every night a free supper would be brought in from Delmonico's, known as America's first restaurant, which was right around the corner. As Arnold watched workmen install teak floors and white mahogany walls, he knew that becoming the next Canfield was what he wanted in life: entrance into the exalted demimonde, a world of high-stakes vice beyond the cheap casinos, fixed boxing matches, and lowly sidewalk action of the East Side ghetto.

To get there, he needed to grow his bankroll, but when Arnold traveled to the racetrack in Saratoga Springs and tried to break into the then-legal bookmaking business, he found that Jews were locked out of the Metropolitan Turf Association, the group of organized bookmakers known as the Mets. The Mets, patrician bookmakers whose lapel buttons sold like seats on a stock exchange, formed an exclusive cartel of bookies who handled betting at all New York racetracks. Since reformers were always trying to eradicate gambling at the track, these bookmakers argued that it was critical to avoid open disputes, and that admitting loud and pushy Jews into their ranks risked hastening their demise.

Relegated to the second tier of bookies, Arnold tried to attract business by offering better odds than the Mets. It was a tough hustle. He racked up debt and fled back to the city. He set up an illegal off-track betting parlor on Forty-Seventh Street and Broadway, an area that beat cops dubbed the Tenderloin for the plush graft money it generated. Up there, the "big smokes," the old-line casino owners from Canfield's cohort, catered to the "swell play." But Jewish gamblers weren't welcome in the Tenderloin either, and when an anonymous letter tipped off the police, Arnold's off-track betting parlor was raided. He told the cops that the place was his "bachelor apartment." But while he tried to explain why the floor was covered in betting charts, gambling clientele knocked on the door and telephones rang with race results, and his operation was shut down.

Arnold could still play billiards and organize roving games of craps and poker, but the lofty underworld that he dreamed of joining remained mostly Protestant, and closed to Jews. That world, however, was tilting.

2

The Crusading Path

ON A SPRING DAY IN 1897, A SIX-YEAR-OLD BOY NAMED Abraham Shoenfeld heard his name called outside. He hurried to the balcony of his apartment in New York's East Side ghetto, where the Shoenfelds lived in relative prosperity at 125 Clinton Street, in one of the neighborhood's first elevator buildings. From the balcony Abe looked left and right. Hundreds of garment workers poured into Clinton Street, shouting, "Shoenfeld! Shoenfeld! Shoenfeld!"

Inside the apartment, Abe's father, Mayer Shoenfeld, paced the floor and shook his head: "They can hound me all they like. I'd be crazy to do it again."

Mayer walked to the balcony and addressed the crowd of tailors in Yiddish. Their cheers turned to groans and hisses when he said that their labor strike was unlikely to succeed and he didn't think he could help them. He apologized. He wished them well, then turned his back and walked into the apartment. The afternoon faded. Tailors lingered on Clinton Street. Some couldn't believe that Mayer Shoenfeld was refusing to lead them. Others were homeless and had no place to go.

Abe went out to gather the newspapers, as he did each evening, and piled them next to Mayer's bed. The boy didn't grasp the economics of immigration and labor, or the intricacies of the garment business, but he knew the struggle he saw around him, and understood that progress in that struggle depended on the participation of people like his father, skilled Hungarian tailors who were in demand and didn't need to strike in order to get what they wanted, who lived in elevator buildings and rarely worried about putting food on the table. Without such leaders, it was thought, the labor movement would have no leverage. As father and son pored over the news, Abe said: "Poppa, if they're already out" — if the tailors had already decided to strike — "then why not help them win?"

Mayer had his reasons. Three years earlier, when he first emerged as a labor leader, newspapers characterized him as calm and understated. "He's a young Hungarian Hebrew of great intelligence, earnestness, and physical power," observed the *Sun,* noting he was "tall and thickset, with an open round face."

A crucial aspect of Mayer Shoenfeld's popularity was his defiance of East Side stereotypes — the savage Polish ghetto dweller, the hotheaded Russian socialist. He told the papers that his battle was not against the garment industry, per se, but its chewing up of workers: "I believe in better education, better homes, better wages, better working conditions — these are all that people need. I have no time to spend on theories."

Mayer's union, the Brotherhood of Tailors, grew. In the summer of 1895, he organized fifteen thousand workers in a walkout, said to be the largest of its kind on the East Side, while he negotiated terms with manufacturers: a pay raise, and a fifty-nine-hour workweek that ended in time for the Jewish Sabbath. The strike was a success, until December, when the busy season ended and employers went back on their promises. The next summer, Mayer convinced an unprecedented forty-five thousand workers to strike, but the result was the same. The busy season ended, employers reneged, and workers faced another winter without work or wages.

For Mayer, the stress of these contests was immense. He no longer looked like the bulky and successful tailor he'd been, but like the stooped and hollow-eyed tubercular masses he led. By the spring of 1897, when the striking tailors appeared beneath his balcony, Mayer felt that his energies were better spent on other social justice initiatives. But his son's urging put new ideas in his head: if he could convince enough workers to strike, not just in New York but in other cities, perhaps he might win more enduring commitments from factory owners.

During the next month, Mayer appeared in cities across the country, speaking to garment workers in Baltimore, Boston, Chicago, Rochester, and Syracuse. When manufacturers saw that a multicity strike was in the offing, they agreed to a substantial raise in wages.

It was another win, for the time being, but it came at a cost. When the Brotherhood of Tailors celebrated with a party, the orchestra, spying the Shoenfelds arriving, started up with "Hail to the Chief" — and that's when Mayer collapsed from a heart attack. SHOENFELD BREAKS DOWN, read the *World* headline. His doctor said the stress of being a union leader could kill him if he didn't quit.

The strike did bring other opportunities for Mayer. Foreign governments solicited his opinion about labor troubles in their own countries. Local political interests invited him to run for office. Patent-medicine firms asked to use Mayer's likeness in ads for hair restorers and pain expellers. He passed on all of them.

That summer, as Mayer recovered from the heart attack, there was a knock at 125 Clinton. Abe, opening the door, encountered a short man in a double-breasted cloak and a flower in his buttonhole. The visitor's white beard was neatly trimmed. His blue eyes sparkled. Abe recognized him from newspapers: the famous banker. Speaking in a clipped manner, his perfect English marred only by a lisp, he introduced himself as Jacob Schiff and asked if Mayer was at home.

* * *

Jacob Schiff was a German Jew who ran Wall Street's second-most-powerful investment bank, Kuhn Loeb, which he had inherited from his father-in-law. Unlike the Eastern European Jews who recently began immigrating to America as refugees, the German Jews had arrived earlier, in the mid-1800s. The German Jews fled from prejudice, but Jewish life there, thanks to a period of enlightenment, was not as bad as it was in Eastern Europe. In America, the German Jews assimilated and succeeded as bankers and captains of industry. They moved into mansions uptown, doled out charity to the poor, and worried about the fate of their downtown co-religionists, a group whose ranks were rapidly exceeding the German-Jewish population uptown.

By the late 1890s, Schiff, the uptown banker, and Mayer Shoenfeld, the East Side activist, represented the two wings of the country's nascent reform movement, a campaign that would reshape American society. The reform movement was national in scope, but it had begun to formalize here, on the East Side, earlier in the decade, following the 1890 publication of Jacob Riis's *How the Other Half Lives*. The book, a powerful work of photography and journalism, drove home the reality that New York was not one city but two, a city where history's greatest concentration of wealth resided miles away from history's greatest concentration of poverty. This revelation, and the fear it caused about instability, helped lead America's plutocrats to a surprising discovery: the laissez-faire system that had made them rich during the Gilded Age was also terrible for the country.

The problem wasn't their own fortunes, the plutocrats decided, but the ruthless competition that characterized the Gilded Age and set off a nasty causal chain: unregulated competition led to overproduction, overproduction led to price cuts, price cuts led to layoffs, layoffs led to social upheaval and labor strikes. It all amounted to a rapid boom-bust cycle that no nation could sustain. The bankers who ran Wall Street—a mix of Yankee Protestants like J. P. Morgan and German Jews like Jacob Schiff, whom the *New York Times* called "the Jewish J. P. Morgan"— believed they had a better alternative to competition: consolidation.

In the summer of 1897, when Schiff, the banking eminence, visited Mayer Shoenfeld, the ghetto activist, Wall Street was embarking on a colossal merger movement, which would later become known as the corporate reconstruction of American capitalism. During the next decade, bankers would merge thousands of competing companies into hundreds of megacorporations, or trusts, including United States Steel, the Standard Oil Trust, the Tobacco Trust, General Electric, and a consolidated railroad system. As Mike Wallace writes in *Greater Gotham: A History of New York City from 1898 to 1919,* this merger mania would afford the ruling class "an empowering sense of legitimacy," a belief that in solving the historic evil of competition, they'd saved the country.

But of course there was still a legitimacy problem—a giant wealth gap, a lack of labor laws, and no government welfare system. The country's growing proletariat could work themselves to death, literally, without any hope of achieving economic independence. Taking these facts into account, Schiff and other wealthy uptowners knew that business reform could not be uncoupled from "the social problem"—from crime, disease, illiteracy, overcrowding. So, for the masses down below, the immigrants whose toil and patterns of consumption helped make the American economy boom, the elite sought to carry out, in addition to business reform, *social* reform. "Their goal," writes Wallace, "was to alleviate the bad conditions without radically altering relations of power and property; they sought both social reform and social stability."

The German Jews from Schiff's uptown crowd were pioneers of the reform movement, using their untaxed wealth down on the East Side to build orphanages and reformatories, hospitals and employment bureaus. Nathan Straus, the German Jew whose family owned Macy's department store, focused on public health. Straus halved the death rate in the Infant Asylum by introducing pasteurized milk, then built his own pasteurization plant on East Third Street and opened milk stations around the city that sold milk for pennies, or gave it away. The German Jews built the United Hebrew Charities Building on Twenty-First Street, where the destitute could apply for relief, and financed Lillian Wald's Henry Street Settlement and her visiting nurse program.

If the German Jews led the way in reform, they also had more at stake than their Yankee Protestant counterparts. Ever since the Eastern European Jews began arriving, the German Jews worried that these unwashed co-religionists, with their Orthodox religiosity and radical politics, would undermine their own hard-won social respectability among the ruling patrician class. In building their fortunes, reputation had been everything for the German Jews, and now it was in jeopardy. Thus many of their reform efforts were aimed squarely at assimilating the downtown newcomers. The German Jews organized the Educational Alliance on East Broadway like a factory of Americanization. The *New York Times* called it "a center of civilization in parts of our town most given over to savagery."

To administer these programs, the elite reformers needed an on-the-ground army — settlement-house workers and teachers, nurses and doctors, and a class of professional politicians who could wrest power from Tammany Hall, loosening Tammany's grip on the immigrant population. The reform movement was shaping up to be a kind of civil war, a fight both within the Jewish community and American society at large for the future of the country. The war would require money and foot soldiers, Schiffs and Shoenfelds.

As Jacob Schiff and Mayer Shoenfeld spoke about ideas for betterment, Schiff proposed a "colonization scheme," an experiment in which Mayer would remove a community of tailors from the city to decongest the ghetto. Schiff had purchased land in the New Jersey countryside, and would fund a garment factory there as well as homes for 100 families. Mayer agreed, and for the next few years he and his son Abe — the second-youngest of Mayer and Dora Shoenfeld's six children, but the oldest son — commuted regularly between the East Side and Kenilworth, New Jersey.

These were golden years for Abe. In the country, he learned to fish, hunt, swing an axe, and raise livestock. "We lived in an area of deserted farms and abandoned orchards, the woods filled with chestnut and hickory, a road lined with black walnut, all sylvan and aromatic," he would later recall. During one memorable autumn, the workers voted to quit for the day when they heard that Jacob Schiff, in his high silk hat, had driven out to join them for Thanksgiving dinner. "After all," they said, "we are his nephews."

Back in the ghetto, Abe's best friend was Louie Rosenberg, who, like Abe, was the child of middle-class Hungarian-Jewish immigrants. Louie's father was a flour broker at the Produce Exchange, the commodities market on Beaver Street that architects considered one of the city's best structures, with a twenty-two-thousand-square-foot main hall that rose sixty feet to the skylit ceiling. Among Jewish immigrants, Hungarians, who represented 10 percent of the East Side population, came from a more progressive part of Eastern Europe than the Russians, Poles, Slavs, and Lithuanians. To the uptown German Jews, the refined Hungarians were familiar and approachable, but in the eyes of fellow downtowners they were aloof and toplofty, and Abe and Louie, with their talents and privileges, did little to alter that perception.

Abe and Louie played baseball in Seward Park and Hamilton Fish Park, which had been established as part of the reformers' "organized play movement," an attempt to keep immigrant children off the streets. They listened to the Enrico Caruso albums that Mayer brought home, the first commercial recordings of a major singing talent, and enjoyed father-son evenings at Little Hungary, a favorite Houston Street restaurant. There, among murals of menacing brigands and rural love scenes, the boys dined on beer soup and fried chicken and listened to their dads tell stories about their own childhoods in the old country.

But these good times didn't last long. Mayer's New Jersey colony, unable to sustain itself in isolation, folded in 1901, and the East Side's green spaces were soon flattened beneath a rate of immigration that now averaged a hundred thousand Eastern European Jews a year. Meanwhile, the East Side became an incubator of delinquency, and Abe watched a Jewish underworld coalesce in real time.

This was no mere crime wave. Each block had a gang and a poolroom, where boys learned to be gamblers, pickpockets, and pimps. The poolroom boys gathered on the sidewalk, calling one another sons-a-bitches and bastards and insulting girls as they walked by. Allen Street, referred to locally as "the gut," was the heart of the Jewish red-light district. On Abe's walk to school at PS 20, he passed one of Mother Rosie Hertz's many brothels, where, it was said, a dozen prostitutes per brothel might service a hundred and fifty clients daily and three hundred on the Sabbath.

Like any city, New York had always had crime, but this was different. On the old East Side, the Irish East Side, crime had been disorganized. Back then, gangsters were ragtag street thugs and petty thieves who could help keep Tammany Hall in power but generated no money. The Jewish immigrants changed that, organizing the underworld into crude clubs that got out the vote for Tammany *and* poured graft money into Tammany's machine, dynamizing Tammany's system of corruption. Casino owners banded together to protect their interests. Jewish pimps formed their own union, a "mutual benefit society" incorporated under state law. There were arson specialists who defrauded insurance companies, and horse poisoners who extorted businesses that relied on horse transport. Each criminal fiefdom had its own royalty, such as the King Pimp and the Queen of Fences. These kingpins, the essential players in their respective spheres, were retrograde corporate leaders who lobbied politicians, managed client relationships, scouted talent, and dispensed payroll.

*　　*　　*

For reformers like the Shoenfelds, backed by the uptowners, vice and crime now felt like reform's most urgent frontier, and it was in 1901 that Mayer Shoenfeld decided to pursue a new path, one that would shape Abe's own future. Mayer pivoted from a progressive, advocating for better housing and working conditions, to a *repressive* — a vice warrior who took on the "social evils" of gambling, prostitution, and saloons. This so-called moral reform had, in previous decades, been the realm of religious figures. But now, as immigration grew to unthinkable proportions and crime spread, moral reform became a more popular idea, regarded as a crucial avenue to civilized life in twentieth-century America.

The idea for a vice crusade surfaced when a high-powered group of academics, publishers, and businessmen formed the Committee of Fifteen, led by Jacob Schiff. Working for the Fifteen, Mayer was one of several middle-class reformers who organized young East Siders into bands of detectives who searched out the locations and operating details of brothels and gambling dens. The detectives gathered evidence including affidavits from prostitutes, copies of real estate transfers to pimps with names like Pincus Lovenfeld, and clever advertising. Whenever one madam moved locations, she would send out postcards entreating her patrons to renew their "membership in the library," promising a selection of "new books on file in our new quarters." The intelligence showed that there were brothels all over the city. Black prostitutes worked on Greene and Wooster Streets, as well as up along Broadway, where they ran into French prostitutes and their pimps, the *maquereaux*. But the East Side was the clear capital of the sex trade. Every address between 1 Allen and 205 Allen contained a Jewish prostitute, if not a full-blown brothel. Schiff, confronted with boxes of such evidence, hung his head and wrote: "Prostitution in our once great city has become, one can almost say, *Semitic*."

The Fifteen discussed putting in motion the kind of initiative that was possible in this era, when the monied elite could purchase its own state-backed repressive bodies. Thus the Fifteen obtained warrants for raids on dozens of addresses. To provide legal cover for the raids, they chose William Travers Jerome, a crusading attorney. Jerome, assisted by Mayer Shoenfeld and other "stalwart young men," smashed their way through more than a hundred gambling dens and brothels, with a journalist always in tow. Once inside, Jerome set up a makeshift court among the shattered furniture and exploding flashbulb powder and issued verdicts on the spot.

The rampaging Jerome made great newspaper copy and drew harsh criticism. Beyond the city's limited niche of moral reformers, it turned out, lay the majority of New York's population, who were more or less content with the status quo. After all, aside from its particular Semitic flavor, Allen Street was nothing special in America. Prostitution proliferated there because people wanted it, just as they did on Gayosa Street in Memphis, the Levee in Chicago, the Barbary Coast in San Francisco, Storyville in New Orleans, and Hooker's Division in Washington, DC. At the turn of the century, only two states had laws prohibiting traffic in women, and red-light districts existed in almost every major city. What, many New Yorkers wondered, was the big deal? As for the decades-old temperance movement, which sought to curb alcohol consumption, it was popular in some places, but New York was New York: a fast-paced, pleasure-loving city. New Yorkers drank on Sunday, the Sunday drinking law be damned. They played cards and bet on horses. And a sizeable constituency *provided* this vice market: not just prostitutes and pimps, but the police and judges who were paid to look the other way.

Schiff and his Committee of Fifteen saw that they'd misjudged things. Mayer Shoenfeld tried to embolden the bankers, imploring them not to give up on vice-crusading, but to no avail, and the Fifteen disbanded.

* * *

Without the backing of the Fifteen, Mayer Shoenfeld and William Travers Jerome carried on alone, as a political team. Mayer managed Jerome's campaign for district attorney, while Mayer himself ran for alderman in the East Side's eighth district, a Tammany stronghold. Under the headline HEBREWS WORKING FOR DECENCY, the *New York Times* reported: "A corps of 150 young Hebrews who want to have the stigma wiped out from the 'red light' district have organized as volunteer canvassers for Mayer Shoenfeld." Mayer, referring to Tammany's dirty election tactics, told the *Times*: "The usual system of purchasing votes on the East Side will fail in this campaign."

In Jerome's campaign, shaming was a central gambit. Barnstorming the East Side, speaking to immigrants, he waved a leather belt studded with "brass checks," the poker-chip-like currency that madams gave to johns after they paid. The john presented the brass check to the prostitute of his choice, who later returned it to the madam in exchange for her earnings. "Is the honor of Jewish women sold for brass checks nothing to you?" Jerome shouted, waving the belt. "If these conditions existed in other communities, there would be a vigilance committee organized and somebody would get lynched."

Before the election, Mayer and his corps of young Hebrews roamed East Side streets in true vigilante style, carrying axes and breaking down brothel doors. On election day in 1901, Mayer narrowly lost his own campaign to a Tammany-backed brothel keeper, but Jerome won his bid for district attorney. As DA, Jerome set his sights on the city's leading gambler, Richard Canfield, hero to Arnold Rothstein.

Jerome raided Canfield's casino. But when he tried to force testimony from two witnesses, young men identified as Canfield customers, Jerome hit a surprising political blockade: the German-Jewish uptowners. The two witnesses were not Vanderbilts or Whitneys, as many expected them to be, but rather Jesse Lewisohn, an heir to the German-Jewish mining fortune, and Mortimer Schiff, Jacob Schiff's only son — both of whom refused to testify and successfully challenged subpoenas to do so.

In the end, the aging Canfield closed his casinos and left town, unwilling to endure the raids of reformers. Jerome remained DA but abandoned vice-crusading for more traditional prosecutorial activities, such as high-profile murder cases. As for Mayer, his bitter experience with Schiff and the uptowners changed his thinking. Uptown intervention in the ghetto, he decided, was not the means to uplift: charity, urban removal programs, even labor strikes — they were all forms of reliance that created classes of dependents, what he called "pathological parasitism." "A nation that cannot fix itself cannot be fixed," he said at the dinner table. Mayer believed that the fate of the Jewish people would be settled in their time. They could thrive in America as never before, or they could founder. If East Siders wanted to improve their condition, he said, they would have to do it themselves.

As Abe Shoenfeld grew into his teenage years, he was torn between formal education and the crusading path of his self-taught father. Abe was a natural student. After he finished eighth grade at PS 20, the principal wrote: "I cannot speak too strongly for his mental powers or say too much for him as a young man of sterling integrity and honesty of purpose."

Abe had once shared those traits with his best friend, Louie Rosenberg, but Louie was drifting. That drift began with Louie's status as a baseball star. Being the cleanup hitter for the East Side Swatmores exposed him to the street element, to the gang leaders who were always looking for new talent. At thirteen, Louie was arrested for disorderly conduct, then for stealing, and at fourteen he served his first term at the House of Refuge, a juvenile reformatory. He got out in time to start ninth grade with Abe at Stuyvesant High, but Louie was rarely in attendance.

That winter, in early 1906, the Shoenfelds and the Rosenbergs looked forward to an East Side visit from President Teddy Roosevelt, the country's top reform politician, who was to be honored at a banquet at their old haunt, Little Hungary. There Roosevelt told the crowd: "I doubt it would be possible to find a more typically American gathering than this one. For Americanism is not a matter of birthplace, of ancestry, of education, or of creed. It is a matter of the spirit that is in a man's soul." It was an electric evening for Abe, a time to remember, but Louie missed it.

A few months later, at the end of Abe's freshman year at Stuyvesant, he sat in the principal's office. The principal was overwhelmed. A new round of pogroms in Russia had sent over new waves of Jewish refugees, turning the East Side into the most crowded neighborhood in the world. The *New York Times,* in a comparison of global ghettos, reported that Bombay, India, had once been the world's most densely populated area, with an average of 759 people per acre, whereas New York's East Side now had more than a hundred blocks with densities of between 700 and 1,600 people per acre. There were sixteen thousand East Siders for every acre of East Side park space.

In the city's schools, classrooms of seventy were commonplace. Thousands of children attended half-day sessions, while thousands more were turned away. The Stuyvesant principal, struggling with a mandate to thin the school's ranks, gestured at Abe's record of achievement and said he didn't think Abe would learn much if he stayed. He urged Abe to consider leaving school and pursuing a career.

Abe thought about it. He'd grown up watching Mayer follow one failed reform attempt after another as he tried to elevate the community. School, on the other hand, was attractive for a kid who spent much of his free time in libraries. Abe loved math and history. He admired his little brother, Dudley, who planned to be a doctor. And still, Mayer's words rang in Abe's head: *The future of the Jewish people in this country will be decided in our time.* If not in Mayer's time, Abe thought, then perhaps in his own. In 1906, reformers were no longer seen as spoilsports or puritanical bluenoses. The country's fear of rapid urbanization, population explosion from immigration, and the spread of venereal disease had turned reform into a socially acceptable and even glamorous avocation for young people on the rise. Abe decided to leave school and join his father's fight.

It was an important moment in that fight. Charles Evans Hughes was running for New York State governor on a classic reformer's ticket. Hughes vowed to regulate Wall Street, replace Tammany Hall with "a decent and unbossed" administration, end labor abuses, and achieve vice reform. Hughes, who needed the immigrant vote to win, tapped Mayer Shoenfeld to organize what Hughes promised the newspapers would be "a vigorous campaign in the Jewish quarter."

One evening, when Hughes came to 125 Clinton to discuss campaign tactics, Abe walked into his father's study with an issue of *Popular Mechanics*.

Abe was developing a stentorian voice. The depth of it sounded a little comic, coming from a fifteen-year-old, but it also lent his pronouncements a certain authority. He said there was a new type of Victrola that allowed you to record sound on a record. He suggested they record Hughes's campaign speeches, in English and Yiddish, then make copies of the records and set up phonographs with "morning glory" horns on street corners. The men shrugged: *Why not? How else to persuade half a million immigrants?* So they made recordings, mounted phonographs on wagons, and marshaled a traveling brass band to draw attention to the spectacle. The press was enchanted. PHONOGRAPH TALKS HUGHES: MAYER SHOENFELD MAKES AN EXPERIMENT ON THE EAST SIDE, read a *New York Times* headline.

But not everyone loved it. During the campaign, as Mayer and Abe were setting up phonographs, thugs who represented the Tammany interest attacked their wagon, knocking Mayer unconscious and shooting

Abe in the shoulder. Abe's mother, Dora, berated Mayer for dragging their son into the violent world of East Side politics. Abe wondered if he really wanted to take up his father's mantle. He recalled the pleasures of a quiet library and considered returning to school. Then November came, election day arrived, and something glorious happened: Hughes won.

3

Making Your Mark

WITHOUT CHARLES EVANS HUGHES, ARNOLD ROTHSTEIN might have remained an obscure figure.

By the time of Hughes's election in 1906, the business side of reform was complete. The plutocrats had achieved their vision: they tempered competition in the marketplace by creating a combined corporate economy, in which the top 4 percent of American concerns produced 60 percent of its industrial output. New York City was now home to the headquarters of half the country's largest entities, which resided in Lower Manhattan, near the bankers who created the corporations and sat on their boards. This merger boom coincided with the biggest economic boom the country had known, and further widened the wealth gap, as industry sped up and ground down its labor force. When that boom ended in the 1907 market crash, during Hughes's first year as governor, corporate scandals and the excesses of Wall Street spilled into the open, and helped create an opportunity to advance *moral* reform.

Having legitimized the business world—organizing it neatly into those 366 buildings of nine or more stories that rose in Lower

Manhattan, four times the number that had existed a decade earlier—reformers decided it was time to clean up society too, to add a moral sheen to the rising corporate state by balancing economic growth with social justice. The current laws concerning racetrack gambling, reformers said, were fundamentally unjust: they protected betting at the track, where the wealthy went, and criminalized off-track venues, or poolrooms, where the poor wagered. Religious constituencies, such as the New York Board of Jewish Ministers, denounced "the injustice" of allowing "the rich man to enjoy pleasures which are made a crime to the poor," and in 1908 they backed Governor Hughes in the anti-gambling cause. That cause was strongly opposed by Tammany Hall and racetrack owners, but Hughes, ignoring death threats, "lashed the racing interest" and pushed through New York's Hart-Agnew law. This law banned organized bookmaking at the track but permitted a more informal kind of betting, defined as oral bookmaking between friends and associates. To those who decried the consequent loss of revenue and the violation of personal liberties, Hughes said, "The test of respect for the law is where it is upheld in its majesty even though it hurts."

And the pain was significant. The Hart-Agnew law, which was later imitated by many states, including California and Texas, put out of business racetracks that had prospered as gambling enterprises. At the larger tracks, such as Saratoga, the legal cartel of bookmakers, the Metropolitan Turf Association, now dissolved, and the racing world turned to second-tier bookies like Arnold Rothstein, Sol Lichtenstein, and Mannie "Cock-eye" Mannheimer—Jews who were willing to work in the new gray area of oral bookmaking.

This lesson would guide Arnold's career. The reformers' puritan enactments couldn't eliminate enduring human behavior. Arnold saw how, in the gaps and gray areas created by anti-vice legislation, he could create his own marginal business world, operating under no recognized authority but himself.

For Arnold's ancestors, though, this idea wasn't new at all. Across history, in many countries, whenever the establishment wanted to prohibit something on religious or legal grounds — moneylending, liquor, prostitution — it delegated the resulting black market to Jews to organize. In Russia and Poland, where Jews had handled the liquor trade for centuries and presently ran most of the licensed brothels, vice prohibition was another method of marginalization. It was a way to benefit from an oppressed community while creating an aura of sin around it, thus providing an abiding pretext for persecution.

On their first date in 1908, shortly after the passage of the Hart-Agnew law, Arnold told Carolyn Green, an eighteen-year-old Broadway actress, that he was going to be a big man someday. In Arnold, Carolyn saw a well-tailored twenty-five-year-old whose subdued style and spruce appearance stood out against the garish fashions of Broadway. He had dark hair and a complexion that was remarkable for its smooth pallor, as if he never had to worry about razors. She was taken with his solicitousness and gentle manner, qualities that she couldn't emphasize enough when describing them to friends. She fell too for his laughing eyes, even though the laugh itself often sounded artificial to her.

Carolyn understood Arnold. She too had distanced herself from her background, having been raised poor by her Catholic mother and Jewish father, a butcher. She changed her last name from Greenwald to Green and enrolled in the Rodney School of Elocution to prepare for life on the stage. She found some early success in shows like *Havana* and *Fascinating Flora*. While she was playing in *The Social Whirl,* a poll of the audience voted her the prettiest young woman in the cast. At the time she met Arnold, Carolyn had a small role in the comedy hit of the season, *The Chorus Lady,* which played in New York before hitting the road. Hurtling through Pennsylvania and Kansas, Carolyn would look out at the country houses, at kerosene lamps burning cozily behind curtained windows, and idealize a quieter life of peace and security. She was tired of putting on and taking off makeup, sick of sleeping in a new hotel each night. She wasn't cut out for show business. She was ready to settle down. She knew Arnold gambled, but he told her that he planned to quit and go into legitimate business when he made his goal of $100,000.

During these years, Arnold adopted a pattern that he'd stick with for the rest of his life. He spent all night at a restaurant called Jack's Oyster House, on Sixth Avenue and Forty-Third Street, a surf-and-turf joint whose décor bespoke a men's club and a fairy tale. The walls featured stuffed wildlife and murals adapted from the Brothers Grimm and Hans Christian Andersen. The real show began after midnight, when, as one regular recalled, "the red-hot sports came piling in: rowdy actors, college boys with their tender insides all stirred up by rum, roistering young millionaires throwing dad's hard-earned money to the bow-wows, visiting celebrities, prizefighters, wrestlers, outright bunco steerers, and every variety of sure-thing man and grafter that the city knows."

Pretty much anything was tolerated at Jack's, until it wasn't. When college football players and fans from Harvard, Yale, and Princeton poured into Jack's after a game, fights often broke out between the young men. If the college boys failed to heed a warning, waiters wrapped napkins around their fists, formed a "flying wedge," and advanced on the troublemakers, throwing them onto the Sixth Avenue streetcar tracks. Stumbling along those tracks, the revelers gazed up at the twinkling red and green lights of the gargantuan Hippodrome Theater, where eight thousand spectators watched shows on a stage that was twelve times larger than that of any other theater on Broadway — enough space for a thousand performers to act out realistic battle scenes alongside a 750,000-gallon tank that did service as a lake or a river.

Broadway, Manhattan's oldest street, had emerged from the darkness of Arnold's youth, when the marquee for David Belasco's Criterion Theatre was the only thing illuminating the future Times Square. Now, in 1908, four years after the Times Building went up, Broadway, if not yet widely known as America's celebrated thoroughfare, was perhaps as beautiful as it would ever be, with its wrought-iron façades and low-slung vaudeville houses. Even the skyline was a giant stage. Using new technology known as flashers, which allowed groups of lightbulbs to be turned on and off in sequence, simulating movement, and rheostats, which allowed lights to be dimmed and raised, advertisers erected cartoonlike figures that turned the New York nightscape into a phantasmagoria. The Heatherbloom Girl, her petticoat blown about by gusts of electrical wind and rain, revealed a naughty glimpse of leg. Boys boxed. A girl walked a tightrope. A giant kitten played with a ball of Corticelli silk and got tangled up. Fountains of White Rock Table Water gushed into a basin seven stories down.

"Arnold never wanted to be anywhere except on Broadway," Carolyn recalled. "He never liked the country. He didn't care for any other city except New York, and Broadway, for him, was New York. To leave it for only a few days was a hardship."

For Arnold, Broadway nightlife wasn't so much about socializing — he didn't drink or smoke — as it was about developing business. At Jack's he met chorus girls whom he used to attract "plungers," wealthy gamblers, to his roving poker games. He was a poker master, in part because he looked nothing like one. His face appeared to be an open book. He smiled at hands of cards he supposedly liked and grunted over ostensibly bad cards. He scowled and laughed. He simulated "worried" or "pleased." Whatever opponents wanted to see in him, they found it, and by telling them everything, he told them nothing. Out all night, he bragged to these companions that his beautiful girlfriend was at home, waiting, and called her repeatedly throughout the evening to prove it.

Carolyn knew there was a hole in Arnold that could never be filled, a childlike neediness that she accepted as part of his strange charm. He was good-humored and surprisingly self-aware. He was also controlling and wounded. He would come home at six in the morning and sleep until three in the afternoon, and the first thing he usually said upon waking was: "I don't feel well." Between his gambling and all-night life-style, his coffee intake and his sugary diet of sweet cakes, it was no wonder that Arnold suffered from indigestion and headaches, and he was always treating these maladies with milk of magnesia or bicarbonate of soda, whatever new proprietary medicine was being advertised on the electric billboards of Broadway.

Six months into their relationship, Arnold asked Carolyn to meet his family. "Believe me," he assured her, "it doesn't matter what they say or think. I'm a stranger to them."

When they sat down in the parlor room at the Rothstein family brownstone on West Eighty-Fourth Street, Arnold's father, Abe the Just, asked Carolyn: "Are you Jewish, Ms. Green?"

She said that her father was Jewish and her mother was Catholic, and that she'd been brought up Catholic and still attended Mass.

"But you will change your religion if you and Arnold marry?"

"No, Mr. Rothstein."

Abe the Just nodded, as if he'd been expecting this disappointment. "My son is a grown man. If you marry him you have all my wishes for your happiness, but you cannot have my approval. I cannot approve of losing my son."

"But you would not be losing him," Carolyn said.

"If he marries outside the faith, he will be lost to me. That is the law."

On the way home Arnold laughed bitterly. "It was just the way I knew it would be," he said.

But Carolyn had second thoughts about the relationship. She imagined that one day Arnold would hate her for coming between him and his family. To this, Arnold said: "You heard him. My father said I live my own life. Well, it wouldn't be much of a life without you." He broke out an engagement ring: a setting of white diamonds clustered around a brown four-carat diamond, creating the effect of a daisy. "Sweet, let's get married," he said.

In the summer of 1909, during the August racing season in Saratoga, Arnold and Carolyn tied the knot in a tiny ceremony attended only by two of their closest friends—the up-and-coming journalist Herbert Bayard Swope, a gambling buddy of Arnold's, and Swope's future wife, Pearl. Pearl liked Carolyn because she was glamorous and dignified. "She was more of a lady than most ladies I know," Pearl once said. But with Arnold and Swope, it was a more complicated friendship. Swope, an inveterate gambler, borrowed money from Arnold, and Swope's habit interfered with his job. One editor fired him for covering too many stories from the racetrack. Which was perhaps why Swope—though he would later learn to separate play and work and become one of the top journalists in the country—was, at the moment, writing for the *Morning Telegraph,* a paper that covered horse racing. For Swope, Arnold was both an enabler and a source of information. For Arnold, Swope could help manage public perception, shifting attention this way or that. Swope's piece about the wedding treated Carolyn as the chief attraction and mentioned the groom only briefly, describing Arnold as a "broker."

In Saratoga, their first night together was not as Carolyn imagined it. No sooner were the newlyweds alone than Arnold said, "Sweet, I had a bad day today, and I'll need your jewelry for a few days." It was an odd beginning to their life together, but Carolyn was blissed out and in love. He told her he was merely borrowing the jewelry, her engagement ring plus a brooch, but she never saw the pieces again.

Back on West Eighty-Fourth Street, when Abe the Just heard of the wedding, he tore his clothes, donned his shawl, covered the mirrors, and said kaddish, the prayer for the dead, for his second lost son.

That fall, Arnold and Carolyn were back in the city, where they attended a dinner of powerful Tammany Hall politicians.

As the first decade of the new century came to a close, Tammany was embattled—divided by leadership strategies, lacking a vision for the future, and in need of shoring up its voter base. It was a tough base to nail down. The new Eastern European immigrants, the million or so who came after 1900, were less meek and more educated than those who came in the late 1800s, when Mayer Shoenfeld was organizing the garment industry's first labor strikes. Many of the new arrivals had stayed in Russia and fought as revolutionaries, refusing to flee until the czar put in motion a plan of extermination. For Tammany, widening the electoral base among such an unwieldy population was no longer as simple as it once had been. For one thing, these new immigrants knew how to organize labor unions and raise armies. They wanted more than free shoes and Passover meals. And this would be a problem. Because beyond Tammany Hall's founding idea—protecting immigrants from the law in exchange for loyalty on election day—Tammany had no social-welfare platform. It was pro-labor only in its rhetoric. In reality, Tammany voiced little objection to the class structure. On the contrary, it profited on social *in*justice, insofar as the proceeds from crime kept the machine running.

A primary middleman in that corruption machine was Big Tim Sullivan, the Tammany state senator who had been a mentor to Arnold since the 1890s, when Arnold and Herman Rosenthal operated craps games on the sidewalk outside Big Tim's East Side poolroom. Since the days of Arnold's youth, Big Tim had expanded. He opened a new office on Broadway and formed a nationwide chain of burlesque houses, music halls, and vaudeville theaters. These investments were all supported by crime. With his corrupt police and judges, Big Tim controlled the city's unofficial gambling commission, handing out "licenses," or police protection, for this illegal activity that generated $3 million in graft per year.

At the dinner, Big Tim told Carolyn, "Your husband is going places." Then he gave Arnold an incredible wedding gift: protection for a casino in the high-rolling district around Times Square, the Tenderloin, where, a few years earlier, Arnold's attempt to set up an off-track betting parlor had been foiled when the place was raided and Arnold lacked the requisite connections. This was a big deal. Arnold would be the first Jewish gambler to get "a Tenderloin concession."

The couple moved to a three-story brownstone on Forty-Sixth Street, where Arnold and Carolyn lived upstairs, while, downstairs, he would build a casino and set about becoming the city's new Richard Canfield. The first thing Arnold did was hire a Black butler to help manage the casino, but he had a long way to go to become the next Canfield. The place was shabbily furnished, with broken fixtures and mismatched chairs. There were several music publishing concerns on the block, which created noise, and a stable next door that drew rats. The Rothsteins summoned exterminators, even kept a pet ferret, but the brownstone never would be free of the rats. Again, Carolyn's expectations of married life were upended, but, as she later wrote, she decided to content herself until Arnold could get "established in a sound business" and she could "enjoy a normal life with him, and a normal social life with our friends."

Desperate to make the most of this opportunity, Arnold went in search of plungers or marks, rich men who thought they could beat the house. "Making your mark" meant proving the sucker wrong. He read the papers, looking for announcements of marks visiting the city, and in time he drew many of his idol's former patrons, fleecing the same plutocrats whose merger mania and reform movement had created the gray area in which a Jew like Arnold could make good. One night, the son of John Gates — inventor of barbed wire, creator of U.S. Steel — lost $40,000 in

Arnold's place. The story, printed in newspapers, identified Arnold as a professional gambler who played for high stakes. It was wonderful advertising, Carolyn recalled, and it marked the beginning of Arnold's career as a big-time gambler, a professional who would "go the limit" against all comers. And he now had the capital for renovations. He turned the first floor into one great room adorned in green and gold, with crystal chandeliers and secret recesses into which tables and roulette wheels could be slipped should cops breach the reinforced doors.

Back at Jack's Oyster House, Arnold's success drew resentment from his underworld peers, some of whom tried to undermine him. One night they lured him into a game with a pool shark imported from Philadelphia. When Arnold beat the shark in a thirty-six-hour match, the incident became the talk of Broadway, made national news, and initiated a parade of business at the Forty-Sixth Street casino.

4

Tony the Tough

D OWN ON THE EAST SIDE, FAR FROM THE BROADWAY
of Arnold Rothstein's New York, Lillian Lieben and Antonia Rolnick lived on "Jewish Broadway," or Grand Street. Back in 1900, the *New
York Tribune* wrote that "Grand Street is Broadway plus Fifth Avenue, only
very much more so. Its wide sidewalks show more fashion to the square
foot on a Sunday than any other part of the city." By 1910, the population
had multiplied and the neighborhood was more seedy. The clothing shops
shared the thoroughfare with casinos, saloons, and "coaling stations" where
*nafke*s, prostitutes, could refuel with coffee and cake at 3 a.m.

Lillian and Antonia were both Russian-Jewish immigrants from the
Pale of Settlement, but Lily, with her blond ringlets and peach complexion, looked more French than Russian. Antonia, who went by Tony, was
traditional: full crimson lips framed by masses of black hair. Whereas
Lily arrived from the Pale in 1897, at the age of three, with her family
intact, Tony came over in 1906, at thirteen, with only her father, after
narrowly surviving that year's pogrom in Bialystok. In New York, Tony
spoke English haltingly, unable to pronounce sounds like *th* or *ing. Cloth*

came out as *clot, singing* as *sin-gin*. Struggling to adapt, she compensated with grit. At PS 20, when gang girls bullied them and pulled Lily's flaxen curls, Tony attacked, never hesitating to strengthen an argument with a blow. This brassiness earned her a nickname: Tony the Tough.

In the afternoons, they begged pennies from Lily's mother, a dressmaker, and hung out in one of the many candy stores, or "cheap charlies," that dotted the East Side. Over frozen tortonis served in fluted cups, the girls traded dreams. Lily wanted a family. Tony wanted to dance like Isadora Duncan and act in movies.

Soon, however, these ambitions gave way to reality. Both girls dropped out of PS 20 in eighth grade and joined New York's garment industry, whose workforce was more than 70 percent female and comprised mostly teenagers. Lily worked in a millinery factory, making artificial flowers and fashioning feathers for one of the prewar era's more emblematic accessories, its gigantic hats. For her part, Tony labored in a laundry, working the foot-operated iron presses, a job akin to climbing steep stairs all day while holding a pipe above your head. Her legs rippled with muscle. Her arms were always covered in burns.

During the first decade of the twentieth century, the city's Jewish garment industry matured. As "skyscrapers" went up each week to create new factory space and house the increasing number of corporations headquartered in Lower Manhattan, the old tenement sweatshops moved into street-level storefronts and large lofts. This transformation created efficiencies, and by 1910 New York manufacturers produced 80 percent of all clothing worn in the United States.

But even as the infrastructure of the business evolved, labor law didn't catch up, and working conditions remained much the same as they'd been in the late nineteenth century, or worse: more immigrants meant more competition for jobs, and this dynamic helped strengthen a conviction among employers that labor *should* be cheap and disposable, per the law of the marketplace. Employees worked eighty-hour weeks without a minimum wage or safety regulations. And garment work was still seasonal, which meant that there was no guarantee of steady employment in the "slack season," the cold winter months.

As a result, the Russian-Jewish girls who supplied most of the industry's workforce perceived prostitution as a pit that always loomed, a fate they were constantly trying to avoid. "The danger of corruption," as one female researcher of the period wrote, "is more intimately connected with Jewish girls than with Irish or Italian. The Jewish girl, while perhaps not personally so proud as the Irish, is in many ways more ambitious and purposive. She desires to have all that the world offers. This purposive characteristic, so noble if devoted to high ends, and so dangerous if directed to pleasure alone, is seen more evidently in the Jewish girl than in any other."

Of the nobler kind, several East Side daughters became famous for their visionary leadership. In 1908, the *New York Times* called Pauline Newman "the East Side Joan of Arc" when the nineteen-year-old led the largest rent strike the city had ever seen, leading to the establishment of rent controls. The following year, Newman joined fellow activists Clara Lemlich and Rose Schneiderman to help inspire the Shirtwaist Makers' Strike. Among the thirty thousand who joined that strike, many were of the sort who supported themselves on five dollars a week, wearing spring jackets through winter and renewing old hats with a bit of ribbon. Many lived alone and rented a "half sheet," a shared bed, in someone else's apartment. Whether battered by thugs whom manufacturers hired to break up picket lines, or arrested and sent to the workhouse, their enthusiasm for striking only grew with their hardship.

The Shirtwaist Makers' Strike was a cause célèbre, the first garment strike to win broad public support. The Russian-Jewish girls galvanized both the wealthy suffragettes uptown, who looked at the strikers and found their own movement wanting, as well as their native-born working-class colleagues. "It's a good thing, this strike is; it makes you feel like a real grownup person," wrote a Russian-Jewish immigrant named Theresa Malkiel in *The Diary of a Shirtwaist Striker,* a novel that Malkiel wrote from the perspective of a native-born garment worker who is inspired by her immigrant colleagues to join the fight for labor rights. "But I wish I'd feel about it like them Jew girls do. Why, their eyes flash fire as soon as they commence to talk about the strike—and the lot of talk they can put up..."

One could only speculate as to what made "them Jew girls" special, particularly given that the tribulations of Eastern European immigrants meant that they were not, in the aggregate, physically privileged. The shortest and skinniest of all European arrivals, they were cursed with anemia and poor musculature. But they also came with advantages. Their leadership in New York's labor movement could be attributed to a background of labor fights in Russia. Their durability derived from a culture in which daughters did double duty as wage earners and mother's helpers so that their brothers could study.

Certainly, they were motivated by the opportunity that America offered. In this new ghetto, they might have labored to stand upright (spinal curvature) or to breathe through inflamed pathways (rhinitis, bronchitis). They might have scratched themselves raw from ringworm and dust-induced skin ailments ("baker's itch"). They might have choked down their vegetable-free diet of bread and herring with defective teeth, and endured the dull misery of chronic constipation. But here, in a place they called Dollar Land, at least no one was *literally* trying to murder them, and this freed them up to take their own elevation in hand. East Side girls of this generation could hardly hope to go to college, as their brothers were now doing, but that didn't stop them from putting aside something of their meager earnings for theatergoing and membership in the Jewish Girls' Self-Education Society, where, for a fee of one dollar a month, they read Gorky, Hugo, and Tolstoy.

At night, in Manhattan, dark desertion characterized the Upper West Side, where Irish girls worked as domestic servants and feared going out, as well as the Lower West Side and Little Italy, where, per custom, unmarried Italian daughters were kept at home. "On the East Side, below Fourteenth Street and beyond Broadway, in contrast, the streets at night are ablaze with light and gay activity," wrote Mary Van Kleeck in *Working Girls in Evening Schools,* a survey of the city's burgeoning night school scene for young women seeking to advance. "We seem here to be in another city. Open shops line the way; noisy voices of push-cart peddlers cry their wares; and men, women, and babies crowd the sidewalk. In this neighborhood the evening schools flourish," observed Van Kleeck, who found that more Jewish girls, those eighteen or younger, attended night school than all of the city's native-born females combined.

And yet: Despite the presence of such girls in the East Side immigrant population, the ones kept straight by a higher purpose or some positive force, there were others, perhaps most, who were too *normal* not to seek respite from the monotony of the factory, too vital and spirited to pass up the seductive pleasures of Dollar Land. While their brothers lit bonfires, rolled dice, and played cards, the girls gathered around street organs, stepping and swaying to the music, and thronged East Side dance halls. Some of these places were branded as dance schools. Some were open during the lunch hour to lure pale-faced factory girls, who, once inside, were invited into the bathroom by older girls and treated to free makeovers and dresses. Other dance venues were rentable arenas where underworld figures arranged "rackets," or dances, advertising: DOLLAR ADMISSION! DAMES FOR NOTHING!

In *Jews Without Money,* his fictionalized autobiography, Michael Gold recalled this seamy dance-hall culture: "The pimps were hunters. A pretty girl growing up on the East Side was marked by them. They watched her fill out, grow tall, take on the sex bloom. When she was fifteen, they schemed to trap her. Pimps infested the dance halls. Here they picked up the romantic factory girls who came after the day's work. They were smooth storytellers. They seduced girls the way a child is helped to fall asleep, with tales of magic happiness. No wonder East Side parents wouldn't let their daughters go to dance halls. But girls need to dance."

One Saturday night in late 1910, Tony proposed that she and Lily attend their first racket. Lily was reluctant, but Tony argued that if they could take care of themselves at work, then they were equally able to do so at play. At the dance, waltzes and two-steps pounded on the piano, accompanied by a drum flow. The girls danced together in a block as men watched from the sidelines.

The foot-operated presses had thickened Tony's lower half, leaving her with the kind of figure that East Siders referred to, not unfavorably, as a "battleship." Her figure was accentuated by the S-curve silhouette, the popular look of 1910. The shirtwaist, tucked closely in front, bloused loosely over the back of the new "short skirts," which grazed the top of ankle boots. These skirts, gathered at the center back, fit closely around the hips and flared toward the hem, creating a swaybacked posture that resembled, in profile, the letter S.

Someone cried out, "Take partners for a dance!" Two men at a time stepped out, broke the block, asked a girl to "step up for a turn," and away they gyrated in the turkey trot or the grizzly bear. Other men circulated among the girls, saying they had sample shoes and dresses in the back. *If they fit they're yours.* Lily dodged these *pezevenk*s, lowly pimps, but Tony spent her attentions freely. She danced with a young man who said he ran a photography studio and passed photos of beautiful girls like Tony to a casting agency for moving pictures. Tony's eyes lit up. When he asked why she kept touching her jaw, she said she had a toothache. He called over a friend, an older man who happened to be a dentist.

The East Side was full of dental offices — on some blocks they seemed as common as tailoring shops and bathhouses — but this dentist looked a bit odd. He wore a pinstripe suit and blue-tinted glasses that obscured a glass eye. His hands were heavy with rings and his necktie glimmered with a diamond horseshoe pin.

In 1896, a one-eyed Jewish soldier in the Russian army abandoned his garrison in Warsaw and decided to become a pimp.

Pimping wasn't a random career choice for Motche Goldberg. In the Russian Empire, prostitution was a regulated and stratified occupation, extending from famous Jewish courtesans down to the "wolf girls" who slept in public parks. Jews comprised 4 percent of the population of Russia, where legal restrictions confined them to the Pale of Settlement, but they dominated the sex trade. At the Congress Against the Trade in Women, held in London in 1910, a Russian representative said that the participation of Jews in prostitution was "inversely proportional to their legal and social position."

In *Sonia's Daughters: Prostitutes and Their Regulation in Imperial Russia,* Laurie Bernstein writes: "To anti-Semites in Russia, such activities only confirmed their impression of Jews as clever exploiters of the trusting Russian people." It was about structural oppression, not race, and the laws made Jews into what the oppressors reviled.

No one in Russia was surprised to discover that a *strashnyi yid,* "a dreadful Jew," ran a brothel in this or that city, writes Bernstein, or that a Russian-Jewish gang known as the Maccabees tricked women into prostitution by running fake ads for maids and nannies, or that Jewish men sold their wives abroad and returned to Russia with a passport stamped "Divorced" in order to find new victims. In *Yama,* a best-selling novel about Russian prostitution, a pious Jew known as Horizon supports his elderly mother and observes the Sabbath while he marries girl after girl and sells them all into brothels. When Horizon meets a military general on a train, he presents himself as part traveling salesman, part broker, and says, "*Nu,* what can a poor Jew do in times like these?"*

After Motche Goldberg escaped the army, he seduced a fifteen-year-old girl and took her to London, where he joined a group of Jewish pimps known as the Stamford Road Gang. When a reform association closed in on them, the pimps pulled up stakes and fled, prostitutes in tow, to new frontiers of the global sex trade: the diamond mines of South Africa, then on to Argentina and Brazil and the cities of America, to Seattle and St. Louis, to Philadelphia and Boston, and at last to New York, where, after so many years of wandering, Motche Goldberg finally felt at home.

On the East Side, Motche joined a fraternity of pimps, a kind of union called the Independent Benevolent Association. The IBA, incorporated under state law, supplied its members with employment insurance and burial plots, since Jewish cemeteries refused to accept pimps. Over the years, reform ebbed and flowed and the IBA adapted. During a reform administration, the IBA pimps kept out of sight. When the city was "open," they invested in real estate and posed as movie agents and fashion designers, dentists and doctors. They trolled dance halls and department stores, candy shops and employment agencies, on the hunt for poorly paid working girls, whom they called "chickens" or *frisch' schore,* fresh goods.

After the dance, Tony visited Motche at what appeared to be a dental office on Fourth Street. He "cocainized" her gums and examined her teeth. When Motche, who must've been in his mid-thirties, told the sixteen-year-old that he would like to take her out, she demurred. "I am not a girl keeping company yet," she said.

---

* In *Prostitution and Prejudice: The Jewish Fight against White Slavery,* Edward Bristow calls "white slavery"—a phrase coined by a London doctor in 1839, with explicit reference to Jewish involvement—"the sexualization of blood libel." Just as many gentiles believed that the Jew needed the blood of Christian boys to make his matzoh, they now thought he also required the purity of Christian virgins to keep his flesh mills running. There were all kinds of crazy theories. One Russian author posited that circumcision made sex more pleasurable, and this amplified sensitivity explained the Jew's enormous vitality, his tireless struggle for existence, etc.

"Then maybe it is time," Motche said.

They ate dinner at a restaurant. Motche explained how he lost his eye. He said that his mother, confronted with the grisly dilemma that many parents faced in the Pale of Settlement — maim your son or risk losing him to the forced recruitment of the czar's army — had removed Motche's eye, but to no avail. The czar's army recruited him anyway. Tony knew this story well. Back in Bialystok, prior to the pogrom that took her mother's life, her brother had been sacrificed to the czar's army too. She assessed Motche. A peculiar figure, she thought. But they shared a culture and a past, and that meant something in the anonymous city.

A few days later, Motche presented Tony with a diamond ring and proposed marriage. It was moving so quickly, Tony thought, but perhaps decisiveness defined success in Dollar Land, lest one work in a steam laundry forever. She accepted Motche's offer, agreed to premarital sex, and from there Tony's world fell apart in a series of nightmarish episodes.

One day Motche explained that he had hosted a "party" at his dental office and that a woman had "dropped dead in the chair." As a result, he said, his "diploma" to practice dentistry had been revoked, and he needed $100 to retrieve it. Tony said it took her several months at the laundry to earn $100. Motche suggested that they pawn the engagement ring instead. Tony looked at the ring. If they pawned it, then what did their relationship mean? Motche, referring to oral sex, asked, "Can you French?"

Tony, misunderstanding, said, "No, I am Russian."

Motche said he had a way for her to keep the ring *and* make more money than she made in the laundry. And this was how Tony wound up in a moving-picture house that reeked of stale food scraps and reverberated with the sounds of a blaring organ. There, Tony had sex with a string of men, an inaugural ceremony that the pimps referred to as a "line-up" or "koshering the chicken."

Two months after Motche introduced Tony to prostitution, she began feeling sick in the mornings. By 1910, abortion was illegal in every state, so Motche took Tony to a back-alley door marked ELAMEF—"female" spelled backward. Motche said he didn't find motherhood attractive, then held down Tony's legs while the doctor gave her something to drink. Her vision blurred. She awoke to the doctor wrapping in cotton what he called the *fleisch* and handing her a bottle of laudanum, an opium tincture, for pain.

After the abortion, Tony became melancholy and disobedient. Motche tried to put her in a brothel, but she fought it. He said he had changed his mind about the engagement. He took back the ring and disappeared. Tony tried to go home, but like many Jewish girls who fell into prostitution, she was turned away, in her case by her one remaining family member: her father.

A week later, Tony saw Motche walking down Grand Street with another girl, and noticed that this girl was wearing her ring. As Tony passed by them she said, "Young lady, do you know that this gentleman was engaged to me, and that the ring you have on your finger was mine?" Motche advised Tony to be careful, but Tony, her old self returning, shot back, "I should be careful? With all that you done to me, taking my honor, you tell *me* to be careful?" Before she could say more, the elevated train arrived and the couple ran up the stairs and disappeared, but Tony was not finished.

She didn't know about the Independent Benevolent Association, about the protection money pimps paid into the Tammany system, nor about the lengths the IBA went to in order to protect its members. She knew, however, that this was America, and there were courts and laws for people like Motche Goldberg.

5

Night of Ruin

T HE WORLD'S LEADING YIDDISH NEWSPAPER, THE
Forward, estimated that 3,800 girls went missing from New York
City each year. Many of the missing were Russian Jews who lived on the
East Side. Some got tired of their work and decided to seek their fortune
elsewhere. Some fought with their parents and eloped with a lover. But in
many cases prostitution played a role in the disappearance.

By 1910, Abe Shoenfeld, now nineteen, understood this reality. Four
years earlier, after leaving school and helping his father campaign for
Charles Evans Hughes, Abe began following Mayer up to Albany to
watch lawmakers debate new reforms. Moral reform, a small niche during
Abe's youth, gravitated to the center of the larger reform movement, a
movement that reached deeply into both political parties. The years 1906
to 1910 marked the dawn of moral reform, a period that originated many
of the state-level prohibitory laws, soon to become federal laws, that
would define life in twentieth-century America. During these years, the
first bans of marijuana, cocaine, and opium came about, and alcohol prohibition swept through Southern states. New York wasn't ready to give

up its drink, but it did begin to regulate narcotics and experiment with ways to curb alcohol consumption.

The reformers' capacity for moral indignation was often couched as a generalized concern over "urban moral breakdown," a phrase that functioned as a byword for the subversive alien, the unassimilated outsider. In the limited context of American history, this shifting dynamic felt new, but it had big historical echoes. Throughout the ages, moral reformers had argued that vices fostered by the anonymity of city life had been the undoing of great empires, and claimed that it was at the point when a civilization's urban population came to outnumber its rural population—America's present dynamic, thanks to immigration—that wrecked republics tended to go down. In this age, reformers considered prostitution to be the great republic wrecker, and their anti-prostitution movement became America's top moral crusade.

In New York, Abe Shoenfeld watched the subject of Jewish prostitution, once a local concern, become front-page news.

The frenzy had begun a couple of years earlier, in 1908, with the subject of Jewish crime generally. The commissioner of the New York Police Department, Theodore Bingham, published an article in the *North American Review,* a national publication launched by a group of Boston brahmins. The same group had formed the nucleus of the Immigration Restriction League back in the 1890s, an anti-immigration and nativist movement that was now growing apace with moral reform. In the piece, entitled "Foreign Criminals in New York," the police commissioner blamed the city's crime problem on "Russian Hebrews." It should come as no surprise, the commissioner wrote, that people so unsuited for physical labor, and lacking language skills, should turn to poisoning horses, defrauding insurance, and selling their daughters on the street: "They are burglars, firebugs, pickpockets and highway robbers—when they have the courage; but, though all crime is their province, pocket-picking is the one to which they seem to take most naturally."

According to an anonymous letter purportedly written by a Jewish detective in the NYPD, Bingham truly had it in for the Jews. "Commissioner Bingham has always shown contempt and hatred for the Jews," the letter begins. "He terms them 'kikes,' never anything else." The writer quoted the commissioner as having ordered the police force "to arrest every kike you see anywhere that you can get away with it.... Russia is the place they should stay." The letter continues: "Now Bingham can make good his figures [as stated in the *North American Review* article]. He is counting the same [Jewish arrests] over and over again. They are altering the names, and, wherever they can add a 'sky' or such like [to the end of an arrested person's name], they do."

Bingham's public commentary, coming from one of the country's leading law-enforcement professionals, garnered global attention and kicked off a new media genre: Jewish crime. In 1909, the year after Bingham's article, a respected journalist named George Kibbe Turner published an article in *McClure's* magazine entitled "The Daughters of the Poor: A Plain Story of the Development of New York City as a Leading Center of the White Slave Trade of the World, under Tammany Hall." Turner wrote, "The exploitation of young women as money-earning machines has reached a development on the East Side of New York probably not equaled anywhere else in the world." Turner observed tens of thousands of East Siders marching in the streets for Big Tim Sullivan's political rallies, and wrote: "Out of the Bowery and Red Light districts has come the new development in New York politics — the great voting power of the organized criminals. It is a notable development not only for New York but for the country at large. And no part of it is more noteworthy than the appearance of the Jewish dealer in women, who has vitiated, more than any other single agency, the moral life of the great cities of America." Politicians joined the pile-on, and the US Senate's Immigration Commission claimed that there were two important organizations of pimps, "one French, the other Jewish."

In New York, and around the country, many rejected the hysteria. They claimed that prostitution was voluntary, or that reformers had an economic motive to stir things up so they could raise funds to carry out their "work." One prosecutor claimed that white-slave narratives were "a sort of pornography to satisfy the American sense of news." Yet, as over-wrought as the narratives could be, Abe, who lived in a place where a corporation of pimps operated from a local café, saw truth in them, as well as a cause for himself, a cause backed by a new legal movement.

The anti-prostitution drive led to the 1910 passage of the Mann Act, which made it a federal felony to transport women across state lines for "immoral purposes." Although it was later overshadowed by subsequent developments in anti-vice legislation, such as federal bans of drugs and alcohol, the Mann Act was a pivotal moment in American history. In the old notion of vice reform, reformers sought to alleviate bad conditions, such as drunkenness or gambling, through compromise: variable regulations concerning the purchase of alcohol, or reducing legal racetrack gambling to oral bookmaking. These half measures, it was thought, satisfied reformers while leaving a gray area open. As David Langum writes in *Crossing Over the Line: Legislating Morality and the Mann Act,* no one, until now, had thought vice could be eliminated altogether. But in the Mann Act's breadth and ambiguity, one could see how, by 1910, the give-and-take approach to vice regulation was being superseded by the can-do-ism of the Progressive Era, with its bold faith in social engineering and universal solutions for aberrant human impulses that had never before been "solved."

Abe had no premonition of what the Mann Act would mean for the country. But it provided him with a warrant to pursue his obsession, a fixation that was some mix of sympathy with and aversion to prostitu-tion, an eternal fact of life as chronicled in the Old Testament and any number of history books Abe had read.

He knew that many prostitutes chose the life, and yet in the early 1900s there were few ideas in the air about the legitimacy of sex work:

whether one believed it should be legal or illegal, it was the hallmark of a failed community. And in the end it was *this,* the submerged status of Abe's neighborhood, that he hoped to reverse, however unlikely that goal was for a teenager living among what was then one of the planet's most complex underworlds.

In 1910, Abe began to spend time at Essex Market Court, on the northeast corner of Second Avenue and First Street, where he could observe "the whole panorama of the slum frontier." There he listened to the stories of arrested prostitutes, some as young as thirteen, as they came before the magistrate, arms akimbo, their hats pulled down over their braids, their princess dresses short enough to show silk hosiery.

These girls recounted having been kicked in the stomach or slashed with a knife. One declined to give evidence because her friend was killed after testifying against the IBA. Not all the prostitutes were Jewish, but most were. When the magistrate asked when they had come to America, they would often remember the date in relation to a Jewish holiday or the Hebrew calendar.

> *Two weeks before Yom Kippur, 1903.*
> *Three days after Rosh Hashana, 1905.*
> *It was 1907, your honor, in the Hebrew month of Eydr.*

One case in particular caught Abe's attention. Antonia Rolnick, known as Tony the Tough, pressed charges against Motche Goldberg, head of the IBA, for "seduction," luring a lady into sex with a false promise of marriage — a crime that reflected society's view of itself as the protector of female virtue. Most seduction cases failed, but Tony's courage in bringing the case at all was exceptional. At the trial, after Tony took the witness stand and related the whole saga with Motche, the judge asked:

"After the night of your ruin, as you characterize it, why did you save your underclothes?"

"A respectable Jewish girl keeps the underwear for a year," Tony said, citing no real religious law or tradition. If she was trying to bolster her case, perhaps it was because she sensed that a fix was in.

The defense attorney produced the photographer from the dance. He claimed that he met Tony not at a dance but rather when she came to his studio to get her picture taken to become an actress. "She sat on the couch, and I seen the purpose she came for, so we had connection," the photographer testified, referring to sex. "A toothache? She never mentioned it."

In rendering a verdict, the judge explained that the crime of seduction had three elements: (1) a promise of marriage; (2) sexual intercourse; and (3) the previous chaste character of the complainant. As to the third element, the judge held that the prosecution had failed the burden of proof, and Motche Goldberg went free.

After the trial, Abe pursued Tony as a research subject, hoping to find out more about the IBA. Instead he fell in love, and fell hard. There were steamy afternoons in abandoned tenements and romantic Chinatown nights. They shared plates of chop suey and listened to a crooning boy waiter named "Little Georgie" Gershwin.

For a while, Tony made Abe forget all about the reason he'd met her in the first place. He felt that what they had was real, and believed that Tony felt it too. But when he asked her not to return to the streets, to stay with him instead, she balked. "You must be joking," she said. "Look at these legs — a million dollars in stock!"

Something in Tony was broken. She'd adapted to her new means of earning an income. Abe pleaded: "I'm not your father, Tony. I don't care who you've been. I love you." He said he'd never lie to her, never betray her, but Tony the Tough pushed him away. Later, discovering she was pregnant, she returned to the door marked ELAMEF, disposed of their child, and departed with another bottle of laudanum to ease the pain.

*   *   *

Among the German-Jewish uptowners, the subject of Jewish prostitution had been floating since the 1890s. Jacob Schiff, having headed the Committee of Fifteen back in 1901, knew all about it. Schiff's son-in-law, Felix Warburg, who financed countless charitable endeavors on the East Side, knew plenty about it. The Lehmans, the Guggenheims, the Lewisohns, the Ochses, the Goldmans — they were all aware of Jewish prostitution. But it was too shameful to address. And too potentially damaging to their collective reputation.

But to Judah Magnes, the firebrand who ministered to the uptowners at their fancy Fifth Avenue synagogue, Temple Emanu-El, the congregation's feeble response to downtown crime was indefensible. And now, during the 1910 Passover holiday, Rabbi Magnes planned to tell his congregants how he felt.

Four years earlier, the German Jews had hired Magnes, a Sacramento native, to be the youngest rabbi in Emanu-El's history. The image-conscious uptowners liked his laid-back California vibe. It didn't hurt that he was strikingly handsome, with olive skin and the smile of a matinee idol.

When Magnes joined the congregation, he expected to lead them in the secular tradition, known as Reform Judaism, but he wasn't prepared for just *how* disengaged his wealthy congregation would be from genuine Jewish concerns, and it rankled him to see how that detachment filtered down: Emanu-El, in his eyes, was "a childless congregation." Magnes was stretched. Downtown, when he led rallies to protest pogroms in Russia, he experienced a sense of purpose. Uptown, he felt like the help. "Can I serve two masters?" he wrote to his father back in Sacramento. "The plain people...of Russian descent, in whom some Jewish life is still left, and on the other hand, the rich Jews, who would buy the soul of their servants for coin?"

As he worked through these doubts, Magnes tried to remain

benevolent — to never sneer and always seek to see the best in others, to reserve his judgment for institutions and systems rather than people. But the uptowners challenged his patience. The rich Jews had a knack for dragging Magnes into the most trifling affairs. At the moment, for instance, he was locked in a futile power struggle with Felix Warburg, who insisted that his son and his nephew be bar mitzvahed without doing the work.

This sort of thing was typical — it was always less, less, less. First they wanted Magnes to preside over intermarriages. Then they wanted him to do the weddings at St. Patrick's. And so it went with the downtown issue. When it came to negative press about the East Side and ongoing revelations of Jewish crime, Magnes felt that the uptowners responded too weakly, if at all.

His critique wasn't completely fair. In 1908, after the NYPD commissioner wrote his article blaming crime on Jews, the uptowners wrote letters of outrage. The commissioner renounced his article, and Jacob Schiff praised him for his "manly retraction." It was then that the uptowners started the New York Kehillah to deal with local matters and appointed Magnes as the Kehillah chairman. A Hebrew word that means "community," *kehillah* described an ancient form of self-governance in which a committee of elders moderated the tribe's relationship with the local power structure. But in its first two years, the New York Kehillah all but ignored crime, focusing instead on education and health care. The uptowners wanted to assimilate the downtown Jews as quickly and quietly as possible, and hoped the crime problem would simply go away without damaging their own privileged position in the Wasp-ruled hierarchy.

Now, on Passover, Magnes scanned the pews. He had once believed that he'd never tire of Emanu-El's lofty spaces or the organ melodies that rained down like a chorus of angels. But, as he recently wrote to his father, he had now woken from his dreamland and realized that he could not, in fact, serve two masters. If the uptowners would let him, he would continue on as chairman of the Kehillah, a position in which he might have some influence over how the rich Jews deployed their money, but he wouldn't waste any more time at Temple Emanu-El. And since this was his last night, there was no reason to hold back.

"I shall speak to you without reserve," he began his scathing Passover sermon of 1910, an act of defiance that would make headlines. Many congregants walked out before Magnes finished his tirade, and two weeks later he resigned.

If the German-Jewish uptowners felt little urgency about Jewish crime, it was partly due to the city's leadership. Mayor William Gaynor, elected in 1909, portrayed the German Jews as they wished to see themselves, as virtuous caretakers of the city's Jewish poor, and referred to East Side crime the way the German Jews preferred to regard it, as a matter of bias. "I am sufficiently familiar with the Jewish character to know that Jews are just as quick to denounce and disavow Jew criminals as any other kind of criminals," Gaynor said. "What people has not its backward race?"

Gaynor's opinion was that Jews had their share of offenders, same as any population, and that guarding the rights and liberties of "the weak, uninfluential, and friendless" ought to be the chief aim of government. As for social evils, he took the pragmatic view: "The natural tendency of unfortunate women is to congregate in districts, and no law is needed for that," he observed. "I would rather see that they are not driven out of their natural congregations and scattered all over into thousands of flats."

Many German Jews felt that Gaynor, a former judge, was rescuing the East Side in his own way, by recasting vice as a corruption problem.

Once elected, Gaynor refused to give patronage jobs to Tammany Hall flunkies, a radical move for a mayor who'd been supported by Tammany in the election. Instead, he appointed the best person for each municipal job. He also came down hard on the Tammany-backed police force. He barred warrantless raids, prohibited the use of clubs, and banished the NYPD tradition of the Rogue's Gallery, which displayed photos of anyone whom police suspected of being a criminal.

Gaynor, even though he was not a reformer, appeared to have turned the city government into the kind of efficiently run, anti-Tammany operation that many reformers envisioned. By the summer of 1910, after Rabbi Magnes's resignation from Temple Emanu-El, the *New York Times* editorialized that Gaynor's first year as mayor had been "an epoch in the history of the city," and predicted "the new standards of administration established would take years of misrule to eradicate." It wasn't just his policies that won him fans. He walked from his Brooklyn Heights home across the Brooklyn Bridge to City Hall each morning, gave speeches composed of reading lists, and responded to every letter he received, engaging with citizens across the country on the best methods for lettuce farming and the plight of single women looking for good men. He hated subway riders who sat in the first seat, forcing those who came after to climb over their legs, and once suggested "making this selfish practice a misdemeanor." He was funny and serious, generous and irascible, more wise grandfather than glad-handing politician.

Many pegged Gaynor as a presidential hopeful, but his time was limited. In August 1910, as he embarked on a family vacation to Ireland, he was giving an impromptu press conference near the entrance to the ship when a laid-off dockworker emerged from the crowd, shouted, "You have taken my bread and butter away!," and fired two shots below Gaynor's ear.

When Gaynor emerged from the hospital, one bullet still lodged in his throat, he was different: less patient, more quick to anger. If 1910 had been a year of triumph, the remainder of Gaynor's term would be full of problems, most of which stemmed from his handling of crime and the police department.

William Gaynor stood for many principles — political independence, freedom from oppression — but his most closely held conviction, and what made him unique for his era, was his opposition to moral reform. Laws that couldn't be enforced, that sought to eliminate eternal human behavior — such laws, he believed, only enhanced corruption by putting too much power in the hands of police to collect graft. If reformers hadn't criminalized gambling, he reasoned, then cops and politicians wouldn't be able to profit from ducking a law that didn't exist. Gaynor described his vision of policing as the preservation of "outward order and decency," not a vice-free city but not a wide-open city either — a city in which police respected the sanctity of private property instead of misusing their power to effect an immense system of blackmail.

As mayor, Gaynor couldn't do much about the laws. But he did hold sway over the police department and therefore could take a shot at curtailing blackmail. After the shooting, when he returned to City Hall, the first item on his agenda was reducing police graft in the precincts by centralizing and consolidating vice patrol, such that average beat cops would no longer be able to take bribe money. He tried to accomplish this by ordering the new NYPD commissioner to form two central vice squads to cover the entire city.

Responding to Gaynor's command, the police commissioner assigned two veteran cops to run the squads. To lead the first squad, he assigned Lieutenant Dan Costigan, known as Honest Dan for his incorruptibility. But in a confusing move, the commissioner, who would later face allegations of corruption or ignorance, assigned the second vice squad to Lieutenant Charles Becker, a well-known grafter. This assignment would put

Becker in a tricky position, forcing him to shut down some of his long-time business partners, casino owners who paid him for legal protection. In doing so, Becker would divide the underworld—pitting those jilted gamblers he turned on against those he continued to protect—and seed the ground for a war between them.

6

The Girl Who Earns Her Own Living

A RNOLD ROTHSTEIN'S FORTY-SIXTH STREET CASINO WAS exceeding expectations. One night in 1911, a chorus girl who worked for Arnold as a "steerer" steered Percy Hill, the head of one of the country's largest corporate trusts, the American Tobacco Company, into Arnold's place. When Hill proceeded to drop $60,000, all on credit, and then asked for more credit, Arnold had a decision to make. If he cut Hill off, it would depreciate Arnold and his establishment in the eyes of the big-ticket gamblers he courted. But if he said yes, then he would have to offer Hill unlimited credit, since, in Arnold's mind, it would appear cheap to extend credit piecemeal to such a major plunger, and Arnold abhorred the appearance of cheapness. He sized up his mark: a bad gambler. Amateurs, Arnold knew, played it safe only when they were winning; when they lost, they pressed their bad luck, hoping it would turn. "Mr. Hill," he announced, "your credit is any limit you want to set. Good luck."

At the end of the night, Percy Hill gave Arnold an IOU for $250,000.

Arnold ran upstairs, sweat pouring from his head. He woke Carolyn and asked her to come into the library. He sat in a big leather chair, unbuttoned his shirt at the throat, removed his collar and tie, and sipped bicarbonate of soda. Carolyn thought something was wrong. Then he handed her the IOU. He'd finally done it! He'd made his $100,000 and then some. "If it's good," he said, "I'll buy you the biggest diamond in New York."

She didn't want a diamond. "What I want won't cost anything," she said. "All I want is a promise that you'll stop gambling if this IOU is good."

He didn't answer her. Instead, he went to get his milk and cookies. They were waiting for him, as always, in his bedroom. He came back to the library. "I've got butterflies in my stomach," he said. He spread the IOU before him. "I'll know tomorrow if this means anything."

The next morning, at the downtown headquarters of the American Tobacco Company, Arnold collected a check for the full sum. But the executives treated him like scum and said that this was the last IOU they'd cover. Their reproach stung, but Arnold went home and told Carolyn that he had a quarter-million bucks, which made him as good as them—and hungry for more. Now he wanted to keep on until he had a million.

Carolyn urged Arnold to leave gambling behind and go into legitimate business. He did have offers to go straight. More than one gambling client had wanted to make him a stockbroker, but he always declined, remarking that a man had a better chance in a gambling house than he had on Wall Street. "You're brilliant," Carolyn said. "You can do whatever you want."

"We'll see," Arnold said. "It's too early to make plans."

In a period of such rapid transformation, Arnold had no idea what was coming, and this uncertainty excited the gambler. He loved the challenge of changing with the times, of capitalizing on whatever opportunity the moment tossed up—a new law, a novel proposition, a ball game or boxing match whose outcome might be engineered. To relish that challenge with strength and poise was the essence of the "sporting man," an idealized figure in early twentieth-century America.

A sporting man lived in the gray area, straddling overworld and underworld. He played for big stakes and survived on a sprawling network of support that he maintained with generosity. If you helped people, they'd do anything for you, and the network would grow. Carolyn noted that many people associated the sporting man with horses galloping over green turf, baseballs thumping into gloves, and lithe bodies socking it out in the ring. These associations, she saw, obscured the "sordid foundation," the reality that a sporting man was, in truth, "a wolf trailing the fat herd," uninterested in sport aside from the odds and percentages involved.

If the sporting man was artifice, though, so was sport itself. "Baseball and betting were allied from the beginning," writes baseball historian Eliot Asinof. In the mid-1800s, when the game was played in private clubs, the clubmen saw the game as a vehicle for a wager: runs were called "aces," turns at bat "hands." It was the desire to win those bets, in fact, that professionalized the sport, motivating clubs to hire ringers — boys from the mines and mills who could hit and throw better than the sons of the rich. "There was hardly a game in which some wild, disruptive incident did not alter the outcome," writes Asinof. An outfielder, positioning himself for a fly ball, would be stoned by a spectator. One gambler ran onto the field and tackled a ballplayer. Another insured his bet by shooting bullets at the ground around an outfielder's feet. By the 1870s, newspapers were already publishing obituaries for the sport. "The amount of crooked work is indeed startling," wrote a St. Louis paper. A Buffalo paper wrote that its local club "should fold up if they can't play a square game."

But the national pastime endured, as did the crookedness. During the 1912 World Series between the New York Giants and the Boston Red Sox, someone put the word out that a Tammany Hall politician had fixed it for the Giants to win. The rumor resulted in a rush of New York "sucker money," tipping the odds in favor of New York and against Boston. Later, an investigation uncovered no evidence of a fix. Rather, the gamblers who spread the rumor were taking bets from the suckers while putting their own money on Boston to win. For that Series, the Rothsteins had a private box at the Polo Grounds, but Arnold never sat down. While Carolyn and her friends enjoyed the games and cheered for the Giants, Arnold stalked the stadium, looking for bets.

Meanwhile, Mayor Gaynor's experiment with police reform meant that some casinos and brothels were raided by the two centralized vice squads, but many were left alone — unmolested by cops but also unprotected by cops, and this, ultimately, was how the plan backfired, failing to create the outward order and decency Gaynor envisioned. Gangs overran the city in 1911, to such an extent that even Tammany Hall worried that gang violence was out of hand.

Unlike the Irish roughnecks of the previous era, the new Jewish gangster was small, quick, and deadly. According to NYPD records, he weighed, on average, 125 pounds, and openly carried pistols on each hip — until 1911, the year Tammany state senator Big Tim Sullivan, Arnold Rothstein's mentor, introduced a bill that made it a felony to carry a gun on one's person. Gun manufacturers fought the bill, but Big Tim, in an unusual political alignment, had the backing of respectable uptowners *and* the police, since his gun bill gave cops leverage over gangsters. The Sullivan Act became a model for gun-control legislation across the country, but it didn't pacify the streets of New York.

As Jewish crime peaked, casino and brothel owners, unsure of whom to pay off, increasingly turned to criminals for protection. By 1912, the underworld and upperworld were paying tribute to a young Jewish gangster named Big Jack Zelig. East Siders were grateful to Zelig for protecting both legitimate and illegal businesses from competitors and predators, including the Italian gangsters who were trying to extend their domain beyond Mott Street. Zelig, the son of a Russian tailor, had dark eyes and wide shoulders that tapered to a small waist — "a handsome bastard, built like an Adonis," wrote Abe Shoenfeld, whose best friend from childhood, Louie Rosenberg, was now the leading gunman in Zelig's gang, the Avenue Boys. Zelig, Abe wrote, was "afraid of nothing" and "crazy as a bedbug when it came to fighting." In the chaos created by Mayor Gaynor's policies, Zelig, a Robin Hood character with his own moral compass, held the underworld together, if tenuously.

While Abe's old friend drifted further into the underworld, as Zelig's sidekick, so did Abe himself, but in a different way. In 1911, Abe began taking freelance assignments from uptown reform committees, who paid him to gather intelligence on the city's prostitution scene. For Abe, the anarchy that Zelig's rise represented brought into relief the difficulty of his own work, and its dangers.

By the second decade of the new century, philanthropy in New York and other cities had taken on the structure of an industry, funded not by government but by self-selected elites who established committees to investigate social problems, both locally, in American ghettos, and abroad. Wealthy reformers went to Europe to see social welfare programs in action. They studied health insurance in Germany, municipal housing in England, and public milk stations in France.

As a moral reformer with a specialty in prostitution, Abe did his own version of the reformer's grand tour. In 1911, he visited the red-light districts of Albany, Chicago, and Washington, and took an eye-opening jaunt to Cuba, where he observed state-sanctioned prostitution in action. If reform now felt like the right path for a self-taught scholar like Abe, the movement had come to exude more of the aura of the laboratory and lecture hall than that of the pulpit. The old moralistic appeals, wrote one observer, were replaced by a new-age emphasis on reformers' superior factual grasp of the urban environments that needed to be purified, by force if necessary.

Back on the East Side, the old-school reformers who'd helped start the movement in the 1890s, such as Lillian Wald and Jacob Riis, had become iconic. Riis was now busy building playgrounds and gyms. Wald's program sent visiting nurses into tens of thousands of homes a year. Wald and Riis were financed in large part by the German-Jewish uptowners, with especially large donations coming from Jacob Schiff and his son-in-law, Felix Warburg. Their money now also funded young reformers who taught vocational courses in settlement houses and interviewed ghetto dwellers about their struggle. Among this new guard of reformers were both East Side natives and children of wealthy uptowners, including the first generation of young women to graduate from American colleges.

Women couldn't vote yet, but some were beginning to move into professions beyond teaching and nursing. *The Girl Who Earns Her Own Living,* a 1909 career guide, laid out what a lady could expect to find in paths such as sales, commercial art, cosmetology, and elocution. The job of telephone operator was recommended for those who possess "keen powers of observation, persistency, and the wisdom of secrecy concerning her employer's affairs," though "the girl with the strident, harsh voice has no place in a telephone exchange, and will not be tolerated." The author of *The Girl Who Earns Her Own Living* wrote approvingly of social service: "Modern philanthropy presents a congenial method of self-support for educated, ambitious, earnest women. The organized uplift movement offers a field in which the intelligent, tactful woman may reap the double harvest of a fair livelihood and the knowledge that the world will be the better for her having worked in it." For ladies who dreamed of becoming the next Edith Wharton or Ida Tarbell, the organized uplift movement was a triple harvest because they could get paid to research and write.

Thanks to the plutocrats, German Jew and Wasp alike, philanthropy was a frothy enterprise, funded by, among others, the steel-rich Carnegies, the oil-rich Rockefellers, and the railroad-rich Sages, all of whom endowed foundations, such as the Russell Sage Foundation, whose publishing arms disseminated books and reports. If the rationalization of American business had been about creating economic efficiency, the plutocrats now believed they could apply a similar principle to uplift — that, by gathering and analyzing facts on the ground, the moral universe could also be wrangled into order. Privileged children, those who in a previous era might have done missionary work abroad, could now get the same enriching experience without leaving their city. In New York, young reformers flocked to East Side settlement houses — local bases from which the rich could reach those they were trying to reform. They furnished the settlements like Ivy League social clubs, with pillows in the window seats, flower boxes, and brass plates on the door.

In this era of muckraking journalism and realistic fiction, the settlement houses gave aspiring writers an ideal vantage on the picaresque drama of ghetto life. When Ernest Poole, who would later win the first Pulitzer Prize for fiction, went from Princeton University to the University Settlement on Delancey Street, he discovered that nearly all the residents were working on books and articles. For those with literary ambitions, the East Side, with its coffee-drinking freethinkers and political radicals, was all fodder and inspiration. The film industry, ragtime music, American fashion, Ashcan art — they were all being invented here, below Fourteenth Street and east of the Bowery. There was also good food. Delicatessens, the first stirrings of that great New York institution, offered kosher and nonkosher items, from pig's feet and foie gras to smoked jowls and game pies.

After an evening in cafés with anarchists and actors, poets and labor leaders, Ernest Poole would hustle back to the University Settlement and jot down, as he later recalled, "chunks of life intensely real." The center of the intensity was Second Avenue, from Houston Street to Fourteenth Street. This strip of the city struck many as New York's most Parisian thoroughfare, lined as it was with Yiddish theaters and underworld haunts.

The subset of reformers and writers who specialized in underworld matters tended to be East Side locals, freelancers like Abe Shoenfeld.

At first, when Abe started doing this work in 1911, the vice-focused committees that hired him were composed not of German Jews — who, to the distress of Rabbi Judah Magnes, still preferred to ignore East Side crime — but of their Wasp counterparts in the upper crust, the kind depicted in Edith Wharton novels. This was an important distinction, because the motivations of these two uptown categories differed. For the German Jews, the downtown Jews were problematic, a potential setback. But to the Wasps, the downtowners presented an *opportunity*. If you promoted eugenics and immigration restriction, as many Wasps did, then information about ethnic crime was wonderful validation for those policies, and the young Abe, as yet unaware of the agenda he was serving, always delivered.

In fact, it was the blowback from an old piece of moral legislation that gave Abe his start as a paid moral reformer. In an attempt to weaken the power of saloons, which Tammany leaders historically used to galvanize constituents, New York's 1896 Raines law mandated that only "hotels," places with at least ten bedrooms, could serve alcohol on Sunday and past the 1 a.m. closing time for saloons. But the Raines law backfired when saloon owners decided to enter the brothel business, adding ten bedrooms on the second floor, converting their establishments into "Raines law hotels," and hosting prostitutes upstairs. The newly formed Committee of Fourteen, a Waspy successor to the failed Committee of Fifteen, hired Abe and a female counterpart in the vice-reform community to pose as a married couple, checking into Raines law hotels and reporting back on their findings.

Abe's partner in these missions was a non-Jew named Natalie de Bogory. The daughter of exiled Russian revolutionaries, Natalie had recently married an American journalist, becoming Natalie Sonnichsen. It was never clear what motivated her career as a vice reformer, but she and Abe were devoted investigators. One report that Natalie wrote for the Committee of Fourteen, entitled "Investigation of Five Hotels," gives a sense of their cloak-and-dagger life together:

At 10:15, Mr. S. and I entered the hotel. When Mr. S. asked for a room, the man hesitated, but after glancing him over said that he had just one room free. He produced a register in which Mr. S. wrote "C. Omner & Wife." We were then taken up a flight of stairs and given a front room on the left, for which one dollar was charged.

The room was small and shabbily furnished. On the wallpaper over the mantel were a number of foul inscriptions written in lead pencil. The bed showed indications of recent occupancy: the lower part of the counterpane being streaked with mud, evidently from boots. The wash basin was still wet and the slop jar was half full of dirty water.

Mr. S, wishing to survey the floor, stepped into the dark hall, where he saw a figure receding. He followed it into an empty room, where the man seemed frightened and explained that he was fixing up the rooms.

We made our mark (a big "C" containing "XIV") on the righthand side of the fireplace. Going out, we were obliged to ring, the door having no knob and being opened by some invisible means from an interior room.

The vagueness of this report, and ones like it, underscored the dubious utility of such investigations. Was the hotel really being used for prostitution? And if so, who was going to do anything about it? But Abe was getting his bearings as a researcher in the underworld. Whether working with Natalie or alone, he evinced a knack for getting vivid and comprehensive material. To the city's one-dollar brothels he would bring sandwiches for the madam, then sit in the parlor, order a beer, and offer two dollars to any prostitute who was willing "to toss up" her life story. In the five- and ten-dollar houses he could hang out and chat in exchange for an overpriced bottle of wine. In this way he learned everything about the sex trade, from the medical risks of curetting a syphilitic prostitute to the special health considerations of a woman who sleeps with two thousand men a year.

Abe's immersive style sometimes carried him beyond reporting, which wasn't unusual in this line of work. Since 1901, when the Committee of Fifteen became the prototype for anti-prostitution committees, vice investigations had popped up in dozens of American cities, and researchers were known to achieve a fragile but authentic intimacy with the objects of their study. How far that intimacy went was anyone's guess. But later, looking back, Abe seemed to suggest that sex was, if not part of the job, then perhaps an occasional by-product: "It was difficult to work in the fifty-cent houses because you couldn't buy anything," he recalled. "You had to either take a woman or get out, and who wants those women?"

If Abe consumed the thing as he grassed on it, he was animated by some of the same patrician prudishness and hypocrisy that characterized his Wasp sponsors, many of whom visited prostitutes, drank on Sundays, and enjoyed drug-fueled benders even as they lobbied for laws that would ban those activities. That's not to say Abe wasn't in it for the right reasons: his concerns about his neighborhood were genuine and went beyond vice and violence.

Most of all, he hated crime that targeted regular people — the fraudsters who sold fake steam-liner tickets, the synagogue thieves who reaped a golden harvest on the High Holidays, and the rabbis who counseled married couples and prisoners and then traded the information for kick-backs from divorce attorneys and prosecutors.

He was aggravated by the noise of the ghetto, and felt that it was this noise, as much as anything, that drew negative attention. The late-night rackets. The gangsters motoring about in autos* with "muffler cut-outs." The hideous cries of tenement cats. And the *filth*. Who could abide the dank movie theaters, the ubiquitous dead horses that gutter children played on like jungle gyms, or the dark, reeking fish market on Delancey with its ankle-deep slime?

When describing such conditions, Abe often walled off his emotions with irony, using sarcasm and caustic wit to conceal a pain that was actu-ally big and deep. Of his motivations, he later recalled, "I was, plainly, very angry; maybe this is an understatement of my feelings. I keenly felt the shame and disgrace that the men and women [of the underworld] were heaping on the body of law-abiding and respectable Jews."

He was above it, and done with it. While other ambitious East Siders of Abe's generation attended college and graduate school and used what-ever connections they could find to climb the career ladder — in fields such as law, medicine, engineering, and entertainment — he resisted those conventions and status markers and moved from one freelance vice-reporting job to the next. With his prematurely receding hairline and an aristocratic bearing influenced by rectitude, Abe looked like a no-nonsense, baby-faced man. He grew to six feet, inherited Mayer's thick forearms and Hungarian arrogance, and spoke with that deep, booming voice. Like his father, he wore Bull Dog suspenders from Hewes & Potter ("Will outwear three of the ordinary kind"), and like the college kids in the settlement houses, he carried a Waterman's fountain pen ("Free from dip, skip, blot or blemish").

---

* In prewar vernacular, at least in New York City, "car" had not yet replaced "auto" or "machine."

A composite of uptown and down, he listened to Enrico Caruso, wore a pince-nez, and followed fitness regimens from the popular men's health magazine *Physical Culture*. But he also watched Yiddish theater, smoked Turkish cigarettes, and consorted with prostitutes who knew him as "that writer," and toyed with him, saying, "Hey, girls, feel the hard-on this kid has. He'll fuck the whole lot of us!" It all went into his reports. To Abe's dismay, those reports went nowhere.

The Wasp uptowners that Abe worked for weren't interested in elevating his neighborhood. They wanted to issue pamphlets and generate headlines that could advance some other agenda—birth control, religious purity, fear of immigrants.

Prosecuting criminals, after all, was tough; inevitably it meant outing corruption in both political parties and interfering with the leisure activities of voters.

Back in 1910, for instance, when the Waspiest of reformers, John D. Rockefeller Jr., started his Bureau of Social Hygiene, he convened a grand jury to look into the Independent Benevolent Association, the pimping union. The inquiry, though it produced reams of newspaper coverage about "Jewish involvement in the white slave trade," led to no legal cases or prison time. Ridiculing the Rockefeller grand jury, the tongue-in-cheek *Sun* wrote: "In response to a call from the Women's Municipal League, about two-hundred women representing more than fifty organizations met at the Waldorf Astoria to discuss plans for stamping out the white slave traffic. As the delegates had not been empowered to take any final action in the matter, it was decided after a discussion of nearly three hours to appoint a committee to nominate tentative officers for a central committee, which in turn is to organize other committees."

For a while Abe, now twenty, tried a different tack. Under a pseudonym, he wrote an English-language column about police corruption for the *Kibitzer,* a Yiddish paper that his father came to own in lieu of payment for a debt, but this got Abe into trouble. In early 1912, three cops cornered him in an alley. These cops, who grafted from pickpockets, were livid because their names had appeared in Abe's column. Though it was anonymous, they had somehow discovered his identity. Clubs out, they beat Abe to the ground and were preparing to teach him a lesson he'd never forget, when Big Jack Zelig and Louie Rosenberg appeared and sent the cops walking.

Abe was shaken. In the streets, he'd always followed a rule learned from his father: If you never took graft and never, unless in defense, harmed another person, then you had nothing to fear. The rule wasn't literal. Abe hadn't taken graft or hit anybody when he caught a bullet during the 1906 Hughes campaign. But for the Shoenfelds, the rule served as a kind of religion, a faith that if you refrained from bribery and violence, then, come what may, you remained untouchable in a moral sense. You could fight your battles knowing that you were, as they said, "well on." Now, lying on the ground, Abe thought: *In a world turned upside down, what good is such a faith?*

Louie picked Abe up. Abe looked at Louie's earnest face and Zelig's broken Roman nose and wondered if perhaps these criminals were better for the city than any reform group he could join. Legitimate business owners worshipped Zelig and would do anything for him. As for Louie, the underworld now called him Lefty Louie because he shot a pistol left-handed, practiced obsessively at Coney Island shooting galleries, and once hit a sprinting Italian from the running board of a speeding auto. Louie, who was newly engaged to an East Side girl, brushed dirt from Abe's shoulder and said, "Be careful out here, friend. And give my best to your father."

That evening, Abe did not pass on Louie's regards to Mayer. Instead, he did what vexed young men sometimes do when the world doesn't bend to their will. He went home and blamed his frustrations on his dad.

7

Vengeance

B Y 1912, NEW YORK CITY WAS CORPORATIZED, BEAUTIFIED, and supersized. The Chelsea Piers, Carnegie Hall, and Abe's personal mecca, the New York Public Library, were complete. Penn Station, based on the buildings of ancient Rome, with its breathtaking steel-and-glass concourse, and Grand Central, with its oyster bar and art gallery, were nearly finished. It was the age of superlatives in New York: The greatest show on earth. The most spacious parks. The largest theaters. The busiest harbor, overseen by a fifteen-story statue, "mother of exiles," who welcomed immigrants to a city whose population was now 40 percent foreign-born. New York exuded to the world the image of a global hub, a futuristic city where trains shot through tunnels beneath the sea and ran a hundred feet aboveground, leaping across rivers.

Beneath all of that grandeur, on the other hand, there was rot. If New York had the grandest mansions, it also had the worst slums, inhabited by a massive underclass who worked in the city's thirty thousand factories. The plutocrats who financed reform were keen on social control: they passed laws regulating gambling and drugs and prostitution, but nothing about minimum wages or meaningful limits on working hours. The city's largest industry, garments, had shifted to factory lofts, where conditions were in some respects worse than what they'd been in the old tenement sweatshops.

New York became the central arena in which fundamental questions were finally being explored. In an advancing society of modern industry and great economic inequality, what did social justice really mean? What responsibility did the privileged few have to those foreign poor who filled their factories and mines and made them rich? Should the rich pay taxes? Should there be a formalized welfare program? Universal health care? Factory regulations?

In the city's garment factories, foremen and forewomen known as speeders were charged with maintaining a breakneck pace. The habit of locking factory doors and ignoring calls for safety mechanisms and fire escapes — it all added up to a kind of bondage. Sexual assault, like tuberculosis, was a fact of life in the factories, as was death: In the spring of 1911, 146 employees of the Triangle Shirtwaist Company, located on the top floors of the Asch Building near Washington Square, died in a fire because they'd been locked in by the company's Russian-Jewish owners.

Friction between Abe and Mayer began in the wake of the Triangle tragedy, when Mayer decided to pursue a new line of work, becoming an advisor to the Clothing Manufacturers' Association, the putative enemy of the same garment unions he had once organized. To Abe, Mayer's decision was a rejection of everything the Shoenfelds stood for. Hadn't Mayer once preached that industrial slavery *was* white slavery, that the greed of manufacturers created the poverty that created prostitutes and criminals? Now, years later, this way of thinking was gospel for Abe's contemporaries, who viewed labor unions as sacrosanct.

The argument between father and son was far from academic. Where one stood on the labor question was as defining and divisive as any issue of the day — for the Shoenfelds, it was one of those monumental topics that could even color other family debates, such as the recent treatment of a Russian-Jewish immigrant who came to work in their home as a servant.

Mayer and Dora Shoenfeld paid the servant girl $10 a month plus room and board, which was like making $30 a month in a factory. Not a bad deal. After two months, they raised her to $11. After the third month, she asked for $12 and they gave it to her. After the fourth month, she asked for $13, and they agreed. The girl drove a hard bargain, but she was good, she had no one else in the country, and the Shoenfelds could afford it. After the fifth month, however, the girl asked for $14, and that's when things turned nasty.

To his son's horror, Mayer shared this saga publicly in a newspaper interview. For Mayer, the story served as an example in the larger context of an argument he was making about uptown reform committees, the kind that employed his son. Uptowners didn't understand East Siders, Mayer contended, didn't get how certain kinds of giving, such as the ghetto's prevalent breadlines and soup kitchens, could ruin an immigrant community by reinforcing a sense of helplessness and creating dependence.* For a *Tribune* column entitled "Vengeance," Mayer told the paper that the servant girl didn't just come out and ask for the $14:

> She was ashamed to ask again; so what does she do? She comes to
> my wife and says she is going away. "A lady uptown," she says,
> "she will give me fourteen." It makes my wife mad. The girl is
> greedy. It makes me mad too. This is what I told my wife: "We
> will get even with that girl. You tell her that you will pay her,

---

* There was evidence for Mayer's point of view. A contemporary report from the United Hebrew Charities showed that the East Side problem of missing husbands was exacerbated by the fact that husbands with desertion on their minds could be "pushed into vanishing" by the "happy consciousness" that aid for their families would be forthcoming.

not fourteen, but twenty dollars. Then, in a month, we will fire her, and she will never get another job as long as she lives, and she will starve to death." Now, that is the East Side way! So that is what I say to the uptown committees. You leave the East Side to an East Sider. We are wise to ourselves.

Mayer's prediction about the servant girl's dire fate was surely inflated. Still, Abe insisted that his father's treatment of the girl, whose presence dredged up bitter memories of Tony, was unnecessarily harsh, and the public airing of it absurd. Mayer's betrayal of the unions only furthered the divide.

The evening Abe came home from his scrape with the police, the running tension between him and Mayer finally snapped. What extra help, Abe asked Mayer, could the garment manufacturers possibly need? The legal system already sided with them. Cops corralled strikers, and judges put them in prison. One judge ruled that strikes were "against God." As for the shirtwaist girls who struck before and after the Triangle fire, they were left to their own devices. Many of them were assaulted by the thugs whom manufacturers hired to break strikes and obstruct protests. Who could forget their plucky leader, Clara Lemlich, arrested seventeen times, lying in the hospital with a busted-up face and six broken ribs? The girls out there marching and dying, whoring and disappearing, were Abe's peers.

But Mayer had his own ideas about betterment. He saw the future not in what the Jewish ghetto lacked but in what it already had: an industry that produced most of America's clothing. In that industry, Mayer argued, the downtowners held the means to create their own future. And he was right that the garment trade reflected a kind of communal upward mobility. In 1897, when he led his last strike, nearly all clothing manufacturers were German Jews. Now, fifteen years later, most were Russian Jews. Mayer joined the manufacturers as their adviser because he believed that the Triangle fire would open legislative opportunities for labor law, and that it would be easier to reform the garment industry from the inside rather than pressure manufacturers from the outside, as he had once tried to do without much success.

Besides, Mayer didn't recognize the new unions. They were led by recent Russian-Jewish immigrants who'd taken the violent style of revolutionary politics and labor wars from the Pale of Settlement and imported those hard-line tactics to the New York garment industry. Many East Siders, Abe included, saw this aggression as just reprisal, but Mayer's problem with the new labor leaders was personal. In 1910, during a big strike in the men's garment industry, Mayer's friend, a tailor named Herman Liebowitz, was murdered because he had "scabbed" (worked during the strike) in order to put food on the table for his five children. That murder, which occurred openly in the street, in the middle of the afternoon, was never investigated—an indication, Mayer said, that unions had as much political power as manufacturers.

The topic was charged, and the argument devolved into barbs. Abe called Mayer a sellout. Mayer mocked Abe's generation of reformers as self-important writers, mere "graduates of the settlement houses," who investigated this and that but took no action beyond the brothel bed.

Later, in his own bed, Abe tried to sleep but was incensed—angry at the state of the city and ashamed over having crossed a line with his father. While he stewed, musicians at a saloon across the way played into the midnight hours. At 3 a.m., Abe burst onto the fire escape and screamed, "Stop this noise! It is not alone criminal but immoral!"

After her relationship with Abe, Tony returned to the streets. She slept in cheap Bowery lodging houses and ate from breadlines. She tried to be an independent prostitute, a so-called trotter. Late at night she would carry a milk can, so that if stopped she could make a "grandstand play" and claim to just be out looking for a quart of milk. But it wasn't long before she was arrested by the cops who earned their graft from the pimps of the Independent Benevolent Association. Sent to the Hawthorne School, the overcrowded reformatory built by Jacob Schiff, Tony escaped; arrested again, she was sentenced to six weeks at a women's prison on Blackwell's Island, the future Roosevelt Island.

When she got out, she selected a two-dollar brothel on Fourteenth Street, where the trade tended to be middle-class business owners, a notch above the coal heavers and sailors who frequented the fifty-cent houses. Here, Tony was protected from the law — and exploited to the hilt. "Men are very fussy and you have to cater to them if you want to keep their trade," the madam said as she sold the girls dresses and silk stockings at exorbitant prices. But Tony learned to maximize her physical assets, and earned two dozen brass checks per evening.

Tony was still young and desirable, but she knew that the shelf life of a prostitute was short. She had to move on and up, lest she travel the downward path back to the Bowery, where the "old stock" was traded among the fifty-cent houses, and eventually left to join the colony of "fire lighters," wretches who lived on dimes by lighting lamps and starting fires for pious Jews on the Sabbath.

In the late winter of 1912, while Abe was fighting with his father, Tony was standing on Fourteenth Street, "booming up trade," when she ran into her childhood friend, Lily Lieben. More than a year had passed since the two had seen each other at the fateful dance where Tony met the pimp Motche Goldberg. Lily, knowing little of Tony's hard times, embraced Tony and explained her own recent good fortune. She'd met a boy. They were getting married!

Then Lily stepped back and took in all of Tony. Her old friend's smiling mouth was a straight, cruel line, Lily noted, and Tony's once-soft face was pinched yellow by opium. "Tony," she said, "whatever became of your fellow, the dentist?"

Tony the Tough raised her hand as if to slap Lily, as if to deliver the kind of blow she'd once doled out in their joint defense, and then said, "My fellow? He rode away. And that's all there is to it. They all ride away in the end."

8

The Killing of a Jewish Gambler

W HEN LILY LIEBEN FIRST MET LOUIE ROSENBERG, at a ball hosted by Big Jack Zelig, she didn't know much about Louie's past. She didn't know that he'd spent his teenage years in and out of reformatories and prisons. She was smitten. *That dashing flop of hair!* Louie was thin but his face was broad and he carried himself like an oak tree.

As they courted, enjoying evenings in Coney Island, Louie spun a tale about his life that sounded good to Lily. He told her that he used to work for his father, a flour wholesaler at the opulent Produce Exchange, but then discovered that he could do better working for himself, running a cigar store on Second Avenue. Lily thought: *What a smart boy I will marry!*

But gradually the truth about Louie revealed itself. When Lily learned that his cigar store was a front for a gambling den, she took this information to her mother, a dressmaker who had moved Lily and her sister from the Pale of Settlement to New York when Lily was three. Her mother told her not to worry: gamblers made *good* husbands. They had fine homes. Their wives were well dressed. If this was questionable advice, it was also an indication of how crime was viewed in the old country, where capricious laws held little moral significance for the poor and marginalized Jews of the Pale.

When Lily thought about it, she couldn't really argue with her mother's point. She liked the restaurants, the feel of her jeweled fingers toting around a silver mesh bag with foxtail drawstrings, and the auto rides. "I do not know a girl living in the circumstances I did who did not envy me my marriage to a gambler," Lily would later recall. "Especially when the girls saw me driving in an automobile. For to an East Side girl an automobile ride is heaven. . . . It stands for the very summit of riches." Aside from the pleasures of Dollar Land, a family of her own was what Lily wanted, and with Louie she could envision having it. If she was being naïve, well, as Lily herself later observed, one cannot always expect great wisdom from a girl of seventeen.

When Lily and Louie got married at the Rivington Street Synagogue, she wore a white silk gown made by her mother, and considered herself the happiest bride in New York. Afterward, at the reception, Zelig gifted the couple $100. Zelig gave Lily a kindly, searching look, then took her hand in his big paw and said, "Nice to meet you. I hope we will be friends."

The newlyweds moved up to the Bronx, where some East Siders were migrating for fresh air and fresh starts. Developers dynamited the cliffs around Southern Boulevard and transformed the area into rows of new dwellings with all the latest improvements. Their six-room flat included a library and a dining room, a porcelain bathtub, and an electric bell to ring in visitors downstairs. Everything sparkled. At night, while their music box ground out "The Gabby Glide," the husband and wife danced and sang as joyously as children. For Lily's eighteenth birthday, Louie surprised her with a yellow canary in a gilded cage.

It was the summer of 1912, the summer when "auto polo" was the new lethal fad* and the six-day bicycle races at Madison Square Garden pulled larger crowds than baseball. It was the summer when events taking place far above Lily's head would bring the city to a climactic moment, a time when everything would flip over and never flip back again.

A month into their idyll on Southern Boulevard, the honeymoon came to an abrupt end when a few of Louie's friends began to stay at their apartment. The boys went out at night and came back later and later each evening. One night while they were gone, Lily went out for a walk and was assaulted by a thief who tried to wrest the rings from her fingers.

"You ought to stay home at night," Louie said when he learned what happened. "That is the place for a woman."

"And it is the place for a man, too, at such hours!" Lily shot back. But Louie just shrugged, and a few nights later their situation darkened. Downtown, during a gang war with the Italians, Zelig was shot in the back of the head, though not fatally, and Louie was shot in the foot.

When Louie came through the door, Lily gasped in horror at the sight of his foot. He said he was playing baseball when it happened. He asked Lily to call a doctor, and retired to the bedroom.

A doctor came. Then there was another knock at the door. Lily

---

* Surprisingly, this writer found no record of an actual fatality resulting from the sport, whose brief period of nationwide popularity peaked in the mid-1910s. In New York, one could catch a match inside, at Madison Square Garden, or outside, at the Polodrome in Hempstead Plains. A match consisted of two autos, or "metal ponies," stripped to their steel frames, and two players per side—a driver and a mallet-swinger who stood on the running board. Each period began with the autos at either end of the field, and the ball positioned at the midline. The umpire dropped his arms and away flew the roaring autos in a smoking shower of sparks, the mallet-swingers stamping and dancing on the running board to help gain speed. Observed one reporter: "As the machines came head on at the ball, the players whooping in defiance, it seemed as if the next instant must witness an awful crash and the blotting out of four lives; yet no one could look away from the fascinating peril."

opened it and found a strange-looking man. He was bald and nearly albino, without eyebrows or lashes. He had red lips and freckled skin that smelled of jasmine talc. He introduced himself, smoothly and politely, as Jack Rose. "Bald Jack Rose is known as one of the best poker players there are," wrote Abe Shoenfeld, adding that Rose had stolen his wife, "a very beautiful woman," from a Second Avenue stuss dealer — stuss being a New York version of the old Western game of faro — and put her to work: "The child Mrs. Rose has bearing Jack's name came into this world by the fatherly instincts of a worthy 'sucker' who is paying Mrs. Rose $200 a month. So it is that Rose always has an income."

Lily asked Jack Rose if he knew how Louie got hurt. Rose explained that Louie was wrestling with a friend at the bathhouse and scratched his foot. He went to the bedroom to speak to Louie while Lily, pretending to read a book, listened to their conversation from the library.

"Lieutenant Becker is going to frame you up," Rose told Louie.

"But why?" asked Louie.

"Becker has the goods on you. He knows your record. He will plant you as he did Zelig." Rose was referring to a recent incident in which cops, using the new Sullivan law, had planted a gun on Zelig as a pretext for arrest. It wasn't Lieutenant Charles Becker who'd done the planting, but Louie didn't know that. "Becker can give you fourteen years," Rose said, "and he'll do it, unless you do something for him." Rose wanted Louie to believe that he was there as a messenger for Becker, the grafting cop who headed one of the two centralized NYPD vice squads. If Louie was quick to believe this story, it was because Rose was indeed a graft collector for Becker.

During the next two weeks, Jack Rose visited frequently, and often he took Lily around, as if courting her. Lily's home was now a club where men smoked, played cards, snorted cocaine, and talked about secret business. When Louie's foot healed, he said, "Lily, what do you think about putting our furniture in storage and going to Far Rockaway?"

"Will you come?" she asked.

"Not at first. Me and the boys have a job here in town, but when that is finished, yes, of course I will come."

They packed up the apartment, moved out, and parted ways.

In mid-July, as Louie and Lily dismantled their home, Arnold Rothstein summoned Herman Rosenthal, his old childhood friend and fellow gambler from the East Side, to Arnold's brownstone casino on Forty-Sixth Street to discuss a delicate matter.

As gamblers, their careers had both taken off during the rise of the Jewish underworld that began in the 1890s, when a pubescent Arnold and a twenty-year-old Herman ran craps games outside Big Tim Sullivan's poolroom. Over the years, the native-born Arnold cultivated a subtle and understated style. He renounced jewelry and confined his monogram, "A.R.," to his shirt cuffs. Whereas the immigrant Herman, born to the Russian ghetto and raised in the American ghetto, harbored no genteel pretensions. He sported sparkling jewelry and emblazoned "H.R." on gleaming cufflinks, tie clasps, and belt buckles.

While Arnold gravitated to Broadway, Herman stuck mostly to the East Side, where he ran stuss houses. Recently, though, their paths had converged. In 1909, after Arnold got permission from Big Tim to open a Tenderloin casino, Rosenthal also got permission. Herman did as Arnold did, leasing a brownstone on Forty-Fifth Street, one block away. Like Arnold, Herman installed a casino on the first floor and set up house on the upper floors with his wife, a former prostitute. But while Arnold came into his own, Herman struggled to build a business. He lacked that salesman's touch, failed to attract the right clientele, and overextended himself on lavish furnishings that lacked popular appeal — too much pink satin, it was said.

Herman had other problems, too. He fought with East Side gamblers such as Bald Jack Rose, with whom he had a long history. "It was Herman

Rosenthal who started Rose off right," wrote Abe Shoenfeld. "Most of the time Rose was employed by Rosenthal directly or worked in houses in which Rosenthal was interested." But the dynamic between them shifted when Bald Jack Rose became the graft collector for Lieutenant Becker, and lorded his new power over his former mentor. As Becker's collector, Abe wrote, "Rose was abetted by a raffish subaltern named Bridgey Webber," another East Side gambler with whom Herman had a rivalry. As kids, when Bridgey stole Herman's pet dog and held it for ransom, Herman repaid Bridgey with a broken jaw. Now, hoping to move Herman out of the Tenderloin, Bridgey was playing pranks again. He'd been sending anonymous letters to Mayor Gaynor's office, saying Herman was using rigged equipment in his casino. Gaynor passed the letters to the NYPD, and cops from the local Forty-Seventh Street precinct shut Herman down.

Instead of taking his lumps and keeping quiet, Herman fought back. One recent day, when temperatures reached into the nineties, he cranked up the furnace and locked the occupying cops inside his brownstone. To get them out, a fellow cop broke through with an axe, which was why Herman's place no longer had a front door. Then, on July 11, he went to court and asked a magistrate to enjoin the police from occupying his premises, an audacious move that put his crusade on public record. Some observers said that what Herman was doing took guts, but most thought he was crazy. *Holy gee, to go looking for trouble like this!*

At the moment, Herman was trying to convince the district attorney to make a corruption case against the cops, and this is why Arnold had asked Herman to come by. One didn't need Arnold Rothstein's keen understanding of power to know that infighting among gamblers was a threat to their collective business. No gambler, no matter how rich, could operate without approval from the top of the underworld's power center, Tammany Hall, which itself was presently in a state of transition. At forty-nine, Big Tim Sullivan had been stripped of his senate duties and hospitalized with progressive dementia, a symptom of late-stage syphilis.

Big Tim was gone, Arnold reminded Herman, and it was common knowledge that the current Tammany leader, Charlie Murphy, corrupt though he was, lacked Big Tim's affection for gamblers and street vice. During this time of uncertainty, it was all the more important to avoid drawing attention to themselves or the grafting police who ensured their survival. The best way to deal with a reform wave, Arnold advised his old friend, was to let it pass. Make your graft payments. Keep your mouth shut. Even Arnold had submitted to the ritual. A few months earlier, in the spring of 1912, his own gambling operation had been raided by Becker. It was an inconvenience, but Arnold made some repairs, spread some bribes, and reopened a few weeks later.

"What they been doing to me ain't right," Herman said, referring to the raids. "Used to be, you took a man's money and took care of him. Now they take your sugar and beat your place to pieces anyway." He added: "If the Big Feller [Big Tim Sullivan] were here, Becker would be pounding a pavement."

"The Big Feller isn't here," Arnold said. "And if he was, he'd tell you to keep your trap shut. All you can do is make trouble for a lot of people."

Herman said, "I don't want to make trouble for anyone, only Becker." He promised to name no other cops and no one in Tammany Hall.

Arnold tried a different approach. "Beansy," he said, using Herman's old street name, "you need to get out of town." Arnold knew the Sam Paul Association—the coalition of Jewish gamblers, described by the *New York Times* as "one of those loosely constituted organizations peculiar to the East Side, a combination fraternity and gang"—would sooner kill Herman than let him jeopardize their industry.

And that was only one constituency that wanted Herman dead. After all, Herman's transgression, his squeal, was the exact thing that had angered the former police commissioner, Theodore Bingham, back in 1908, when Bingham wrote the article that blamed the city's crime problem on Russian Hebrews. In the anonymous letter regarding Bingham, ostensibly written by a Jewish detective, the detective quotes Bingham as having told police: "Hold every damned kike you can. They are making such a squeal." Now, up in the Tenderloin, the old-line, non-Jewish casino operators also felt that the tribal jealousies of Jewish gamblers were screwing things up. The *Sun* had written recently, "The members of the [Tenderloin] fraternity, who had been enjoying the field to themselves before the East Siders flowed in, complained that the small fry were ruining the whole business by their treachery to each other, their 'squeals' to the police, and their greed for small profits."

Arnold told Herman, "Lay away until this thing blows over." He extended cash: "Here, take five hundred."

Herman glanced at the money. He looked at Arnold, who was eight years Herman's junior yet always telling Herman what to do. Well, this here was Herman's game and he had it all worked out: he would get a newspaper to publish his allegations against the police, and the district attorney would put him before the grand jury. "They only call you a squealer if you lose," Herman said. "I'm not leaving town."

Arnold pocketed the cash and walked away without another word.

In rejecting Arnold's advice, Herman offended what Carolyn Rothstein described as her husband's "inordinate vanity" — the pride he took in his information, in his uncanny ability to know what would happen next. Failing to respect that prescience, Carolyn said, was an offense that Arnold rarely forgave, and never without fashioning a punishment: "Arnold never had further use for a person who didn't follow his instructions."

On the night of July 15, Manhattan's district attorney, Charles Whitman, sat in his sweltering office and listened to Herman Rosenthal tell the same story he'd told Whitman several times during the past month.

Little had changed. Rosenthal still lacked corroboration for his corruption charges against the police. It wasn't that Whitman didn't want to take on a police corruption case; he wanted a case that won support up and down the class ranks of reform, and an anti-corruption crusade certainly fit that bill. But he wasn't willing to press forward without more evidence. Whitman told Rosenthal that he couldn't put him before a grand jury unless other gamblers could testify to the alleged widespread police corruption. Rosenthal nodded and vowed to return.

From the window of the DA's office, Whitman watched Rosenthal speak to reporters on the steps below, assuring them that he was going "to see this thing through." Then Rosenthal hopped in a taxi and headed uptown. Normally, Whitman wouldn't let a potential witness leave his office without security, but an attack on Rosenthal could confirm the gambler's allegations, morally if not legally.

The Café Metropole was on the first floor of the Metropole Hotel, on Forty-Third Street, a few doors west of Broadway. Inside the hotel entrance, two large electric fans whirred loudly. The breeze swayed the potted palms, fluttered the lace curtains, and flickered the table candles behind red shades.

It was after midnight when Herman Rosenthal came into the restaurant, his shirt open at the throat, his coat unbuttoned. A ragtime pianist, having recently replaced the five-piece band, played a cheerful version of "Oceana Roll," a hit song of 1911, and leaned into the syncopated beats:

You see that smoke so black sneak from that old smokestack
It's floatin' right to heaven and it won't come back...

Rosenthal sat at the nearest empty table. He ordered a steak, a Havana cigar, and a horse's neck—ginger ale and lemon.

His wife had begged him not to go out, but he had told her not to worry. The city was his home, he said, and he was the last man in New York anyone could kill right now. Feeling loose, he lit up the cigar and called out to a nearby table of fellow crooks: "What do you think of the papers lately?" He laughed. "You boys aren't sore at me, are you?"

"You're a damn fool, Herman," one shouted back.

Rosenthal finished his dinner, then walked to the hotel entrance and bought several newspapers, fresh off the presses. Back at his table he ordered coffee, read the *World* headline, and smiled at his handiwork: GAMBLER CHARGES POLICE LIEUTENANT WAS HIS PARTNER. The story had been written by the *World's* Herbert Bayard Swope, the journalist who was one of Arnold Rothstein's gambling friends. When Swope had finally agreed to publish Rosenthal's claims against the police, Rosenthal was led to believe that Arnold had changed his mind and decided to help him. In any case, he believed that Swope's article would give his allegations credibility in the public mind, forcing DA Whitman to take the case seriously — particularly if Swope, as promised, also published the contents of Rosenthal's affidavit, the same one he had sworn to in Whitman's office.

Across the dining room, the pianist broke into another ragtime hit: "Oh, you beautiful doll, you great big beautiful doll..."

Shortly before two o'clock in the morning, as the fellow crooks walked out, Bridgey Webber came through the hotel doors, made a wide circuit of the restaurant, and stopped at Rosenthal's table: "Hello, Herman." Despite their fractious past, Bridgey seemed courteous, and, stranger still, Herman showed no surprise at this, nor did he pause when Bridgey said someone wanted to see him outside. Later, this fact led many to postulate that Rosenthal must have figured Bridgey and the others had seen the stories in the papers and now wanted to join his cause.

Outside, he clutched a burning cigar in one hand, newspapers in the other, and stepped onto the sidewalk. He saw two of Bridgey's partners.

There was the hatchet-faced Harry Vallon, crouched on the other side of the entrance. And there was Bald Jack Rose, talking to someone in a dark doorway across the street. Suddenly, there appeared a gray Packard, with steeply arched fenders, and a glass flower vase on the hood. The vase was a not uncommon touch in those days, when a speed of twenty miles per hour was considered reckless. Four men—all young, all wearing clothes of the latest cut—emerged from the auto and formed an arc in the street.

This being Broadway, the brilliant night—even without the Packard's enormous headlights shining in Rosenthal's face—was blinding in a way only New York could be. High atop the building next to the Metropole was an illuminated lion. Down below, the stage was cleared.

"Over here, Herman," came a voice from beyond the lights.

Herman was crossing the sidewalk when a burst of shots erupted from the street. Two bullets hit him in the neck and head. One entered his cheek, passed through the root of his tongue, and lodged in his spine. Two others pierced his chest. A fifth bullet missed him and came to rest in the wood trim of the Metropole. As Herman dropped, the newspapers beneath his arm fanned around his feet. The Packard charged away. Bridgey Webber stepped over and leaned down, bending at the waist, hands in pockets, and studied Rosenthal's bloodied face. "Hello, Herman," he said, then straightened up. "Goodbye, Herman."

All of this happened while several police officers were patrolling Forty-Third Street, and an off-duty detective was dining in the Metropole. Yet no one tried to prevent the shooting or apprehend the gunmen.

There was, however, one person who found the event disturbing. An unemployed cabaret singer, Eddie Gallagher, was on his way to audition for a new job at the Metropole when the fleeing Packard nearly ran him over. Gallagher hurried to the scene of the crime and tried to relay the Packard's license plate number to a police officer, but he was told that the cops already had the license number. In fact, it later came to light that of the four different numbers the police possessed, none were correct.

Gallagher, figuring that his Metropole audition was canceled, went to the West Forty-Seventh Street precinct to tell his eyewitness story and register the license number, but he was ignored again. When he persisted, a cop carried him to the rear of the station, threw him into a cell, and walked away, telling a nearby reporter, "Nobody likes a squealer."

Perhaps the cop was speaking, indirectly, to the ghost of Herman Rosenthal, whose own voice rose from the beyond, the following day, when the *World* published his affidavit, his formal allegations as presented to DA Whitman, in which Herman proclaimed: "I have been called a fool for attacking the police—a squealer because I would not stand for police oppression. I have lost some of my best friends and made a lot of enemies. I can't help that now. Perhaps, if I had the thing to do over again, I might not go into it, but now that I'm in, I'm going to stick."

Part Two

Mister Prettyfield

9

Waking Up

A DAY AFTER THE ROSENTHAL MURDER, JACOB SCHIFF WOKE in his Fifth Avenue mansion and made his daily to-do list on a small school slate that he carried in his breast pocket. The sixty-four-year-old trotted down the marble stairs to the mahogany morning room, where a dumbwaiter carried breakfast up from the kitchen and Schiff ate alone, accompanied by a yellow canary and a bronze bust of Moses Mendelssohn.*

Schiff then walked from Seventy-Eighth Street to Union Square, where he met his driver for the remainder of the commute to Kuhn Loeb, the investment bank he ran. Piled next to Schiff in the Fiat were journals and newspapers. He picked up the *World,* read the lead article, and gasped. Ten days later, the Kehillah convened at the United Hebrew Charities building, on Twenty-First Street.

---

* Back in Germany, in the fall of 1743, Mendelssohn, at the age of fourteen, walked one hundred miles to Berlin and entered by the Rosenthaler Tor, the only gate in the city wall through which Jews and cattle were allowed to pass. Mendelssohn became a philosopher, and paved the way for the German-Jewish epoch, a nineteenth-century enlightenment that produced, among others, Marx, Freud, Mahler, Einstein, Kafka, and Schiff himself.

For the German Jews, the Rosenthal murder was a disorienting torment. The spotlight that the case shined on Jewish crime was a gift to those who wanted to close the country's borders, and, for them, the timing was ideal: the next anti-immigration bill was set to come up for a vote at the end of the year. Meanwhile police circulars with photos of the wanted gunmen, above the words "American Hebrew," were distributed internationally, as authorities scoured cities from San Francisco to Paris.

At the Hebrew Charities Building, Kehillah chairman Judah Magnes took control of the meeting. After Rabbi Magnes's 1910 resignation from Temple Emanu-El, he held on to his Kehillah position. If he was infuriating to some, he was also too valuable to lose. Those close to Magnes would later remember him as "a great appreciator of ideas," "a perennial underdog," "a prophet," "an idealist," "a self-centered egotist," and "a sledgehammer." He went his own way, and this made him magnetic even to those whose pieties he harpooned. Now, finally, momentum was on his side, and he pushed, urging the uptowners to take action against Jewish crime. He picked up the *Ottawa Journal* and read aloud: "We take up our paper to see how those poor heathen in New York are getting on with the upheaval over the killing of a Jew gambler by some equally useless members of the underworld. It would be a good thing if a few thousand of such cattle would kill each other; the pity of it all is that there is only one wiped out, and the matter of who is responsible of small consequence." Then he picked up the London *Times* and read a more generalized commentary: "Trades and occupations in which gambling is a large element are everywhere peopled by Jews. They are attracted to the rise and fall of stocks. 'Bulling' and 'bearing' and 'arbitrage' have a fascination for them of something gained for nothing, of profits derived without labor."

Magnes paused, letting these words hang in the air. When a Kehillah member suggested sending letters to these papers, as they had done in the past, to complain of anti-Semitism, Magnes waved off the idea. "The time for public gestures and super-sensitiveness has passed," he said. He suggested that the Kehillah organize a "vigilance league" and hire investigators to ferret out information, then pressure the mayor and police commissioner to take action.

Schiff flinched. He recalled the public relations disaster of the Committee of Fifteen's vice crusade. In the intervening decade, Schiff, who himself was a first-generation immigrant—unlike most of the German-Jewish uptowners, who *descended* from immigrants—had made many efforts on behalf of immigrants. He sponsored the Hebrew Orphan Asylum, Montefiore Hospital, and the Hawthorne School for wayward children. Abroad, he lobbied for sanctions against Russia, as punishment for the czar's treatment of Jews in the Pale of Settlement, and financed Japan's successful war against Russia in 1905.

As an activist and philanthropist, Schiff was a tireless innovator. In 1907, when Americans groused about the glut of immigrants on the Eastern Seaboard, Schiff shot off letters to Minnesota farmers, asking what agricultural background one needed to work the land there, and coordinated with shipowners to take new immigrants to Galveston Bay. When the immigrants arrived in Texas, Schiff's lawyers matched them to cities according to vocation. Butchers went to Kansas City, carpenters went to Grand Rapids, tanners to Milwaukee, and so on.

Still, addressing Jewish crime remained a thorny subject. There was a fear among the German Jews that the historical experiment in America could end in catastrophe, and that calling attention to Jewish crime would not only hasten that fate but also alienate the downtowners, who often bridled at reform efforts. The relationship between Jewish rich and poor was an old story. Back in the towns and villages of the Pale, there was always a local kehillah, a body of influential Jews who exercised its power over the lower class. In New York, the most famous downtown playwright, Jacob Gordin, known as the Yiddish Shakespeare, produced a biting satire in 1903, *The Benefactors of the East Side,* that skewered Schiff and his pretensions as "the second coming of Abraham Lincoln freeing the slaves."

But Schiff reconsidered the matter of a vice crusade. The America of 1912 was a different country than that of 1901 or 1903. The rise of moral reform and anti-vice laws now supplied legislative backing for a war on crime. And if such a war was politically risky, there were also risks in doing nothing — like the risk that this place of asylum would cave under its chronic xenophobia, close its borders, and go down in Jewish history as another false promised land.

Schiff liked Magnes's idea. Schiff's son-in-law, Felix Warburg, also liked it, as did others: the lawyer Louis Marshall; the bankers William Solomon and Isaac Seligman; *New York Times* publisher Adolph Ochs; and the philanthropist Sam Lewisohn, the son of the copper-mining mogul Adolph Lewisohn. (Sam's cousin, along with Schiff's son, had been put on the spot back in 1901 when the lads were found gambling their inheritances at Richard Canfield's casino.) But most Kehillah members disagreed with such a bold move as that which Magnes suggested. Why draw more negative attention to their own kind? Sure, Jews had their share of criminals, but so did other groups. If there was to be a vice crusade, these dissenters argued, let it be waged *by* all *against* all. The dissenters resolved to give their money instead to the Citizens Union, a coalition of Waspy reformers known as the Cits. The Cits were financing District Attorney Whitman in the Rosenthal case, giving the DA money to hire investigators and pay witnesses.*

The dissenters left, while those keen on a vice war stayed. Magnes said they would need someone to lead this crusade, and on this point Schiff was prepared. He pulled out a prepublication copy of a forthcoming report, entitled *Commercialized Prostitution in New York City*. It was a four-hundred-page document commissioned by John D. Rockefeller Jr.'s Bureau of Social Hygiene. The report's author, ostensibly, was the lawyer

---

* Paying witnesses was a common trial practice, along with other procedural oddities like publishing the names, professions, and addresses of jurors.

who ran the bureau. But Schiff had heard through uptown connections that the actual writer was the son of Mayer Shoenfeld, a downtown tailor whom Schiff once partnered with on a variety of failed reform endeavors. Schiff passed around the report, which was unrelenting in its depiction of violence and pornographic in its detail, shocking for its time. After the members glanced over it, they agreed that this author, the tailor's son, was their man.

On August 8, three weeks after the Rosenthal murder, Abe Shoenfeld lay on the floor of his bedroom in the back of his family's apartment at 125 Clinton Street and completed his morning regimen. Chin tucked, hands clasped behind his skull, he pulled his head away from his body to stretch and strengthen the spine, as instructed in *Physical Culture*. He stood up, extended his left leg, bent his right knee, and dipped until his hip touched his heel, then repeated the movement on the other side, back and forth.

He checked his watch. It was 8 a.m. He walked to the window and looked across the courtyard. Right on schedule, the back windows of the building opposite his opened, and the parlor-house girls heaved the contents of their trash bins into the air. The hefty napkin bundles, evidence of a palmy evening, dispersed and splattered on the courtyard below. He rolled his eyes. Six years had passed since Abe left school to become a reformer, and no real progress had been made. He was only twenty-one, but his enthusiasm for the work was fading.

In the kitchen he poured a cup of Postum, cracked a fist of black walnuts over wheat and cream, and read the papers. Two of the Rosenthal gunmen had been found. One was caught in an upstate village. Another hadn't gotten farther than Harlem, where he fell asleep with his girlfriend in one arm and an opium pipe in the other. Splashed across every paper was Abe's old friend, Louie Rosenberg, who, along with the fourth gunman, Harry Horowitz, was still wanted for the murder.

Abe shaved, wrapped a fresh collar around his neck, and shouldered into a light worsted coat. In summertime, most men favored a Sennett boater hat, but Abe preferred his Howard hat with the dented crown. It went better with a pince-nez. Dress to impress. It was a big meeting for Abe. He walked up to the Hebrew Charities Building and found Judah Magnes in his office. They shook hands and laughed. They had both been expecting something different. Abe figured a rabbi would have a beard. Magnes assumed the author of the prostitution report would be older. Magnes tapped a copy of *Commercialized Prostitution in New York City* and confessed his surprise that Jewish people could do the things described therein.

Abe said: "If it is any consolation, sir, there is no Jewish way of being a whore."

He was flattered to have been called by Magnes, a maverick whose principled rejection of Temple Emanu-El and embrace of the East Side made him, at thirty-five, one of the most famous rabbis in America. Later, Abe would deem Magnes "the one person I could fairly say was a paragon of virtue." But Abe didn't care much for the Kehillah, which he saw as another naïve committee of rich people, Jewish or not.

So many of these committees had come and gone since Abe's childhood. Every few years a criminal reform effort materialized, and it tended to play out the same way. Some cops might see prison time. A reform mayor might get elected. But the officials who enabled crime were never prosecuted. True reform, Abe knew, wouldn't come about until the connection between the underworld and the upperworld was severed. He was fed up with false reform: "investigations," like the Rockefeller report, that were conducted for the sake of publicity. He expected to be pitched another such project. What he heard surprised him.

Magnes, by way of introducing the subject, said, "Investigation without action is a habit that ranks high among the credentials of hell," and went on to discuss a vice crusade in which Abe would bring the Kehillah information about the underworld, and the Kehillah would take that information to Mayor Gaynor. He asked Abe who the biggest East Side gambler was. Abe said it was Dollar John Langer, who ran at least eight casinos. Magnes asked what it would take to shut down Dollar John. Abe said they would need the name of Dollar John's bagman, the cop he pays off.

This plan sounded different from anything Abe had heard. What about publicity? he asked. He was concerned about his safety, of course, but he also wondered whether the Kehillah was out to get headlines, like the other committees. Magnes assured him that nothing would appear in newspapers. Abe had never had a conversation like this. Maybe he was wrong about the Kehillah.

Like the uptowners, Abe was embarrassed by Jewish crime, but for more personal reasons. His former best friend was on the run from a murder charge. The girl he fell in love with had left him to live the life of a prostitute. His one burning desire was to finish what his father's generation had started. He wanted to clean up the neighborhood and crack down on crooked politicians who were abetting crime on the East Side. This sense of purpose would make Abe Shoenfeld a crucial asset for the Kehillah, if he could stay alive.

They agreed on a plan: identify Dollar John's bagman in the NYPD. Magnes wrote a check for $2,500, with no further guidance or instructions for how to use it, and told Abe to get in touch when he had information.

Before Abe left, Magnes said there was one more thing he wanted to discuss. He handed Abe a report from another Kehillah investigator and asked for Abe's opinion. The report, about crime at an East Side bowling alley, had been written for Magnes by a young attorney named Jonah Goldstein. Jonah and his brother were Tammany lawyers, Abe knew, and their law firm, Goldstein & Goldstein, defended East Side gangsters. The bowling alley in Jonah Goldstein's report was next to the

Forsyth Bath House, where many of those gangsters lived. The gangsters, Abe assumed, wanted to get rid of the bowling alley in order to extend the bathhouse. Jonah was using his position with the Kehillah to advance his clients' agenda. Abe explained this to Magnes and said he couldn't work with Goldstein: "If you'll have him, please don't have me."

Magnes called out to his secretary: "Ms. Levinson, please phone Jonah Goldstein. Tell him that we've suspended operations and will no longer need his service."

Abe, seeing what his word meant to Magnes, reconsidered. He wondered if Goldstein could be a kind of decoy. On second thought, Abe said, "Perhaps it's better to keep Jonah on and tell him nothing. Let him make the *tumel*" — the commotion.

Magnes called back to the secretary: "Ms. Levinson, let Jonah be!"

Abe pocketed the $2,500 check and walked out.

Magnes retained no evidence of the payment, but he did record the contents of the meeting in a letter to his Kehillah colleagues: "We've made connection with an excellent young Jewish man who has considerable experience in ferreting out what we want to know. We hope his results will merit further action, for it is high time we wake up and stay awake."

While Abe Shoenfeld pursued the Kehillah's secret plan and his own vision of a vice-free community, Arnold Rothstein was trying to salvage his own future.

Back in July, the situation with Rosenthal had worked out more or less as Arnold predicted, insofar as Rosenthal was dead, but the fallout had taken Arnold by surprise. He hadn't expected that the murder would light such a fire under the district attorney to take on police corruption. Arnold paced his casino, trying to puzzle out some plan that would give reformers what they wanted in the Rosenthal case while preserving his political benefactors in Tammany Hall.

He began to spend his afternoons at Delmonico's, the fancy Fifth Avenue restaurant where Tammany leader Charlie Murphy dined. Unlike Big Tim Sullivan, whose underworld association was public knowledge, Murphy had tried to cultivate a more respectable image. Instead of taking money from gamblers and pimps, Murphy preferred to plunder state budgets and bilk city contractors. He purchased a weekend estate in East Hampton, and moved his meetings from Tammany headquarters on Fourteenth Street up to Delmonico's, where, in a private area known as the Scarlet Room, he received a procession of bankers and lawyers, teachers and reporters — the unofficial secret service that supplied Murphy with his own legendary intuition. Arnold got in line.

Arnold understood that Murphy's new Tammany Hall could mean new opportunities for himself, too, so long as Tammany came through the Rosenthal Affair intact. The trick, Arnold and Murphy agreed, was keeping the case about police corruption rather than political corruption. Recently, Lieutenant Charles Becker, who'd been assigned to run one of Mayor Gaynor's two vice squads, had been arrested in connection with the murder. Murphy and Arnold made no secret of their belief that Becker had nothing to do with Rosenthal's execution. And yet Becker, one of several cops named by Rosenthal, *was* a grafter. If a sacrifice had to be made, Becker was the obvious candidate, but a big question remained: how to manufacture the evidence that Whitman would need in order to make a case against Becker? Arnold had a solution in mind.

He fetched his gambling buddy, the journalist Herbert Bayard Swope, and together they visited the district attorney at his apartment.

10

To the Wall

WHEN ARNOLD AND SWOPE KNOCKED ON THE DOOR OF the DA's Madison Avenue apartment, they found Charles Whitman distraught and drinking heavily, worrying that the Rosenthal case would become another blown career opportunity. A high-functioning alcoholic with a jutting chin, a craggy nose, thin, downturned lips, a broad forehead, and hair worn in a center part, Whitman had the look of a schoolmaster in a boy's academy — a job that he had in fact held between college at Amherst and law school at NYU.

In 1902, Whitman climbed out of a dreary career in private practice by getting named to the magistrate's bench, the lowest-ranking judicial office. Five years later, the city's magistrates met at Delmonico's and chose Whitman as their president. On the night of his promotion to president of magistrates, a well-lubricated Whitman stumbled down Broadway and stopped into a bar for a nightcap. By the time he drank up, he realized that the time was twenty-three minutes after one o'clock, the legal closing hour. He stopped at more saloons, enjoying an illegal drink at each one, and then reeled into the Forty-Seventh Street precinct. "I am president of the Board of Magistrates!" he announced, and berated the police for failing to enforce the law.

This bald-faced hypocrisy made Whitman an ideal political candidate for the city's Wasp power center, those republican reformers — known as the Holies, as in holier-than-thou — who tended to use reform as a cudgel, enforcing the same drinking laws that they themselves routinely broke, and soon Whitman's life changed. He became a regular guest at uptown dinner parties and Newport mansions. In 1909, the Wasps got him elected to district attorney. As DA, Whitman cultivated the press, but that big career-making case, something that could advance him to mayor or even governor, eluded him. And the Triangle Shirtwaist fire of 1911 still haunted him. In the Triangle case, Whitman rushed indictments against the factory owners, then stumbled at trial and failed to achieve a single conviction, leaving 146 deaths unavenged.

But now it was 1912, and things were looking up for Whitman, as Mayor Gaynor lost support over the city's increased lawlessness. For Whitman, as for Arnold, the Rosenthal murder presented a chance: if he could prosecute a cop for the murder of a man who'd given testimony in Whitman's own presence just hours prior, he would have a good shot at beating Gaynor in the next mayoral election. And, at first, the Rosenthal case had looked good for Whitman. After the murder, he went to the West Forty-Seventh Street precinct and found Eddie Gallagher, the singer who was jailed for trying to give the police information about the crime. Whitman got the license plate number from Gallagher, then tracked down the owners of the murder vehicle, two young East Siders who rented out the gray Packard from a stand on Second Avenue. That led to the arrests of the accomplices who rented the auto: Bald Jack Rose and Bridgey Webber. As for the gunmen, the authorities already had two in custody. The case now appeared largely solved — and this, for Whitman, was the problem: a trial of lowly Jewish gamblers and thugs was not a career case. He needed to nail someone higher up, such as a cop or a

Tammany politician, but he had no evidence. Whitman was considering how he might drop the case quietly when he answered the knock at his door.

Whitman would not have recognized Arnold Rothstein, but he had a history with Herbert Bayard Swope. An intensely ambitious reporter, Swope often used his platform at the *World* to drive stories, literally creating news. Earlier that year, for instance, he led coverage on the sinking of the *Titanic*. The previous spring, on the morning of the Triangle fire, it had been Swope who brought fellow reporters to Whitman's office, dragged Whitman to the scene of the fire, and then wrote Whitman's press statement, in which Whitman vowed to move quickly and seek justice. It was justice that Whitman then failed to get because he moved too quickly. In the Rosenthal Affair, it had been Swope who printed Rosenthal's allegations in the *World,* the very article that Rosenthal gloated over before his head was blown off.

Swope, like Arnold, was driven, and together they made a formidable combo. They differed in some respects — where Swope was flamboyant, Arnold was conservative — but they were the same age, both Jewish (Swope from Germans, Arnold from Russians), and of a similar mind about living on the edge. Of Swope, Carolyn Rothstein recalled: "Herbert had one of the most remarkable personalities I've ever known. The feature about him that most impressed me was that he succeeded in making you think that you of all the persons in the world were the one he most wished to be with at that moment. He had an astonishing gift for making valuable friendships, and of having his own way with his friends."

Swope and Arnold told Whitman that they could help him make a case against Lieutenant Becker, so long as Whitman agreed to limit his investigation to Becker, leaving Tammany officials out of the trial. According to their plan, Swope would run Bald Jack Rose's "confession" in the *World*. It would be a story of how Becker used Bald Jack as the go-between to arrange the murder of Rosenthal. At trial, the state's other gambler-witnesses would then parrot Bald Jack's story in their testimonies. Whitman thought about it. The plan entailed relying on the worst witnesses, those who *did* in fact order the gunmen to murder Rosenthal, but there were no other options. So Whitman summoned Bald Jack and the other gamblers from jail to complete the deal: immunity in exchange for testimony that everything they did, from renting the auto to hiring the gunmen, was done at Lieutenant Becker's behest.

After a grand jury indicted Becker, Whitman's uptown backers — the Waspy Cits — rewarded him with a war chest and an audience at Cooper Union. When reporters asked Whitman about rumors connecting the Rosenthal murder to Tammany Hall, Whitman, per his agreement, was careful: "We're investigating a murder," he said, "not conducting some sociological investigation." He said he wasn't "directly concerned with the general gambling situation," and promised to avenge the murder "as a challenge to our very civilization."

All that remained, Whitman added, was to capture the two gunmen who were still on the run.

Lily Rosenberg was back living with her parents on Grand Street, where she received letters from Louie. "Don't worry," he wrote from Yonkers, "I've been pretending to be an actor." From the Catskills, he wrote: "Now I pose as an insurance agent, because no one wants to talk to an insurance agent." These letters bucked Lily up, and her attitude changed. No longer just an obscure ghetto dweller, she was now page-one news, part of a great caper, and she behaved with the chutzpah of someone who believed notoriety was its own kind of protection.

When a deputy police commissioner called Lily into NYPD headquarters and asked her where Louie was hiding, she said, "I wish I knew." She blinked her blue eyes and patted her golden ringlets. "I do hope this affair blows over soon and you fellows find the right man."

In August detectives followed Lily. She took trolleys and elevated trains all over the city, slipping into buildings by the front and leaving by the back. One day she met a friend who said, "Come, we are going to see him." They boarded an auto and motored out of Manhattan.

From across the street, Abe Shoenfeld watched the auto speed away, then hailed a taxi and followed.

For the past month, Abe had bankrolled a squad of investigators who employed their own spies, including doormen and casino dealers. He logged the addresses and details of dozens of East Side gambling dens. But the one detail he needed, the identity of Dollar John Langer's bagman, his graft collector in the police department, eluded Abe. If the underworld was tight-lipped, it was because gamblers had been flooding the streets with money in the wake of Rosenthal's murder, paying off anyone who might have betrayal on their minds. No one did, not after what happened to Rosenthal. And not after what happened since. The bartender who fingered one of the gunmen was shot dead the next day. In East Side streets, people extolled the virtues of silence, and prophesied: *Long life if you stick.*

It was impossible to get anyone to speak. By the time Abe tracked Lily to Louie's hideout, he'd spent the Kehillah's $2,500 and gotten nowhere. He had one idea left.

Downtown, on the courthouse steps, Abe joined a crowd of reporters gathering around Big Jack Zelig, who'd unwittingly become the most important witness in the Rosenthal Affair. Zelig's journey to this point had begun back in June, when he was sitting in the Tombs jail with a gunshot wound in the back of his head and facing a long sentence for the planted gun. It was then that Bald Jack Rose approached him. Bald Jack wanted Zelig to handle the Rosenthal murder, but Zelig said no. Zelig then accused Bald Jack of being behind the planted gun and using it as leverage to compel Zelig to murder Rosenthal. Bald Jack denied it. But, to avoid Zelig's wrath and get him out of the way, Bald Jack provided bail money for Zelig, plus funds for Zelig to take his wife and son to Hot Springs, Arkansas, the era's popular underworld vacation spot. Bald Jack was then free to approach Louie Rosenberg, Zelig's second-in-command, about doing the Rosenthal murder.

After a few weeks in Hot Springs, Zelig sent his family home and traveled to Boston to pick pockets in a new city. It was in Boston that Zelig read about the Rosenthal murder, the job that he had turned down, and wondered whom Bald Jack got to do it. When Zelig learned the identities of the alleged shooters, his own pals in the Avenue Boys, he returned to New York. By that time, the *World* had published Bald Jack's "confession," a document that detailed how Lieutenant Becker arranged the Rosenthal murder. In the confession, Bald Jack described his visits to Zelig in the Tombs, and characterized his request that Zelig arrange the murder as having originally come from Becker. This was the key evidentiary point that put Becker in the hot seat and made Zelig the most important witness in the case. People wondered: When examined, what would Zelig say?

Now, on the courthouse steps, was an opportunity to find out. Reporters wanted to know what Zelig had just told the grand jury. Zelig wouldn't go that far, but he did make several clarifying remarks to the press. First, he said he didn't know Lieutenant Becker. Then he confirmed that Bald Jack had approached him in the Tombs and provided him with bail money — but not because Zelig agreed to orchestrate Rosenthal's murder. Rather, Zelig explained, Bald Jack knew that if Zelig had been sent to prison for the gun charge, then Zelig's friends would have killed Bald Jack. At which point Zelig's lawyer interrupted: "Would have *avenged* you," the lawyer corrected.

"That's what I said — would've *avenged* me." Zelig smiled and the reporters roared with laughter. In a world of duplicity and injustice, in which the powerful peddled what East Siders called "soft music," Zelig, at least, was no "bull slinger."

The crowd dispersed, and Zelig boarded a crosstown trolley. Abe hopped on and took the seat next to him. As the trolley lurched along, Zelig said, "G'morning, Abe, writing another article?"

Abe and Zelig had known each other since they were kids, when Zelig would stand up against the knife-wielding Italians who screamed "*Matacristo*," Christ-killer, and cornered the Jewish boys in alleys. Now Abe and Zelig were on opposite sides of the fence legally, but they both wanted a better neighborhood. To Zelig, Abe was a harmless reformer gathering facts. But now Abe was asking for something different: the name of Dollar John's bagman. Normally, Abe wouldn't bother asking Zelig for such a favor, because Zelig didn't squeal, and he certainly didn't talk business with reformers. But Zelig was in a tight spot, and Abe had no other options.

"No articles. I was hoping to talk about the boys," Abe said, referring to Louie Rosenberg and Harry Horowitz, the two gunmen still at large.

"What about them?" Zelig asked.

"Their wives have been playing hide-and-seek with the detectives," Abe said. "They think it's a game." Zelig suppressed a wince. This was Abe's leverage. He pushed: "By the end of the month, Louie and Harry will be in custody."

"I don't want to know where they are," Zelig snapped.

"I wouldn't tell you if I knew," Abe said, but he *did* know.

Zelig sighed. "What do you propose?"

"We all know it was Dollar John and Bald Jack Rose and the Sam Paul Association that were behind the Rosenthal murder," Abe said, offering his own theory of the case. "If we drive Dollar John to the wall"—destroy his gambling empire—"the gamblers will turn on each another. The case against Becker will be exposed as a fraud. Whitman will drop it. Louie and the boys will walk away. No one cares about a gamblers' war." This scenario was speculative, but it made some sense in the moment.

Zelig said, "What do you need from me?"

"The name of Dollar John's bagman."

"Forget it." For Zelig, the underworld's no-squeal law — taken from the Pale of Settlement, where Jewish traitors identified the most able-bodied boys for the czar's army — was sacred. Even after Zelig had been shot in the head by the Italian earlier that summer, he refused to testify against the shooter, saying he'd get "hunk," revenge, in his own way.

Abe pleaded. "Soon everyone will be squealing. And then what? When Louie and the boys are facing the chair, then what? For years, Zel, gamblers cleared their measure in peace because *you* made the wops toe the line at Mott Street. The cops didn't do that for them. *You* did. And whenever it came back on you, you always stuck" — refused to name names.

"And I'm stickin' now," Zelig said, then hopped off the trolley and disappeared into the noonday crowd.

If Abe didn't get Dollar John, the Kehillah's crusade would die an early death. He wrestled with an impossible decision: whether to turn Louie and Harry in. If all four gunmen faced the electric chair, Zelig might change his mind about helping Abe take down Dollar John. Abe's life had paralleled two decades of failed reform efforts. He felt the pressure of that history. Magnes and the Kehillah got him to care about reform again, to believe that a more aggressive approach could work. He remembered his father. Mayer used to say that reform wasn't a pretty business, that it entailed tough decisions and even turning on friends. But...*Louie?* There was a chance that the conjectural scenario Abe offered to Zelig could bear out, that pressure on Dollar John could somehow benefit Louie. If it didn't, though, Abe might be sending Louie to the chair.

*　*　*

Louie Rosenberg and Harry Horowitz hid out on the top floor of a brownstone in Brooklyn. The back balcony overlooked an open-air moving-picture show, and at night the two married couples — their wives were both named Lily — watched free comedies and thrillers from the fire escape.

"We won't have to hide long," Louie told Lily. "They'll soon find the fellow that did it." If Louie felt comfortable lying through his teeth like this, his confidence in his situation reflected a blinkered perspective of the case: thanks to Bald Jack's manipulation, Louie and the boys had carried out the Rosenthal murder because they thought the order came from the police department.

So they carried on. Each morning, after the delivery man left a piece of ice at their door, the wives shopped for food while the boys read about themselves in the papers. The days were tinged with hope, and Lily wondered if they might live this way forever — it wouldn't be so bad.

Abe wrote down an address — "756 Woodward Avenue, Brooklyn" — and sent it to an NYPD detective.

Bored with their confinement, Louie and Lily decided to pull hats low over their brows and head to Coney Island. On the boardwalk, they passed the Gen-u-wine Somali Warriors and the Ubangi Women, whose lips enclosed ten-inch-wide wooden disks. They passed the Human Fountain, Spider Boy, and the Thyroid Woman, who weighed 689 pounds. A man in a bowler hat barked: "All aboard the aero-plane shooting gallery! Wing a plane in flight! Considerable skill is required, for the platform on which the marksman stands is constantly moving! Fifty cents for five shots! Get a buck for each plane hit!"

Louie took the rifle and sprinted up the steps to the aero-plane wing. When the barker turned on the motor, a propeller blew Louie's suit against his body while the wing pitched side to side. In the distance, against a painted cloud panorama, mini aero-planes moved along a slotted track. Louie spread his legs, took aim, and shot five planes in quick succession, then hopped down and collected five dollars. By now Lily knew that people didn't call her husband Lefty because he played baseball with his left hand.

As the boardwalk lights came up against the darkness, she pointed at the Mile Sky Chaser and said: "Take me on the big ride!" The coaster climbed to a peak. Its plunging descent pushed Lily's diaphragm into her throat and the upward surge snapped her head back, the white sands below a blur in the night.

After he turned Louie in, Abe wrote dozens of pages—some for his report to the Kehillah, some for his own personal file—about the Avenue Boys and what the gang had meant to the neighborhood. The story began, he recalled, on a spring day in 1909. Zelig walked to a thieves' hangout on Broome Street, where Louie Rosenberg and Whitey Lewis sat on the shoeblack chairs outside. Louie and Whitey had been arrested for picking pockets. The judge could have given them "a short poke" on Blackwell's Island but instead held the pair over for the grand jury and a possible trial.

"No chance to get it away from his term?" Zelig asked.

"Not a chance," said Whitey. "The rat looked down at us and said, 'I know your kind. You're a menace to society.' I was going to reply: 'Sure you know me, judge. Don't you remember when you were my defense lawyer? And I had to go out and steal so I could pay your fee?'"

Zelig threw up his hands. "What do you expect from a rat like that? He hasn't any principle."

Later that night, at the Chatham Club on Doyers Street, two Italians attacked one of Zelig's friends. Zelig hit one Italian in the jaw and sent him flying, then took the other and "commenced to pound his head on the table, steadily, like a pestle in a mortar." Before this evening, Abe wrote, "Zelig had taken as many beatings as he'd given, but his graft was stealing. What did he want with gangsters? Nothing. But that night became the christening of a new gang man, the likes of which the town had not known. Zelig became a target and realized that in order to remain in New York he'd have to fight his way through the streets. He went back to the shoeblack chairs and organized the best mob the East Side had ever seen — notorious, murderous."

The Avenue Boys ran the Italians out of East Side dance halls, prevented robberies, and came down hard on pimps. "Boldly, foolishly, Zelig's enemies challenged his rising star," Abe wrote. "They came heeled with irons [pistols] and rarely lived to tell the tale. To those who wished to return to an earlier time — a time of shaking down casinos and businesses — Zelig was a menace, augmented by his two fearless lieutenants, who would die for him, who would never say no."

Of Louie, Abe wrote: "He is well-educated, refined in manner, and one would never think that he is as bad as his actions related herein denote." Of Lily, Abe commented: "She fell in love and is steadfast in her conviction that as a wife she should not desert him."

Louie and Lily awoke to a knock and heard Yiddish spoken outside. "It must be okay," Louie said. "Answer it."

When she opened the door, several detectives loomed. The deputy commissioner who had interrogated her a few weeks earlier said, "Hello, Lily. I see you've found Louie." Her answer was a scream.

11

Pal Zel

A WHIZ, A FLASH, AND THEY WERE PAST!
Round and round they went, clinging like flies far up the outer edge of the velodrome's sloping surface. Since the introduction of the six-day bicycle race in 1891, interest in the sport had grown rapidly as foreign riders, from Jamaica to Tasmania, worked up enthusiasm among the many nationalities of New York, the world's most diverse city. New reforms in the six-day race meant that riders no longer went the whole 142 hours alone. No competitor could ride more than twelve hours each day, but the sport lost none of its excitement.

On the first Saturday in October, days before the Becker trial was to begin, Big Jack Zelig, looking for a distraction, attended the six-day race at Madison Square Garden, on Twenty-Third Street. Louie and Harry had been found. Zelig was sick about it, and felt responsible for his comrades' plight.

The six-day race didn't provide much diversion. Before Zelig could finish a beer, two Italians grabbed him from behind and threw him to the floor. He took punches to his head and ribs, the attackers shouting, "You dumb Jew bastard!" After attention from surrounding spectators forced the Italians to flee, Zelig, blood running from his nose, pursued them up the steps, his fist descending across the head of one Italian, whom Zelig then heaved, with a twist, down the stairs.

Outside, he dusted himself off and hailed a taxi downtown to Siegel's Café, a hangout for thieves at 76 Second Avenue. He collected his mail at the front and took his regular table in back, where a waiter delivered Zelig's usual, seltzer with lemon. But not long after he sat down he was bothered again.

Witnesses would later say that Red Phil Davidson, a red-haired Russian-Jewish pimp, tall and bumbling, looked nervous as he approached Zelig in the café. Two nights earlier, Zelig had hosted a ball to raise money for the gunmen's legal defense fund. At the ball, Red Phil, who was held in low repute even by fellow pimps, hoped to buy his way into Zelig's good graces by offering to purchase wine for Zelig's group. Zelig had declined, but when Red Phil persisted, Zelig accepted the bottle. Nevertheless, Red Phil's largesse failed to purchase Zelig's respect, and now Red Phil wanted his money back.

Zelig was dismissive. "I did not ask you for money. You were trying to show everyone that you were my friend. Now get out of here."

When Red Phil pressed the matter, Zelig stood up and slapped Red Phil across the face, blackening his eye and sending the pimp slinking out of Siegel's. Zelig returned to his table and opened his mail. There was a letter from Louie, written from the Tombs:

> *Dear Pal Zel: I received your letter and I was certainly glad to hear from you, and you certainly know how I more than appreciate what you are doing for me. Zel, old man, I ain't worrying a bit.... You tell me that you are going to stick to me and to the boys to the end. I know that, Zel, as I know what you are made of...*
>
> *I remain your sincere friend and pal,*
>
> *Louie*

Zelig must have felt wretched. *What was he made of?*

He had been portrayed as a swing vote in the Rosenthal Affair, a witness whose testimony could determine the outcome of the two October trials, first Lieutenant Becker's and then that of the four gunmen. No one knew how Zelig would testify, although he'd certainly tipped his hand on the courthouse steps, following his grand jury testimony, when he indicated that he didn't know Becker and hated Bald Jack Rose. It seemed that Zelig intended to refute Bald Jack's testimony, destroying the prosecution's case. Zelig's comments had rattled powerful entities who were invested in the success of the case, including Tammany Hall and the East Side gamblers of the Sam Paul Association — of which Zelig, as their protector, had been an esteemed member until now. After Zelig's remarks on the courthouse steps, DA Whitman was so desperate that he'd been feeding his own hoped-for version of Zelig's testimony to the *World,* saying that Zelig "was so afraid of Becker that he had no alternative but to hire the quartet of murderers and then flee the city in terror of the policeman."

For Zelig, the decision about how to testify remained an impossible one. If he did echo Bald Jack's story on the witness stand, then he would be sending his friends to the electric chair. If he testified in Becker's defense, however, it might help Becker, but it wouldn't necessarily help the boys, whose guilt wasn't much in dispute. Herein lay the conundrum: Becker probably hadn't ordered the murder, yet due to Bald Jack's trickery, Louie and the boys committed it because they thought the order came from Becker, who — in their eyes — *was* the police department. What complicated matters further, for Zelig, was the fact that much of the East Side underworld, even beyond the Sam Paul Association, was pulling for Whitman. Like Arnold Rothstein, the underworld hoped that speedy prosecutions would preserve the power of Tammany and hasten a return to the wide-open city of yore. Hence Zelig was a dangerous wild card, and many preferred him dead.

In Siegel's Café, while Zelig dealt himself a game of solitaire, an idea came to him. A terrible idea, but it was all he had. He wrote a name on the back of a bathhouse ticket. He summoned a "lobbygow," an errand boy, handed the kid the ticket, and gave him delivery instructions. The lobbygow ran off. Then Red Phil Davidson returned, asking to make amends. They shook hands, and Zelig gave Red Phil five dollars as a peace offering.

Later, Zelig left the café, stopped in for a shave at the barber next door, and jumped a trolley. As the trolley rolled along, Zelig lit a cigarette and smiled at a young boy and his mother. He didn't notice when the motorman turned around and addressed a crazed-looking character behind Zelig. "What's the matter?" asked the motorman, moments before Red Phil aimed his gun and pulled the trigger. Zelig was shot in the back of the head, for the second time in four months, and this time he flopped forward and died.

The streets filled with people. *Zelig's been shot!*

Red Phil ran but was apprehended.

On Second Avenue, Dollar John Langer paced the sidewalk: "Is he dead? Is he dead? He is? Oh . . . thank *God*."

Sometime that evening, the lobbygow arrived at Abe Shoenfeld's door, handed Abe the bathhouse ticket, and ran away. Abe turned the ticket over. There, in Zelig's looping script, was the name of a New York cop: Inspector Cornelius Cahalane, the bagman for Dollar John.

The next afternoon, on the North Shore of Long Island, a newspaper reporter reached William Gaynor at the farm where the mayor spent weekends with his family. Gaynor was sitting on the porch, reading a well-thumbed copy of the Old Testament, when the reporter asked if he had anything to say, in view of the fact that a man who figured prominently in the Rosenthal case had been shot in the back of the head.

Gaynor rubbed his neck and swallowed painfully. He said he had no comment, and returned to his Bible.

On Monday, Abe Shoenfeld and Rabbi Judah Magnes sat in the mayor's office in City Hall, watching Gaynor hold the telephone to his ear. For Abe, Zelig's death was a blow. Zelig was no saint but he *was* the ghetto's source of stability, the reason that some center held on the East Side, and now that he was dead Abe expected that someone worse would take his place.

Gaynor put his hand over the mouthpiece and said, "The police commissioner has Inspector Cornelius Cahalane in his office. Inspector Cahalane says that whoever says these things about him is a liar."

Abe looked at the clock. "At this moment, Cahalane's lieutenant can be found at the Prince George Hotel, waiting to receive a bag of money."

Gaynor repeated this information into the phone and the call ended. He assessed Abe and Magnes. Gaynor disliked reformers. The ones he knew were hypocrites who wanted to tell the poor when they could consume alcohol or conduct business. Too often, in Gaynor's view, reformers were the same people who paid slave wages, then turned around and called East Siders prostitutes and criminals. "Such people think it is the mayor's job to not have a single criminal on the streets," Gaynor once wrote. "I ask these good people what they have done to rescue a single unfortunate woman from the life she is leading."

But if Gaynor had to deal with reformers, then these Jews, he suspected, might be the best way to clean up the city, to achieve the ends of reform without invoking the reformer's circus, bowing to hollow moralism, or letting DA Whitman, who was gunning for Gaynor's job, ride herd over the NYPD.

"Twenty years of empty reform committees has left me doubtful that citizens can address problems in their own communities," Gaynor said. "I should've known that it would be you people who might bring it off. We hear a great deal about Christian charity but the Jews are different—you do not go together clannishly in one party as other races do." He told Abe and Magnes to bring him whatever they discovered about crime and corruption.

Magnes thanked Gaynor and said that he hoped Mr. Shoenfeld's identity would remain anonymous. To this Gaynor nodded agreement. "I know only a Mister Prettyfield," he said, translating Shoenfeld, and ended the meeting.

That afternoon, Inspector Cornelius Cahalane took a squad of patrolmen to Second Avenue and smashed Dollar John Langer's gambling empire to pieces.

Down in the financial district, Abe waited on Pine Street while Magnes went up to Jacob Schiff's office in the Kuhn Loeb building and returned with a check for $5,000. Abe handed Magnes an itemization of expenses for the first $2,500 and Magnes handed it back. "Rip up the receipts," he said. "I don't need to know how you're spending it. Just let me know when you need more."

Along Delancey, thousands of mourners joined the funeral procession for Selig Harry Lefkowitz, who had lived as Big Jack Zelig, "East Side Emancipator," and died at the age of twenty-four. A cantor conducted hymns while a coach conveyed the body across the Manhattan Bridge to Washington Cemetery, where Zelig would be laid to rest next to the Yiddish playwright Jacob Gordin.

The passing of Zelig exposed a disunity among East Siders. Not all were sorry to see him go. From windows along the funeral route came the shouts of hecklers.

What licentiousness reigns among us!

In the old country murderers received a donkey's burial!

The divine word, "I chose you among the peoples of the earth," ends this way?

From a street corner, Tony the Tough watched the spectacle with fellow madams. While the fortunes of Tony's old friend Lily plummeted, Tony, now a brothel manager, was coming up in the world. When Tony asked the other madams if they planned to attend a benefit ball to raise funds for Zelig's widow, one madam scoffed: "Who is Mrs. Zelig? Let her go out on the street and sell it the same as we do."

Tier on tier, the grand criminal courts building, which occupied a full city block downtown, rose to a central rotunda crowned by a soot-encrusted glass roof through which a soiled and viscous light was filtered into the courtroom. There, on the day of Zelig's funeral, the four gunmen appeared for their arraignment while Lily Rosenberg sat in the gallery, wearing a brown dress and a black turban hat made of crinkled satin.

The case had turned Lily into a tabloid sensation. The press called her Lefty's French Doll and depicted her as gorgeous and naïve, with, as one paper wrote, "some nameless quality that reminds one of kittens and babies." Reporters wrote of her confidence in Lefty's innocence, and how she discussed the grave charges against her husband as if he'd been ticketed for speeding in an auto. But Lily had reason to keep her spirits up. Actually, few people expected Becker to be convicted. And if Becker wasn't convicted, Lily assumed that Louie would be deemed innocent as well.

The judge remarked on how many Roses there were in the case. The state's lead witness was Jack Rose. The victim was Herman Rosenthal.

One of his killers was Louie Rosenberg. The judge laughed. "It's the War of the Roses! But it won't do for the trial. We'll have to come up with new names." He turned to Louie and said, "You're the one known as Lefty Louie?"

"We are only too glad to be identified, Your Honor, and to get this case over with as soon as possible and cleared up," Louie said. "But identify us the way everyone else is identified. This isn't square."

Outside, autos rambled past and wagons clopped over cobblestones and trolley tracks. Inside, even on a high floor, little could be heard above the din below.

"Lift up your voice," the judge said. "It would be difficult to get a more noisy corner in the city. Again: you are the one known as Lefty Louie?"

"I am now, Your Honor. Since this case started."

"What is that? You must raise your voice."

Louie bent double over the wooden rail, shouting, "Yes! I am Lefty Louie!"

Lily tensed as reporters scratched away on notepads, recording their impressions of the gunman's impudence. For the first time it struck her that Louie could really die. This was no game. The realization flipped a switch, and she decided she would do whatever it took to save her husband from the electric chair.

In a nearby courtroom, Red Phil Davidson convulsed with sobs and shuffled along, one reporter noted, "like a child experiencing his first roar of busy-hour traffic."

At his own arraignment, Red Phil told conflicting stories about the murder of Zelig. First he said he was told that if he killed Zelig then he would be "the big man." Told by whom? When asked to elaborate, he insisted that no one was behind him, and that he was getting revenge on Zelig for slapping him around. At other times, Red Phil boasted of having done a job that not even the police could do, eliminating a gangster who had menaced the neighborhood and stolen for years. But some facts did come out. The revolver that Red Phil used to kill Zelig was traced back to a cop. The cop claimed to have lost the weapon months earlier. In a statement, the NYPD said Red Phil acted alone.

Red Phil's arraignment ended at the same time as the gunmen's, and all defendants were escorted over the Bridge of Sighs, a covered skyway that connected the criminal courts building to the Tombs jail across the street. When Louie spotted Red Phil, he broke free and mauled his friend's killer until he was subdued and dragged away.

When Lily was permitted to visit Louie in the Tombs, she tried to speak to him about the upcoming trial, but he remained preoccupied with Zelig's death and the mystery surrounding it. "He didn't have the nerve to do it alone," Louie said of Red Phil. "He's been a low pimp and a messenger boy all his life, just a lobbygow, and a cheap one at that."

"Louie!" she interrupted. "Is there anything that you know about *this* case? About *your* case?"

He lowered his voice. "Becker has been sending me notes tucked on the inside of books."

Lily's eyes widened. "What does he write? Tell me!"

" 'Keep up heart.' 'I am working hard for you boys.' 'I'll get you out of here.' That sort of thing."

"You saved the notes?" Lily asked. "Please tell me that you saved them!"

"Of course not," Louie said. "They could get us into trouble if the guards found them."

"Whitman says that if you tell all you know you could receive only two years in prison."

Louie seemed offended. "Two years? I wouldn't take two days. I'd rather die than squeal. Zel was going to stick till the end and so are we."

*   *   *

If the notes sent to Louie were genuine, Becker had good reason to be optimistic. The trial appeared to be a disaster for DA Whitman, who compensated with exaggeration and embroidery and instructed his witnesses to do the same. Whitman told the jury that the Rosenthal murder was "the most cunning and atrocious of any time, in any country." Whitman's lead witness, Bald Jack Rose, was similarly over-the-top, depicting Becker as psychotic and acting out long bits of dialogue between him and Becker regarding the Rosenthal murder. Bald Jack claimed that Becker said, "I want that squealer's tongue cut out and hung on the Times Building!" Bald Jack portrayed himself as the voice of reason: "Don't excite yourself, Charlie. This man Rosenthal isn't worth taking any such chances with." Whitman's other gambler-witnesses told muddled stories. One, when asked about the timing of alleged events in the case, said, "There is no use in asking me questions about time. Time means nothing to me. I don't keep track of days, months, years."

Even with a prosecution-friendly judge accepting Whitman's contentions as fact, the case made little sense. Why would Becker order the murder of Rosenthal when the supposed secret about Becker's grafting was already out? If Becker ever considered harming Rosenthal, he would have known that in doing so he would become a prime suspect. Meanwhile, Becker's defense was clear. A reporter who had called Becker on the evening of Rosenthal's murder to tell him about it took the witness stand and testified that he had been with Becker throughout the rest of the night and into the morning. If true, this meant that Becker couldn't have met Bald Jack Rose at 6 a.m., as Bald Jack claimed, to "congratulate" him on a job well done. By the time Becker's case went to the jury, not even assistant prosecutors in Whitman's office expected a win.

And still, to much of the public, Whitman's case represented high-minded citizens, fighters for a better world, while Becker represented

crooked Tammany Hall riffraff, grafters who despised the Jewish criminals they took money from. To help Whitman, Herbert Bayard Swope
pushed this anti-Semitic narrative along, inventing phrases from Becker
and even running one as a *World* headline: BECKER SAYS HE IS SATISFIED:
"I'LL NEVER BE CONVICTED OF ANYTHING ON THE TESTIMONY OF THIS
BUNCH OF DIRTY JEWS."

The jury came back with a guilty verdict for Becker. Two weeks later,
a different jury returned another guilty verdict for the four gunmen, and
in November, all five defendants were sentenced to die in the electric
chair at Sing Sing.

A crowd formed outside the West Side Prison on Fifty-Third Street, now
known as the Whitman Ritz because DA Whitman had been treating the
state's witnesses to freshly pressed suits and manicures. After the trials,
the celebrity squealers, most of whom were terrified of retribution, slipped
out by a side door and planned to leave the city — all except for the preter-
naturally confident Bald Jack Rose, who lingered to chat with the crowd.

During his testimonies, Bald Jack had related an interesting background, claiming to have been a garment manufacturer, a theatrical
producer, a boxing promoter, a baseball coach, and, yes, a gambler. What
slippery shit, people wondered, would comprise Bald Jack Rose's next act?

Bald Jack said he planned to parlay his fame into new endeavors,
such as chronicling his underworld experience in articles and films. He
donned a black wig and announced his desire to shake off his cognomen.
He declared that henceforth he preferred to be addressed as "just plain
Jack," then hopped in a taxi and whirled away.

At the Astor Hotel, where the Cits feted DA Whitman, Abe Shoenfeld
watched the prosecutor tell the crowd that the convictions meant the end

of gang rule in New York. Whitman held up a copy of *Collier's,* one of the world's most popular magazines, and pointed to its lead feature on the Rosenthal trials, headlined: THE DEFEAT OF THE UNDERWORLD.

But the underworld, Abe knew, was convinced of a different reality — that the Rosenthal case marked the beginning *and* the end of this reform wave, and that the old Tammany system of corruption and impunity for crime would return. Just look at what happened with Dollar John Langer: that fall, a magistrate threw out the case against the gambler, citing a lack of evidence that the raided casinos belonged to Dollar John. It was a common ground for dismissing cases against gamblers who funneled millions into Tammany's political machine, and this outcome emboldened casino owners, who concluded that "Dollar John's pinch was a right fall," meaning strictly for show. Writing to the Kehillah, Abe documented the response of one confident casino owner: "This is the country of laws! You can't smash a man's place any more than I can smash your home. Gaynor plainly says that if you have the evidence on a place, apply for a warrant and make your arrests. This is not Russia. If we are doing wrong, let them come out and get us."

Abe was back to square one. Zelig, the person who had helped him, was dead, and Louie had been sacrificed to no purpose. But, undeniably, there was also ground gained, he knew, particularly when he reflected on his ineffectual vice-reporting days. He'd tasted triumph in Gaynor's office, and acquired the confidence of Magnes and the Kehillah sponsors. Having seen what was possible with their backing, Abe felt momentum and refused to quit. "Gamblers are all out on the streets looking around," he wrote. "Word has been passed that things are about to come to a showdown, which is why we must keep after them."

12

Bridging the Wires

BY THANKSGIVING, MANY EAST SIDE CASINOS WERE
up and running again, while brothels remained in a state of limbo.
The pimps of the Independent Benevolent Association gathered at 92
Second Avenue, a café owned by the president of the IBA, who went by
Rabbi Rebelle, or simply Rebelle, a slightly belittling term meaning Little Rabbi.* In a Kehillah report, Abe described Rebelle as "a fifty-four-
year-old Russian-born Jew with a clean-shaven head. One of the pioneer
East Side cadets, he has the notorious reputation of being the downfall of
many respectable East Side girls."

Here, at Rebelle's, where the unofficial uniform ran to bright-colored
pinstripe suits and neckties that sparkled with the IBA's common symbol, a diamond horseshoe pin, the pimping brethren played cards, collected money orders from prostitutes they had sent to work abroad, and
talked business. Collectively the IBA, it was estimated, operated more than
half of the city's brothels, a marketplace that was driven up and down by

---

* His real name was Abraham Levinstein.

the psychology of reform. If a public official indicated that he was in favor of an open town, business boomed, whereas agitation in the opposite direction, from reformers, sent pimps scrambling to divest their shares.

For the pimps, the past six months had been a time of uncertainty. Prior to the Rosenthal murder, a one-third share in a brothel could sell for as much as $2,000, and the market was rich enough that a pimp could buy into a house at those high rates and have plenty left to cover furnishings and the inevitable plumbing nightmares. Now, given the post-Rosenthal skepticism, an entire lease could be had for $400. It was tempting, particularly to the younger pimps, to buy in at the bottom, but it was also risky. What if the end days really had arrived?

At Rebelle's, IBA members speculated about the future.

"If what the papers say is true, that it is a permanent thing, then we'll have troubles," one pimp said.

Other pimps were more dismissive. They recalled how Rockefeller's 1910 grand-jury investigation of their society turned out to be almost purely for show. "The papers always say it's a permanent thing, these cleanups, but houses were and always will be," another pimp said. "DA Whitman? He's just out to send a few cops to jail and con his way along until the next election."

A third pimp offered his socioeconomic theory: "If they're after anyone, they're after the poor slob who spends a dollar. The rich guy will still be able to get it anytime he wants."

Rebelle yelled across the café: "Motche, what do you say?"

Rebelle was the IBA president but Motche Goldberg was the fraternal order's king. Each year Motche delivered an estimated half-million dollars of IBA protection money to the powers that be, and thus served as the IBA's tipster, giving his fellow pimps the yea or nay on whether to proceed with investments. The identity of Motche's contact was considered to be a *heylik zakh,* a holy thing, such that when Motche came around each month to collect their *moos,* their measure—each pimp's share of the payoff—no one asked whom Motche "saw." Thus few knew that Motche had no direct relationship with a politician, but that he delivered the IBA's protection money, instead, to the city's most powerful pimp, a woman named Mother Rosie Hertz. Mother Hertz, who owned brothels all over the East Side, gave Motche instructions to pass on to the IBA.

Motche hadn't heard from Mother Hertz lately, and thus had no idea what the future looked like. In fact, he had recently spent $30,000 just to allay squeals from the madams and prostitutes who worked for him. Yet, at Rebelle's, Motche withheld all caveats, confessed no doubt, and remained bullish. "Just lay low and let everything blow over," he advised. "And do not wait to gobble up shares, because they are soon going to be worth a lot."

The pimps nodded, believing fully in the words of their king, for what bound the IBA together was confidence—not in Motche per se, but in just how shrewdly their ancient profession could be handled. *They come and go but we are here.* No other enterprise adjusted so promptly to conditions: exploited, beaten, infected, jailed, scraped out—the Jewess remained steadfast. Or so the pimps thought.

At Mother Hertz's Ninth Street brothel, Tony the Tough began her days by rubbing a paste of Delatone powder between her buttocks, brushing Silmerine into her hair, and dusting her body in talc. There, in the unventilated air, thick with tobacco and perfume, disinfectants and the pungent aroma of abortifacients from ergot to mustard baths, Tony toiled.

During the past year she had transformed herself from an ordinary young prostitute, a "quimbo," into a "star," a savvy earner who was looked upon with envy by her rivals. She had risen through the ranks by "wearing the rose." A rose in the hair signified her status as a "can," a prostitute who sold anal sex for ten or twenty dollars, many times what could be charged by the "middle-bridgers" who stuck to vaginal intercourse.*

As her earnings rose, Tony used the money to purchase fine dresses and fancy stylings at Barth's Salon, the "whore's hair parlor" at 16 Second Avenue, where she absorbed the wisdom of big-name madams like Jenny the Factory, Becky Wetdream, and Sadie the Chink. They talked about menstruation, gossiped about johns and pimps, and traded tips on how to maximize profits. There was a feeling of camaraderie at Barth's. They sang ragtime songs such as "Everybody Is Doing It" and "We Will Do Some Cooing," substituting nasty words for the lyrics. Soon Tony was spending afternoons in the back of Barth's, playing poker with Mother Hertz herself, who wore the wig of an Orthodox Jewess, talked of God, and pinched the cheeks of her favorite girls. Out on the street, Hertz winked at cops and treated children to pennies, spreading coins around like fertilizer.

Now, as madam of Mother's Ninth Street house, Tony showed an aptitude for exploiting the quimbos in the same way Tony had been exploited when she entered the trade. Once a week, she invited peddlers in to sell the girls dresses and toiletries at triple prices, and kept business running at a steady clip. The life had certainly hardened Tony, but she was smitten with one girl, a sixteen-year-old Russian Jew who went by the name Kitty Blonde. Tony and Kitty shared movie magazines and smoked opium, which rendered Tony oblivious to her surroundings and the flight of time. She dreamt of success in the movies, of lighting up the screen for the entertainment of thousands.

Soon Tony and Kitty discovered another side of their sexuality, and fell in love. Pirouetting up the stairs, gliding down hallways, they lost themselves in drug-fueled fantasies of a different life, elsewhere, with

---

* In the garment industry, a "bridge" was a pocket. A "middle bridge" referred to the popular front-center pocket on skirts, a practical feature for working girls.

each other. But it wasn't meant to be. One night, when the watch boy signaled that the cops were coming — making one of the "for show" raids that had been popular since the Rosenthal murder — the ladies darted from the house and ran toward the Bowery. Kitty Blonde, confused, darted in the wrong direction, was mowed down by an auto, and died.

As Tony mourned Kitty, she paid more attention to what was happening outside her window, where the same Russian-Jewish girls she once worked alongside in the garment industry were out in the streets again, protesting child labor and advocating for better working conditions. Since 1910 these marches had increased in size and power, summoning the memory of those who died in the 1911 Triangle fire, the ones who had choked and burned, had plunged down the elevator shaft and broken their skulls or jumped from windows and landed on the pavement with a sickening thud.

Tony considered her circumstances. She was twenty. The easy money didn't interest her as it once had. And she had a pretty good idea of what the future held: she would catch a disease, if she hadn't already, or grow old and join the fire lighters on the Bowery. If she was going to die in this city, she wanted to die like those girls in the street, fighting for something better. But how?

"We need a lawyer," Rabbi Magnes told Abe Shoenfeld as they sat across from one another in Magnes's office in the Hebrew Charities Building. "Someone who can go to court, urge prosecutors to see cases through, and ensure that evidence is presented properly." Abe knew Magnes was right, though he couldn't think of one East Side attorney who wasn't too close to the underworld, too beholden to Tammany's influence to be the bulldog that the vice crusade required. But Magnes had someone in mind.

He took Abe to Lüchow's, the fashionable restaurant on Fourteenth Street, these being the prewar years when German cuisine still enjoyed enormous prestige in the city. Over a lunch of goose liver in aspic and roast capon, Magnes introduced Abe to a young lawyer named Harry Newburger. A Kentucky native, Newburger attended Columbia University and NYU law school and then got a job with the corporate law firm of Benjamin Cardozo, the future Supreme Court justice. Magnes knew Newburger because they lived in the same Gramercy Park building. As a neighborhood, Gramercy, just north of Fourteenth Street, was popular with reform-minded professionals who sought involvement in immigrant uplift. After putting his kids to bed, Newburger often wandered upstairs to share a nightcap with Magnes. In those late-night chats, Newburger confessed that he was disillusioned with Wall Street and sick of kowtowing to rich clients. He was twenty-seven, and, like Tony, he wanted a more purposeful path. When Magnes mentioned his anti-vice work, a light came into Newburger's eyes. He wanted in.

At Lüchow's, Abe assessed this Newburger, with his bow tie and gleaming banker's cut, and could hardly imagine a more unlikely candidate for a vice crusade. The Kentucky accent was charming but it only underscored Newburger's alien status. He didn't know a lick of Yiddish, nor had he ever practiced law in a criminal court. But the Wall Street lawyer surprised Abe. Newburger explained that he'd been hanging out at Essex Market Court. He detailed the mechanics of the "bondsman's graft," the scheme by which a "trust" composed of lawyers, judges, and cops turned the legal system into a cash machine. By keeping bail amounts low and delaying trial—so that prostitutes and thieves, when arrested, could return to the streets immediately and continue working— the bondsman's graft literally skimmed the profits of crime.

Newburger also said he'd forged relationships with honest cops. "There are inspectors and captains who are incorruptible," Newburger said. "The problem is that they must depend on court clerks to prepare affidavits and submit warrant applications. Invariably the clerk works for the rats"—the corrupt attorneys and judges. Newburger was impressive, and Abe saw how his outsider status could be an advantage: Newburger had no connection to Tammany Hall, and he didn't care about politics. They discussed the failed case against Dollar John and the necessity of getting hard evidence — evidence that even a corrupt judge couldn't disregard.

Newburger had a plan. He took Abe to a building on Centre Street, next to the new NYPD headquarters. A door opened onto a room of women who sat around a table with some kind of apparatus in the middle that made a clicking sound. Each woman wore a listening device connected to the apparatus, and took notes on school slates. Circling the table, observing their work, was a cop with an elaborate mustache. Newburger introduced Abe to Joseph Faurot, head of NYPD detectives.

This setup astounded Abe. Detective Faurot was a straight cop with a reputation for being on the cutting edge of technology. Years earlier, Faurot went to Paris to study the Bertillon method of fingerprinting, then came back to New York and helped the prosecutor's office get its first murder conviction using fingerprint evidence. He was also a minor celebrity, having appeared in a 1911 movie called *The Thumb Print*. In the movie, a wife is about to be found guilty of murdering her husband when Faurot shows the court the difference between the wife's thumbprint and that of the man who left his mark on a pair of tailoring shears, the murder weapon.

Faurot now explained to Newburger and Abe how his "listening-in squad" solved cases by "bridging" telephone wires. At the moment, Faurot said, they were gathering evidence on a gang of Wall Street thieves who stole cable information from J. P. Morgan. To Abe, this wire-bridging capability was extraordinary, and he thought about what it could mean for his Kehillah mission. He told Faurot and Newburger that Dollar John kept his mother in an apartment across from the Comanche Club, his main gambling den on Second Avenue. There was a phone in that apartment, Abe knew, and at night Dollar John sat next to it, awaiting updates on daily profits at his casinos.

A few days later, Newburger and Abe joined Detective Faurot in the cellar of 60 Second Avenue, across from the Comanche Club. Faurot scraped the insulation from the ends of the two wires that formed the building's telephone circuit, then clipped each wire to a receiver. He ran a third wire through a hole in the wall and into the building next door, 62 Second Avenue, where, with Kehillah funds, Abe had rented an empty apartment on the top floor. Up in that apartment, Faurot's listening-in squad connected the line to the clicking apparatus and waited.

Later that night, Dollar John picked up the phone and discussed his gambling business in detail, tallying the evening's take from craps, roulette, and stuss. Newburger went to court, represented himself as a lawyer for a group of concerned citizens, and passed the listening-in evidence to the prosecutor. Not even a tainted court could dismiss listening-in evidence, and soon the *World* announced: FIRST GAMBLER IN PENITENTIARY, noting that Dollar John's one-year sentence dealt "a novel shock to his mates."

This prosecutorial coup tipped the scales in Abe's favor. Several informants who had been reluctant to give him information now helped him, leading to more than two dozen gambling prosecutions in December of 1912 — so many cases that the Kehillah hired two more attorneys to assist Newburger.

These cases sent a message not only to East Side gamblers but to the "big smokes" in the Tenderloin too. BIGGEST GAMBLERS QUIT; BROADWAY SECTION CLEAN, reported the *World*: "When news of what happened to downtown roulette wheels and poker tables reached New York City's uptown gambling belt — the 'green-cloth district' north of Forty-Second Street, where the principal temples of chance were located — talk of lawyers was abandoned, and it was deemed more practical to hire a furniture mover than a student of Coke or Blackstone. Croupiers have been discharged. Some proprietors still use their houses as private residences, including Arnold Rothstein of West Forty-Sixth Street."

* * *

Now, in the mayor's office at City Hall, William Gaynor, intrigued by the Kehillah's success, entertained frequent visits from Harry Newburger to discuss the status of the vice crusade. Gaynor, the former judge, and Newburger, the lawyer, debated constitutional issues surrounding policing, such as warrantless raids, undercover stings, and bridging wires. This was the aspect of reform that Gaynor resented most: government creeping into the home, surveillance trumping privacy.

Newburger lobbied for broad leeway, an easing of the restrictions that Gaynor had put on the police department when he came into office. Gaynor, despite his objections, was inclined to let the Kehillah proceed. Most reformers came to him with complaints and demands. At least these Jews had a plan to clean up their own quarter rather than simply tell others how to live. And there was some self-interest involved, too. Now that the Rosenthal trials were over, DA Whitman had commandeered the inquiry into NYPD corruption and was trying to tie every instance of police malfeasance to Gaynor's alleged mismanagement. Supporting the Kehillah could be an investment in Gaynor's own political future.

Gaynor knew that if this vice crusade was to continue, however, some bending of the law would be necessary. He only wished there were people in the NYPD whom he could trust with these decisions, people like Newburger and Abe Shoenfeld themselves. In a letter to Jacob Schiff and Judah Magnes, Gaynor proposed installing Newburger as third deputy police commissioner and Abe Shoenfeld — or Prettyfield, as Gaynor called him — as Newburger's secretary. Gaynor suggested that Newburger could oversee the NYPD's new internal affairs division, where he could dispose of dirty cops quietly, depriving Whitman of further headlines.

Newburger agreed to Gaynor's plan. This kind of impact was more than he had imagined when he left Wall Street. For Abe, though, the decision was harder. He fantasized about breaking the connection between politics and crime, about finishing what his father started, and now here was the chance. Yet once the crusade was public, he would likely lose his anonymity and it would become trickier for him to protect informants, without whom there would be no crusade.

During the holiday season, as Abe weighed the pros and cons of running the crusade out of the NYPD, the threat of exposure grew more serious. He was at Lüchow's again, eating lunch with Newburger and Magnes, when Jonah Goldstein pushed through the door. Goldstein was the defense attorney who, prior to Abe's Kehillah hiring, had been feeding Magnes information, albeit questionable, about the East Side underworld. In Abe's initial meeting with Magnes, he had suggested that Magnes keep Goldstein around in order to distract from the work Abe would be doing.

Goldstein marched over to their table and addressed Magnes. "I was at Essex Market Court today," he said. "And an attorney, this man here"—pointing at Newburger—"was presenting evidence on behalf of concerned Jewish citizens. You can imagine my surprise, learning that there was another attorney privy to Kehillah activities of which I myself am unaware. Must I remind you that I've given up evenings, at considerable cost to my practice, to work for you?"

Unfazed, Magnes said, "If you feel you are not getting enough out of your position, then I wish you luck."

"Why are you treating me this way?"

"Your investigations have furnished little, and your promiscuous use of the Kehillah's name hasn't helped our work any."

Goldstein shook with anger, and hurried out of the restaurant.

Newburger, Abe, and Magnes looked at one another and laughed. "So much for improved community relations," Newburger said, joking, but the truth was that Jonah Goldstein scared them.

Abe knew that if Goldstein tipped off the underworld to the

Kehillah's plans and the vice crusade's existence, police support would be important—for reasons of safety, of course, but also because the crusade could become quite violent. He told Magnes that he would take the NYPD job on one condition: that he and Newburger lead a "roving strong-arm squad" of twenty cops of their choosing. It was a tall order, given that neither Abe nor Newburger possessed a day of law-enforcement experience, but Gaynor agreed. So they assembled a list of upright cops who would attempt to do what no reform committee had done— eradicate the underworld of a refugee population that had lived under the yoke of oppression for centuries.

Abe was ready. In the five months since his first meeting with Magnes, word of his financial backing spread among stool pigeons, and his sources expanded. The East Siders may not have believed in the promise of reform, but they understood the language of money. And his experience with Faurot's listening-in squad inspired Abe to cultivate sources among the city's telephone operators, the "hello girls" who worked the jacks and plugs of switchboards at hotels and offices, where they became privy to all kinds of useful information. Abe was accumulating so much intelligence that he could envision what an all-out vice crusade might look like, taking on not just gambling and prostitution but also thieves and drug dealers, horse poisoners and gangsters—the kind of thoroughgoing cleanup that few reformers imagined possible, if they imagined it at all.

Abe could see it. His mind was a grid of the city's underside. He carried a phone book's worth of names and addresses. He knew, for instance, that Tony the Tough had come up in the underworld and was now managing one of Mother Hertz's brothels.

Posing as a john, Abe visited the Ninth Street house and requested Tony. Once inside the bedroom, he took off his hat and coat and dropped the pretense. It took a moment for Tony to recognize him. Two years had passed since their fling, but Abe had changed: His face was more square, his features sharper, his hairline in retreat. He looked more thirty-one than twenty-one, but Tony remembered him, the guy who wanted to set things right.

Abe told her about the Kehillah and the police department, and said, "You don't belong here. Help us."

"Squealing can get me killed," she said.

"Yes, it can," Abe said.

She thought about it. Like many East Siders, Tony didn't hold the rich Jews in high esteem, and from her experience in the old country she knew that a kehillah often put its own interest ahead of the community's. She remembered when the czar's recruiters came to Bialystok. Her father had sent her brother to hide in the forest, but the kehillah's agents hunted him down.

Abe said, "You live here now. You're not a Russian. You're not a Jew. You're a New Yorker, and this is your city." He walked across the room and placed a bankbook on the dresser. He said there was a thousand dollars in an account at Jarmulowsky, the immigrant bank. If she joined them, there would be another hundred each week. He put on his coat and hat and prepared to leave.

"Why should I trust you?" she asked.

"I promised that I would never betray you," he said, "and I never will."

13

Everyman's Friend

I N EARLY 1913, AS ABE AND NEWBURGER PREPARED TO
enter the police department, the fate of America's open borders shifted
daily. In January, Congress passed a sweeping anti-immigration bill that
featured a literacy test, the functional equivalent of immigration restriction for non–English speakers. A week later, the outgoing President Taft
vetoed the bill, but said that he was doing so reluctantly.

In New York, the German-Jewish uptowners cheered the victory.
One Kehillah member wired another: PRESIDENT VETOED IMMIGRATION
BILL THIS AFTERNOON GOOD SHABBOS.

To celebrate, the uptowners gathered at the mansion of Felix and
Frieda Warburg, on Ninety-Second Street and Fifth Avenue. The Warburg place, future home of the Jewish Museum, was one of the poshest in
the city. Thirteen servants lived on the sixth floor. A squash court, where
Felix played against a pro each morning, took up the fifth floor. The
fourth floor contained the children's rooms, connected by a giant toy train
set. The third floor was designed for Frieda's weekly tea gatherings. The

second floor featured a dining room for eighty and rotating pedestals that displayed Botticellis and Rembrandts.

Felix Warburg was the fourth and youngest son of the oldest private banking family in Europe. But unlike his brother Max, who ran the family business back in Hamburg, and his brother Paul, who invented the idea for the US Federal Reserve, Felix was not a great banker. And unlike his other brother, Aby, whose pursuit of rare books would culminate in a famous library, Felix lacked a singular driving force.

People called him Fizzy because he was spontaneous and lively and dressed with flair: a Tyrolean cape on mountain hikes, a green suit for important meetings. At home, after dinner, he pumped away on a full-size organ while his five children danced and sang around him. He loved his fast car, a French De Dion-Bouton, and his hundred-foot yacht. At his five-hundred-acre weekend estate in White Plains, visitors could swim in an indoor pool with trapezes above the water, play tennis on grass courts that lured stars from Forest Hills, and ride show horses down a bridle path lined with hand-carved benches, each one displaying the names and dates of office of an American president.

"He liked to spend money, and knew well how to do so, especially on the ideals and visions which he had in such profusion," his wife Frieda later recalled. Felix gave a lot of money away, and might've been the only uptowner whose charity exceeded that of his father-in-law, Jacob Schiff, who remarked: "One can be extravagant even in giving, and Felix is that." Felix's biographer called him "a philanthropic colossus, a one-man social welfare agency." For Felix, it would be good deeds that gave his life purpose, saving him from being just another Gilded Age swell.

It started in 1895, when he came to New York to marry Frieda Schiff. At twenty-four years old, he was already the big Warburg spender, unselfconscious about enjoying what his family's money could buy. As an outsider with an ability to laugh at himself, Felix also had a clear view of the absurdity of society life, scorning what he called "the silly layer cake" that separated the arrogant German Jews from the Eastern European immigrants. Felix, like Jacob Schiff, was an immigrant too, after all. Down on the East Side he encountered the same ragged Russian Jews he'd seen as a boy at the port in Hamburg, where the starving refugees, having trudged across Europe, waited to embark for America.

In New York, some of Felix's first friends were downtown reformers like Lillian Wald. Wald helped Felix get into educational reform and build the playgrounds that Abe Shoenfeld and Louie Rosenberg played on as children. Soon Felix and his father-in-law were at the head of a bewildering array of charities and causes. Behind Felix's desk at Kuhn Loeb, he built a wall that comprised fifty-seven file cabinets, each representing a different committee on which he served. In bed at night, in his dreamy tone, Felix would say, "I could imagine...," and Frieda knew there was another project in the offing.

His biggest vision was a state-run system of health insurance, a plan of universal health care rooted in Germany's "compulsory sickness insurance law," which Bismarck invented in the 1880s to outflank Germany's rising socialist movement. In America, the push for universal health care ultimately failed to win broad support and died in 1912, but such programs were the kind of pressure valves that Felix and others in their uptown crowd were thinking about — ways of easing the tension between rapid industrialization and preindustrial legal codes that accorded no rights to the masses. Even as the German Jews defended capitalism, they were pervaded by an uneasy feeling that they were living over a tinderbox of discontent, the kind of populist rumble that, down through history, had been their undoing.

And yet, what of America's present system were any of the reform-minded elite, Wasp or German Jew, Republican or Democrat, really willing to change? What of their own exalted positions might they actually sacrifice? Sure, the German Jews initiated the national campaign to bar child labor; built hospitals, schools, and orphanages; and financed education for other minority groups, such as southern Blacks. They gave a lot, but they also paid few taxes.* At the heart of American life, they believed, was the right to accrue wealth without interference. This was a right that the turn-of-the-century merger boom effectively codified, helping to create the ultimate in unreachable private property—that all-powerful, cash-minting shield of impunity, the modern corporation.

That night, someone invited two Russian Jews to the Warburg mansion. With their baggy sack suits and red ties, the Russians stood out. Felix overheard the pair admiring his paintings. One said he hoped that when the revolution came and there was a division of property, he got *this* house. For limousine liberals like Felix, such jokes hit close to home, as Socialist political candidates made headway and America endured the most violent period of industrial strife in the country's history.

"I hope that if you do get my house, you will also invite me to be your guest, because I have always enjoyed it," Felix told the guests, and walked away.

If the German Jews had taken an unseemly abundance of pride in being benefactors to the Eastern European downtowners, their feelings about all that giving were changing by 1913. To many, the endless charity felt like a heavy tax rate, while the endgame—uniting the two communities—remained hard to fathom.

And it's not as if the German Jews received much gratitude for their efforts. Within a year of arrival, the typical downtowner learned the East Side habit of casting aspersions on their "snobbish German brethren." For their part, the German-Jewish sense of superiority struggled to reconcile itself to brotherhood with the dregs of Europe, with those "wild Asiatics"

---

* The Sixteenth Amendment to the US Constitution was ratified in 1913, providing for an income tax ranging from 1 to 7 percent. Before then, federal revenues came mainly from excise taxes and tariffs on imports. As a regulatory measure, the 1913 income tax was joined, in 1914, by two new antitrust laws that strengthened the original antitrust law, the Sherman Act of 1890.

who shot each other on East Side streets, gorged on ice cream and chop suey, and couldn't feed their babies without passing on typhoid. Interestingly, though many German-Jewish families married their children off to Christians, the idea of their offspring marrying downtown Jews, *immigrants,* terrified them. If an uptown boy married a downtown girl, a whisper often went around: *He must've gotten her pregnant!*

Resentment between the groups was real and often turned violent, a trend that could be observed in the criminal courts. In one case, a young Russian-Jewish immigrant who worked as a delivery boy shot his German-Jewish boss dead for withholding wages. In another, a Russian-Jewish baker removed the eyeball of his coworker for insulting his corned-beef sandwich and calling him a *kike*—a slur that the German Jews were said to have invented to distinguish themselves from the downtowners.

The relationship was knotty. In many respects it would've been easier for the German Jews to *favor* curbs on immigration. They stood to lose a great deal should disapproval of the Eastern Europeans rub off on them, at a time when they believed they might be nearing acceptance. The dean of Columbia University, who felt that his school's reputation as a "Jew college" was hindering fundraising, was okay with German Jews: "The Jews who have had the advantages of decent social surroundings for a generation or two are satisfactory companions," wrote the dean. The problem, he said, was pushy East Siders, ambitious grinds who were "not particularly pleasant companions."

The downtowners were loud and aggressive. And that *language.* Although it was actually Judeo-*German,* Yiddish was, to the uptowners, "piggish jargon." Many understood Yiddish but hated it. It was another savage symbol of the buried past, that mean legacy of eons from which the German Jews, even as they fought for wider tolerance and open borders, wanted to break away. Could they do it with the ghetto dwellers? A better question: Could they do it *without* them? After all, it was the garment industry, running on immigrant labor, that put New York on top.

The uptowners were caught between their loyalty to these precarious co-religionists and their own established position in America, which, to be realistic about things, was still dicey. Recently, a few select Germans had been "invited" to help finance cultural institutions and serve on boards. The president of the Metropolitan Museum of Art was looking, as he wrote, "for an agreeable Hebrew, because the Zoo and Public Library have done so and our attitude is becoming conspicuous."

But even as the Wasps let them into their social institutions, the German Jews were careful not to press it. They knew their place. They'd read Edith Wharton's *House of Mirth,* in which the tragic fall of Lily Bart is counterweighed by the rise of Simon Rosedale, the crude Jewish financier "who is mad to know the people who don't want to know him." Some speculated that Otto Kahn, the German-Jewish banker who was Jacob Schiff's number two at Kuhn Loeb, was the inspiration for Rosedale. Kahn himself surely knew that when it came to the world of the Wasps, he was on thin ice. After he used his money and musical expertise to help revive the Metropolitan Opera, he declined to buy a box in the Met's elite Diamond Horseshoe out of concern that invading this precious Wasp stronghold would provoke resentment. To the Wasps, Kahn observed, a kike wasn't Russian or German. A kike, Kahn said, was any Jewish gentleman who'd just left the room.

Kahn knew that the German Jews could segregate from the downtowners all they wanted. They could live on Fifth Avenue with the Carnegies and Vanderbilts, turn their drawing rooms into museums, wrap their wives in French lace, and cosset their sons at Connecticut boarding schools. They could mimic the Wasps down to the last oyster ladle. But decent social surroundings would never fully cleanse them of the taint, as Kahn observed, because to the Wasps a kike was a kike.

Surely more than one motive drove the German Jews in their mission to elevate the downtowners: among them were a sense of moral duty and their self-identity as stewards of a community at a crucial moment in history. But by 1913, it was the idea of their linked fates — reinforced by the

general population's tendency to lump all Jewish-Americans together—
that provided the most powerful incentive. In the end, whatever lot befell
the downtowners was likely going to be shared by the uptowners. Which
is why Kehillah member Louis Brandeis, soon to be the first Jewish justice on the Supreme Court, addressed the gathering at the Warburg mansion and affirmed what they all knew: The recent veto of the
anti-immigration bill, Brandeis said, was not a victory but a temporary
escape. "The snake," he promised, "will return."

The Kehillah vice crusade needed to work. It also needed to be covert.
No one could know that the Germans orchestrated it. So far, so good. The
crusade's public front, the bow tie–wearing Newburger, suggested no
obvious uptown connection, much less a genuine attempt to fight crime.
As one Yiddish paper commented: "The Police Commissioner has
appointed Harry W. Newburger to the position of Third Deputy Police
Commissioner. Mr. Newburger is the first Jew to hold this rank. He is not
a regular member of the police force and has no training."

In January, on the first Sunday of 1913, the night before Abe Shoenfeld's
first day in the New York Police Department, he joined his family for
dinner at 125 Clinton Street, where the atmosphere was tense. When
word got out that Abe was joining the NYPD as part of a "cleanup force,"
there was speculation in some quarters that he would come home in a
pine box. Not wanting to expose his family to the risks, Abe had moved
into the Kehillah's rented apartment at 62 Second Avenue, where he slept
with a gun, his old .32 Iver Johnson, under his pillow.

His mother, Dora, was accustomed to stress, having seen her husband
through countless crusades, and she knew that her oldest son would follow some similar path, but she hadn't envisioned *this*. Earlier that day,
Sam Paul, the head of the East Side gamblers' association, had stopped by
125 Clinton and extended an invitation to Abe to address the membership.

The ominousness of this invitation hung over dinner, and Mayer's nonchalance about it did little to soothe Dora's nerves. "Come now, Dora," Mayer said. "You think your son is brainless. He believes he is fearless. He is certainly heedless. But no one was taught to stand down in this family." The relationship between father and son remained distant, but Mayer did care about Abe's safety, even if he had a funny way of showing it.

After dinner, he called Abe into his office and asked how he was outfitted for firearms. Abe said he still used his .32 Iver Johnson, the pistol Mayer had given him years earlier, and he showed Mayer a new weapon, a Colt Special with a flashlight on the barrel. Colt had sent prototypes to the NYPD, and Detective Faurot passed this one on to Abe. The weapon was impressive, if impractical: the flashlight ran on a heavy battery housed awkwardly between the grip panels, which made the weapon almost too clunky to handle, much less fire with any accuracy. Mayer walked to his artillery cabinet and fetched a pair of modified Bull Dog suspenders with holsters stitched to the front and back. He gave the suspenders to Abe and advised him to carry the Iver Johnson out front and the clunky Colt in back, so that he had speedy access to the lighter revolver. This was as much advice as Mayer would offer.

It was an unceremonious send-off, but that's how things were in the Shoenfeld family. Sometimes you organized thousands of people in a labor strike, or tried to resettle families in the countryside, or became a vigilante. The Shoenfelds were heedless and fearless, and if they were lucky to be alive they chalked that up to the old family rule: So long as you never took a bribe and never, unless in defense, raised your hand in violence, you were untouchable.

The next morning, when Abe appeared at the Sam Paul Association, Paul told the audience: "Here is Abe Shoenfeld, our good old friend, our member." Abe was certainly not a member, but Sam Paul was keen to claim the newly appointed NYPD employee as his own. "It pleases me that one of our boys is in the department. He knows we'll stand for a pinch, so long as it's a *right* pinch" — a fake arrest. The crowd laughed.

Abe gripped the podium and looked out at the gamblers, thieves, and murderers. He saw a thief named Benjamin Fein, who'd recently killed two people in a bid to fill the power vacuum left by Big Jack Zelig. The audience cheered.

You know us, Abe!

Hope you won't be too strict!

Take! No one will ask where you got it!

The criminals wanted assurances, a sign that Abe was the harmless puppet of another reform show, and perhaps some intimation that the recent spate of casino shutdowns was only temporary. None of them knew that Abe himself was the mysterious force behind those shutdowns, nor that he wanted no gold or power, that he'd never even considered working for the NYPD until his Kehillah work thrust him into it.

"Unfortunately," Abe said, "I was always too busy to become a member, but I am everyman's friend. And let me be clear: There isn't a politician in the city who can say he got me this job. I got it on my own. And I'm going to do the right thing as a sworn official. I'm going to fight to clean New York. My partners and I cannot be reached, except to receive just treatment, an ear to complaints, and the carrying out of every detail, no matter how trivial."

Sam Paul's smile dissolved. Of this moment, Abe later recalled, "They were going to poison the milk at my door and pee on my grave." There was silence as Abe exited the clubhouse. He wondered if he would be stabbed or shot, but he walked off into the cold morning sun, heading for his first day of work as a New York City cop. "I had a great desire to go out and face them," Abe recalled. "I had but one aim, to get at it, to fight, to suppress, to set things right wherever possible."

14

Misfits

Back in 1904, when Arnold Rothstein was still chasing that Richard Canfield ideal, another young upstart was electrifying circus audiences in Coney Island. This English daredevil, known as Tourbillon, had a crazy act called "The Circle of Death," which entailed a cage of lions. Above the cage was a giant funnel, and separating the funnel from the caged lions below was a circular platform that could be pulled away. Tourbillon, meaning "whirlwind," rode his bike around the platform, and when speed was attained he mounted the funnel, riding round and round, defying gravity, at which point his assistant pulled the platform away, exposing the "cycle whirler" to the lions, who swiped at him hungrily.

In the early 1900s, writes David Maurer in *The Big Con: The Story of the Confidence Men,* "The American circus was a grifter's paradise on wheels." It was in the circus that Tourbillon learned to separate people from their money, but circus life was a hard grift and the Circle of Death didn't always go as planned. Sometimes the platform, once pulled away, got stuck. Other times a lion escaped into the nearby town. So, in 1910, Tourbillon ditched the circus and drifted into Manhattan, where he discovered the crowd at Jack's Oyster House.

Above, Lower Manhattan, 1912. Below, the Lower East Side, at Catherine and Cherry Streets, 1910. (*Author's collection*)

Uptown, police helped affluent children cross the street in 1909. Downtown, "young 'Oliver Twists' are arrested for pickpocket work," according to words penciled on the back of this 1904 photo. *(Author's collection)*

East Side delinquency and vice proliferated during the first decade of the twentieth century. Penciled on the back of the middle photo: "Addict preparing a shot of cocaine, 1910." *(Author's collection)*

East Side children, often
shoeless and hungry,
roamed the streets looking
for food. Herring and
tea were neighborhood
staples, but knishes and ice
cream were favored treats.
(Author's collection)

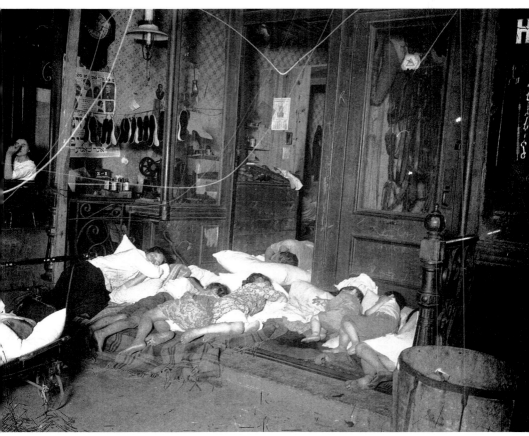
For the immigrant poor, the promise of America did not always match the reality. An East Side family sleeps outside in summer to escape the sauna-like temperatures of the tenements. *(Author's collection)*

The wealthy German-Jewish uptowners congregated at Temple Emanu-El (left) and spawned countless philanthropic plans to elevate their downtown co-religionists. Their milk pasteurization program was a public-health landmark. Below, a milk depot dispenses bottles of milk for pennies. *(Author's collection)*

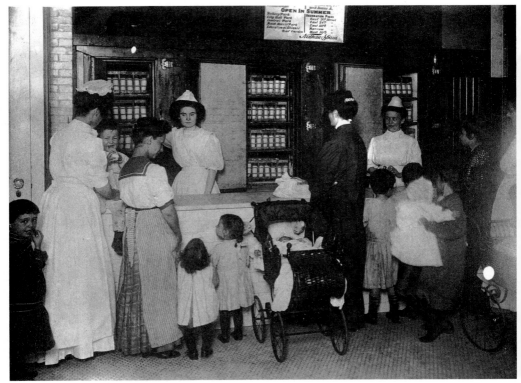

Like their uptown counterparts, the downtown Shoenfelds—Mayer (above right) and seventeen-year-old Abe (above left)—wanted to elevate the East Side. Part of reform was weakening Tammany Hall. Below, Tammany leader Big Tim Sullivan, whose picture hangs prominently on the wall, sponsors a shoe giveaway to assuage his ghetto constituency. (*Author's collection*)

Mayer Shoenfeld believed that uptown-sponsored breadlines (above) and soup kitchens (below) were no different than Big Tim's charitable offerings. They created reliance, he said, and perpetuated a ghetto mentality. *(Author's collection)*

East Side girls inspired the country with their protests and garment-industry labor strikes. Below, garment workers are inducted into strike culture, learning what they called the old Hebrew oath: "If I turn traitor to the cause I now pledge, may my hand wither from the arm I now raise." *(Author's collection)*

Many East Side girls were kept straight by a higher purpose. They marched in the streets, learned their numbers on a wall, and pursued education wherever they could. For others, the dance hall was a distraction. *(Author's collection)*

Mayor William Gaynor (above, in black hat) survived the 1910 assassination attempt, but never fully recovered. Below, months after the shooting he supports himself on a chair as he initiates his plan to tackle the graft problem in the NYPD. *(Author's collection)*

Broadway, 1912. "Arnold never wanted to be anywhere except on Broadway," recalled Carolyn Rothstein. "He didn't care for any other city except New York, and Broadway, for him, was New York. To leave it for only a few days was a hardship."

(Author's collection)

Jack's Oyster Grill, Carolyn wrote, "might be likened to the water hole in the jungle where beasts of prey and their natural enemies gather under a very real, but invisible, flag of truce for refreshment." *(Author's collection)*

Bald Jack Rose (right) orchestrated the murder of Herman Rosenthal (above) at the Metropole (below) and recruited Louie Rosenberg to do the job. A judge referred to the case as the War of the Roses. *(Rose, Library of Congress; Rosenthal and Metropole Hotel, author's collection)*

Louie's teen bride Lily (left) became a witness in the murder trials. For another key witness, Big Jack Zelig (above), the six-day bicycle race kicked off a very bad night. Below, a six-day competitor takes a breather. *(Author's collection)*

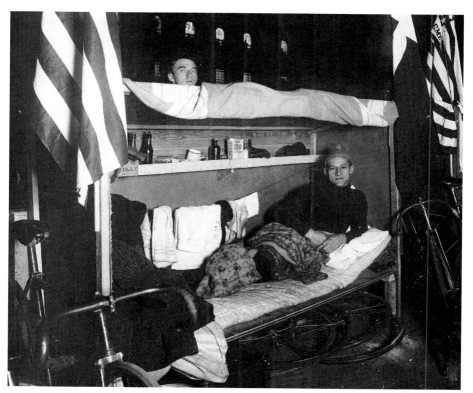

The Rosenthal murder initiated a new phase in the vice-crusading career of Abe Shoenfeld, pictured here in 1913. That winter, Abe — who stayed fit with exercises from *Physical Culture* — was twenty-one when Mayor Gaynor installed him in the police department. *(Author's collection)*

MARCH "STARTING THE DAY RIGHT" IN THIS
15 CENTS INFORMATION OF VALUE TO EVERYMAN. ISSUE
PHYSICAL
CVLTVRE

HORACE FLETCHER
on "EATING for
HEALTH and WEALTH"

PTON SINCLAIR on "FASTING EXPERIMENTS and EXPERIENCES"

"Here," wrote Carolyn Rothstein, "Tourbillon met workers of the badger game [sexual blackmail], gamblers, thieves, racketeers of all descriptions."

In the city, Tourbillon's appearance — tall and blond, with a British accent that went down a treat — helped him execute one unlikely con after another. A lawyer who represented Tourbillon remarked that his client could meet a woman in the evening, be holding her hand in ten minutes, and be holding her bankbook by morning. It helped that he worked as a model for a Fifth Avenue tailor, where he got the fine duds that facilitated his nighttime exploits. In 1911, when Tourbillon was charged with robbing a hotel, the judge said: "He is as smooth a rascal as ever came before me. A real Raffles."

Raffles, a literary character invented by the brother-in-law of Sherlock Holmes creator Arthur Conan Doyle, was a potent reference in the prewar era. The success of the Holmes franchise inspired many knockoffs, but Raffles, designed to be an inversion of Holmes — not a gentleman detective but a gentleman thief who remains on the periphery of "decent society," fearing rejection from the same snobs he steals from — was said to be Conan Doyle's favorite Holmes imitation, and a fair comparison for Tourbillon. Raffles was thus added to Tourbillon's aliases, but his friends at Jack's took the initials of his full name — Robert A. Tourbillon — and called the beautiful man Rat, or Ratsy, and the incongruous name stuck.

In early 1913, Arnold sat in the back of a Manhattan courtroom while Ratsy stood trial for running a casino. Arnold viewed Ratsy's case as a test, one whose outcome might point to new opportunities in the post-Rosenthal underworld. He'd bribed plenty of cops before, but he'd never attempted to fix a trial until now, and it worked. Leveraging his new status with Charlie Murphy and Tammany Hall, Arnold made the evidence against Ratsy vanish from the police precinct. Ratsy walked away, the *New York Times* reporting: EVIDENCE DISAPPEARS: COP SAYS HE WAS DISMISSED FOR REFUSING TO COMMIT PERJURY.

The day Ratsy went free, Arnold returned to the brownstone on Forty-Sixth Street. He looked around the great room, now stripped of its roulette wheels and other paraphernalia. It had once represented everything he wanted — the Canfield dream, entrance into the illustrious world of high-stakes casino gambling — but that world was moving on. Gambling, which had long been commonplace in American life, would now gradually become quarantined and sanitized in state-sanctioned venues, and Arnold would have to change with the times. He and Carolyn moved six blocks north, to a modest apartment on Fifty-Second Street. "The age of the New York casino ended with the murder at the Metropole," Carolyn recalled, but as one age faded, a new one racked into focus.

One writer who orbited Jack's, and later published the first biography of Arnold, wrote that, following the Rosenthal Affair, "Rothstein kept out of the public eye for the next seven years." Another Rothstein chronicler, looking back, remarked: "Within less than two years of the [Rosenthal] shooting the great war had begun and life changed. But it was in that period that Rothstein became the master. Just how and just why no one seems to know." Whether it happened in two years or seven years, Arnold transformed during the mid-1910s, from a successful gambler into something much larger, and that metamorphosis, though tenebrous and furtive, could be traced in the recollections of his wife and associates, and in the headlines and trial transcripts concerning his friends at Jack's.

Jack's was full of figures like Ratsy Tourbillon and Nicky Arnstein. Nicky, like Ratsy, was European-born and a real Raffles. According to a biographer of Nicky's one-time wife, the famous Jewish comedian Fanny Brice, the teenage Nicky was drawn to professional cycling and he liked to throw races, a habit that brought him into alliances with gamblers and confidence men of the sporting underworld: "He felt at home in their world, and they quickly saw how this well-educated, polished young man could be valuable in many operations." Nicky was arrested in Monte Carlo and Paris. From London, where he was accused of being part of a ring of con men that stretched to Hong Kong, he was extradited to the States in 1912 and managed to stay out of prison thanks to his friends at Jack's.

Ratsy and Nicky weren't small-time crooks or immigrant ghetto dwellers. They were assimilated people who could discourse on art and foreign places even as they disdained snobbishness, disregarded laws, and hunted up suckers. That they never employed actual violence to separate the mark from his money was a point of pride. "Of all the grifters, the confidence man is the aristocrat," writes Maurer in *The Big Con.* "The trusting victim literally thrusts a fat bankroll into his hands."

Generally, artists of the "big con" were people who grew up in the early days of the American confidence game, when it was limited to small cons like circus grifts and three-card monte, and practitioners needed only to pay off the local cop to secure protection for their swindles. But by 1913 the big con was entering its decade-long golden era, alongside the rise of moral reform and corporate America, and it was these three phenomena, taken together, that created the new Arnold Rothstein.

In many ways, the moral-reform movement of the 1910s was a partner of the business-reform movement happening alongside it. If the earlier merger boom, the first phase of the corporate reconstruction of American capitalism, was about limiting competition by combining businesses into vertical behemoths, this next phase was about establishing a web of regulations to check the behemoths: antitrust law to limit monopolies, an income tax to make the rich pay something back, a federal reserve to stabilize the economy, and, later, stock-market regulation. The first phase consolidated power and wealth. The second phase checked power and wealth. Both phases, taken together, would circumvent socialism and transition the Gilded Age to a sustainable corporate-capitalist future. Vice repression was another way to guarantee that future by legitimizing corporate power. Prohibiting casinos was thought to legitimize stock speculation. Prohibiting narcotics was thought to legitimize the pharmaceutical industry.*

These new laws that shaped America sprang from a desire for something higher, for ethical business and clean living, a set of rules that could purify the country by upholding the superiority of the wealthy and justifying surveillance of the hordes. And yet moral reform was also inconsistent with America's propensity for vice, for gambling and imbibing and drug-taking. That fissure, between biological impulse and the Anglo ideal, would need to be rationalized, or managed, by someone who was more than just a grafting cop. The advent of the big con introduced Arnold to this role.

As we've seen, the purification movement gained steam around 1906, following the merger boom, with state-level laws, regulations, and outright bans of alcohol, drugs, and gambling. Then, for the first time, vice repression jumped to the federal level with the 1910 Mann Act, the anti-prostitution law that made it a felony to transport women across state lines for "immoral purposes." This broad and ambiguous law was a perfect harbinger of moral reform, establishing a pattern that would play out again and again in the twentieth century.

At first, the mere passage of the Mann Act satisfied those who fretted about immigration and changing sexual norms. But few of the law's supporters had considered how the Mann Act, once passed into law, might

---

* At a 1909 Senate hearing, when a skeptical lawmaker asked William Jay Schieffelin, the head of the Drug Trust, an informal group of pharmaceutical executives, if he thought that drug prohibition would drive drug traffic into the hands of "bootleggers," creating a dangerous underworld market, Schieffelin said he hoped it *would do* precisely that, leaving his industry "free to sell them only for legitimate medicinal purposes and have nothing to do with supplying the victims of the habit." Schieffelin, who inherited his family's legacy drug company, was also the leader of the Citizens Union, financing DA Whitman in the Rosenthal case.

be implemented. It was finally decided that the Department of Justice's policing division, the new Bureau of Investigation (the future FBI), would handle enforcement. Since its 1908 birth, the Bureau had been a small agency, its two dozen investigators operating out of Washington and handling miscellaneous federal crimes such as Postal Act violations. The Mann Act provided the Bureau's first takeoff, converting it into a national institution with agents in every large city.

In the first years of the Mann Act, the federal government prosecuted the few actual cases of cross-state sex trafficking that investigators could find. But in 1913, the law's breadth resulted in a landmark case of cross-state romance that happened to entail adultery, and was therefore deemed "immoral" even though no prostitution was involved. A conviction in that case, later upheld by the US Supreme Court, meant that any man traveling across state lines with any woman who wasn't his wife was now a potential Mann Act violator, and a bustling industry in sexual blackmail, known as the "badger game," emerged. The game was simple: A woman seduced a man and asked him to take her on a trip. Once across state lines, her outraged "husband" barged into the hotel room and threatened legal action. As Carolyn Rothstein recalled, the badger game was refined by Arnold's associates, Ratsy lead among them.

Not all big-con games exploited moral legislation. Some cons, such as "the wire" (a fake off-track betting parlor with actors to make it look real) and "the rag" (a "bucket shop," or fraudulent stock brokerage), relied on the mark's own greed.* The leading practitioner of the wire was an Irishman named Charles Gondorff, while the top bucketeer was an Eastern European Jew who went by George Graham "GG" Rice. "It was during this period,"

---

* Bucket shops posted their worthless stocks on a "second-tier exchange" called the New York Consolidated. While reputable stock exchanges like the NYSE made efforts to ascertain that listed stocks were legitimate, the president of the Consolidated, a friend of Arnold's, didn't feel so compelled. Buy or sell, lose or gain, the Consolidated received a kickback of one-eighth of a point for every share traded, a commission known as a "kosher eighth."

wrote Carolyn, "that I met GG Rice, one of the most famous and talented bucket shop operators. Born Horowitz, he had a strong Semitic appearance despite his change of name.* He educated himself by reading newspapers and looking up unfamiliar words, and it was said that he could write the most brilliant and convincing stock letters in the world."

The big con brought about some major changes in confidence games. In the old days of rigged card tricks, a con man could buy protection from a cop. "The fix was a simple transaction between con men and officers," writes David Maurer, "with influential saloon-keepers or politicians occasionally acting as intermediaries in difficult cases." But now, in the golden era, where con men separated important people from large amounts of money and thus risked heavy repercussions, a stronger fix was needed — the fixing of judges and juries, police chiefs and prosecutors, as well as political parties. Writes Maurer: "It is not implied that a fixer is necessarily a part of any party political machine — a good fixer can weather many a change in administration — but he usually pays off to that machine, directly or indirectly, in cash. This fixer is sometimes a respectable and legitimate citizen, often an attorney, but in some places he had a hand in the rackets. His underworld connections are legion."

Arnold cultivated notorious figures such as Ratsy, Nicky, Gondorff, and GG, offering to lend them money, funnel kickbacks to the right people, and provide bail and attorneys when the badger game, the wire, or the rag went sideways. From his table at Jack's, he took investment meetings and loaned money to anyone who had a plan. He didn't refer to these plans as crimes. He called them "stories," and Carolyn described how he brought these stories into being: "The banks loaned Arnold large sums of money without security, which he in turn lent to persons of more or less questionable morals, such that the banks themselves were financing the underworld."

---

* Carolyn was mistaken. He was actually born Jacob Simon Herzig.

*   *   *

It was a busy churn, connecting the worlds, but Arnold whirred like a transmission belt and became addicted to the role of fixer. A lawyer who worked for Arnold said, "He wants to be known as the greatest fixer in the world. He likes to help everyone with bail, rescuing the boys from tough traps, shining in the eyes of tough fellows as being their friend." Later, in a rare interview, Arnold himself affirmed this view. When asked what was worthwhile, besides making money, he said, "Doing things for people, for your friends. I'd lie and steal and hang for a friend. What else is life for?" He added: "My code of life is absolutely simple. Help a friend, be a friend, use your brains and fear nothing."

Carolyn saw her husband's code in more personal terms — she noticed that he took on the character of his estranged father, Abe the Just, who had acquired his sobriquet by donating time and money to mediate difficulties between groups in the garment industry. "I am not trying to compare the social, religious or moral qualities of the father and son," wrote Carolyn. "I am merely submitting the fact that where the father in legitimate channels made sacrifices to help persons in trouble, the son did exactly the same service in the purlieu of the half-world."

The incessant movement, the rush of chance, the adoration that desperate people showed for the genie who materializes out of nowhere — these things were drugs for Arnold. "He would hound a man for fifty dollars which was owed him, but he would cheerfully sacrifice thousands to maintain his reputation for being a big man among big men," Carolyn wrote. "He had to be a big shot, and a big shot couldn't afford to be cheap. It was one of the many ways he fed his inordinate vanity, a vanity which grew hungrier and hungrier as the years rolled past."

Sustaining that role became the reason that Arnold *wanted* money, so that he could loan it out again, to have it always be working. At night, on her way home, Carolyn would have herself driven slowly up Broadway, the taxi going at a crawl. It might've been cold and rainy. It might've been snowing. But more often than not she would find Arnold pacing the sidewalk and ask him to come home. He'd wave her on: *I'm waiting to see someone to collect from.* He knew if his debtors had had a good day, and he would stay out all night in order to catch the person in funds. "He was always desperately in need of money," Carolyn recalled. "No matter if he made hundreds of thousands in a day, there were always notes to be met at the bank, losses to cover. I was always and forever rushing to banks to deposit money at the last minute to take care of [to cover] checks that were due in the morning."

Whatever glamour others projected onto Arnold and his Broadway crowd, they were compulsive gamblers, self-destructive addicts consumed with getting money to make the next bet. There was little joy in winning, just the high of relief. "A deal has been written of the honor of gamblers," Carolyn wrote. "It is largely a myth. For the most part they are a neurotic, unreliable, hysterical, unfortunate, debt-ridden collection of human misfits. If one of them happens to have a large roll of bills at any given moment it doesn't mean anything. Someone else will have the roll within a few hours or days."*

In the early days, Carolyn hadn't understood Arnold, hadn't seen him as a man who was going to take a certain delight in breaking the law. And even now, at the wizened age of twenty-three, she still relished his gentleness with her, still felt their mutual love, and still nourished the faith that their situation was temporary, that eventually they were going to be like other people in "the great world, trying to live for the best that was in us."

Carolyn eased into the role of "loyal woman," what she self-effacingly called "the Mrs. Grundy." They had no children. Instead, she played wife-mother to her thirty-year-old man-child. Late at night, while working on

---

* Maurer makes a similar point: "Most con men gamble heavily with the money for which they work so hard and take such chances to secure. In a word, most of them are suckers for some other branch of the grift."

his little black books, his ledgers, he would call out to Carolyn. *Just sit over there, Sweet. You don't have to do anything or say anything. I just feel better if you are near me.* "He rather expected, as a small boy does, that I would forgive him for his shortcomings and keep right on being the woman to whom he might come with his troubles, his aches and pains, his worries, and later, his fears." Carolyn was the only person in whom Arnold had absolute faith, she believed, and there was a bond between them that endured until the end. "If I lived with Arnold without regrets, and would do the same thing all over again if the conditions were reproduced, it was because I was very much in love. That love? That love explained everything. It made forgiveness and toleration unnecessary."

Still, it was easier for her to forgive Arnold in the early days, when she was certain that he loved only her. In 1913, Carolyn was at the hairdresser when she picked up a copy of *Town Topics,* a high-society gossip rag, and read: "A tailor-made man prominent in the guessing fraternity is seen nightly in the Broadway restaurants with beautiful Bobbie Winthrop." Everyone knew Barbara Winthrop. She danced in the Ziegfield Follies, and her photo often appeared alongside that of film star Mary Pickford. When Carolyn confronted Arnold about Bobbie, he promised to stop seeing her, but he didn't stop and Carolyn rationalized this too: "Keeping a woman was the thing to do. So Arnold selected a woman for the part who was one of the most glamorous and compelling of the day. He was keeping in the fashion of his set with a vengeance."

One day, Arnold and Carolyn went shopping on Automobile Row, a string of Broadway blocks running from Forty-Ninth Street up to Columbus Circle. For decades this strip had been home to the horse-and-carriage trade. Now, as automobiles went mainstream, these same blocks glimmered with new auto showrooms: Benz, De Dion-Bouton, Ford, Fiat. They settled on a striking Edwardian speedster, a red Métallurgique-Maybach imported from Belgium. After buying the auto, Arnold made an appointment at the dentist to get a new set of gleaming white teeth.

The money, the image, the connections—he was gathering the threads he'd use to twist and transform crime into big business, organizing it all into a grand industry worthy of the corporate age.

His position, though, depended on the power of his political overlords in Tammany Hall. Tammany appeared to have survived the Rosenthal Affair but was in disarray, fighting for its existence against the forces of moral reform and facing a righteous enemy that no one, not even omniscient Arnold, saw coming.

Part Three

The Incorruptibles

15

Whacked Unmercifully

A T THE EAST SIDE POLICE PRECINCT ON CLINTON
Street, where new security bars were being installed on the windows, Third Deputy Commissioner Harry Newburger expelled the
newspaper reporters and introduced Abe to the twenty cops gathered in
the back room.

Here was the team he'd asked for. In addition to Detective Faurot,
there was Honest Dan Costigan, the lieutenant who had formerly led one
of Gaynor's two citywide vice squads, both now defunct. There was Frank
Cassassa, an Italian detective who specialized in catching pickpockets. (It
was Cassassa whom Abe had tipped about Louie's whereabouts.) Another
notable selection was Isabella Goodwin, the NYPD's first female detective, whose specialty was undercover stings of unlicensed doctors and
"palmists" who sold false medical remedies. The rest of the squad was
composed of patrolmen with a reputation for honesty, plus a mix of Irish
and Jewish "bruisers"—Cohen, Finn, Levy, McKenna, Miller, Murphy,
and Sheridan. One bruiser, Moe Stein, whom Abe knew from childhood,
carried a weighted umbrella instead of a club. And lurking in the back

corner was a surprising selection: Cornelius Cahalane, the grafter whom Abe had outed, months earlier, in the pursuit of Dollar John Langer.

Abe said: "It's true that Harry and I are here because concerned citizens went to the mayor. But this is no reformer's show. What we have in mind is a crusade to clean the Jewish quarter and we've enlisted you because we know you cannot be touched." Abe said they would separate the squad into two groups. To start, Detective Cassassa would lead his own group in a roundup of pickpockets and fences, while Abe and Newburger would lead the second group in raids of casinos, narcotics dealers, and law-breaking saloons.

After this introduction, Cahalane, the grafter, addressed Abe privately. "I know it was you who turned me in," he said. Abe acknowledged that it had been him. "I want you to know that I only took money from gamblers, never from a whorehouse," Cahalane said. "I go to confession. I'm a practicing Catholic." Abe nodded, but Cahalane was curious. He asked why, in light of his history, he had been selected. Abe parroted something else that his father often said: To get anywhere in this world, he explained to Cahalane, it helped to be an "ex"—an ex-lawyer, an ex-tailor, even an ex-grafter. Knowledge gained in one world was often put to its best use in another context.

If Abe was liberal with his selections for the vice squad, he knew that the present legal landscape was in many ways new and largely untested by law enforcement. Moral reform had created new categories of crime but, as yet, few limits on how that crime was patrolled. For Abe and Newburger, these anti-vice laws were tools, and in using them to the utmost they would become early spearheads for the expansion of police power that vice reform would generate in American life.

The first weeks of the vice crusade were swift and hectic. Up and down Second and Third Avenues, and across Eighth Street and Houston, the cops smashed through reinforced "ice-box doors," tore out phone lines used for off-track betting, and carted wagonloads of roulette wheels and "stuss layouts" back to the precinct. They needed all this—as "marked," or labeled, evidence—for potential trials, but Newburger emphasized that its condition didn't matter, so the cops sank their axes up to the haft in the lacquered wood of gambling paraphernalia, and the precinct sounded like a shipyard on a busy day. GAMBLERS' TOOLS SEIZED IN RAIDS "MARKED" TO BITS, reported the *World,* noting, "Anyone wanting good mahogany kindling ought to be on hand."

For Abe it was a pleasure to raid, to decimate "the conditions" and see things torn down. His satisfaction was evident in early Kehillah reports chronicling the vice squad's progress: "One man came flying out of the saloon with his trousers slit so that they looked like skirts—another rolled out into the gutter. Women never cried the way these dirty scoundrels howled and yelped.... They can do almost any kind of dirty work, but they cannot take their medicine, and if they ever got any, they certainly got it on this night in the saloon here." After raiding a place, Newburger would assign a patrolman to the door to turn away customers. If the proprietors responded to a raid by installing new doors and locks, Newburger would break out a statute book and demand admittance under the pretext of fire prevention, and the squad would wield their axes and break through again.

They had been handed incredible power, and they used it. On occasion Abe and Newburger applied for a warrant, but raided largely without them, simply using Abe's anonymously sourced information as daily to-do lists. His probable cause may not have held up in court, but it didn't need to. Whatever he said needed raiding, they raided. Ike's Pool Room, on Broome Street, with a soda stand out front that drew neighborhood children, was, Abe wrote, "nothing more than an incubator of vice and crime. It is filthy, dirty, the language used is vile, and it should not be tolerated." Jake's Pool Room, on Delancey, was "a resort wherein congregate young men who are started on the road to thievedom. . . . It is filthy and disgusting, and the place should be whacked unmercifully." At Harry's Pool Parlor, on Avenue C, Abe wrote, "Many boys who play are under age, and morally they have no right to be here, also legally." At a pool parlor on Rivington, "The boys all have their hats, coats, and collars off, as the odor is vile and hardly any ventilation whatsoever. A crowd is always seen outside, thieves and pickpockets who delight in insulting people who pass by. They are a boisterous bunch and should be cleaned out." Of the rowdy scene outside Gold's candy store, Abe, already beyond his remit, wrote: "It is bad enough when boys throw dice—but nothing could be worse when young girls are taught the game and hang around candy stores until midnight, laughing and talking with the boys when they should be home and fast asleep at this hour. We should get after it."

As Tammany-allied judges, lawyers, and cops scrambled to protect their underworld cash cows, Newburger kept pace, overseeing every prosecution. Abe wrote: "We have investigated the conditions around the courts and know the inner workings of the leeches who infest them. For instance, a thief is arrested—we find he is making connection with a fixer around the court to see the policemen in the case. The Third Deputy Commissioner then rings the precinct, asks for the detective bureau to which the police are attached, and drops a gentle hunch requesting to know the status of the case. Then the report is immediately circulated that Newburger wired, and then of course there is nothing doing in the case."*

In drug cases, when it came to preserving evidence, no tactic was off-limits. In one raid, when the wife of a drug dealer choked on broken glass while trying to swallow tubes of cocaine, Abe poured cooking oil down her throat to keep her alive so she could testify against her husband. In

---

* Newburger would call the police who'd been contacted by the fixer, and ask about the status of the case. This question was enough to convey Newburger's hunch that a fix might be underway, and, if so, squelch it.

other cases, Abe hauled addicts into court and jabbed their arms with morphine to stave off withdrawal, so they could face the judge. To capture dealers, Newburger implemented a new law-enforcement method, the "buy-bust," and Abe taught patrolmen how to behave like addicts, or "fiends." But Abe didn't always get what he wanted. When he urged raids on pharmacies, otherwise legitimate businesses that used "runners" to deal narcotics on the sidewalk, the warrant issue became a problem. "Something should be done about the drug stores," he complained in Kehillah reports. "We have so many that are selling this stuff, and if we can only get some judge who will give us search warrants, of course, we need not require a terrible large amount of evidence."

Judges and politicians tried unsuccessfully to recruit Abe and Newburger into the Tammany fold, and by late February their squad became known within the police department as the Incorruptibles.

Detective Cassassa's unit, meanwhile, chased pickpockets through trolley cars and elevated trains. "Women screamed and jumped on the seats while Cassassa and his quarry surged and pushed and thumped their way among the frightened passengers, but the detective did not loosen his grip," the *World* reported of a bust. "Cassassa knocked the heads of the men together, pounded their noses into the floor, and told them he would kill them if they didn't quit."

That winter, they arrested legions of thieves — Fannie Diamond and Toothless Kitty Davis, Candy Kid Phil and the Thirteen-Dollar Jew, Rosie Cheesecake and Hymie Rubbernose. At Essex Market Court, Cassassa refused open bribe attempts as he walked down the hallway to testify, throwing aside his coat and saying, "Here's my badge. Talk to this." In courtrooms, Abe identified himself as "Max Prettyfield, a sociology student" and functioned as a translator, ensuring that nothing was lost when the criminals testified in their Yiddish slang of *gazlunim,* zhits, and *shtanges.** Sometimes testimony revealed the details of grafting cops. One thief confessed that with the help of a detective, he fenced more than $500,000 worth of stolen goods per year, which led to that detective's quiet dismissal, the first of many. This was the Gaynor way — handling corruption on the down-low — and it suited the Kehillah's secretive agenda as well.

As the Incorruptibles worked, Abe's informants and agents supplied him with an ever-growing pipeline of information. One agent, a fellow Hungarian Jew named Marcus Braun, who had once been an immigration inspector, posed as a pimp and reported back to Abe about the movements of the Independent Benevolent Association. Another informant, whom Abe referred to as his "top man," was a seventeen-year-old who hung out at the saloon across from Essex Market Court, where Tammany lawyers congregated to make deals and buy cases. A third informant was a young woman named Natalie Sonnichsen, with whom Abe had worked on earlier reform assignments, when they posed as a married couple and infiltrated the seedy Raines law hotels. Now Natalie was working undercover in department stores, where pimps and madams, disguised as shoppers, went to headhunt immigrants who worked in the stores as poorly paid shopgirls.

Abe kept his informant reports locked up in the Second Avenue apartment, where, surrounded by the same people he was chasing, he returned each morning, bathed in the clawfoot tub, and fell asleep until the water got cold. Then he did his exercises from the latest issue of *Physical Culture,* made Postum, put Enrico Caruso on the Victrola, organized notes from informants, and wrote.

For the Kehillah, Abe funneled facts and narratives, opinion and strategies, literary references and biblical allusions, personal asides and

---

* Criminals, nickels, and dollars.

plenty of sarcasm into 621 reports, which he called "stories," such as: "St. 24, Becky Wetdream," or "St. 231, New York Independent Benevolent Assocation." If these raw and detailed reports about prostitution seemed calculated to provoke a response, it was because Abe, Newburger, and Magnes worried that the uptowners might be too satisfied with the crusade's early successes and shut it down prematurely.

Of one prostitute, Abe wrote: "Flossy is a half-breed — having Indian blood in her veins. She is up against a Jewish mack* who hounds her and pounds her and is at her heels continually, and holds her down like a dog or a prisoner." Of another: "Rae is a Jewess — 5 feet three inches — a little stocky shrimp — dark complexion — black hair — black eyes — weighs about 150 pounds — lives with an Italian pimp. She always brags that 'No Jew pimp can get my money, he must be a wop and a good one.' After work she is always in the company of another Jewess, Lena the Musketeer, and they have their coffee and cake around three o'clock in Berger's Restaurant at 107 Second Ave. One morning we had to carry Lena out of Berger's because she was gripped with a paralytic stroke in her legs. Of course this comes not alone from the length of time she has been in the graft, but from the unnatural practices she must undergo with johns."

In the streets, what Abe facetiously called "the field of study," his eye was often drawn to the seedy and the debauched. About Jennie Silver, a prostitute who lived with her pimp and her two-year-old daughter, Abe wrote: "If she does not make enough money for him, he kicks and beats her. He would let the baby go hungry for milk, and take the last few pennies out of the house for drink." Of another prostitute, Abe wrote that "a baby of eight months, whose skin is all broke out with sores, lies in the very room where she practices her iniquities." At a "50 cent disorderly house," he observed: "The women themselves were filthy enough, but the

---

* From the French slang for pimp, *maquereau* (literally, mackerel). Elsewhere in Kehillah reports Abe uses his own invention, "mackanolean."

floors, ceilings, and walls are all loaded down with disease, and the beds are full of vermin." Describing the scene at a so-called *weisbier stube,* a cheap kind of saloon-brothel, Abe noted: "When a john enters, the girls sit on his lap, rub him up, and coax him for drinks. Then he is asked if he desires any pleasurable moments in life (this is not the language used — the language being unfit for print), and if he acquiesces he is ushered into a rear room where sexual intercourse is performed on a dirty couch, but no dirtier than the underclothes the woman wears. The work of a woman in a *weisbier stube,* prior to intercourse, is 'SQUEEZING THE LEMON,' since the woman squeezes his privates and often, behind the sideboard to be found in every *stube,* masturbates him if he is a thick-headed foreigner."

Whenever possible, he noted the cheek-by-jowl proximity of prostitution to the wholesome side of ghetto life. There were brothels above, below, and next to synagogues and schools, soup kitchens and wedding halls, and all around them swirled the pimps, a group for which Abe reserved special disdain: "A man with pimp blood in him is a dog." Of a pimp named Pearlstein, Abe wrote, "He cannot read or write in English. He is an animal." Of another: "Shtumi (Dumb One) has two gold teeth in the front of his mouth and a general deceiving appearance as his face is covered with small-pox holes." Another: "Max Weinstein, alias Max the Paroch, had a Jewess named Helen, alias Helen N****r, at work for him on Second Avenue until two operations she had to undergo and became worthless. To use the vernacular of the underworld, 'her belly is cut to ribbons.' Helen had to turn all her money over to him, and when she held out a little for herself he beat the life out of her."*

---

* In these prewar years, the N-word was used among New York's dark-complexioned Russian Jews, frequently as part of a person's underworld name. In Kehillah reports, one finds N****r Rue, N****r Mike, and so forth, and newspapers often printed these aliases, putting, for instance, Yoshke N****r in headlines. Interestingly, many didn't consider German Jews to be "white" either. When Kuhn Loeb became the second-most-influential bank on Wall Street, J. P. Morgan, who referred to Jacob Schiff as "that foreigner," consoled himself, telling a friend that his firm remained one of the only all-white banks in New York.

At Barth's Salon, the Second Avenue hair parlor where prostitutes like Tony the Tough went to network and get their hair puffed, Abe set the scene: "On the corner is a drug store, next to that is a candy store, next to that is a milk store, and then comes one of the dirtiest and filthiest hangouts for degraded women.... This place is to the very bottom ditch not only a public nuisance but a public disgrace."

Barth, the eponymous barber, acted as bondsman for the women when they were arrested, Abe noted, and ran a rich graft with the Tammany defense lawyers, who bribed judges and sold cases at Essex Market Court. In the courtroom, the father-son team of wardens who guarded the pen in the back corner sold cocaine, opium, and whiskey to prisoners. "If this city is to be made a decent and habitable place for Jews and Gentiles to live in," Abe wrote of the courthouse grafters, "we must meet this nefarious gang with sledgehammer blows."

These immersive chronicles, set down with a stylish pace and rhythm, had little precedent in the canon of American writing as it stood in 1913. If Abe's oeuvre had a literary forebear, it was perhaps the French writer Eugène Sue, whose novel *The Mysteries of Paris* was popular among Abe's cohort.* In that book, East Siders saw their ghetto world reflected in the prostitutes, madams, and thugs of the French capital. Abe himself might have found inspiration in the book's central character, a duke who goes undercover as a Parisian worker, speaks in underworld argot, fights for the lower classes, and navigates all layers of society while diagnosing the nobility's complicity in vice.

In his own Kehillah reports, Abe resisted indicting the wealthy for the problems he described. He felt apprehension about alienating the benefactors without whose money and power there would be no vice

---

* In an interview, Big Jack Zelig once cited Eugène Sue as his favorite author.

crusade. But just in case any German Jews were inclined to shut the crusade down early, Abe submitted a report about prostitution at Macy's, the department store owned by a Kehillah member. Abe's informant, Natalie, discovered that Macy's floor managers did double duty as scouts, breaking underpaid shopgirls into the sex trade and selling them off to madams and pimps.

Taken together, Abe's Kehillah reports sustained the interest of the uptown benefactors, and more vice-crusading funds flowed.

After Louie's sentencing, Lily took a job in the millinery department of Macy's. In the city's largest department store, she hoped not to be recognized, but on her first day, other shopgirls figured out who she was. *That's the girl whose husband shot Rosenthal.* As Lily observed those shopgirls turn to prostitution to supplement their pitiful wages, she wondered if she would ever sell herself in order to continue being a loyal wife to Louie, whose case, now headed to an appeal, she was determined to win.

Traveling to Sing Sing and Albany, hiring lawyers, soliciting signatures for petitions—it all added up, and she needed the Macy's job, so she tried to remain chipper, even as customers pointed her out like an animal on display. *My, how you look like Lefty Louie's wife. What an unfortunate resemblance, for she is a bad girl!*

16

Year of the Red-Light Drama

URING THE SPRING OF 1913, ABE AND THE INCORRUPTIBLES chased pimps and madams down dumbwaiters and through cellars. Eyes ablaze, blood rushing to his head, Abe led raids of massage parlors and *weisbier stuben,* fake hospitals where prostitutes masqueraded as nurses and dance halls that served as recruiting grounds for the IBA.

The crusade against the million-dollar sex industry seemed to enjoy some kind of providential oversight. In one raid, a squad member's pocket watch deflected a bullet headed for his heart. In another, a pimp rushed Abe with a rusty bayonet. Moe Stein, the patrolman Abe knew from childhood, shouted "Look out!" Abe fumbled his .32 Iver Johnson, dropping it. He reached for the heavy Colt Special, but the extra-wide grip, which housed the battery for the mounted flashlight, rendered the weapon unwieldly and he couldn't get a shot off quickly. The pimp was about to hurl the bayonet at Abe's head when Moe Stein leaped forward and rammed the spear end of his weighted umbrella into the pimp's mouth, impaling him to the pine wall.

Across Allen Street, up and down the Bowery, the Incorruptibles shut down some fifty brothels, a development that generated the cleanup's first publicity, with headlines such as POLICE PURGE EVIL RESORTS and EXODUS OF EXPLOITERS FOLLOW RAIDS. From a hotel lobby, Newburger gave an interview to the *Sun,* while other papers wrote about Newburger and Mayor Gaynor riding through the East Side and remarking on the improved conditions. The Kehillah was never mentioned, nor the German-Jewish uptowners, but the *World* reported "a secret movement afoot to rid the Jewish quarter of its notorious criminal field," and credited "a quiet, effective police campaign behind the fact that the city is cleaner than ever." Whoever was behind it, the cleanup had led to "shocking and lurid revelations" about the underworld, supplying fodder for authors, filmmakers, and playwrights, who almost instantaneously created ripped-from-the-headlines stories with titles like *Damaged Goods, The Lure,* and *Traffic in Souls,* hard-hitting blockbusters that would give 1913 a place in American cultural history as the Year of the Red-Light Drama.

In one best-selling red-light drama, a novel called *The House of Bondage,* a pimp named Max Crossman stalks Mary, an unhappy sixteen-year-old, and plies her with alcohol. She wakes up in an East Side brothel where she entertains an "unending procession of visitors." When Mary asks one customer to help her escape, he says, "Why, don't you know that that yid who got you into this makes a business of such things? Don't you know there's a whole army of them that do? I wish to the Lord I could do something, but there isn't a policeman or a magistrate in the city who'd listen to me — they know too well where they get the jam for their bread and butter." Mary contracts venereal disease, then plots revenge: she gets Max drunk and passes him a case of VD. *The House of Bondage* was so popular that its publisher had to order ten new printings in as many months.

These works revealed the "East Side underworld" to a national audience. At the same time, thanks to the Kehillah's success, some people from that actual underworld were learning the identities of the vice crusaders, "Newburger and Shoenfeld." The IBA president, Rabbi Rebelle, stalked Second Avenue, swigging whiskey and shouting, "That Newburger is some cock-sucking Jewboy!" As Abe spun down Second Avenue in a Black Maria, one of the five hundred Model Ts that Ford adapted for the NYPD in 1912, beleaguered prostitutes gathered on the sidewalk and raised their hands as if to pray: *"Lieber Got,"* they said, *"nem em zu heint nacht." Dear God, take him tonight.*

The notoriety brought the vice crusade a new set of problems. Rebelle vowed to spend his last cent — his life, if necessary — fighting the police, and said that under no circumstances would he be put out of business. The Incorruptibles couldn't expect to interrupt the city's most profitable vice without resistance. The underworld battled back, and the human cost was significant. Prostitutes suspected of squealing were turning up dead. Abe's "top man," the seventeen-year-old who worked as a spy in the lawyers' saloon across from Essex Market Court, fell asleep one night in the bar. He was discovered with incriminating notes on his person and killed with an ice pick through his heart. These tragedies haunted Abe and drove him harder.

Sure, the Incorruptibles had made surprising progress in the first few months of the crusade, but if no officials were prosecuted, then the cleanup might only be temporary. In that case, the Kehillah vice crusade would be, he worried, not much different from the fake reform efforts gone by, "an investigating committee looking for a little excitement." If the Kehillah was going to wipe out Jewish prostitution, he had to break that lucrative connection between the upperworld and the underworld, between Mother Rosie Hertz and whomever she paid off. "Mrs. Hertz," he wrote to the Kehillah, "has always bragged that she's been running houses for twenty years, that she saw the police come and go, made and broke, people born and people die, and that after everyone is gone she will still be running a little natch for her last customers. If Hertz may get the best of us, it will lower our stock as a fighting mob in the opinion of the underworld."

Abe needed the same thing he'd needed at the outset of the crusade: the name of a bagman. Not a lieutenant but someone higher, someone whose exposure might shut the system down. He needed Tony the Tough to come through.

During the peak decades of globalized Jewish prostitution, in the late 1800s and early 1900s, whenever morality crusades would seek to push Jewish pimps out of a city, the crusade's success often coincided with a kind of Spartacus moment, an episode in which a prostitute, or a group of prostitutes, decided to break the chain of bondage and join the crusade. In Johannesburg, in 1908, Jewish prostitutes revolted against the so-called Immorality Trust, South Africa's version of the IBA. In Asia, Nathan Spieler, whose name was a Yiddish byword for pimp, trafficked women and owned brothels across the continent—until 1912, when a prostitute went to the Shanghai police and swore out a complaint against him.

In New York, Antonia Rolnick knew nothing of this larger context. She knew only of Dollar Land, a place where immigrant daughters, surrounded by new energies in the streets and new ideas in the lecture halls, longed to shed the past and seize liberation in a place where it was finally possible. "I would like to write a poem / But I have no words," one garment worker etched into her cutting table. "My grammar is ladies waists / My schooling skirts." Whether joining the Jewish Girls' Self-Education Society or simply teaching one another their letters by writing on brick walls, liberation energized them. The yearning to be free also expressed itself in acts of defiance, a word so rooted in East Side dialect that it was shortened to "defi." Some defis were historical, such as the mass movements for labor rights and housing reform. Other defis were smaller acts of resistance, such as the day a garment worker named Sarah Rozner decided that she'd had her breasts grabbed for the last time. When the offending foreman came around again, Rozner put her long-knife cutter in his face and said, "Son of a bitch, I'll run this through your fucking nostrils."

In the winter and spring of 1913, a spirit of change possessed Tony the Tough, and she turned on the underworld with a pitiless vengeance. She reported to the Kehillah every brothel she knew of and the passwords to get into them. She named every cop she paid off and every "procurer" who sold girls. She broke into the offices of real estate agents — the *mecklers*, or middlemen, who rented out brothel space on behalf of rich property owners — and stole the leases that linked those brothels to noted people, including a local judge and the newspaper owner William Randolph Hearst, who fashioned himself a voice of reform while profiting from the same thing he deplored in his papers.

After the Incorruptibles carried out raids that Tony's information facilitated, she set out to burn her own organization, the empire of Mother Rosie Hertz, by arranging for one of Abe's undercover detectives to sneak in and photograph a prostitute undressing. The next day, the brothel was raided, and the photographic evidence meant that Mother had no recourse to the customary protection that her bribes had always guaranteed. She was soon arrested and, for the first time in her career, put on trial.

Tony appeared in the parlor room of an East Side building owned by Mother Hertz, who sat in a chair perched on a dais. Diamonds hung from her neck, and fine lace secured her wig. Below her, on floor level, were a chair, a table, and a tea service. Following the weekly ritual, Tony came before Mother and proffered the chamois money bag that contained the final weekly profits from the brothel that Tony, until recently, had managed. Mother passed the money bag back to her husband, who sat at a desk behind her and kept the accounts. Then Mother gathered her skirts, stood up on the dais, and kicked Tony across the chin.

From a heap on the floor, Tony dragged herself into the chair and rubbed her jaw.

"Tell me!" Mother shouted. "Why cannot a smart kike whore like you remember what even the dumbest wop on Mott Street knows?"

Simulating contrition, Tony apologized and said she hadn't seen the *shomis,* the detective, when he came in, posing as a john, to take the photo.

Mother was incredulous. "The *shomis* blew the butter factory without so much as a moozle?* And no one thought to mention it?"

"Please, Mother, forgive me. Cannot the case be fixed?"

Mother threw up her hands, saying, "Who knows when this moral outbreak will subside."

Such anxiety was a new feeling for Mother Hertz. She'd seen her way through many moral panics, going all the way back to the 1880s, when Mother's own mother had been, according to Abe's Kehillah report, the first Jewish prostitute on the East Side — "routinely taking on," as Abe wrote, "five Pollacks in a coal cellar for ten dollars." Mother herself came into the trade in the 1890s and weathered two decades of reform efforts. But now things didn't look good. The younger pimps could no longer afford to "eat from *ongegreiten,*" money saved. Angered over what they saw as mismanagement by their pimping elders, several younger pimps had decided to ignore the IBA's orders to *halt den pisk,* hold your mouth, and squealed. The putative IBA king, Motche Goldberg, had recently disappeared. Some pimps speculated that Motche was hiding out in the Catskills until the *geruder,* the rumpus, died out. Others said he had fled to South America, but no one really knew.

Mother called back to her husband: "Have we received any word from Winnie yet?"

"No," her husband replied. "No word from Winnie."

---

* Translation: "The detective left the brothel without so much as a kiss?"

Tony bowed out, vowing to Mother Hertz to do better, and remembered that name: *Winnie.*

Before he grew into what Abe Shoenfeld would call "New York's chiefest grafter," Winfield Sheehan came to the city from Buffalo, an eighteen-year-old with bright blue eyes and a cherubic face, and worked as a crime reporter for the *World.* There he cultivated connections with Tammany Hall and used his platform to poke fun at reformers and their "divine mission."

After six years in journalism, Winnie went into politics, attaching himself to a war veteran named Rhinelander Waldo, the son of wealthy patrician uptowners. In 1909, after Winnie helped Waldo become commissioner of the New York Fire Department, Waldo repaid Winnie by taking him on as his secretary. In this role Winnie wielded his political power in the Tammany style. For instance, he routinely fixed charges against the film mogul William Fox for fire-code violations at Fox's theaters. When Fox, an Eastern European Jew (born Fuchs), wanted to expand, he found—as most of the pioneering East Side movie moguls did—that he couldn't get loans from German-Jewish bankers, who tended to regard the fledgling industry as disreputable and unpromising. Fox, whose movies featured sex and violence, was particularly controversial. Winnie introduced Fox to Big Tim Sullivan, who, from his own entertainment business on Forty-Third Street, bought and sold theaters nationwide, until his recent incapacitation.

In 1911, when Waldo moved from fire commissioner to police commissioner, Winnie moved with him. As secretary to the NYPD commissioner, Winnie organized the graft system on a giant scale, collecting money from the city's pimps and gamblers while hiding behind the naïve Waldo. Whenever complaints about Lieutenant Becker's grafting arrived at the NYPD, Winnie would ask Becker if the allegations had any merit,

Becker would deny them, and such was the extent of any internal investigation.

At first, the Rosenthal murder hadn't seemed like a problem for Winnie. On the contrary, he was relieved by the death of a gambler who threatened to expose the graft system over which Winnie presided. The difficulties began when DA Whitman decided to build a murder case against Becker, because soon thereafter Winnie's name spilled into headlines: WALDO'S SECRETARY INVESTIGATED AS SUPPOSED GRAFT COLLECTOR. Headlines alone weren't enough to dislodge Winnie, though, not when he had friends like William Fox, who barged into NYPD headquarters and told Waldo that if he didn't stand by Winnie, then Fox was prepared to spend a million dollars of his own money on Winnie's defense.

Now, Abe compared Tony's information with intelligence from his undercover agent in the IBA, Marcus Braun, who wrote: "It is my opinion that Winnie Sheehan, Waldo's secretary, is the man the pimps look to. Several of the group have dropped hints in my presence. While the name itself was not mentioned, they have a peculiar Yiddish conniving way of conveying their innermost thoughts. They try to be *shtum* [silent] but are given to boasting and unconsciously hand themselves" — reveal their secrets.

That spring, when Mother Hertz took the witness stand in her own trial, for charges stemming from raids of her brothels, she held the power to disclose decades of business dealings with cops, prosecutors, and judges. Here was the moment Abe had long envisioned, when the kind of high-level corruption that facilitated crime would be laid bare and severed. The fact that the prosecutor in Mother's trial was an assistant district attorney, James Smith, only heightened the drama. Smith, Abe learned from his undercover agent, was the "backstop" for the IBA, quietly disposing of cases against pimps. These same pimps now pressured Smith to drop the case against Mother, calling him a double-crossing rat and threatening him with exposure.

Smith was in a bind. He couldn't drop the case because his boss, DA Whitman, was in the midst of a law-and-order campaign. At the same time, Deputy Commissioner Newburger was urging a mortified Smith to denounce Mother at trial and demand the maximum penalty. Smith couldn't do that either, because Mother knew too much, so much so that on the witness stand she bragged of her power. "I treated Joe Wasserman like a good mother would treat a good son," she said of one former cop, and pantomimed how she used to slip money and presents to Wasserman. "Why, it was a pleasure to give up." Even so, when asked to incriminate those higher up in the chain of corruption, Mother wept. She said she would not drag in respectable men, husbands and fathers. It was a sham trial. The judge sentenced her to a year in prison, though she would be out in a few months.

After Mother's trial, a rattled Winnie Sheehan summoned Newburger to NYPD headquarters and told him to get rid of Abe Shoenfeld, screaming, "We don't need spies in the department! I don't care who put him here!"

Uncowed, Newburger said, "Sir, if the department had ten Abe Shoenfelds then it could dispense with you *and* me. If he goes, I go."

Abe should've been happy. Newburger kept telling him so. But to Abe's mind the Hertz trial was a setback, a reminder of the limits of reform. High-level grafters were protected. Many drug dealers were slipping through the law's hands on technicalities. Pimps and prostitutes were already moving into tenements, where married men, as Abe wrote to the Kehillah, "now took the heavenly joys just down the hall from their families."

Abe wasn't naïve. He had read W. E. H. Lecky's *History of European Morals,* in which Lecky remarks that prostitution appears in every age as the perpetual symbol of sin.* Having descended from the moderate reformers of the early Progressive Era, Abe had never believed it was possible to rid the earth of vice, certainly not prostitution, until anti-vice laws swept the nation and the Kehillah came along, gave him an army, and put him at the head of a wide-ranging crime fight. This experience, as he later reflected, turned the moral reformer in him into a kind of moral revolutionary, and if it was the habit of revolution never to be content with the limits of its gains, it was the tendency of moral reform to exceed the limits set for it by reasonable people and the possible means of enforcement. The remote fringes of moral lapse nagged at Abe, and he felt himself coming apart.

In early June, Abe stood on the edge of Seward Park, where, at the turn of the century, he and Louie had played baseball until immigration quadrupled and turned Seward Park into "Sewer Park." He was accompanied by Honest Dan Costigan and a thirteen-year-old girl. Earlier that day, the girl had wandered into the Clinton Street precinct to ask the cops to find her friend. She explained that they often came to Seward Park to ride the swings, and men would watch them. The girls had names for these men. One was Steady because he never missed a day. The old one was Father Time. The men dropped pieces of paper on the ground — vouchers for penny ices at Dorman's candy store on Madison Street.

One day, the girl went on, "They dropped movie tickets to Fox's Theater. So we went up to Fourteenth Street and they let us watch all the movies we wanted so long as we gave up to the fellows. After they copped us out they asked if we wanted to be kept for a good thing. We said no. But they took Rachel anyway."

---

* Lecky: "Herself the supreme type of vice, she is ultimately the most efficient guardian of virtue....On that one degraded and ignoble form are concentrated the passions that might have filled the world with shame."

The story wasn't unique. Parents complained that their daughters, one as young as ten, came home with syphilitic sores after playing at Seward Park.

A few minutes later, Abe and Honest Dan Costigan rolled up to Dorman's candy store in a Black Maria. Looking into the store, Abe mulled over his family credo: *Never, unless in defense, raise your hand in violence.* The Incorruptibles hadn't shied away from violence, of course, but in light of the task they had been given, none of it seemed egregious. He turned to Costigan, who, as if reading Abe's thoughts, said, "Less law, more fight: that is my argument."

The veteran Costigan, having led an effort to clean up Chinatown in 1903, understood the limits of vice crusades. They weren't endless. If Mayor Gaynor lost reelection in November, the Incorruptibles would be disbanded, and between now and then any number of other factors could intervene to cut their mission short. Thus it was important to move on, to address the gangsters and horse poisoners before the clock ran out. "If you boys want to see this through," Costigan said, "you'll have to break some of your rules."

Abe reached for the cumbersome Colt Special, the pistol that nearly got him killed, and wondered if perhaps the weapon would finally be good for something. Inside Dorman's candy store he walked behind the counter and asked, "Who pays for the penny ices for the girls in Seward Park?" The moment Dorman feigned confusion, Abe grabbed him by the shirt and slammed the butt of the Colt against his head, again and again, until the gun's grip panels broke apart and the battery came loose, and then he let Dorman fall to the floor.

Back at the Clinton Street precinct, Abe gathered the Incorruptibles and conveyed Costigan's sentiment in his own terms: "I don't think we should be very much enamored with the possibilities of court convictions, because it seems that in the most important cases we cannot get them," he told the squad. "My firm belief, however, is that since the means justify the ends, we should admit for the present time that it is necessary to fight the evil with less law and more force" — and not just for the most important cases, but for all cases.

If the Incorruptibles couldn't develop charges on a "known criminal," Abe instructed them to "vag the punk," arrest the person for vagrancy, the era's catchall crime. He said they could use the vagrancy law to round up "fake peddlers" who sold broken watches as authentic gold timepieces and colored water as cologne. He said they could use the excise law to shut down lascivious dancing at any saloon or dance hall that served alcohol after 1 a.m., and cite the public nuisance law to justify a raid of any establishment, public or private. Some of this aggressive policing was arguably legal, while other tactics crossed the line into vigilantism.

But once he got going, it was tough to stop. He advocated rounding up panhandlers who begged too aggressively, and urged raids on movie theaters for the crimes of poor ventilation and showing love scenes. "This is one of the filthiest houses on the East Side," he wrote of an Avenue B theater, describing a mud-caked floor strewn with rotting fruit scraps. "Added to this is a three-piece band consisting of a piano, violin and drum, and whoever accused these men of being musicians certainly did a great wrong. The noise they make is enough to give anyone a headache."

As the Incorruptibles policed the neighborhood, the Kehillah helped professionalize the police department, an overhaul that reformers saw as a crucial part of Tammany Hall's ousting. Jacob Schiff and Felix Warburg funded new training and recruiting programs, while Newburger managed the NYPD's new internal affairs division, presiding over trials of corrupt cops, including a few members of the Incorruptibles who succumbed to bribes or tipped off criminals to raids.

At the same time, Abe used the back channel available to him, via Mayor Gaynor's office, to carry out his own reorganization of the NYPD ranks. In a Kehillah report entitled "St. 258, Transfer the Detectives," he submitted a list of detectives who took bribes from thieves. "The East Side today is infested with as many police thieves as there are regular thieves of the ordinary type and caliber who do loft and safe jobs, and pickpocket work," he wrote. "Is there no way that a Society of Jews numbering into the hundreds of thousands [the East Side neighborhood] can ask for relief of such scoundrels!" The grafters named in Abe's report were subsequently moved uptown and put on desk duty, a development that led to the Kehillah's first newspaper mention. The *World* reported that many of the transfers were from the Clinton Street station, "where the Kehillah, or Hebrew Vigilance Association, has been active in keeping tabs on the police."

With the secret out, the Kehillah decided to blow its own cover.

17

Il Nostro Get

I N MAY OF 1913, RABBI MAGNES ASKED ABE AND NEWBURGER
to advertise a public meeting of the Kehillah at Kessler's Theater, the
new venue for Yiddish drama on Second Avenue, and to make sure that
the East Side underworld was aware of it. "The time for a showdown was
at hand," Abe recalled. "We placed an announcement in the Jewish press.
I personally called on shopkeepers and tenement dwellers, and caused the
story of the coming meeting to reach the guts of the vice field. I implored
Dr. Magnes not to hold his punches, to bang away at them."

At Kessler's on the night of the meeting, Magnes walked onstage and
took the podium while Abe and Newburger, armed and ready, blended
into the overflow crowd. Until that night, Abe had known Magnes only
at his desk, calm and deliberate. Onstage at Kessler's he became something else — tall, daring, an angered Elijah hurling defiance at Jezebel
and King Ahab. He lambasted Mother Hertz's lawyer for extolling the
"pure and spotless character" of a woman who had ruined hundreds of
Jewish girls. He denounced lewd dancing and slutty attire. "Jews are
passing through a crisis and decisions must be made by each individual,"

he said. "Shall the race be stained and blotted in reputation? Or shall its members rise to moral heights such as their history might lead Americans to expect them to do?"

Magnes jolted the audience, screaming, "We know the whole Second Avenue mob! Aliases! Addresses! In the name of Sarah and Rachel, I want you to hear me in plain words and not forget them: You pimps, you thugs, you fixing lawyers — we will drive you from pillar to post, every last rat, out of your holes and into the sewers where you belong!"

If the Kehillah had carefully avoided publicity for the past ten months, it now flooded the zone with messaging in an effort to convince citizens to stand with the vice crusaders as they turned toward the underworld's final frontier, the extortionate gangs who controlled the East Side community with intimidation and violence.

A *New York Times* headline read: VIGILANTES TO RUN GANGSTERS DOWN. The headline of a Yiddish paper said: VIGILANCE LEAGUE ALREADY FOUNDED: BATTLE AGAINST JEWISH GANGSTERS BEGINS IN EARNEST, and reported, "The plan was to keep the league and its members a secret, but Newburger and Shoenfeld declare it high time for a large scale effort to free Jewish neighborhoods from murderers and gangsters. Currently, East Siders fear stepping out of their businesses and homes. Many pay large sums for protection." *Outlook* magazine likened the story to an urban Western, describing the Kehillah as "a modern vigilance committee brought into being by the same conditions that brought about vigilantes in the old frontier days."

But the *World,* as always, offered the most extensive coverage. KEHILLAH OPENS GANGSTER WAR ON EAST SIDE, read the headline of a multipage spread: "The Apaches of Paris are timid compared to the quick-acting gunmen of New York's East Side, who, under pain of death, levy tolls on merchants. The police have failed to bring them down. But the Kehillah, a great Jewish organization of businessmen, backed by a war fund, is out to exterminate the gunmen. Can they do it?"

*   *   *

It wasn't clear whether they could do it.

The initial phases of the Kehillah vice crusade were perhaps destined for victory. The Rosenthal murder helped generate opposition to casinos, giving the Kehillah the push it needed. Similarly, the crusade against drugs and prostitution dovetailed with nationwide crackdowns on those vices. But there was no movement against gangsterism, the ghetto phenomenon in which a thug class, protected by business, politics, and bribery, extorts its own people with impunity.

To those who lived in the America of 1913, the "ghetto" seemed uniquely American, another symptom of immigration and urbanization, another harbinger of national decline. But the modern ghetto, as fact and concept, originated centuries earlier in Europe: the word itself was coined in Venice, after Jewish refugees, fleeing a nearby war, arrived there in 1509. This new Jewish presence created tension between the state, which saw Jews as useful, and the Church, which viewed them as problematic.

By 1509, Jew hatred had been metastasizing for roughly four centuries, ever since the High Middle Ages, when Christian theologians — the so-called Scholastics — discovered the work of Aristotle, the ancient philosopher who regarded the lending of money as inherently unproductive and morally suspect. This idea was interesting to the Scholastics, because during the eleventh and twelfth centuries they were still puzzling out what it meant, legally and morally, to be a good Christian. Infatuated with Aristotle, the Scholastics decided to make the law against moneylending a central tenet of Christianity: moneylending, they decreed, was appropriate only for those outside the faith, the Jews.

For future historians it would be tempting to cite the Church's ban on moneylending as the source of Jewish success in business, as if it gave them a head start as creditors and investors. But their business career predated the ban, stretching back to the very beginnings of the commercial revolution. During the sixth century, Jews who had settled in Germanic lands, often living under the protection of a former Roman soldier, owned vineyards along the Rhine.

For the next several centuries, their status as outsiders shaped the talents they developed. At a time when even local trade in Europe was largely nonexistent, Jews became international merchants. The big money was in Mediterranean long-distance trade, and this was controlled by three groups: Syrians, Greeks, and Jews. The Syrian merchants focused on Asian markets. The Greek merchants tended to wait for customers at home. By the seventh century, Jews were the leading importers of Eastern spices, silks, ivories, and slaves to Germanic courts, and the leading exporters of Western furs and weapons to the Mediterranean. By the ninth century, the words "merchant" and "Jew" became synonymous in Germanic chronicles and legal codes, which referred to *Judaei vel ceteri* ("Jews or other traders") and *mercatores et Judaei* ("merchants and Jews").

In *The Commercial Revolution of the Middle Ages,* Robert Lopez writes: "So long as the Jews were allowed to retain their profits and reinvest them more or less as they pleased, they quickened the economic development of every country where they lived."

During these centuries, enmity toward Jews was limited to the Church, which was not yet confident enough in its converts, and the converts not yet Christian enough to be wary of Jews. Church leaders prohibited Christians from eating or drinking with Jews, in order, as one bishop said, "that no shadow may fall on the sons of light through social intercourse with the children of darkness." The Church objected to the Jewish slave trade, not for reasons of morality but because Jewish slave traders, like Christian ones, proselytized their slaves and the Church begrudged the loss of souls. "Here, Christians and Jews were rivals in virtue no less than in vice," writes German-American historian Marvin Lowenthal in *The Jews of Germany: A Story of Sixteen Centuries.* Laws were passed that forbade Jews to buy Christian slaves.

Laws changed, but Jews, as trading intermediaries, remained mere pariahs—until the late eleventh century, when their status began to shift. In 1095, France's Pope Urban II delivered a speech, known as the Indulgence, in which he urged all knights and soldiers who believed in Christ to go forth from Europe and take back Jerusalem from the Muslims. Jews were not directly targeted in the First Crusade of 1096, but the general hysteria over allegations of defiled Christian monuments and tortured Christian believers led to splinter groups of Crusaders slaughtering Jewish communities along the Rhine. Those communities rebuilt, but Jewish life got steadily worse, generation by generation, as crusades continued for the next four centuries. Even while popes prodded and coerced Jewish moneylenders to finance crusading soldiers, the bias against moneylending—usury—was codified as Christian law in 1179, with an absolute ban whose violation carried the punishment of excommunication. The Church regarded usury as a crime on the same scale as homicide, sodomy, incest, and simony—the Tammany-like buying and selling of ecclesiastical offices, privileges, and pardons.

During this era, the narrative about Jews changed. Now they baked with the blood of Christian children and poisoned wells with plague. Restrictions on them increased, in Germany and elsewhere in Europe. Discriminative Jewish dress was introduced—horned hats, yellow armbands. Their legal text, the Talmud, was burned by the wagonload. Jews, writes Lopez, "were gradually crowded out of honorable commerce and herded into highly dangerous lines of business that would make them hated because of their ruthlessness and ruthless because of the hate they encountered."

But there was one major problem with this moral legislation: it was a really inconvenient time to ban moneylending. In Europe between 1050 and 1300, new agricultural surpluses were making greater commerce and urbanization possible, but only for those who could access credit. Thus moneylending, a mortal sin of theology, became a mortal *necessity* of commercial life. This contradiction was summed up in a popular quip: "He who takes usury goes to hell, and he who does not goes to the poor house." In *A Distant Mirror: The Calamitous Fourteenth Century,* Barbara Tuchman writes, "Nothing so vexed medieval thinking, nothing so baffled and eluded settlement, nothing was so great a tangle of irreconcilables as the theory of usury.... This was left to the Jews as the necessary dirty work of society, and if they had not been available they would have had to be invented."

In *The Jews of Germany,* published in 1936, shortly after America's fourteen-year experiment with Prohibition ended, Marvin Lowenthal wrote, "Moneylending suffered in Christendom the same taint as liquor-dealing in America. It bristled with vexations and restrictions, it might be necessary but the devil was in it, and the cost of its services mounted accordingly." The prohibition of moneylending established a cycle that would play out again and again across the ages. The risks that a gray-area moneylender (that is, one unprotected by law) took in dealing with bad-faith and vengeful debtors enlarged the interest rates and narrowed the terms of the loans. This increased the burden on borrowers, who in turn expressed that burden through hate and violence. When tensions became acute, angry debtors, on whatever passing pretext, gave themselves over to pillage and slaughter of their local Jewish quarter.

In 1509, when the Jewish refugees appeared in Venice, the Venetian Church wanted them out, but the Venetian government saw how they could be useful as moneylenders and peddlers of used clothing to the poor. The senate resolved the tension in a way that would serve Venice's economic needs *and* satisfy its religious hostility. Jews would henceforth be required to reside on an island that once housed a copper foundry, or *ghetto* (from the Italian verb *gettare,* meaning to pour, cast, or throw).

Gates were erected at the island's two access points, where footbridges reached the city. Guards opened the gates at sunrise, so Jews could go to jobs, and closed the gates at sunset. When Venetian Jews realized that these living conditions would be permanent, they began to refer to their enclosed quarters, jokingly, as *il nostro get* — a pun that combined the Italian word for "our" with the Hebrew word for "divorce," as in "our divorce from society."

Here, then, was a model for modernity: a reviled minority appraised for the advantages it could bestow on this or that class. And since what was advantageous to one class was often disadvantageous to another, the minority, caught in the middle, became subjects of persecution on one side and protection on the other.

Later in the 1500s, this bind played out dramatically in the Kingdom of Poland, where the Polish lords, the aristocrats, turned the Jews into their liquor agents. The lords leased to the Jews licenses to manage Poland's grain estates, converting grain into mash and mash into vodka, which the Jews then sold, via Jewish-owned taverns, to Poland's peasants, including those in the eastern borderlands of Ukraina (pronounced *Ookraina,* meaning "border"). By leasing out the liquor trade, using the Jew as a buffer, the Polish crown could have it both ways, retaining a major profit center while disowning responsibility for the vice that decimated peasant communities.

In Poland, Jewish liquor dealers and tavern-keepers prospered until 1648, when the backlash arrived. Those peasants of Ukraina organized into warlike companies, or Cossacks, to fight off the liquor-slinging Jews. This agitation by the Cossacks led to an important geopolitical shift in Eastern Europe: the Russian tyrants in Moscow, seeing an opportunity to overthrow the Polish liberals in Krakow, aligned with the Cossacks in a campaign to take over the borderlands between Russia and Poland. When Russian troops overran those borderlands, they were struck by the spectacle of villages populated entirely by Jews, a strange people about whom most Russians knew little more than the rumor that once upon a time they had crucified Christ.

During the 1790s, the Russian empress Catherine the Great formalized the borderlands as the Pale of Settlement. About her plans for the Jews there, now under Russia's dominion, Catherine sent mixed messages. She promised to respect their former Polish "liberties," though the promised toleration remained mostly notional. For instance, when Jews attempted to participate in government, they were blocked on the basis that, via control of the liquor trade, they exploited the peasantry. Catherine decreed that Jews would live exclusively in the Pale, forbidding them to live in Russia's interior. At first, Russia's Jews were permitted to keep the liquor trade. Then the trade was pulled away when Catherine's grandson, the new ruler, sought to drive Jews out of "parasitical" endeavors and into "useful" occupations.

For the next century, between the creation of the Pale and the emigration of Eastern European Jews to America that began in 1881, the quality of Russian-Jewish life rose and fell as broad-minded czars traded power with despots. In dark times, agricultural Jews would be kicked off their farms and herded into the Pale's towns, where they crowded together in airless spaces or froze to death. In more liberal eras, such as the 1850s to the 1870s, the so-called Czar Liberator, Alexander II, relaxed residential restrictions and limits on professions. Jews returned to the countryside, where their capital found new outlets in timber and railroads. Some moved to the interior of Russia, where they attended universities and became lawyers. But then Alexander II was assassinated in 1881. And even though only one of the plotters, a pregnant woman, was Jewish, Russians responded to the assassination with a wave of pogroms against Jews. They were kicked out of Moscow and St. Petersburg, except for some Jewish females who were allowed to stay but obliged to register under the "yellow ticket," as prostitutes. Rural Jews were forced back into the cities of the Pale, where the underworld grew gigantesque. Up and down the Pale, from the northern city of Minsk to the Black Sea port of

Odessa in the south, Jews became smugglers and sex traffickers, horse thieves and horse poisoners.

There was a circular logic to *il nostro get*. Overcrowding and isolation produced certain traits in the ghettoized people, traits that could be invoked to rationalize further negative attitudes toward those people, justifying more isolation and more restrictive laws to control the teeming rabble. For the average citizen trying to get by in such an environment, the choice between paying off the cop or co-religionist shaking you down, versus challenging the extortionists, was pretty easy. Bribery was just business.

When the uprooted community settled in New York, this aspect of ghetto culture moved with it, until someone decided to take a stand.

Months before Herman Rosenthal was murdered at the Metropole and Abe Shoenfeld was summoned by the Kehillah, one brave East Sider tried to confound the old logic of *il nostro get*. In January of 1912, Louis Blumenthal, a Russian-Jewish farrier, one who made horseshoes for a living, called a meeting of his fellow stablemen on Cherry Street.

Cherry Street was down along the water, in the far eastern section of the East Side. If the East Side was a tough place to live, the Cherry Street section of it was especially brutal. Harry Roskolenko, a Russian Jew raised there, described the area as a ghetto within a ghetto, "a do-it-yourself slum cast in its own unalterable image."

In a memoir, *When I Was Last on Cherry Street,* Roskolenko depicts constant danger. An older sister was killed by a truck. When Roskolenko and his mother tried to filch ice, she crawled beneath a truck and lost an arm. "In horrifying block fights," writes Roskolenko, "the Jews of Cherry Street fought the Irish from Front Street. We loaded our stocking hats with glass and stone and charged away, slugging until a dozen kids were left sprawled and bleeding in the gutters — their eyes half-blinded, their arms or legs broken. When the losers recuperated, the violence — everything short of murder — was on again."

Reigning over this hardscrabble world, Roskolenko writes, were the horse-poisoning gangsters who extorted businesses that relied on horse transport. The gang was referred to as the Yiddish Camorra, or the Yiddish Black Hand, having modeled its tactics on those of the ruthless Italian gangsters who shook down the businesses of their own paisanos with the threat of bombs and kidnappings. And this was why the farrier, Louis Blumenthal, called the meeting of stablemen in early 1912, to discuss the attack on their livelihood.

Horse poisoning wasn't new. On the East Side, the trend dated to at least 1891, when the *World* reported that horses were being poisoned at the rate of three per week, an average that soon rose to a hundred per week. The standard method of poisoning was arsenic, but there were also stories of "hamstringing" and cutting out tongues. In 1905, the *New York Times* reported that the police had arrested a Jewish immigrant "whose mania for killing horses caused him to be driven from Russia," and noted that he went free because his New York victims feared the consequences of testifying.

In New York, life for horses had always been harsh. Dozens died each day from sunstroke and mistreatment. Roskolenko recalls: "Horses, horse cars — everything had a horse pulling it — and often there were fat dead horses lying on the mounds of garbage made into snow mountains. And some kids, in ugly bravado, would find broomsticks and stick them up the horses." In *Jews Without Money,* Michael Gold draws an equally ghastly portrait: "When a horse lay dead in the street, he was seized upon to become another plaything in the queer and terrible treasury of East Side childhood. They leaped on his swollen body, poked sticks in the vents. They pried open the eyelids, and speculated on those sad, glazed big eyes. They plucked hair from the tail with which to weave good-luck rings."

As the number of autos multiplied, the rumbling engines and shrieking crescendo of Klaxon horns adding noise to an already loud city, equine tragedy became its own newspaper genre. On any given day, citizens read accounts of man-versus-nature chaos. A runaway horse dashed up Lexington Avenue, glanced off an auto, and landed in a baby carriage, sending the infant flying into the gutter, miraculously unharmed. In another story, a windblown newspaper sent a horse galloping through crowded East Side streets and onto the Williamsburg Bridge, where it plunged through an opening and fell to Kent Avenue, crushing the hood of a passing car. Given this peril, the horse-poisoning gang was the last thing that Blumenthal and his colleagues needed in 1912.

The Yiddish Black Hand was led by a twenty-eight-year-old Russian-Jewish immigrant named Joseph Toblinsky, known in the underworld as Yoshke N****r. He had been poisoning horses since at least 1902, when he served his first term in prison for animal cruelty. Arrested again in 1909, he skipped bail and fled the city. Police tracked Toblinsky to San Francisco and extradited him back to New York, where he told reporters, "I am glad to be with you again. But say, won't some of you fellows get me some winter clothes? I'm freezing to death." If he was relaxed, he knew he was protected, and indeed the indictment against him disappeared.

Toblinsky, known as King of the Horse Poisoners, consolidated the gang at a Suffolk Street saloon, where, Abe informed the Kehillah, a "fall fund" of $5,000 was always on hand to beat cases. "Now Mein Herr Yushki is in our midst again and has mobilized a new crew," Abe reported, observing that those who pursued this foul enterprise tended to be as dense as they were unyielding. Later, a bullied stableman recalled his own experience with a horse poisoner named John Levinson: "I says, 'Mr. L., you are ruining me, poisoning me three horses worth a thousand dollars. Now, when you poison me a couple more, I got to go out of business. I ain't no millionaire....Look, I want to ask you a civil question: Haven't you got some principle in you? Can you take a man's hands off and then make the same man stick his hands in his pockets and give you money?' And he said, 'I don't know what you mean.'"

In the halcyon days of horse poisoning, Toblinsky's crew pulled off an impressive stunt, collecting $2,000 a month in extortion payments from the Adams Express Company, a horse-powered logistics outfit that Abe called "the largest and toughest trucking company in Manhattan." At first the proprietors of Adams Express doubted Toblinsky's tenacity, until they found half of their stable poisoned.

Now, on Cherry Street, Blumenthal informed his colleagues that he was standing up to the Yiddish Black Hand. So far, the results weren't great. A week earlier, after Blumenthal refused to pay the horse poisoners $500, telling them to go to hell, a bomb exploded in the hallway outside his apartment, blowing his door off its hinges and nearly killing his wife. The stablemen admired Blumenthal, but looked away. They remembered the last poor schmuck who challenged the horse poisoners, an ice-delivery man killed with his own ice tongs. Blumenthal was well aware of the danger. Still, he reasoned that taking on the gang in court was worth the risk, lest the horse poisoners extort them all out of business. The following morning, he said, he intended to testify at the trial of a horse poisoner, and he urged his colleagues to join him. But as Blumenthal rallied his mates, the ultimate argument prevailed against him. A man broke through the stable door, drew a revolver, and put two bullets in Blumenthal's heart.

In the summer of 1913, eighteen months after Blumenthal's murder, Abe gathered the Incorruptibles and said, referring to the Yiddish Black Hand, "The time has come when we must wipe out this bastard firm unconditionally. If we cannot do it lawfully, we will take the law into our own hands and fight them with their own weapons. Poison for poison. Shot for shot. There must be no quarter shown."

18

Your City

THE SUCCESSES OF THE KEHILLAH VICE CRUSADE, followed by its exposure in the press, didn't embolden the East Side community as one might have expected it would. For one thing, eliminating so much crime so quickly upset an East Side economy that had relied on crime. Wide-open gambling and prostitution kept money flowing, and now that money was gone.

Other consequences were unforeseeable. The many pawnshops that once fenced stolen goods shut down, and some were sneaky about it. The East Side's largest pawnshop staged a burglary of its own goods and announced it was closing. When customers mobbed the place to see if valuables and heirlooms brought from the old country were gone forever, a two-year-old lost his mother in the scrum and crawled into the street, where a truck crushed his foot so badly that it had to be amputated.

Immigrants likened the Kehillah's agents to the Black Hundreds, the czar's ragtag militia that carried out pogroms in the Pale of Settlement. Now, when Abe and Newburger appeared in a café for coffee and a roll, they were regarded with suspicion, East Siders whispering "*Zechs!*"

Stop talking, the Kehillah is here. One resentful tobacconist refused to sell Abe his Turkish cigarettes and kicked him out. If the underworld was disappearing, what system would replace it? Without a guarantee of something better, people weren't about to put their lives on the line.

Further doubt was sowed by the ghetto's intelligentsia, the Yiddish playwrights and editors who criticized the German-Jewish uptowners for selling out the underclass in their drive for assimilation. One Yiddish paper complained about "half-baked reformers instructing them on decency" and "missing no opportunity to smear the East Side in the eyes of the world." A Tammany-allied attorney told a gathering: "For every gunman there are a hundred boys going to college. But you never hear about that! No, they come down here and tell us we produce all the murderers and gamblers and pimps. We don't need these kinds of friends!"

One of the most active anti-Kehillah agitators was its first hire, the defense attorney Jonah Goldstein. Since the confrontation in Lüchow's, when Goldstein felt he'd been used by Magnes, he had pursued a campaign of revenge, sending anonymous letters to the press calling Abe and Newburger drug addicts and grafters who took bribes even as they earned "fancy figures," big money, from the uptowners. Then Goldstein made a big move of his own. He established the East Side Neighborhood Association as a competitor, and sought funding from the same German Jews who financed the Kehillah. When Magnes sent a letter to Felix Warburg, urging him not to give money to the ESNA because it was supported by the underworld, Goldstein saw the letter and promptly sued Magnes for libel.

In late July, at the first meeting of the ESNA, Goldstein addressed the audience, which was composed largely of business owners, plus a few incognito Incorruptibles. "I am sick of reformers coming down here and assuming to tell us what we need," he said. "What does this Newburger really know? From his smug demeanor you'd think he's Heracles championing the Olympian order against the chthonic monsters. They say his stool pigeon, Shoenfeld, is some crack detective. But must a sleuth inform us of prostitution? When a lady whistles at you on Allen Street, you know she's not calling you to a minyan!"

At this, Abe himself emerged from the crowd and interrupted. "Any attorney who defends a criminal, knowing him to be guilty, is worse than the criminal," he told the crowd, taking a swipe at Goldstein. "The attorney takes no chance of the crime, yet happily divides the spoils with his client. And where do those spoils come from? They come from you." Goldstein protested. Abe continued: "I know why you pay the gangsters. You have your trade and your families, and you are legitimate. And unlike gamblers and pimps you cannot simply move. You're tied here, to your city. That leaves no choice but to contend with the gangsters, to resist them and starve them out! In so doing, a factor is attendant upon you to stand up, and stand firm, and dare anyone to molest you!"

Events of the last few months, including the speech by Magnes at Kessler's Theater, press coverage of the crusade, and Abe's own preaching — together it all seemed to achieve something, to boost confidence, and in the following days business owners appeared at the Clinton Street precinct, timid but interested in cooperating.

One informant, an ice cream merchant named Hyman Bernstein, helped focus the investigation. Bernstein said that if few people in his own industry volunteered to cooperate against the horse poisoners, it was because many ice cream merchants were *themselves* horse poisoners. Originally, Bernstein said, East Side ice cream merchants had organized the Horse Owners Protective Association in an effort to pool their power to keep down the price of milk and sugar. Soon, however, membership became mandatory. Asked to join the association, Bernstein said he declined and explained what happened next. He was out on his ice cream delivery route, a hundred feet from the Brooklyn Bridge, when his horses stopped and suffered a bout of diarrhea. "Their eyes turned orange," he recalled. "They started in kicking and making all different kinds of turns and so forth and trying to lay down and trying to get up and finally after torture of an hour they died." With traffic accumulating behind him, a cop came along and said, "You have a lot of nerve to leave a horse drop right in the entrance of the bridge!"

Bernstein, traumatized but angry enough to do something about it, said he was willing to cooperate. Newburger suggested the idea for a "marked-bill sting," a new tactic that had been used successfully in a recent case. Bernstein would pay the poisoners with marked currency, which would serve as hard evidence of the extortion. Using this method, which became common police practice in a later era, the Incorruptibles arrested low-level horse poisoners, who led up the chain to Joseph Toblinsky, who in turn double-crossed the Horse Owners Protective Association and provided testimony that led to more than thirty arrests. The headlines read: ICE-CREAM DEALERS HELD FOR HORSE POISONING. MERCHANTS PAID GANG CHIEF TO DESTROY THE STABLES OF RIVAL.

In the criminal courts of Lower Manhattan, the Kehillah vice crusade was transforming legal practice. Just as Newburger implemented new law-enforcement techniques to make arrests, defense attorneys also adapted their schemes to the times and created a new kind of advocacy, which entailed an appeal for tolerance and urged a consideration of history and the defendant's environment.

In the trial of the horse poisoners, for example, a defense lawyer told the jury:

The system of jurisprudence we are under here is the Anglo-Saxon system. And yet we are not all Anglo-Saxon. We represent a heterogenous mass, a population gathered from the four corners of the earth. Those who come here early in life may be trained in the dogmas and tenets announced by the makers of this great republic. But those who come here later in life have lived in countries where government is different, where those in power are not the servants of the people but the masters of them.

And here we have men who cold-bloodedly killed poor brutes without a single atom of compunction, regret, or shame. That such viciousness could prevail in this enlightened community, in the twentieth century, seems impossible. What an awful thing it is to poison a horse. *Cowards! Cowards! Cowards!*

But you, ordinary Americans brought up among Anglo-Saxon conditions, you must not judge these defendants upon your own conceptions of morality. You must rather endeavor to fit yourselves, if such a thing is possible, into the workings of their mind. For you are dealing here with refugee Russians, oppressed Jews, whose livelihood was obtained under great duress and dire surroundings, who by reason of suppression have had their minds so—let me use the word—distorted. I have noticed, in the cases we see here of receiving stolen goods, that most defendants do not appreciate the enormity of a property offense. Many do not even realize they are committing a crime. They think they have a right to a bargain. [*Laughter*]

You must be tolerant. You must divorce yourself from prejudice. The Bible says: "I will visit the sins upon the sons and their sons until the fifth generation." No man becomes suddenly vile. No man becomes suddenly evil.

The lawyer's description of the old-world environment was accurate if incomplete. Far from meek, the Jewish gangsters in the Pale of

Settlement often dominated their communities. And in the 1890s a new graft came along. At a time when socialism was inspiring factory workers to organize for better working conditions, Jewish thugs and pimps became soldiers in the labor wars.

At first the criminal class opposed the socialists. The criminals represented manufacturers against the strikes and attacks of the Jewish labor organization, the Bund. It was an intra-ethnic labor war that peaked around 1900, when there was, on average, one strike per day in the Pale. The Bund failed in 1905, wiped out by pogroms and mass emigration. But prior to its demise there was evidence that it was winning the war of ideas, as pogroms convinced Jewish criminals of their common cause with the workers.

Now, in New York, a similar phenomenon could be observed. Back in 1909 and 1910, during the shirtwaist makers' strike, garment manufacturers would hire Jewish thugs to attack striking workers. "Busting up strikes was a lucrative sideline for downtown gangsters," writes David Von Drehle in *Triangle: The Fire That Changed America*. "So-called detective agencies were constantly looking for strikebreaking contracts from worried bosses in shops where there was unrest." Some of these agencies, like the Pinkerton Detective Agency, were famous nationwide, but New York City was full of such firms. They were often founded by former cops who had been ousted for corruption and could use their underworld contacts to staff formidable gangster armies to attack picket lines and protect factories.

But, as with the pogroms in Russia, the 1911 Triangle fire changed how East Siders thought about the labor wars. For Jews, it became shameful to work against the labor movement, and honorable to work on its behalf. And then came the Kehillah vice crusade: by 1913, the elimination of so much vice had left a bewildered criminal class looking for new opportunities. If the old underworld was disappearing, a new one was taking its place.

*　*　*

That summer, Tony the Tough parted ways with the Kehillah. She changed her appearance, converting her black tresses into a "psyche knot," the hairstyle of gang girls. She back-combed the front half of her hair until the roots were sturdy enough to hold a pompadour, then spun the rear half into a twist and wrapped it around itself to form a bun held together with a long gilt hairpin. Flush with savings, Tony purchased an auto and motored to the Forsyth Bath House, at 79 Forsyth Street, where she pushed through the doors and asked: "Need girls?"

The desk attendant gave her a key to a dressing room.

At one time these rooms had been used by garment manufacturers who came during the lunch hour for steam baths and massages. Now, as indoor plumbing made the old Turkish and Russian bathhouses less popular, they fell into disrepair and were colonized by the underworld, the dressing rooms used as dorms by the "soldiers" who worked for labor unions. In the battle unfolding in streets and factories, Tony the Tough's new wheels made her a valuable member of the union's gangster army. She tore through the East Side streets, chauffeuring around the labor sluggers — known as *shtarker*s, heavy-hitting thugs — who terrorized the same factories that had once exploited them.

The leader of the *shtarker*s was a twenty-four-year-old named Benjamin Fein, who went by the deceptively cute sobriquet of Dopey Benny. People called him Dopey because he had a droopy right eye, the legacy of adenoidal problems in childhood, a common East Side affliction, and because he spoke in a distinctive drawl, which was persuasive. In a 1905 profile, entitled "The Artful Dodger," the *New York Times* called Dopey, then sixteen, "a walking recruiting station for the criminal academy." In those days, the apparently Dickensian figure would hang out near PS 20, where Abe went to school, to scout potential child thieves.

Dopey, who became known in the underworld as the Dope, might have remained a simple thief and thug had he not been approached, in late 1912, by Morris Sigman. Sigman was a Russian-Jewish labor leader for the United Hebrew Trades, the umbrella union that covered dozens of smaller garment unions. Like many UHT leaders, Sigman had been a Bund member back in Russia. When he arrived in New York, he had no patience for the shoddy working conditions he found. He exhorted the ghetto masses to rise against industrial tyranny, and drafted the Dope to lead them.

The Dope wanted to fill Big Jack Zelig's shoes, and the labor wars, he felt, could provide him with the authority and cash to do it. Zelig himself had always refused such work on moral grounds. Slugging scabs, after all, meant maiming regular working people — often the most marginalized or vulnerable ones, such as Black women and old Jewish men. Despite the danger involved, these workers tended to fill factory jobs during strikes because they struggled to find work when there wasn't a strike on. They were the kind of people Zelig might stand up for, not punish. But the Dope had a different value system. Channeling Sigman's pro-worker dogma, he spoke with pride about "sticking to the unions" and turning down handsome offers from manufacturers to guard their shops.

In early 1913, after the Dope sacked several garment factories and assaulted scabs, word spread among UHT bosses that he could "settle" any strike in any industry, and his "slugging work" became plentiful. It was a grueling hustle. The Dope's hospital bills often exceeded his pay. By the time Tony joined up, in the summer of 1913, the Dope was so mapped in wounds and scars from knife fights and shootouts that his parts looked sewn together. But, like Zelig, he made money easily and spent it easily, and his generosity attracted the choicest thugs, including women. If these ladies believed in the mission, they also appreciated that, unlike elsewhere in the labor economy, equal pay for equal work predominated in the Dope's gang. Some of his best soldiers were former factory workers and prostitutes like Tony who wielded hairpins with an overhand grip—raiding factories, chasing scabs around cutting tables, and chanting: *Never go walking without your hatpin, not even to some very classy joints. For when a fellow sees you've got a hatpin, he's very much more apt to get the point.*

The manufacturers fought back but the unions never let up, and their defi was captured daily in 1913 headlines: 37,000 GIRLS WALK OUT IN STRIKE; SING AS THEY PARADE. STRIKING TAILORS INVADE FACTORIES; ELEVEN ARRESTED. WOMEN STRIKERS ROUT POLICEMEN IN WILD ATTACK. 20 GIRLS ARRESTED WHILE 200 HURL EGGS AT THE POLICE; STRIKERS PROVE THEY CAN THROW STRAIGHT AND CAPTORS LOOK LIKE OMELETS. GIRL STRIKERS COMPLAIN OF POLICE BRUTALITY, BEAT DOWN MEN WITH UMBRELLAS. TWO BROTHERS ON WAY TO WORK BEATEN BY STRIKERS. STRIKERS' THROAT CUT AS MOB TRAPS NON-UNION TAILOR. STRIKERS THROW TWO MEN OUT OF FACTORY WINDOW. BOMB FROM AUTO HITS GIRL SCAB ASLEEP IN FACTORY. EMPLOYERS WITHDRAW SETTLEMENT FOR GARMENT STRIKE.

Abe recorded the Dope's union-financed mayhem in Kehillah reports, but he put it down—uncharacteristically—without comment: In his mind, the unions fought fair against the manufacturers, who relied on police and detective agencies for their own strong-arm needs. Abe was more voluble when criticizing the mayor for choosing political safety in the labor disputes, writing: "It is my opinion that Mayor Gaynor is working with the manufacturers, because he is seeking renomination, and with the money that they will put up for his campaign he can easily buy back all the votes he has offended. He merely has to come down to the East Side and make a speech in a synagogue or in a Jewish theater, and deny that he ever told the police to go out and break the strike. Worthy, honorable Mayor! This is a fight between guerillas and guerillas, strikers and manufacturers. If one uses a weapon for defense, why not the other?"

Abe refused to intervene in the labor battle per se, but he knew that the crusade would not be complete until Dopey Benny, a gangster who had the fearlessness of Big Jack Zelig but none of the principle, was taken off the streets. On August 9, 1913, Abe sent two of the biggest bruisers on the Incorruptibles — Patrick Sheridan and Honest Dan Costigan — to the Forsyth Bath House with instructions to lure the Dope into a fight.

The Dope sat on a stoop outside when Sheridan beckoned him across the street. Eyewitness testimony would differ on what happened next, but Abe's own self-implicating account seemed as accurate as any: "When the Dope came over, the officer struck him a terrible blow under his right eye without warning or cause, and almost threw him down senseless. The Dope thereupon retaliated by punching Sheridan in the ear. Sheridan then pulled out his nightstick and struck the Dope across the head with it."

As gangsters ran out of the Forsyth Bath House to aid their leader, Abe recalled years later, Costigan and Sheridan "dragged the fallen gang hero down Grand Street." Abe walked beside them, "encouraging shop-keepers to come out and witness the bleeding Dope defeated." During the fracas, Abe looked back at the following crowd of gangsters and did a double take: There was Tony.

Then the sound of shattered glass turned Abe around again. "It was assumed that they were supposed to be taking him to police headquarters for his record, but instead the officers reached the National Hotel, on the northeast corner of Grand Street and the Bowery, and threw their prisoner through the door, and once inside the officers pounced down upon him with their blackjacks and gave the prisoner the beating of his life." After stopping at the hospital, the Incorruptibles took the Dope to the Clinton Street station with two black eyes and two missing teeth, six stitches in his head, a fractured nose, and a few broken ribs, and charged him with a felony for assaulting a cop.

*   *   *

By late August, Abe's Kehillah writings turned to retrospective accounts of the Incorruptibles' victories. One year had passed since Magnes called Abe to a meeting, and look what had been accomplished. Mayor Gaynor, ailing physically but ramping up his campaign for reelection, was telling reporters he hadn't imagined so much could be done in so short a time. Having seen what was possible on the East Side, Gaynor said, he was considering "a general citywide cleanup."

Like any young person who overcomes long odds, Abe, now twenty-two, was as liable as the next to boast and puff about it. "The work done on the East Side, if analyzed correctly and looked into, is such that I will stand up and let another man see if he can do it any better," he declared in a Kehillah report, and recorded what others said about him: "Several remarks have been passed, 'What do you think about that, two Jews running the police department, two young fellows, Jews.'" Having once conditioned his work on a guarantee of secrecy, Abe was now interested in reputation. In one report cataloguing his successes, he wrote about the eradication of a well-financed casino: "It gave us the hardest fight we had from start to finish, but we got it out, and when this place went, the name by which we were known and which had been rising and rising seemed to fade away in the heavens and no one knew what was coming next."

His chesty pose had something to do with a sense of vindication. Reformers were often accused of overstating problems. Abe's rivals, such as Jonah Goldstein and the other Tammany allies, denied the extent of East Side crime, but the Kehillah crusade proved otherwise. "In the beginning they called me a romancer," a fabulist, "until everything came true," he recalled. Newburger made a similar comment to the *Sun*: "When I told Commissioner Waldo what I learned about the different places he'd say, 'Romance! Romance!,' but upon verification he convinced himself that the information was correct."

This was Abe Shoenfeld's moment, the zenith of his wild dream and a generational vision. Seven years earlier he had left high school, helped get Charles Evans Hughes elected governor, and joined a new vanguard of underworld reformers. He had kept on with the work through the heartbreak of Tony's rejection and his frustration with the uptown committees. He had taken the Kehillah assignment on his own terms, chased out the gambler Dollar John, captained the Incorruptibles through a dizzying maze of crime and corruption, and, in a winning bet, gambled away his anonymity to sway East Siders to the crusading cause. Now he stood ready, with the potential reelection of Mayor Gaynor and the possibility of a permanent crime-fighting mandate, not just to secure the uplift of his neighborhood and catapult the Jewish people into the American future, but to outdistance his own father.

Abe's name was rising, and he believed that no one else's information superseded his own. So he didn't think much of it when, on an August morning, while he was at his optometrist getting fitted for new glasses, two former cops walked in. They claimed to be emissaries of a Wall Street brokerage called Hirsch Investments, and offered to create a $50,000 account in Abe's name. Abe didn't know that Hirsch Investments was a bucket shop, a fake stock brokerage named after Maxie Hirsch, a horse trainer and all-around man for Arnold Rothstein. To Abe it was another bribe offer—so many had come his way—and he was curious about the origin of this one. But when he asked the former cops who sent them, they turned around and disappeared.

19

Scarlet Room

WHILE 1913 WAS A CAPSTONE YEAR FOR ABE SHOENFELD, it was a key time for Arnold Rothstein too. Arnold's role as financier and fixer for big-con practitioners made him a hub of information on crime, which gave him currency to trade in the overworld. "Arnold took an enormous pride in appearing to be *in the know*," his wife Carolyn wrote. He often joked that for him the best job in public life would be police commissioner, and he "found amusement in telling policemen in general terms about some law violation before they had heard of it themselves."

In the afternoon, Arnold traded his information at lunches with politicians and judges. At night he supped with criminals. When the supper people got in trouble, the lunch people got them out. If Jacob Schiff was the J. P. Morgan of Jewish Wall Street, gathering and analyzing information about railroads or oil so that he could decide where to invest resources most profitably, Arnold was the Schiff of the underworld, tinkering in the shadows of corporate empire and playing his no-limit game in the big world. He bragged that where others folded in the face of problems, he embraced the opportunity to "dope out methods," as he put it — to remain calm amid the confusion of change, identify latent opportunities, and conjure new ways and means.

Arnold could move more or less freely between the upperworld and underworld because there was no sharp dividing line separating them in the years prior to Prohibition. The underworld shaded off into the upperworld imperceptibly, and Arnold was the shading, shuttling up and down and balancing the post-Rosenthal order. For example, earlier that year he had brokered a relationship between Tammany Hall's Charlie Murphy and August Belmont Jr.

Belmont Jr. was not a typical underworld figure. His father, a German Jew who came to New York in the 1830s as August Schönberg, was a business agent representing the Rothschild banking family. In the Wasp-dominated city of that era, Schönberg worked assiduously to assimilate and wipe his Jewishness away. He changed his last name to Belmont, married Wasp royalty, and financed the Belmont Stakes, part of the trio of races that compose the American Triple Crown. As a diplomat, he used his influence to support President Lincoln and advance the Union cause during the Civil War. Belmont's first son followed him into politics, becoming a member of Congress and serving as US minister to Spain. His second son and namesake, August Belmont Jr., pursued more varied endeavors.

Though Belmont Jr. was in the upper reaches of class, he, like Murphy and Arnold, straddled the worlds. In the early years of the century, Belmont Jr. financed the New York City subway, then built Belmont Racetrack, which was why he now needed Arnold.

To Belmont Jr., Arnold was a spookish figure, someone to be avoided, and yet the times pulled them inexorably nearer. Belmont Jr. had entered the racing business at a tough moment. After he opened his racetrack, in 1905, he faced one reform movement after another, until 1908, when Governor Hughes broke through with the Hart-Agnew legislation and its ban on organized bookmaking. This was the law that drove the old-line patrician bookies out of the field, leaving it open to Jews like Arnold, who were willing to take the risk of operating in the legal gray area of oral bookmaking. Two years later, in 1910, the gray area constricted when the legislature added an amendment to Hart-Agnew, the Owner's Liability Act, which meant the track owners themselves would be liable for illegal betting. Now, with all betting essentially banned, the best jockeys and thoroughbreds decamped for Europe and many tracks shut down.

But people missed gambling, and herein lay the problem that moral reform often confronted: Who was going to enforce a law that didn't have broad public support?

Seizing this opposition to reform's overreach, Arnold introduced Belmont Jr. to Murphy in the Scarlet Room at Delmonico's in early 1913. There, while Abe and Newburger were embarking on the vice crusade, the politician and the racetrack owner designed a political campaign to eliminate the Owner's Liability Act and bring oral betting back to the track, and by the spring that campaign met with success. "And so, the fantastic era known as the Oral Days was ushered in," recalls racetrack journalist Toney Betts in *Across the Board: Behind the Scenes of Racing Life*. "The romantics in racing call it 'the Renaissance.' Bookies took places on 'The Lawn' in front of the grandstand, displaying odds on the official racing program. A player bet with a bookmaker by word of mouth or wrote the wager on a slip of paper." Regarding the track owner's liability, Betts wrote, "Belmont was no longer responsible for action on the Lawn, where local police now and then made friendly pinches with the cases postponed until winter. 'Does this situation still exist?' the kind judge would ask. 'No, Your Honor,' the kind officer would reply. 'Very well, then, case dismissed.' And so racing, after a two years' separation from its soul-mate, betting, enjoyed a reconciliation in a quasi-legal love nest."

The essential role Arnold played in creating the quasi-legal love nest put him in a stratum above the common bookies. He became, instead, one of Belmont Jr.'s select "clubhouse bookmakers," which Carolyn defined as "one whose ability to pay was never questioned." Instead of working the Lawn, he sat up in the clubhouse, a rarefied enclosure with a fancy bar and restaurant. Thus positioned, Arnold announced that bookies could "lay off," or hedge, any bet, no matter how large, with him. He'd cover the bet but give the bookie his own odds, which Arnold often calculated to eat up the bookie's usual 10 percent advantage. His colleagues didn't love this, but if they wanted to hold on to high-rolling customers and remain in business they often had no choice.

This new role, as a bookie to bookies, gave Arnold a national reputation. Soon he was fielding calls from bookies in Chicago and Kansas City who wanted to lay off risk, and from then on he never wandered more than five minutes from a telephone. It was in this phase, as a big-time bookmaker who could also fix cases, that Arnold built his own vision for the future. The enormous earnings from track gambling inspired Arnold to create a role for himself that had little precedent in American life. He wouldn't just be a bookmaker, he would also own racehorses. He wouldn't just finance con men, he would also purchase real estate, to house their schemes; a surety company, to bail them out; and a life insurance firm, to secure his investments.

As quickly as the reformers had taken a sledgehammer to Tammany's old system of corruption, Arnold fashioned a new one, and now, in August of 1913, Charlie Murphy needed help again.

Murphy had led Tammany Hall for nearly a decade. But with reform ascendant, his organization could no longer protect criminals as it once did. Preserving street vice wasn't the problem. Murphy had always known that more money could be made from a legal contract — such as bilking public utilities and rigging bids — than from the petty blackmail of gamblers and pimps and horse poisoners. Murphy wanted to leave behind the era of Big Tim Sullivan, who was suffering through the final stage of syphilis and would be dead in a few weeks. But to keep his party alive Murphy needed a new political strategy, because even though Tammany functioned like an apolitical corporation, a money machine, it still needed *votes* to stay in power.

For decades, Tammany took the support of its core constituency, immigrants, for granted. But Murphy knew that times were changing and Tammany risked extinction if it didn't shore up the immigrant vote. In recent years, Murphy had taken steps to appeal to the underclass in new ways. He became more political, supporting the push for new labor laws in the aftermath of the Triangle fire. But he knew he needed to consolidate the backing of the East Side underworld as well, particularly when vice-crusading reformers were on the march. The drive for a clean city was putting important East Siders, including vote getters, out of work. If you retracted one source of revenue, taking away gambling and prostitution, you had to supply them with a new one. Arnold was there to pitch Murphy on a solution.

All year long, industries across the city had been going on strike — painters and furniture makers, barbers and waiters, actors and journalists. The *Sun* joked that even Bowery hoboes were unionizing, changing their name to "migratory workers" and demanding an eight-hour day. But the general labor unrest was quite serious — labor violence in America peaked between 1910 and 1915 — and some of the most violent strikes concerned the Jewish garment industry.

If the striking garment workers fought like unions never had in Mayer Shoenfeld's day, it was in part because the hard-line Russian-Jewish labor leaders of the United Hebrew Trades were supported by the *Forward,* the largest Yiddish-language newspaper in the world. In a bold move, the UHT held out for a universal "closed shop," an agreement from manufacturers to hire only union labor. This vision was a socialist utopia — unrealistic in America — but it was a viable pretext for a profitable war:

the union violence coerced workers to join the union and pay membership fees, which financed further terror, which brought in more members, more fees, more terror, and so on. Such a protracted war required political power, and this is where Arnold came in.

Recently, Arnold explained to Murphy, a cadre of UHT bosses had visited him. These bosses had taken a liking to Benjamin Fein, alias Dopey Benny. To keep Fein and his ilk on the street, fighting, the UHT needed bail money, attorneys, and a reliable system of impunity. Arnold could supply bail and attorneys. He proposed that if Murphy could take care of the impunity part, then the union bosses, backed by the *Forward*, could be Tammany's new vote getters.

Murphy thought about it. Abraham Cahan, the *Forward* editor, was many things—a socialist, a leader of the East Side literati, a novelist, a globe-trotting advocate for Jewish causes, and a media mogul with a giant reach that went beyond New York. As a recent headline in the *Arkansas Democrat* put it, RUSSIAN REFUGEE HAS HALF A MILLION DAILY READERS IN AMERICA: "There's only one way to get a vital message to the hundreds of thousands of poor people in the crowded tenements of New York's East Side—go see Abraham Cahan. Who is Cahan? A Tammany ward boss, perhaps? No. Cahan is a quiet, unassuming editor of a great newspaper."

Murphy nodded. Arnold's idea was a good one.

This was a significant conversation. It was one thing for Arnold to help Tammany skate through the Rosenthal Affair, or broker a relationship between Murphy and Belmont Jr. It was quite another for him to be propping up Tammany with an entirely new political strategy. Arnold's proposal was all the more striking because it entailed Tammany abandoning its long-held position on labor, which had been to side with wealthy manufacturers by giving tacit permission to the police to suppress labor strikes. But since Murphy was already endorsing the effort to pass new labor laws, and would likely lose the manufacturers' vote anyway, it made sense to go all in, to throw the full weight of New York's Democratic Party behind the labor movement, a decision that would shape the national Democratic platform in years to come.

To fix cases for the union's labor thugs, Murphy and Arnold knew that they would need a friendly district attorney, someone they could elevate to mayor and eventually to governor, an office that would soon be vacant. At the moment, Murphy was waging an effort to impeach the current governor, William Sulzer, who had taken his own reform crusade too far, calling for investigations of Tammany corruption. District Attorney Whitman, on the other hand, had focused his corruption crusade narrowly on police grafters while ignoring the politicians who controlled them. Murphy and Arnold agreed: Whitman was their man.

Sure, Whitman was currently making his name as a law-and-order politician in the Rosenthal-Becker case, but he had a problem: the appellate court had recently set aside Becker's conviction and ordered a new trial. In its opinion, the court disparaged the case and called the prosecution's witnesses "vile criminals" who were "unworthy of belief," and their testimony "pure fabrication." The decision was a setback for Whitman, legally and politically. He fell out of favor with the Waspy uptown Republicans and couldn't turn to the rich German Jews for support, because they hated his self-promoting style and planned to stick with Gaynor for another term as mayor. Murphy speculated that if Whitman's future depended on it, he would switch sides and accept Tammany's backing.

On successive evenings, the Incorruptibles raided Healy's, the city's prime venue for beefsteak dinners. These dinners were a tradition that dated back to the 1890s, when businessmen gathered in "beefsteak dungeons" to don butcher's aprons, drink beer, and eat thick slices of beef dipped in butter and grilled over hickory. By 1913, coed beefsteak dungeons had spread across the country. They were often elaborate. Healy's, for instance, offered themed rooms, such as the Jungle and the Log Cabin. It also featured an indoor ice-skating rink and a ballroom where diners cheered the Royal Belgian Orchestra.

Healy's, at Sixty-Sixth Street and Broadway, was an odd place to raid, way outside of the Clinton Street precinct's jurisdiction. Newburger opposed taking the vice crusade uptown, wary, as he wrote to Magnes, of "causing an impression that we are attempting to regulate the morals of the entire city." But the raid of Healy's had been ordered by Mayor Gaynor himself. Since the winter, Gaynor had been calling for enforcement of the 1 a.m. closing law for saloons and restaurants, particularly in uptown spots frequented by rich reformers. Gaynor hated the closing law, considering it impractical and paternalistic, but he was adamant that uptowners abide by the same rules that they insisted be enforced for the lower classes. And there was another motive: with the election approaching, Gaynor wanted to expose DA Whitman as a fraud who waved the law-and-order flag only when it suited his political ambitions.

Whitman's ambition was to become mayor, but that summer his hopes were dashed when the Republicans chose as their nominee a thirty-four-year-old, John Purroy Mitchel, known as the Boy Mayor. This slight burned the forty-five-year-old Whitman, who, facing stagnation in another term as DA, went on a bender at Healy's. Drinking late into the night, night after night, Whitman wondered what he had done to fail. He had espoused the right moral program. He did what the Wasps of the Republican Party wanted. And still they nominated the Boy Mayor instead of him. Whitman considered his choices. The Republicans had shut him out. The German Jews were backing Gaynor. Whitman had one option: Tammany Hall. For all of 1913, he had campaigned on the notion that he had killed off the city's gangs. Now, in challenging the reformers directly, he would accept the backing of the party that survived by keeping those gangs on the street.

By the night of August 14, when Harry Newburger and Abe Shoenfeld appeared at Healy's at 12:55 a.m., tensions between Gaynor and the restaurant's owner, Thomas Healy, had been building for weeks. Gaynor ruled that unless a liquor-serving restaurant had an all-night liquor license — and Jack's, where Arnold hung out, was the only place in the city that did — then it had to close *all* of its operations, including food service, at 1 a.m. This legal interpretation angered the city's restaurateurs, who insisted that they should be permitted to remain open past 1 a.m., as long as they sold only food. But Thomas Healy actually defied police attempts to shut him down, and took his case to court. If Healy felt emboldened to challenge the mayor, it was in part because he had the city's top prosecutor getting tanked in his place. By mid-August, Gaynor, intending to show up his rival as a scofflaw, was telling newspapers that DA Whitman was "advising and upholding" the resistance at Healy's, and the public expected a face-off.

That night, spectators lined the stairway of the nearby elevated station as the Incorruptibles prepared to shut Healy's down. Inside, patrons nodded familiarly at Healy — *Thought I'd stand by you* — and prepared to resist. When Newburger entered and gave notice that the restaurant must close, there was snickering and booing. Whitman, soused to the gills, stepped forward and raised a glass, prompting diners to jump on tables and chant: "Whitman! Whitman! Whitman!"

"He's defying us!" Abe said. "He's laughing at us!"

Diners surrounded the cops. The cops pushed back. Cameramen photographed the confrontation, creating evidence that Whitman later tried to use in a suit against Newburger for "oppression," a general charge that could cover anything from police overreach to brutality. That suit was dropped, but the fight at Healy's solidified Whitman's transformation. He accepted Tammany's backing, and his approach to crime-fighting changed.

* * *

"Scab, scab, scab!" chanted the *shtarkers* as another defendant was hauled before the so-called Court of Special Sessions, the mock gangster court where the UHT boss Morris Sigman presided.

Though of medium height and build, with a right eye that looked straight at you and a walleyed left eye, Sigman, who'd been a lumberjack in the Pale of Settlement, had great physical strength, and his battles on the picket line were legend among tailors. According to an insider's account of the UHT, Sigman's colleagues called him "obstinate, pig-headed, unreasonable....He had no talent for compromising with his own faith."

If Sigman discovered that a UHT member had been out scabbing, the punishment was never a warning, and it didn't matter what the excuse was. The fellow might say he was only trying to feed his family, or that he had been evicted and his furniture was on the street. "Don't you know you are not allowed to work?" Sigman would say.

"If my children die from hunger? Then no, I don't know it. But I have ten dollars. Here, take it. I will go home and I won't go to work no more."

When such offerings were made, Sigman laughed. The laugh was the signal to the *shtarkers* to pounce, meting out punishments that ranged from broken thumbs and sliced ears to fatal beatings. Some defendants begged to be shot. Others jumped out the window. "We had sawdust on the floor for when a fellow should bleed, and after we got him out, there was a fellow who would clean up the floor and wash around until the next session," one *shtarker* recalled.

As Tony and the other *shtarkers* watched scabs cry and beg, they felt little emotion. For those who had lost sisters in the Triangle fire, who had watched parents die from tuberculosis, who had spent their youth in a hell of child labor, the sacrifice of a few selfish scabs was nothing. "The worst offense that could be committed by any union man was to scab," recalled an East Sider who had been a young girl during the labor wars. "I can remember seeing, as a child, instances of shocking violence. A scab running down the street with his throat slit, and blood gushing out, and my mother saying: 'That's what they do to a scab.'"

Now they did it more and more because there was little consequence. The *shtarker*s never spent much time in prison, and if one did have to serve time, he or she earned the standard *shtarker* rate, five dollars a day, to sit behind bars—money that a family member could collect at the offices of the *Forward* newspaper. But they rarely stayed locked up for long. Some hidden figure covered bail and attorneys. Another ally ensured that defendants appeared before a friendly magistrate. Yet another, the district attorney, "pigeonholed" indictments, allowing charges to pile up without prosecution. The prime beneficiary of this protection was, of course, their leader. After being charged with felony assault of a police officer, following the Incorruptibles' August 1913 rumble with Dopey Benny on Forsyth Street, the Dope was back on the streets.

20

Don't Tell Lies for Me

I N LATE AUGUST, ON A FRIDAY MORNING, ABE APPEARED AT
the kosher poultry butcher on Driggs Street and said: "You wanted to
speak with me?"

Fridays now found Mayer Shoenfeld at the Driggs Street butcher,
taking up an old habit that dated to his days as a labor leader. Back then,
during strikes, Mayer would slaughter and deliver chickens to the families of striking workers in a gesture of solidarity. As a kid, Abe had looked
on this tradition with pride, but now, with Mayer representing the manufacturers, the idea of his father bringing chickens to striking workers felt
to Abe like hypocrisy. Mayer cut a chicken's neck, hung the bird on a line
to bleed out, and said he wanted to talk to Abe about a garment firm
called Klee & Co.

Klee, a manufacturer of men's suits, was run by a German-Jewish
family whom Mayer had known since the 1890s, when Klee became one
of the first firms in New York to offer custom-tailored suits, typically
available only to wealthy men, at readymade prices. It was a risky move
but it paid off. In 1900, when New York manufacturers shipped $300

million of apparel each year, supplying 80 percent of the national market, newspapers called Klee "the largest popular priced merchant tailoring house in New York."

Thus Klee was the kind of firm that Mayer admired. It hired the best tailors and paid them top salaries to turn out a quality product. But now, amid the labor wars, it was Klee's insistence on making its own hiring choices that put it at odds with the United Hebrew Trades and its demand for a universal closed shop. Mayer informed Abe that the Klee factory would soon be bombed by union thugs, and asked Abe to assign police to guard the factory to prevent killing.

Mayer's request was sensible, as Abe later reflected: "He was right, but I didn't want to do it. I'd be accused of helping the manufacturers." His unwillingness to intervene against unions was a widely held policy among his generation of reformers. It was also a position he happened to share with his uptown benefactors, who, in their bid to win over the East Side masses, refused to condemn the union cause.

Abe told Mayer that Klee could hire its own guards, and recalled an incident from earlier that year when a Klee guard had brained a striking tailor, who later died from his injuries. Mayer argued that Klee, by refraining from violence now, would set a standard for other garment firms. But Abe didn't want to be told what to do. And he believed that with Gaynor's continued support, the Incorruptibles could get the gangsters without going after the unions.

Days later, in early September, on a stage in City Hall Park, Jacob Schiff hosted a campaign event for Mayor Gaynor's renomination, but Gaynor didn't look good. He was too weak and hoarse to address the crowd, so Schiff spoke on Gaynor's behalf. He knocked Tammany and Charlie Murphy, telling reporters that he and the mayor would not allow decisions for the city to be made in a dining room at Delmonico's. Friends of

Gaynor's campaign marched through the gathering with shovels over their shoulders and piled them beneath a sign that said, "Way down under these shovels lies the body of C.F.M." — a reference to Murphy. Despite Gaynor's ill health, the event was a success.

But then the Kehillah's future in the police department dimmed. The day after the campaign event, Gaynor, the Kehillah's political sponsor, finally took that long-planned family trip to Ireland, his mother country. It was the same trip he had been trying to take in the summer of 1910, when a laid-off dockworker shot him in the neck. He had soldiered on for three years, but now, due to complications from the bullet still lodged behind his ear, Gaynor died on the deck of the ship, one hundred miles from the Irish shore.

Five days later, back in New York, the Klee factory on Lafayette Street was bombed, just as Mayer predicted. When Klee set up a new factory in New Jersey, which many manufacturers were doing in an attempt to elude the union violence, that factory was bombed as well. There were no fatalities, just terrified employees. But Abe was beginning to see that maybe his father was right about the union-gangster connection, that you couldn't take down the latter without suppressing the former. The Klee bombings, combined with Gaynor's passing, gave him a feeling of urgency.

The Incorruptibles kept after the Dope and his labor sluggers, interfering with their extortionate "fundraising balls and benefits." The *shtarkers* strong-armed storekeepers into purchasing tickets for these as well as ads in "ball journals," the circulars that announced the events — dances, plays, and boxing matches. Abe updated the Kehillah: "During a conversation that Dopey Benny had with our investigator he informed him that he expected to run a $2,000 ball journal, but has only succeeded in obtaining $200 worth of adverts, and for this he says he must thank the

Kehillah Society." When the Incorruptibles "attended the racket and kept out about fifty well-known thieves, including the Dope himself," Abe expressed his satisfaction: "Imagine everyone dancing and enjoying themselves at the Dope's ball and him left out in the cold, not even allowed to get a glance into the place. If he needed a little more to complete his dopiness—he really went dippy that night."

Nevertheless, the *shtarkers* continued to terrorize garment manufacturers and other East Side businesses with impunity.

Before he passed, one of Gaynor's last letters was a note to Rabbi Magnes, expressing his belief that "no single body has done more to better conditions in the city than the Kehillah." When Gaynor's body came back to New York, it was Magnes who delivered the eulogy at Trinity Church. He alluded to the vice crusade and what Gaynor's loss meant for it:

> My friends and I approached Mayor Gaynor but a year ago, at a time when it seemed that the city was forsaking him. Maligned as few public servants have been—the butt of charlatans and professional reformers—the mayor went doggedly and wisely on his way. His learning and sense of history made him understand the great movements that have brought the world's people to our shores, and he looked upon this wondrous city as a place for the gathering of exiles. We offered the mayor help in cleansing a congested district of the vice and crime and filth that had gathered there for years. He welcomed our help, and did not tire of acknowledging service that in reality drew much of its inspiration from him, for, in his leaving us, the edge of that work is suddenly blunted.

For Abe and Newburger, Gaynor's funeral drove home the reality that their wide-open mandate to fight crime was unlikely to survive the year. Feeling the pressure, they barged into DA Whitman's office. They had been sending letters to Whitman, asking about the twenty-nine indictments pending against Benjamin Fein, and now Abe asked: "Is the Dope to be brought to trial or not?"

"As you are doubtless aware," Whitman said, "the court of general sessions has not reconvened and —"

"Bolawala!" Abe screamed. *Bullshit.* "We might as well send a letter to these people saying it's all right to murder one another!"

Abe kept up hope that they would get Dopey Benny, especially after he was arrested for the shooting death of a citizen, a court clerk who was walking home at night when he was caught in gang crossfire. The Dope allegedly orchestrated the ambush to get revenge on an Italian gang for taking strikebreaking work from garment manufacturers and killing a beloved member of the Dope's gang. But as the end of 1913 approached, the vice crusade's political support continued to dry up and Abe's hopes had less and less chance of being realized.

The German-Jewish uptowners had their own vision for the vice crusade's conclusion, and their lack of interest in Dopey Benny and union violence was evident in the mandate they gave to the crusade in the final months of 1913. That fall, the German Jews, reacting to the Year of the Red-Light Drama, formed the Anti-Defamation League, whose initial report complained: "Whenever a producer wishes to depict a betrayer of public trust — a hard-boiled usurious moneylender, a crooked gambler, a grafter, a depraved firebug, a white slaver, a prostitute, a thief, or other villain — the actor is directed to represent him or her as a Jew."

The German-Jewish uptowners wanted to curtail negative depictions of Jews in the media, so Abe and Newburger ran around the city shutting down plays and movies that dealt with Jewish crime. A movie called *The Inside of the White Slave Traffic* caused the greatest commotion. The story opens with a pimp rising from bed as his prostitute turns over her earnings. The pimp promptly loses that money in a stuss game at a Second Avenue café, which a title card calls White Slave Headquarters. The pimp needs more gambling money but discovers his prostitute has been arrested, so he stalks "a sewing machine girl" named Annie, takes her to a movie and a restaurant, and slips something into her drink. Annie wakes up in a bedroom and it's obvious that she's been raped. When Annie tells her parents what happened, her father throws her out. She returns to the pimp, who agrees to marry her. After a fake wedding ceremony, the pimp tells Annie that he's without funds and must place her with friends until his next paycheck. In the style of red-light dramas, things do not get better for Annie.

In December, when *The Inside of the White Slave Traffic* premiered at the Bijou Theater, it took in twice as much money as the year's former number one box-office hit, another red-light drama called *Traffic in Souls*. By the time Abe and Newburger raided the Bijou, they'd already shut down several red-light dramas, but the trial concerning *The Inside of the White Slave Traffic* would determine whether other producers decided to fight their own cases.

At the trial, a lawyer for the producers pointed out that the pictures in the film might have been repellent "but they are not immoral because they are true." In response, Third Deputy Commissioner Newburger argued: "We have taken the red lights off our streets. I can see no reason for setting them up in our playhouses. These defendants are not aspiring to dissuade young people from a life of vice. They are showmen. Their motive is pure gain." For the judge, the decision was easy. It was a crime to run a brothel, he reasoned, and therefore films that depicted the crime were *not* entitled to protection.

This was the last legal victory for the Incorruptibles, as such, and an unsatisfying one, because a few days later, in a different court, an actual criminal was given complete immunity.

*　　*　　*

The Dope's reign of terror, culminating in the death of a bystander, was a headache for District Attorney Whitman. Still gunning for governor and needing Tammany Hall's support, Whitman pigeonholed the homicide case and tried the Dope instead on the old police assault charge from August.

If Whitman believed that the latter case would be an easier one for him, as prosecutor, to *lose,* he was right. The facts were sketchy. Some said the alleged victim, a cop, provoked the Dope and initiated the fight. And the witnesses all lived near the Forsyth Bath House, in the neighborhood around Grand, Broome, and Essex Streets that the Dope and his *shtarker* crew held in their clutches. Indeed, at the trial, where each juror was assigned a police guard, not a single one of the dozen East Siders called to the witness stand was willing to implicate the Dope. The DA's office rolled over: "I don't want you to convict an innocent man," a prosecutor told the jury. "If you think this man is innocent, then acquit him."

The jury came back with a guilty verdict, but the Dope remained confident.

On sentencing day, the *World* reported, "He wore a neatly pressed black suit with a pencil stripe of white. His shoes had a fresh shine and his tie was a quiet, dark blue one. Had it not been for his swarthy, dark face, furtive bearing, and bad eye he might have been taken for a probationary policeman, for he is a big, husky chap with neatly brushed hair and rather the air of a dandy." The Dope told the court: "I was disfigured, beaten up, and a gun put in my pocket and the police knows it. There are many members belonging to this bar in this court that knows that I was framed up by the police. I am ready to take my medicine, your honor, but I want the court and God almighty to know that I am innocent of this charge."

When the Dope was sentenced to five years, Whitman asked the court to review the conviction, requesting to void his office's own legal victory. WHITMAN SURPRISES POLICE BY JOINING IN REQUEST FOR DIS-CHARGE, the *World* headline announced.

Outside, on the courthouse steps, the Dope boasted to reporters that the police had not and would not be able to get him. Sure, he might be going back to Sing Sing for a bit, but he would have the district attorney working to get him out. He took a bottle of whiskey from his pocket, tipped it to his lips, and offered a sip to a nearby prosecutor. Behind him, the Dope's gang taunted the Incorruptibles, one of whom, the *Sun* reported, "hit like a flash from the shoulder and the sneering gangster's head bumped the marble flagging of the corridor," while another gangster "was slapped so hard that his truculence oozed out in a whine."

The frustrated vice squad knew the crusade was finished. The newly elected Boy Mayor, John Purroy Mitchel, was about to take over for the interim mayor who had been filling in since Gaynor's death. As a rule, politicians made a fuss about crime only when they sought to unseat an incumbent. Mitchel wanted nothing to do with the cleanup squad of his predecessor. In early February, a year after joining the NYPD, Abe and Newburger disbanded the Incorruptibles and vacated the Clinton Street precinct.

In April of 1914, during the week of Passover, Lily took the train to Ossining, north of the city, and walked up the hill to Sing Sing prison.

The previous year, when the appellate court had set aside Becker's conviction and ordered a new trial, Lily was hopeful. The court had denigrated the prosecution's case and its witnesses. If the witnesses were discredited in Becker's case, Lily hoped, then surely the same witnesses would be unworthy vis-à-vis Louie. One of those witnesses even appeared to regret his testimony. Bridgey Webber told reporters, "I get sick every time I think of those fellows up in the death house. It's an awful thing to think of sending five men to the electric chair. I'll feel like dying myself on the day they are killed." Bridgey's wife added: "I cheer him up all the time by telling him they were sure to get new trials." But in the end only Becker was granted a retrial. The appellate court held that the reasons for Becker's retrial did not extend to the gunmen, and sustained their conviction. Finally, a petition for reprieve, for which Lily secured the requisite 3,000 signatures, failed to sway the governor.

Admitted through the gate at Sing Sing, Lily walked down "the lane of torment," a corridor lined with shallow cells. The gaunt faces of prisoners stared at Lily, their eyes full of rage. She passed the threshold of the death house and shivered. There, to the right, was the little green door, the famous exit that Louie and the other gunmen were scheduled to slip through the following day.

In the visiting room, she sat across from Louie, separated from him by a wall of metal lattice. She had one idea left. It wouldn't free Louie, but it might return justice to the case and set things right in some moral way. The idea terrified her. She wasn't even sure she could go through with it. "Louie," she said, "I was thinking about what Jack Rose said to you in the apartment that day."

Louie knew what she was referring to, the conversation in which Bald Jack Rose convinced Louie to kill Rosenthal by telling him that Becker had ordered the killing. Louie had always known that Lily overheard that conversation, and that on the witness stand she had lied when she denied hearing it, just as Louie and the other gunmen, observing their sacred no-squeal rule to the letter, had lied when they testified that Jack Rose hadn't said anything to them about Becker. Lily, therefore, would be a key witness in Becker's retrial, the only witness capable of corroborating the prosecution's embattled narrative that Becker ordered the murder.

"At Becker's retrial," Lily asked, "ought I to tell the truth?"

Over the course of their ordeal, Louie had grown embittered toward Becker. Becker often sent notes to Louie to keep up hope, implying that they would eventually go free. In fact, Becker was just passing on the assurances he got from a worried Tammany Hall. Because Becker knew enough to send half the Tammany bosses to prison, a decision had been made to underwrite Becker's pledge of silence and sustain his hopes with money and lawyers. Then, Becker's application for a retrial was granted while the gunmen's was rejected. Afterward, Becker's wife invited Lily for tea, told her how bad Becker felt about the boys losing their appeal, and tried to elicit how Lily planned to testify in Becker's retrial. Arguably, Becker was no less a pawn in the Rosenthal Affair than the gunmen had been, but in the moment Louie and Lily felt certain that they had been played.

"After I'm gone," Louie said, "I don't want you to tell any more lies for me. It is only right that you tell nothing but the truth. And promise me that you'll not hold on to what is gone. Find a straight man who will take care of you."

The guard placed a hand on Lily's shoulder: Visiting was over. Louie smiled: "Brace up. Be a good brave kid now."

Lily implored the guard: "Won't you let me kiss him?" They escorted her away. She stretched out her arms and wept. "Won't you let me touch his hand? Let me feel his body pressed to mine? His breath on my face? For God's sake! Take pity on me!"

"Goodbye!" Louie cried out. "Goodbye, dear one!"

Lily wasn't supposed to be his only visitor that evening. Despite Louie's objection to his mother coming, Mrs. Rosenberg, ailing and bedridden, insisted on bidding farewell to her son. But earlier that day, when the Rosenbergs started out from the East Side, Mrs. Rosenberg collapsed, and Louie's father, Jacob, made the trip alone.

At Sing Sing, Jacob said, "I've come to say goodbye to my boy." For the press, his arrival was an anticipated event. It had been Jacob Rosenberg, the prosperous flour merchant with offices at the Produce Exchange, who financed most of the four gunmen's legal defense. And, indeed, he now looked like someone who had spent everything he had—financially, emotionally, physically. He tried to walk but he stumbled. The prison rabbi took his arm and led him down the corridor of the death house. Midway, they stopped. "I can go no farther," Jacob moaned. "The boy's mother is desperate. She is at home and I am afraid she will die. I can't go in. I can't go in. I must go back to her now. I could not go back to her if I saw him again. It would kill me."

The next morning, as dawn crept over the hill at Sing Sing, Louie was etherized with morphine while "Whispering Hope" played on a phonograph brought in by the warden.

Hope, as an anchor so steadfast
Rends the dark veil for the soul
Whither the master has entered
Robbing the grave of its goal.

The warden, newspapers reported, decided the order of death based on his estimation of each prisoner's mental constitution. He judged Louie the strongest and therefore the last to die. And Louie, the one-time Hebrew scholar, did seem incredibly stoic. Throughout their ordeal, he had always been the most talkative of the gunmen, willing to chat amiably with the press, but now he was reserved. He sat quietly on the edge of his bed, head in hands. In the next cell, whenever Whitey Lewis had one of his outbursts, screaming that he was "going off an innocent man," Louie said, "It's all right, Whitey. We done all we could. What's the use of talking. It won't get us nothing."

As the sun rose, the first three gunmen went to the chair, and the lights at Sing Sing flickered.

The drug took hold of Louie. He talked while the prison rabbi listened. "I want you to tell all those boys on the East Side that they can't beat the game. They may think they have the game whipped, may think they have the backing that puts them above the law, but look at me: We had as many friends as any fellow on Second Avenue, but when it came to a showdown only the synagogue stood by us." He fell deeper. "And yet I must die sometime, and if it pleases God that I die now, then I am ready." And deeper. "To the gentlemen of the press: There is an editorial in today's paper. It speaks of our 'old bravado' and 'swaggering desire for a game end.' As our keepers can attest, there is no talk of a game end. There is no old bravado here."

Going last, Louie ducked through the little green door and sat in the chair, above which a twisted length of wire hung from an iron fixture. The electrician buckled the straps and adjusted the armor that hid Louie's face. Then he placed a row of electric lights, fastened to a board, across the arms of the chair, and disappeared behind the controls. The rabbi stood off to the side, his back to the chair, and chanted: "Hear oh Israel, the Eternal is our God, the Eternal alone."

Louie responded: "Blessed be the name of the glory of his kingdom for I —"

The words died in his throat as the lights on the board flared from white to crimson. His body shot forward, and the chair's leather straps creaked. Water from the head electrode ran into Louie's mouth, choking him. A groan issued from his lips. Ten seconds later he was still alive. The electrician maintained a second shock for twenty seconds, but when the doctors applied their stethoscopes they were not satisfied. A third shock was delivered, for a full minute, and the witnesses in the observation area watched a greenish-blue haze shoot from Louie's head while the odor of scorched skin filled the room. Another misfire. The electrician punched the apparatus with the butt end of his screwdriver and tried again. After the fourth shock Louie was pronounced dead, and the witnesses made a dash for fresh air.

Later that day, the bodies of the gunmen were returned to the East Side, each in a separate hearse. It was one month into a New York spring, and the afternoon sun streamed down. Because Passover was still in progress, many were home from work, which only added to the swells of mourners in the streets, about five hundred of whom gathered outside Lily's home at 296 Grand Street, where her family had settled after arriving from the Pale of Settlement in 1897.

Lily was three when they made that journey. On the ship, she laughed at the sight of the tumbling blue waves. Her mother remembered how the first-class passengers would look down over the rail at Lily and smile. *What a joyous child! She seems to be made for happiness!* That sunny outlook had carried her through the struggles of immigration and an East Side childhood, brought her to the triumph of love and what seemed like a desirable match with Louie, and buoyed her up during the tribulations that followed their wedding, just two years earlier.

The previous night, unable to sleep, Lily had walked miles and miles down the dark, empty streets of the far East Side, along the water, through the rows of tenements and stables. She cried out as she walked, and then, when the sun began to rise and she felt it must all be over up there at Sing Sing, she grew quiet, and what Louie had said to her came into her mind: *Don't tell any more lies for me.* She sighed. The idea of unburdening herself felt like relief, and for the first time in a long while she breathed easy. If young love was both miracle and madness, wonder and folly, Lily had had a wild experience of that paradox, and now it was over — well, nearly.

In May, a month after the executions, Becker's retrial arrived and his chances looked good.

Although Bald Jack Rose stuck to the story he told in Becker's first trial, his credibility as a witness had tanked since then. Earlier that year, in granting Becker's application for a new trial, the appellate court had noted that Bald Jack and the other gambler-witnesses were "indisputably guilty of the murder and . . . subject to the punishment of death." Becker's conviction, the appellate court added, "rests upon the testimony of criminals and degenerates in whose characters nobody has at any time claimed to discover any trace of such conscience or moral sense as would be any more bounded by their oaths as witnesses than by the blowing of the wind."*

In any event, Whitman clearly needed something more to make his case.

Lily appeared in court in a black dress, her blond ringlets trussed up in a turban. When she took the witness stand, the prosecutor asked: "When you lived with your husband, before the murder of Herman Rosenthal, did Jack Rose—alias Bald Jack Rose—ever visit your apartment?"

"Yes, sir," she said.

"And you overheard his conversation with your husband?"

"Yes. He told Louie: 'Becker says he is going to frame you up with a gun charge.' And Louie said, 'Cannot I fix it with Becker?' And Jack Rose said, 'No, because Rosenthal is squealing. The only way to fix it with Becker is to croak Rosenthal. Becker don't want him beat up. He wants him taken off the earth—throat cut, dynamited, anything.' Jack Rose assured Louie that the sentiment at police headquarters was such that whoever croaked Rosenthal would have a medal pinned on him."

Newspapers played up the effect of Lily's testimony, one writing: "Softly spoken and scarcely audible, her sentences rang loud with the menace of the electric chair and whitened the face of Becker. In an instant, the atmosphere of the court underwent a change so radical that it was plainly to be noted in the jury box."

---

* Citizens and jurors may not have read appellate opinions, but many did read the papers. Unlike his co-witnesses who stayed away from New York, afraid of retribution, Bald Jack had stuck around and penned a series of tell-all articles detailing the life of an East Side gambler. These literary efforts, though perhaps honest, didn't do much for Bald Jack's probity in the Becker case. He had written: "I knew hundreds of gangsters who, at a word from me, would have done my bidding with or without pay, save for a reasonable sum to make sure of their getaway and to pay expenses while they were trailing the victim."

"You testified previously that you never heard Jack Rose say anything to your husband about murdering Rosenthal," the prosecutor said. "Did you lie?"

"Yes," she said, "I lied."

"Why?"

"Because I hoped to save the man I loved from the electric chair."

Lily told her truth innocently, not knowing that it contained its own lie, the lie that Bald Jack told Louie to get him to do the job, and it was this lie that led to Charles Becker's reconviction and turned him into the first American cop to be executed by the state. The prosecution put forth other witnesses, remarked the *Brooklyn Daily Eagle,* "but it was the testimony of Lefty Louie's widow that dealt the severest blow to the defense."

Outside, on the courthouse steps, while Lily spoke to the press about Louie and her decision to testify against Becker, Abe watched from the crowd. Since leaving the police department a few months earlier, he had struggled with guilt over defying his father, who "indelibly carved into my makeup a depository of moral and decent principles," providing the model for what he became. Louie's execution added to Abe's remorse, but it also renewed his motivation. He thought back to 1912, when Louie's capture pressured Zelig into giving Abe the info he needed to get Dollar John. It was the first Kehillah victory, the case that led to everything that followed. Abe needed the deaths of Louie and Zelig—and of his "top man," the seventeen-year-old informant who chronicled court corruption until he was murdered with an ice pick—to count for something. He couldn't give up now.

The Becker verdict struck many Americans as the culmination of a long moral struggle against grafting police and Tammany Hall's machine politics, even as the prosecutor in the case, DA Whitman, now catered to that machine in anticipation of his run for governor.

The Rosenthal case was also a boost for Bald Jack Rose, who continued to cash in on his notoriety. He gave speeches at churches, where he explained, "Men and women of the underworld, the submerged tenth, are a primitive people. They love and hate intensely. But there is more affection among them than in your so-called high society. The unconventionality of their life, the freedom which the so-called respectable life does not offer and which good form prohibits — it's in the blood." Bald Jack attacked the new sciences of criminology and psychology and said that to understand the causes of crime, what mattered most was *humanology*, which was why he had decided to call his new film company Humanology Films, and to appear as himself in movies like *The Price He Paid* and *The Wages of Sin*.

He was earnest, it seemed, but he struggled to build a filmmaking career. *Moving Picture News* called his first effort, *The Wages of Sin*, in which Bald Jack appeared alongside his fellow witnesses in the Rosenthal case, "a disgusting film" and predicted: "All the worst elements in the youth of our cities will flock to see this film. . . . All the moral, clean, upright, thinking people will once more refer to the degrading and disgusting condition of Cinematography." The National Board of Censorship rejected the film, but the general committee, a kind of appeals court, overruled the board, which raised questions about whether Bald Jack had bribed the committee.

Still, not everyone could be bought. When Bald Jack offered Lily $2,000 to appear in his next film, *Why Girls Leave Home,* she told him to get lost. She wouldn't be in his movie for a million dollars, she said, wouldn't have anything to do with him if she were starving to death.

21

The Toughest Money in the World

I N THE SPRING OF 1914, ABE AND NEWBURGER SET UP a Kehillah-funded office on Rector Street.

It was a strange moment in time for the world at large — the Great War was months away — and also on the East Side, where union-funded thugs ran free, thanks to Arnold Rothstein and Charlie Murphy's strategy for Tammany's survival. District Attorney Whitman, now running for governor, did not want to go on record as fighting the unions, because he needed their support at election time.

So while the Dope sat in Sing Sing, awaiting the outcome of his appeal, his underlings competed against one another for supremacy in union work and associated fields of extortion. Since the fight with his father the previous summer, Abe had come to realize that it would be impossible to take the gangsters off the streets without reining in the labor unions too. In his first Kehillah report of 1914, Abe wrote: "This year, all gang conditions are written up along with the operations of the unions, for it is reasonable enough to assume that they cannot be separated if they work together." The report continued: "The Jewish newspaper known as the *Forward* is also mixed up in this war, supporting these scoundrels."

Abe chronicled which individual garment union within the umbrella of the UHT hired which *shtarker,* and tracked the organizational disarray within the *shtarker* ranks. The Furriers' Union, for instance, had tapped Joe Rosenzweig, alias Joe the Greaser, to bully nonunion shops. Of Joe the Greaser, Abe, still an indefatigable collector of biographical material, wrote, "He is 26 years old, height 5 feet, 10 inches, built medium, rather slim, complexion dark; neat dresser, speaks a good English, and does not act as his name implies." Some said Joe the Greaser earned his nickname because he looked Italian, while others said he got it because he avoided guns, preferring, as Abe put it, "recourse to the trusty blade," his knife skills enabling him "to grease" whatever stood in his way.

The Greaser's competition for the Furriers' business was a *shtarker* named Pinchey Paul. "Pinchey," Abe wrote, "is short — blondish — stout — rather good looking. His wife has plenty of diamonds, and so has he. Whenever his wife wants another diamond ring Pinchey runs a benefit for himself. The Honorable Pinchey is no more than a bulldozer...and will crack a man's nut for five dollars." In the Dope's absence, Pinchey, like Joe, was making a play for leadership, and in an effort to consolidate his power he opened Pinchey's Coffee Saloon at 204 Broome Street, where an inscription on the window read KOSHER LUNCH ROOM AND COMBINATION HOUSE. The Greaser wanted Pinchey eliminated, so he approached a recent Russian-Jewish immigrant named Benny Snyder, who had been the *shtarker* for the Bakers' Union until Pinchey took that work away.

The friction between Benny and Pinchey intensified when Benny said something offensive to Pinchey, who in turn punched Benny in the jaw. Later, Pinchey remarked that he was sorry, and to make amends he promised to bring Benny a fur coat, since Benny didn't have one. But the Greaser saw an opportunity to oust Pinchey. He riled Benny up about the beating and asked what, by way of retaliation, Benny would do to get his rep back. "I would take care of Pinchey myself," Joe explained, "but you have a clean record and would get no more than a bit at Elmira. If you want to be my friend, go ahead and do it and I will stick to you to the last."

So Benny did it. In May of 1914, he shot Pinchey Paul dead in a Norfolk Street barber shop, where Pinchey, it should be noted, held the fur coat he intended to give to Benny.

Two weeks later, on June 1, the other Benny of East Side gangdom, Dopey Benny, was released from Sing Sing in a rather slick deal. The appellate court granted DA Whitman's application to vacate Whitman's own conviction of the Dope, one of the most prolific murderers in the city's history. Whitman, for his efforts on behalf of Tammany and the UHT, would soon become New York's next governor and possibly more. Woodrow Wilson predicted that Whitman could be his opponent for the presidency in 1916.

The Dope returned home to the East Side and shared a shaky balance of power with Joe the Greaser. On June 5, Abe wrote, "Dopey Benny is on the payroll of the Neckwear Union and the Cloak and Suits Union. From these unions he gets $25 a week a piece and is a walking delegate and has a card and such. He now expects to get the White Goods [ladies' undergarments] Union that he once had, and also $25 a week as a delegate. This will give him an income of $75 each week, and he states that in view of this income he will be legitimate hereafter."

With Pinchey Paul out of the way, Joe the Greaser consolidated the strike work for the Furriers' Union, the Knitters' Union, and the Ladies' Hat Frame Workers' Union, and used his earnings to establish his own saloon, the Warschawer & Bialer Café at 138 Norfolk Street, an establishment that Abe characterized as "wholesale and retail dealers in fine liquors and cigars, and a regular old lager beer saloon to boot." Abe then added what must have been quite a sentence for him to write: "Joe the

Greaser is now living there with Tony, a girl very well known to the underworld."

Tony the Tough tended to rise wherever she went, and the underworld of labor sluggers was no different. Her devotion to their cause earned her respect, and the role of "Joe's girl." A trauma survivor, Tony was addicted to adrenaline and drama as well as opium, and there was the Greaser, providing those things in abundance, along with a mink coat, compliments of the Furriers' Union.

That summer, Tony stood guard in a mass meeting of the United Hebrew Trades. There, among thousands of tailors, she watched a UHT boss explain why a settlement with manufacturers would not be forthcoming. The bosses said they were holding out for a closed shop. But it was becoming clear that such a goal was unobtainable. Tony could see that vanity and petty tensions had fractured the UHT, as *shtarkers* competed for power and union bosses competed with each other for play in the *Forward*. For the bosses, the holdout was more about power than anything; power mattered more than a simple raise and shorter hours. Meanwhile, the striking shirtwaist girls and those who had perished in the Triangle fire—it was as if they had existed only to help these men expand their following.

At the meeting, the union membership grumbled: How long would the strike last? Where were all those membership fees going? But if a tailor spoke up in protest at the meeting, Tony and her fellow *shtarkers* were instructed to pounce.

That night, Tony joined other *shtarkers* at an opium den on Fourteenth Street, where they reclined on beds and twirled a bamboo stem over the flame of a peanut-oil lamp until the black tar paste boiled and turned orange, then inhaled the fumes and lolled on the mattresses. As the sluggers puffed away, some perspective leaked through. Several of them voiced doubt about the UHT work. One cited the new labor laws that had been proposed by New York's Factory Investigation Commission: a minimum wage, a limit on hours worked, and other laws governing child labor and safety — groundbreaking state legislation that would soon be passed and replicated across the country. Their stoned conversation turned to the Kehillah. "You can't blame Newburger or Shoenfeld," said one slugger. "Every case they have on the Dope is right. Like all of us, he used to be an ordinary pickpocket until the UHT made a Frankenstein of him." The slugger broke down. "My poor mother!" he sobbed. "She once said, 'Be what you want to be if you can't help it — a thief, a murderer, a gangster. But don't go out and beat poor Jews like we are.'" He went on: "We haven't any sense! The UHT showed us how to make easy money. It's the toughest money in the world."

Tough money indeed: Later that summer, Tony stalked a factory forelady through East Side streets, waiting for the forelady to walk by an open cellar door so Tony could throw her down the hole. She paced, preparing to bull-rush the woman, trying to muster the requisite rage, but couldn't go through with it.

In the summer of 1914, amid rising chaos in the streets, Abe and Newburger looked for hard evidence, anything that could break the corruption that protected the United Hebrew Trades and their labor sluggers. But the interest in criminal reform was not what it had been in the previous two years, and the conflict in Europe drew away attention, including the attention of the Kehillah benefactors, who continued to contribute vice-crusading funds in dribs and drabs but were largely preoccupied with global concerns. Then, one day in early September, Tony the Tough came through their door.

Tony told them her story, about how she had joined the labor sluggers, believing in the righteousness of their fight against the manufacturers, until she became disillusioned. She had information: the Dope was shaking down the head of the Kosher Butchers' Union, a man named Salmoniwitz.

Abe and Newburger considered how they might capitalize on this information. They met with Detective Faurot, who showed them his newest device, a recording machine called the detectagraph. That September, Faurot and Honest Dan Costigan, both still members of the NYPD, partnered with Abe, Newburger, and Tony for one last job.

Faurot planted the detectagraph in Salmoniwitz's Clinton Street butcher shop. The Dope showed up and conversed with Salmoniwitz in Yiddish, then said he wanted to talk outside. Faurot crouched low and dragged the enormous machine to the window in time to record the Dope threatening to kill Salmoniwitz if he didn't pay up. But when Costigan surfaced to make the arrest, the Dope fled.

Abe and Tony, waiting across the street, followed the Dope south on Allen Street and up to the elevated platform as the train pulled in. Abe and the Dope boarded the same car while Tony boarded several cars behind them. Dodging in and out among passengers, Abe pursued the Dope to the front. They traded blows. A fist to the jaw knocked Abe on his back. The Dope grabbed the handrails, pulled himself up, and was about to stomp on Abe's head when Tony rushed in, unsheathed a hairpin, and jammed it into the Dope's gut, doubling him over.

In the magistrate's court, the detectagraph evidence meant that Judge John Campbell, who had been facilitating the labor sluggers' impunity, had no choice but to set a high bail: $10,000. When the Dope sent out his usual call for bail money and a lawyer, the United Hebrew Trades relayed the call to Arnold Rothstein. Arnold, surveying this anarchy, said: "Sacrifice him."

"They're not coming for me because I know too much," the Dope said. "I'll show them how much I know."

The Dope sent out word to his followers that if they didn't raise the bail money then he would squeal. Joe the Greaser held a benefit for the Dope but kept the money. The Dope's loyalists were shocked at the Greaser's conduct—it wasn't "clubby," they said—and set out to get him as he walked up Second Avenue during a crowded political gathering. When the Greaser heard shots, he dove into a nearby saloon, barely evading bullets that shattered the saloon window. GANGSTERS' GUNS SPREAD PANIC AT POLITICAL RALLY, reported the *World*. FIVE SHOTS FIRED AT "JOE THE GREASER," WHO "HELD OUT" ON "DOPEY BENNY." The shootout led to the arrests of more *shtarkers*, including the Greaser.

So the Dope called for the new district attorney and made a confession about his work for the unions. FEIN ACCUSES EAST SIDE LABOR MEN, BARES CRIMES OF LAST FIVE YEARS, read a *World* headline. Other *shtarkers* confessed as well. GUNMEN, CONFESSING MANY CRIMES, TELL HOW UNIONS PAID FOR MURDERS, read another, noting that prosecutors "declined to say how much Tona Rollick [*sic*], Joe the Greaser's girl, helped in building up a case. Her status as a witness has not been determined, but she said she loved Joe and expected to marry him some day."

As news of the confessions broke, stories of attacks on tailors poured into the DA's office, leading to the arrest of thirty-six union bosses for extortion, assault, and the 1910 murder of Mayer Shoenfeld's friend, the tailor Herman Liebowitz. UNION MEN AND WOMEN INDICTED IN GANG ROUND-UP, the *New York Times* announced. GRAND JURY FINDS LABOR LEADERS HIRED THUGS TO TERRORIZE EMPLOYERS AND WORKERS: "The gangsters, it was learned, are not the product of the streets, as most people believe, but are the product of the union leaders, who hire them to do their 'dirty work.' If they did not pay money for their jobs, the gangster would not exist."

22

Tailor's Progress

A BRAHAM CAHAN, THE *FORWARD* EDITOR, PROTESTED THE case. Given that manufacturers had run thugs against striking workers for years, Cahan asked, why weren't manufacturers charged with crimes?

If he was a passionate partisan, the labor wars were the culmination of an agonizing exodus that began in the Pale of Settlement during Cahan's youth. Years later, when he told his own story in a five-volume autobiography, he began with a childhood memory, a version of which was shared by many Russian Jews of his era: "I can still see my mother holding me at her side with one hand, and carrying in the other a small pot of cooked food. It was for a Jewish recruit being held in chains. The boy was tall and thin. I remember the clank of his chains, his sad face, the look of hunger, and his constant smoking in the hope that by weakening himself he could gain rejection by the military authorities."

By the time of Cahan's birth, in 1860, forced conscription of Jews into the czar's army had decimated Jewish communities in the Pale of Settlement. Elsewhere, such as in Western Europe, Jewish conscription was looked upon as an attribute of *progress,* a sign of emancipation. "Only in Russia was the conscription of the Jews neither ordered nor received as a harbinger of their civic betterment," writes Michael Stanislawski in *Tsar Nicholas I and the Jews: The Transformation of Jewish Society in Russia, 1825– 1855.* Prior to Nicholas's Jewish conscription statute, which took effect in 1827, Jews were exempted from service because they were assumed to be weak and cowardly, disloyal and religiously fanatical. But Nicholas saw recruitment as the antidote to everything that was wrong with the Jews. Religious conversion to Christianity wasn't advertised as the reason for forced Jewish conscription, but, in a memo, a member of Nicholas's secret police gave up the game: he detailed the unparalleled missionary possibilities provided by army life, and recommended that only young Jews, less entrenched in their faith, be conscripted, and at double the usual quota.

Taking this advice, Czar Nicholas lowered the draftable age for Jews to twelve (versus twenty for non-Jews), and exempted only those Jewish children who attended state-sponsored schools, a negligible number of boys. Each Jewish community was ordered to produce between four and eight recruits for every thousand inhabitants. For each local kehillah— or *kahal,* as it was called in Russia—the excruciating decision was whether to conscript fathers or children. A few years into this experiment, Russia's minister of war noticed that the mortality rate among Jewish recruits was disproportionately high. When he asked a military doctor about it, the doctor cited their youth, pointing out that the registrations of many Jewish recruits stated that they were ten years old, but, due to the fact that their baby teeth were still falling out, it was clear that they couldn't have been older than eight.

"Jewish boys who didn't want to go to the service would cut off fingers and starve and do horrible things to themselves," recalled Jacob Ben-Ami, the Russian-Jewish actor. To make their children unfit, parents did the unthinkable. In his *History of the Jews in Russia and Poland,* Simon Dubnow writes: "The most tender-hearted mother would place the finger of her beloved son under the kitchen knife of a home-bred quack sur-geon." Draft dodging, however, resulted in recruitment shortages, which pressed heavily on Jewish communities, who were held collectively responsible for supplying their quotas. Since the proportion of underage recruits was high, and parents fought recruitment strenuously, *kahal* leaders enlisted Jewish deputies, or bounty hunters, to find and abduct draft candidates.

These posses, called *khappers*—from the Yiddish verb *khapn,* to catch—became permanent fixtures in the Pale, and their kidnapping trade grew lucrative. The *khapper* often ransomed kidnapped children back to their families and replaced them with others whose parents couldn't pay. The historical literature abounds with tales of men emerg-ing from a coach, entering a Jewish house, and coming out with a gagged child while a mother runs after them, screaming and sobbing. Sometimes family members were prepared with axes and knives, and a battle would be fought to the death.

During Cahan's childhood, the *khappers* were abetted by a new law that allowed Jewish communities to present, as a substitute for a recruit required from that community, *any* Jew who'd been found traveling without a passport. "The chase was now taken up by every private indi-vidual who wished to find a substitute for a member of his family," writes Dubnow. "Hordes of Jewish bandits sprung up who infested the roads and inns, and by trickery or force made travelers part with their passports and then dragged them to the recruiting station. Never before had the Jewish masses, yielding to pressure from above, sunk to such depths of degradation." The conscription horrors, writes Dubnow, "bred the in-forming disease" among Jewish communities. Cahan and his contem-poraries came of age in a world of hard distinctions. You were either a *moser,* a snitch, or someone who stuck.

During the latter half of the 1800s, after Nicholas's thirty-year rule, laws concerning Jewish conscription fluctuated from czar to czar. Those laws, combined with other forms of oppression, meant that Cahan's post-Nicholas generation was full of people who resented their heritage, saw weakness in their parents' religion, and sought some new identity. Cahan pursued a secular education, replacing Judaism with socialism. Of his conversion, he recalled: "A kind of religious ecstasy took hold of me. I walked in a daze as one newly in love." In the socialist underground, he no longer needed to worry about approval, the impression he made on women, or the fact that his eyes weren't straight. He severed relations with his father and treated "the struggle of our Russian terrorists as something sacred."

After those terrorists assassinated Czar Alexander II in 1881, the twenty-one-year-old Cahan emigrated to America in the first wave of Russian-Jewish refugees. On the East Side he joined the Propaganda Association, a radical club of Russian-Jewish intellectuals that gave lectures to the refugee masses. His first lecture, on Karl Marx, "lit a flame of inspiration," one observer wrote. In a second lecture, Cahan called on the audience to march up Fifth Avenue with "irons and axes" and "take the palaces from the millionaires." Capturing the imagination, he figured out, was about charisma, and simplifying complex ideas. He believed that socialism could fill the void left by religion, if only it were presented properly. A strike was like *charam,* he told audiences, a ban dedicated to a holy purpose. A union card was not so different from a *mezuzah,* the religious amulet that protects against forces of evil.

In the 1890s, Russian-Jewish intellectuals coalesced around Cahan, but their attempt to organize an effective labor movement failed, just as it failed for Mayer Shoenfeld during the same period. But whereas Mayer denounced violence, Cahan came away with a different lesson, writing: "I believed that without violence, genuine socialism could not be achieved." And then the instrument of mayhem appeared.

In 1897, the same year Cahan founded the *Forward* in New York, the Jewish Workers Bund was founded in Russia. Cahan heard reports of secret printing presses and meetings in forests. Organizing strikes, attacking police, standing up against the *pogromchik*s — the lowly Jewish worker "had suddenly evinced a splendid worthiness and an astonishing courage," writes Cahan. After the 1903 Kishinev Massacre, when even Bund members fled Russia, Cahan was ready to receive them. In New York, the *Forward* became the Bund's "organ," Cahan writes, and his newspaper considered it "holy."

In New York, former Bund members, such as Morris Sigman, became bosses in the United Hebrew Trades, and used the *Forward* to tout their exploits and build their unions. There was a revolving door, what Cahan called an "interlocking directorate," between the *Forward* and the UHT. The UHT bosses, writes Tony Michels in *A Fire in Their Hearts: Yiddish Socialists in New York,* "possessed an acute awareness of themselves as historical actors, as if the fate of an entire people depended on what they said and did." In *Tailor's Progress,* Benjamin Stolberg writes: "The *Bundist* union leaders, having risen through aggressiveness from poverty, became fixed in a state of permanent astonishment at their own success, and fell in love with the limelight."

In America, the union bosses shared the view that there was no use for an honest labor boss if he couldn't settle a strike. The bosses carried out strikes in the most oppressive industries, such as the kosher bakeries, where employees worked eighteen-hour shifts in unventilated cellars. In the bakers' strike of 1909, the union bosses and their soldiers poured kerosene over nonunion bread, burned nonunion wagons to ash, and, armed with pipes, rode dumbwaiters down to the baking cellars, where the screams of scabs couldn't be heard. When that strike was settled, with lower hours and higher pay, the Bakers' Union gained eight thousand new members, and the UHT set its sights on the city's largest industry: garments.

What was good for the bosses was good for Cahan. In 1910, he built the ten-story Forward Building on East Broadway, where the illuminated FORWARD sign hung vertically off the façade like a giant glowing key. For the childless Cahan, the UHT bosses became like his brothers and sons. He created an expense account for them at the fancy Prince George Hotel on Twenty-Eighth Street, and the bosses met there over bourbon and claret to reminisce about the old country and strategize the labor wars. It was at the Prince George, in fact, where many UHT bosses were arrested in 1915.

Ultimately, seven UHT bosses, including Sigman, went on trial for the 1910 murder of the tailor Herman Liebowitz. In court, witness after witness recounted how Liebowitz had been clubbed to the ground and beaten to death in broad daylight, how the bosses ran the UHT like a terrorist organization, and how the *shtarker*s collected payment for assault and murder at the Forward Building.

When the Dope, a subject of so much fascination and fear, took the witness stand, he related his backstory. He was arrested for the first time at age nine, and did his first stint at the House of Refuge at twelve. "I learned my education in jail," he explained. At fourteen, he said, he was arrested for assault during a Jewish holiday: "It was kind of a celebration up in the synagogue and I started to celebrate and got myself in trouble." At fifteen, there was a disorderly conduct charge and a stint at Elmira Reformatory. At sixteen, he "rolled a lush," robbed a drunk, and did another seventeen months at Elmira. At eighteen, a hotel burglary sent him to Sing Sing for three years, and after he got out he met the union bosses. The Dope wanted to be the next Big Jack Zelig, beloved by the community, but Zelig never would have fallen for the lies of the UHT or harmed working people.

It was a tense trial, full of tragedy and vituperation. When the Dope's father, a tailor, took the witness stand, he berated the UHT for corrupting his son: "Everyone knows that boy isn't right in the head," he said, then turned to one defendant and said, "You son of a bitch, I have a mind to knock you down right here." The corruption was pretty clear, but prosecutors struggled to connect the defendants to the five-year-old murder, and the inherent dodginess of the witnesses, many of them admitted killers, didn't strengthen the case.

In the closing argument, the defense attorney said that garment workers had, until recently, been "the most miserable lot of workers which our city has ever possessed, so that as a result you have what you have seen here on the witness stand — a generation of stunted, puny, anemic, sickly individuals." The murder of Liebowitz wasn't committed for personal motives or revenge, he said — rather, it was "a logical incident to be explained by conditions and circumstances." In the end, the jury found the UHT bosses not guilty, and the bosses returned to Cahan's Forward Building for champagne and celebratory speeches.

Still, for Abe the trial was a success — the Dope and his sluggers were taken off the street, many of them facing long prison sentences, and the corruption of Cahan's Yiddish press was exposed.

That fall, Abe and Newburger were meeting in Rabbi Magnes's office when Abe said it was time that East Siders were allowed to vote for whomever they preferred, free of Tammany Hall intimidation. He and Newburger decided to organize a political club and run Newburger for a state senate seat. As news of their campaign spread, one of Abe's informants told him that Tammany's Charlie Murphy had offered him $2,500 to kill Abe. The informant warned that Murphy was going to give the job to someone else. That someone else, Abe learned, was Dopey Benny, whom Governor Whitman, still beholden to Murphy, planned to liberate from prison at the time of the primary.

On primary day, the Dope appeared on St. Mark's Place, where he observed a strange sight: orderly voting and police patrols. For a moment the outlaw and the vigilante locked eyes. Something unspoken passed between them. Apparently even the Dope, disillusioned as he was, realized that this was a new East Side, and he walked away.

After Newburger won the primary, Murphy sent for Abe's father and said, "What does that boy want? We'll make him the youngest congressman we ever had." Mayer passed the message along, and Abe said, "Tell him to drop dead."

Abe carried on against Tammany, chasing the high-level corruption that facilitated crime. One afternoon he was sitting in the Rector Street office when, through the window, he saw John Campbell, the magistrate who permitted the *shtarker*s to work with impunity, walking to lunch with a defense lawyer named Nattie Tolk. Recently Tolk had been indicted for precisely what Abe, in Kehillah reports, had accused him of doing all along: managing the elaborate apparatus, known as the bondman's graft, that kept the labor sluggers out of prison. Abe ran to the street and paid a photographer to shoot Campbell and Tolk arm in arm.

A few days later, the *Brooklyn Daily Eagle,* noting a surprise retirement, reported that "some mysterious influence is at work at City Hall to prevent the reappointment of the beloved magistrate John Campbell."

The downfall of Tolk and Campbell coincided with other symbols of the vice crusade's success. East Side "boy detectives"—supplied with badges, clubs, and whistles—helped victims of theft recover their property, called out bakeries for unsanitary practices, and took to the streets and alleys with brooms and trash carts. Young women, eighteen and over, formed "police squads" to monitor dance halls, reprimand tobacconists who sold to children, and report on ice cream parlors "patronized by men who make advances to young girls." A Rockefeller study found that what remained of New York prostitution was "precarious and unsuccessful." Prostitution would continue in New York, in tenements and discrete "call flats," but the city's red-light districts had been closed, rendering the red-light dramas of 1913 historical artifacts of the silent-film era.

After rejecting the offer by Bald Jack Rose to be in one such film, Lily published her own memoir, a four-part newspaper series entitled "The Story of an Underworld Wife." A newspaper said that Lily intended to relocate to Philadelphia and open a hat shop, "a business in which she seems fitted by a natural good taste." Before departing the city, when Lily visited her old friend Tony the Tough to say goodbye, she found an opium-addicted Tony "anxious for the inevitable end."

Their generation of immigrant women was stranded, caught between a history in which they had few rights and a liberated future that posed a perplexing array of questions for women. But thanks to the sacrifices of Tony and thousands of other immigrants, America was on a path to improved labor conditions and a social welfare safety net, developments that helped balance inequity and ease dependence on elite philanthropy. To the delight of Mayer Shoenfeld, the breadlines and soup kitchens all but disappeared from the East Side. In 1915, called to give testimony on labor relations, Mayer told Congress: "It's a fad nowadays to go to the East Side and magnify anything that's wrong in order to play to the galleries."

Future generations of Jewish-Americans would be severed from that fractious past, with little sense of German versus Russian, or uptown versus down. They were free, in the American way, to forget their origin story and fashion a new identity, even as the legacy of *il nostro get* lived on.

In the early morning hours of July 28, 1915, Charles Becker prepared to die at Sing Sing.

Down in the city, Charlie Murphy and his subordinates sat in the Tammany clubhouse on Fourteenth Street, holding vigil for the man who had stuck. Uptown, Arnold Rothstein held court at Jack's Oyster House, where his gold pocket watch lay on the tablecloth.

At 5:42 a.m., the narrow door to the death room swung open, and Becker, carrying a silver crucifix, stooped and entered. Strapped into the chair, he said: "The Lord have mercy upon me. I am sacrificed for my friends"—a statement that many interpreted as referring to Tammany leaders and the former police commissioner's secretary, Winnie Sheehan.* Becker's reputation had been destroyed, his wife had delivered a stillborn daughter, and his mother had died. "I forgive them all. And to those I have wronged, I beg forgiveness."

The Rosenthal Affair, which concluded with Becker's death, was a totem for those who hoped for a new moral purity in America, a purity they believed would be guaranteed by a growing slate of anti-vice laws— against gambling, prostitution, drugs, and alcohol. The *North American Review* hailed the "salutary effect" of Becker's demise and predicted that his execution would usher in "a time of regeneration." But not all believed it. The *World* predicted that there'd be "a new Becker, a resurrection of all the evil we thought we were burying." This pattern would be repeated, the *World* said, "so long as Anglo-Saxon hypocrisy persists in making felonious everything that it considers shocking, so long as it brands as crimes those practices which other broader-minded and equally civilized nations handle as public nuisances." The *New York Times* added, "The hypocrisy that pervades some of the nation's criminal laws, particularly those concerning such 'non-victim crimes' as gambling, and the refusal of society to confront this hypocrisy, is a larger scandal than that of the

---

* After accusations of graft forced his resignation from the NYPD, Winnie Sheehan hooked up with an old Tammany connection, the film mogul William Fox, and used the money he made from Jewish prostitution to become a partner in Fox Film. In 1929, Sheehan would freeze Fox out of his own company and become the new studio head. Sheehan discovered John Wayne, Rita Hayworth, and Shirley Temple. He also adapted the memoir by Carolyn Rothstein, *Now I'll Tell,* for a Fox film featuring Spencer Tracy and Temple in one of her first roles.

police payoffs. To effectively reform the police, it will be necessary to reform the laws the police are asked to enforce."

After Becker was pronounced dead, Charlie Murphy rose from his chair, reached for his hat, and said, "I guess it's over." What was over was Tammany's management of vice. Murphy walked out into a new world, in which local politicians would never again hold the kind of power that he and Big Tim Sullivan once wielded.

For Arnold Rothstein, that new world presented the opposite reality. As the gray-area banker who could underwrite crime and fix cases, he would have more power than ever. At Jack's, Arnold snapped his gold watch shut and said, "Let's go look for some action."

Part Four

Inevitable Chain

23

Subversive Might

IN AUGUST 1915, A MONTH AFTER CHARLES BECKER'S execution, Jacob Schiff and his daughter, Frieda Warburg, stole away for a father-daughter outing in Bar Harbor, Maine. Schiff owned a vacation home on Mount Desert Isle, making himself the first Jew to break into the great Wasp redoubt—and in a state where hotels and restaurants were closed to Jews and would remain so for years to come. As they walked, conversing in German, Frieda felt hostile stares. The onset of war in Europe meant that all things German, from Wagner to Wiener schnitzel, had become verboten in America. Frieda wrapped her arm around Schiff's elbow and pulled close the sixty-eight-year-old, whose hearing had long been in decline. "Father," she said, "we must do this no longer," and the Schiffs never spoke German in public again.

Schiff loved Mount Desert Isle and looked forward to the annual hikes he took there with Harvard president Charles Eliot. That summer, the war dominated their conversation and they weighed solutions, including a "negotiated peace" with Germany. But when Schiff later outlined this plan in letters to Eliot, the letters leaked out, and it was inferred that

Schiff—America's preeminent banker following the 1913 death of J. P. Morgan—wanted not peace but a German *victory,* and that his firm was a pro-German bank.

That fall, back in the city, Kuhn Loeb partners had a chance to dispel any notion that they sympathized with Germany. Britain's finance minister was in New York to solicit Wall Street for a half-billion-dollar loan on behalf of the Allies: England, France, and Russia. The loan seemed like a good idea to Otto Kahn, Schiff's second-in-command, who saw a chance to establish their allegiance. But Schiff felt differently. He couldn't bear to finance his nemesis, the czar, in a war against any country, least of all Germany. Schiff agreed to approve the loan but only on one condition: that not one cent of it go to Russia. "I realize fully what is at stake for the firm," Schiff told his partners. "But come what may, I cannot run counter to my conscience. I cannot stultify myself by aiding those who in bitter enmity have tortured my people and will continue to do so, whatever fine professions they may make in their hour of need."

After Britain declined the loan on Schiff's terms, the London *Times* featured Schiff's face next to the headline APOSTLE OF BERLIN, and, in America, the phrase "German-Jewish banker" entered public discourse as shorthand for "traitor." J. P. Morgan's son, Jack, refused to attend meetings at the Museum of Natural History with fellow board member Felix Warburg. "I cannot stand the German Jews and will not see them or have anything to do with them," Jack wrote. "In my opinion they have made themselves impossible as associates for any white people for all time."

In 1916, the Wasp elite found a new literary hero in Madison Grant, who reflected the Yankee obsession with lineage and destiny. In Grant's best-selling book *The Passing of the Great Race,* he replaced the soft social anti-Semitism of Edith Wharton's fiction with pseudoscientific racial diatribe and hard-line eugenic thinking. Nordics, Grant claimed, were the most recently evolved of all races, and, therefore, when a Nordic mated with a member of a more primitive race, the primitive genes overwhelmed the Nordic's superior-but-still-fragile genes. The mass immigration of recent decades, Grant wrote, was thus a "genetic invasion."

As Grant saw it, the threat from Blacks was mostly neutralized by state laws already on the books, such as prohibitions against interracial marriage, but the threat posed by the foreign-born was insidious. Grant worried about the tainted "germ plasm" of Jews, writing that their "dwarf stature, peculiar mentality, and ruthless concentration on self-interest are being engrafted upon the stock of the nation." Warning of "race suicide," he said, "We Americans must realize that the altruistic ideals and the maudlin sentimentalism that have made America an asylum for the oppressed are sweeping America toward a racial abyss."

As Abe Shoenfeld and Harry Newburger continued to report on crime, they seemed to absorb and reflect the racial paranoia enveloping the country, and they urged another vice crusade.

"We want the East Side clean!" Abe wrote to the Kehillah. "And while it is cleaner than any section of its kind, we want it in the condition that is beyond reproach, a place that will inspire and uplift and not degrade those who come into it, either by birth or migration." Abe had always been driven by shame, by the sense that his community was seen as racially less-than. But the crusading of his teens and early twenties — even when it tipped into vigilantism — had often been tempered by a sympathetic consciousness of the role that injustice played in creating the conditions he set out to alleviate. Now, as the country renewed its Jew hatred, that compassion seemed to cave, his vigilance transmogrifying into fear and bigotry. The city grew. Communities continued to mix. Southern Blacks of the Great Migration flowed into Harlem, joining Jews and Italians. Reporting on Harlem, Abe commented: "Here it is that our young girls and boys are mixed with the black. Here is the source of the coming black-and-tan generation. I cannot help thinking of the two white girls I saw breaking heroin pills with two black men in the rear of a saloon. I felt ashamed for the moment that I was a New Yorker, that I was an American."

Newburger, whose bid for the Senate never panned out, was also concerned with perception: "Our Christian neighbors are fully conscious of Jewish crime. These conditions are the very things in the minds of persons today who are attempting to secure legislation to restrict immigration. Only a few are giving expression to what they think, but these few have the silent approval of thousands and perhaps millions in back of them."

Rabbi Magnes passed these reports to the German-Jewish uptowners, but another vice crusade seemed like a waste of time. They felt they had handled the downtown problem. And still—as promised in 1913 by Louis Brandeis, now the first Jewish Supreme Court justice—the snake of immigration restriction returned. In early 1917, the literacy test for immigrants finally became law, and a few months later America joined the war to end all wars.

Under pressure, even Jacob Schiff came around to the pro-war view, and soon world affairs divided the Kehillah membership and Magnes. The years 1917 to 1921, historians say, are unmatched in American history for hysteria, xenophobia, and paranoid suspicion. At a time when the US attorney general, buttressed by the new Espionage and Sedition Acts, was telling Americans to keep their mouths shut lest they be imprisoned or deported, Magnes, ever the nonconformer, remained loudly pacifist.

Magnes refused to capitulate, and his brother-in-law, the lawyer Louis Marshall, tried to intercede: "You can be more effective if you do not cheapen yourself by permitting the rag, tag, and bobtail crowd to become too familiar with you," Marshall wrote to Magnes of his alliance with the antiwar agitators. When Magnes responded to these concerns by leading an antiwar rally at Madison Square Garden, Marshall wrote: "By taking such a prominent position in this agitation you are jeopardizing other interests which you have no right to imperil. You are the head of the Kehillah." But he was no longer. The Kehillah would soon be absorbed into the American Jewish Committee, and Magnes would have no role in it, and no power. Weeks after the antiwar rally, when Magnes asked Schiff to endorse a judgeship for Harry Newburger, Schiff lashed out, accusing Magnes of using him for his money, and their relationship never recovered.

In Magnes's office at the Hebrew Charities Building, Newburger took the news about the judgeship gracefully, but told Magnes that he was concerned about Abe: "I impress on him that he really ought to get out in search of a job," Newburger said. "But he feels that our old work is about to resume at any moment. I think it would be infinitely more merciful to tell him there is no hope." But Magnes declined to cut Abe loose, and Newburger tried his own tactic.

On June 17, as they wrapped up work at the Rector Street office, Newburger asked Abe to join him and a few lawyer friends for a road trip out to New Jersey and a steak dinner. He intended the dinner as a way to celebrate their five-year partnership and mark its end. Abe, now twenty-six and still a bachelor, didn't often decline such invitations, but he said he had work to do. It was a lucky choice. That night, on the way home from Jersey, the brakes on Newburger's auto failed. He skidded around a corner, hit an oncoming milk truck, and landed on his head. He spent the next six months in a coma, and the rest of his life as a department-store clerk. Abe believed the accident was retribution for the vice crusade, but was never able to prove it.

That summer, as America entered the war, Magnes managed to raise some money from the founders of the newly established Wall Street bank,

Salomon Brothers, to bankroll Abe in an investigation of the Jewish drug trade. The first federal antidrug law, the Harrison Act of 1914, had created a rich black market for cocaine, heroin, and opium, and many who appeared in Abe's drug reports were recognizable from Kehillah papers.

The "Silver & Ream combination" was a "firm" of former pickpockets and labor sluggers from the Dopey Benny gang, Abe wrote, and "Silver used to run hangout joints and crap games with Dollar John." A Jewish dealer in Philadelphia used to be "a pal of Lefty Louie and Jack Zelig," Abe noted, and now "travels with the widow of Lefty, a little blond girl who hasn't been seen on the East Side for quite some time" (which suggests that maybe Lily never opened that hat shop after all). In his overheated style, Abe argued: "The mind and body of Jewry are being attacked and poisoned. Are we to become a drug-crazed people, or shall we rise in battle and overcome this hydra?" With a squad behind him, he wrote, "I could do nationally with the drug problem what was done locally on the East Side. With enough time, help, money and power I could show such results that we never dreamed of."

But there was no one to read the drug reports. Magnes was moving his family to Jerusalem to establish Hebrew University, and would take with him the Kehillah file, about a hundred boxes documenting the East Side's wayward past. As for Schiff, he was working with President Wilson to finance the war via Liberty Bonds, bonds that were sold to US citizens, generating $17 billion.

These bonds were liquid, as good as cash, and invited crime. Messenger boys who ran around Wall Street dispatching the bonds were slugged and robbed. One robber, when apprehended, said he'd never met "the mastermind" behind the Liberty Bond thefts, the person who fenced the millions in stolen bonds, someone known to him only as "Mr. Arnold."

During the war years, Arnold Rothstein became so powerful that he could shoot two cops, albeit by accident, as he did during the raid of a craps game in January 1919, and walk away. The cop-shooting case set a precedent that few who dealt with Arnold forgot. A magistrate named McQuade dismissed the charges, then turned around and charged the detective who testified against Arnold with perjury. Arnold returned the favor immediately when he served as middleman in the 1919 sale of the New York Giants to three purchasers: the Giants coach, John McGraw, whose pool hall Arnold had haunted as a youngster; a bucket-shop owner whose business Arnold protected; and Magistrate McQuade.

Later that year, on a rainy day in early October, Arnold's status in the world of sports and betting was on his mind when he walked through the lobby of the Ansonia Hotel and entered the smoke-filled Green Room, where a telegraph system was set up to relay the first game of the World Series. An announcer read reports of the play-by-play, while a woman stood next to a diamond-shaped chart, altering numbers and arrows. When the leadoff batter for the underdog Cincinnati Reds came to the plate, the White Sox pitcher Eddie Cicotte kicked into his looping windup. Cicotte, a veteran hurler known for his superb control, had won a league-leading twenty-nine games in 1919, and here he was, in his first pitch of the World Series, *hitting* the batter. The hit batter was the sign that Arnold was looking for—the sign that eight White Sox players were on board with the fix. He plunked down another $100,000 on the under-dog Reds to win.

In June of 1920, the German-Jewish uptowners met in New York. The Kehillah had been usurped by the American Jewish Committee but the AJC membership was more or less identical, as was the dilemma the elders confronted: Another public figure was blasting invective. What to do?

An economic boom had powered America through the Great War, but whatever unity the war and its riches engendered dissipated when it ended, and a belief spread that a conspiracy of New York Jews, who were self-interested capitalists *and* un-American communists, had pushed the country into war. They were responsible for the Bolshevism that, by war's end, had overthrown the czar in Russia and would soon perform a similar feat in America, it was alleged.

During the first half of 1920, this nativist anxiety culminated in two events. The first was the implementation of Prohibition. The second event, which began at the same time Prohibition took effect, was the Red Scare, the most extensive peacetime violation of civil liberties in American history. The Department of Justice raided the meeting places and homes of Russian immigrants in twelve cities, but the focus was New York, where hundreds were incarcerated and deported. The attorney general who ordered the raids said the DOJ needed to collect information about radicals in order to meet the threat posed by "the aliens on the steerage steamers" and "a small clique of autocrats from the East Side of New York."

Now, in June, as the Red Scare raids died down, one of America's biggest industrialists took the lead in Jew hatred. Henry Ford purchased a moribund newspaper called the *Dearborn Independent* and converted it into an anti-Semitic bullhorn. That summer, Ford's paper published a series of articles entitled "The International Jew: The World's Problem." The articles described Jacob Schiff and the Warburgs as modern examples of medieval Jewish archetypes, deicidal monsters who sought to apportion the world between them. The fact that most Americans had never heard of "the New York Kehillah," that "center of Jewish world power," was "testimony to its subversive might."

The AJC was divided about what to do. The lawyer, Louis Marshall, favored an aggressive response. For years he'd been running around the country playing whack-a-mole. In Atlanta, when a German-Jewish factory manager named Leo Frank was convicted, without evidence, of murdering a thirteen-year-old employee named Mary Phagan, Marshall raised money for Frank's appeal. When Frank's sentence was commuted to life imprisonment, a priest and two former judges formed the Knights of Mary Phagan, kidnapped Frank from jail, and lynched him. The Knights of Mary Phagan seeded the reemergence of the Knights of the Ku Klux Klan.

Marshall urged the AJC to fight Ford, but Jacob Schiff, his health failing, warned against "lighting a fire." Let it pass, Schiff advised. The controversy didn't pass, though, so Marshall wrote to the editor of the *Dearborn Independent*. He said the "International Jew" articles "constitute a libel upon an entire people" and called them "echoes from the dark middle ages." The editor replied: "Your rhetoric is that of a Bolshevik orator. These articles shall continue and we hope you will continue to read them and when you have a more tolerable state of mind we shall be glad to discuss them with you."

Ford's paper stepped up its attacks. In July, it began to serialize *The Protocols of the Learned Elders of Zion*. A forged document, published in Russia and recently translated into English, the *Protocols* purported to be the plans of a secret Jewish cabal for world domination. Adapting the message of the *Protocols,* the paper alleged that Jews controlled film, music, and theater, and that they had wrecked America's pastime: "Jewish gamblers corrupt American baseball, and every non-Jewish baseball manager lives in fear of the Jews, particularly that slick Jew Arnold Rothstein."

That summer, as the "International Jew" series gained readers, a case began to build against Arnold for fixing the 1919 World Series. Several White Sox players, including the pitcher Eddie Cicotte and the outfielder "Shoeless Joe" Jackson, implicated Arnold in their confessions.

Arnold denied it, telling the *World*: "My friends know that I have never been connected with a crooked deal in my life, but I am heartily sick and tired of having my name dragged in on the slightest provocation whenever a scandal comes up. I have been victimized more than once and have been forced to bear the burden as best I could, simply because of the business that I was in and the peculiar moral code which governs it. . . . It is not pleasant to be what some may call a 'social outcast,' and for the sake of my family and my friends I am glad that this chapter is closed."

This blithe arrogance did little to close the chapter, and the *New York Times* mocked him: "With patience at last exhausted, one Arnold Rothstein, who seems to be a man of commanding eminence in the circles in which he moves, has decided to give no more excuse to the censorious. For years and years he has lived and prospered on the profits of what 'some may call' criminal activities, and the only penalty has been the linking of his name with all the current scandals! One can easily imagine how annoying that would be to him."

Arnold screamed at his lawyer: "I want you to stop this noise!" His lawyer urged him to go to Chicago and testify before the grand jury. "Are you crazy? Of all the dopey advice I ever had, and I'm paying you for it!" But the lawyer had a plan to make the case go away: since Arnold's exposure meant baseball's exposure, no one who had a financial stake in baseball wanted it to become common knowledge that gambling was rampant.

In Chicago, a photo captured the thirty-eight-year-old Arnold emerging from his chauffeured auto, surrounded by press, and striding toward the courthouse. He's dressed in a suit and bow tie. A Sennett boater is tilted on his head. His hands are joined around a piece of folded paper, which he palms like a hand of cards. On the witness stand, he unfolded the paper and asked to read the prepared statement. "I've come here to vindicate myself," he began. "If I wasn't sure I was going to be vindicated, I would have stayed home." The prosecutor treated Arnold like a friendly witness, and in such an atmosphere he became relatively loquacious, speaking of his love for baseball and his longtime friendship with John McGraw.

The case was never resolved, not after the minutes of the grand jury hearings and the players' confessions disappeared, ensuring that the so-called Black Sox Scandal would become one of the most enduring mysteries in American sport. For the *Dearborn Independent,* there was no mystery at all: "If fans wish to know the trouble with American baseball, they have it in three words — too much Jew."

Far from a local crackpot paper, the *Dearborn Independent* would soon reach a peak circulation of seven hundred thousand readers. It must have been strange for Jacob Schiff, in the final months of his life, to see his name bandied about in those pages alongside that of Arnold Rothstein. And yet there was an earlier period in Jewish history when the attributes of a Schiff and a Rothstein could have existed in one figure.

The "court Jew" emerged in Germanic lands in the late 1600s. This was a period, following the Thirty Years War, when the old moral conception of the state, founded on the teachings of the Church, was being supplanted by an all-powerful ruler, a duke or prince, whose state competed for population and wealth. For guidance, the Germanic rulers looked to Holland, Europe's most liberal country: there, the Jewish refugees who'd been expelled from Spain now flourished. If one believed, as many did, that the decline of Spain was due to its expulsion of Jews, and that Holland owed its superiority in trade to Jewish immigration, then a state's path to success was obvious. As the Christian moneylending ban gave way to capitalism, Jewish merchants and moneylenders were viewed in a different light. Their image didn't change, ipso facto, but their necessity was no longer in dispute.

In Germanic lands, court Jews — or *Hofjuden* — broke out of the ghetto as all-purpose entrepreneurs. For the local prince or duke, they ran money mints and gambling houses; established modern credit systems; funded armies and supplied them with munitions from Poland; and imported the luxury wares, such as silk from France and spices from the Middle East, that made the courts models of consumerist aspiration.

In return for these services, the court Jew was taken under the protection of the prince. Instead of the badge and long dark cloaks of the ghetto Jew, court Jews wore the vibrant short clothes and wigs of nobles, while their wives dressed in the high fashion of many-colored garments with puffed sleeves and long trains. They owned multiple houses and furnished them with well-stocked libraries and works of art that rivaled those of the princes. In *The Court Jew,* Selma Stern writes that these figures "took on qualities of aristocratic society: an exaggerated *Ichgefuehl,* an egoism which found satisfaction only in ceaseless activity and in personal success, and an extraordinary degree of self-confidence."

Positioned between the Christian aristocracy and the Jewish ghetto, court Jews were known to combine kindness and brutality, idealism and cold calculation, a lust for power and loyal devotion. In *The Jews of Germany: A Story of Sixteen Centuries,* Marvin Lowenthal writes: "The Court Jews were more than acute businessmen or picturesque gamblers. Their privileged status enabled them to act as pioneers reopening territory long closed to the Jews." Part of their vanity was pride of leadership, the role they took on as shtadlanim—representatives who used bribery, emotional appeals, and political leverage to ease life for their co-religionists, including those of the criminal class. In the early 1700s, when organized bands of Jewish thieves, such as the infamous Long Hoyum, roamed Germanic lands, cutting purses and robbing factories, many *Gauner* and *Spitzbuben*—crooks and scoundrels—found shelter as servants to court Jews, who in turn fenced the stolen goods.

The most famous court Jew was Joseph "Jud" Suess. In the Germanic state of Württemberg, when Duke Karl Alexander wanted to expand and modernize, he turned to Suess, a merchant and banker, for the resources to do it. Under Duke Alexander's protection, Suess became an influential figure in Württemberg, and a giant target for the intolerant German masses, the Puritans who believed in witches and wizards, who saw devilry in capitalism and regarded the court Jew as a threat to their privileges. To the Puritans, competitive business tactics, such as advertising and underselling, were the techniques of lying Jews.

Suess was aware that everyone in Duke Alexander's entourage wanted to oust him. His letters were full of bitter complaints about the prejudice he encountered, the plots prepared against him, and his premonitions of a horrible fate. The duke dismissed these fears as figments of his friend's imagination. But after the duke died in 1737, Jud Suess was arrested, his property was confiscated, and he was put on trial for treason and hanged.

In October 1920, as Arnold testified in Chicago, the Dearborn Publishing Company put out a bound anthology of its "International Jew" series. Dozens of editions appeared in Germany, where one soldier believed that "speculative" capital as opposed to "productive" capital was at the root of Germany's troubles. In the appeal to break "interest slavery," Adolf Hitler saw an essential premise for the foundation of a new party. As Hitler built that party, he kept a photo of Ford on the wall of his Munich office, and said, "I regard Henry Ford as my inspiration."

24

A Tool Like You

IN NOVEMBER 1920, WEEKS AFTER HIS TESTIMONY IN Chicago, Arnold invited an eighteen-year-old named Meyer Lansky to dinner. Arnold had met Lansky, who was small and hungry-looking, at a bar mitzvah for the son of mutual friends. There Lansky gushed to Arnold about how much he admired his sophistication and the way he became a powerful figure in "upper-class society." But Lansky had his own talents. His mixed gang of Jewish and Italian immigrants ran gambling and thieving operations on the East Side, and had recently defended their territory against a Sicilian don who tried to muscle in. Also, Lansky was a skilled mechanic in the decade when mass production of autos, now commonly called cars, would revolutionize American life and refashion its criminals.

Over dinner, Arnold made a proposition to Lansky. The big-con days were fading due to the rise of radio. Communication was speeding up. Information flowed. For a con such as the wire, a fake off-track betting parlor, you could no longer "rope a mark" by telling him you had a corrupt Western Union official to delay the results of a race. The con men of

Arnold's earlier days — like Ratsy Tourbillon, Nicky Arnstein, and GG Rice — were becoming, as the twenties dawned, anachronisms. They were in prison, on the run, or mired in litigation. But the newest anti-vice law held out new opportunities, Arnold told Lansky. Now that booze was illegal, people would pay anything to get the best Scotch whisky, Arnold said, because it was the chic thing to have "the good stuff" to give to your guests, and a lot of it. Prohibition imbued drinking with new meaning. A drunk was no longer an embarrassment. He was a champion of liberty against tyrannical government, a fighter for individuality in a cowardly and conforming world. As Lansky recalled, "Everybody I knew treated Prohibition with contempt."

A fortune could be made by meeting the demand, and Arnold said he had a way to get the Scotch shipped from England to an area just outside the three-mile line, off Long Island's Montauk Point. Arnold offered Lansky and his crew the job of distribution, getting the booze from ship to shore to clientele. "It's illegal, of course, and will require running risks, but I don't think you mind that," Arnold said, and asked Lansky to discuss it with his friends.

The next day, Lansky introduced Arnold to the twenty-three-year-old Charlie Lucania, a Sicilian immigrant who had grown up on the East Side, where he mixed with both Jews and Italians. Among the insular Sicilians, Lucania, who would be known to posterity as Lucky Luciano, was unique. He looked askance at his native underworld culture, at his Sicilian elders, or Mustache Petes, whom Lucania called "shitheels." He poked fun at their dated clothes and bulging bellies, their guttural accents and ancient vendettas. He saw them as too set in their ways, too shortsighted and greedy. He liked the traditions and values of Jews. As a youngster he ran errands for a Jewish garment manufacturer who regularly invited Lucania to his home for Sabbath dinner and once helped get him out of the reformatory when he was arrested for drugs.

Arnold said, "We should sell the whisky in the original bottles, unadulterated. This way you'll reach a discerning clientele. And no stigma will be attached to you as being real criminals. Believe me, it's the right way for you to set out on your careers."

Lansky and Lucania looked at one another, then turned to Arnold and with one voice said, "Count us in."

During the next six months, a freighter made ten trips across the Atlantic, carrying twenty thousand cases of King's Ransom Scotch each time, and by the summer of 1921, eighteen months into Prohibition, the Lansky-Lucania gang were among the country's first modern gangsters. Arnold retreated from direct involvement, but bootlegging wealth turned him into a colossus of the gambling world even as his new affiliations cut him off from the business elite of that world.

In the summer of 1921, after Arnold won two record-setting bets at the track, August Belmont Jr., owner of Belmont Racetrack, wanted to put distance between himself and Arnold. He didn't mind Arnold's winning, or his cheating. Cheating was common.

The problem, for Belmont, was that bookmaking on the Lawn operated under the sheerest veil of legality, and if politicians looking for publicity ever wanted to investigate racetrack gambling, Arnold's reputation as a bootlegger and fixer of the Series would give them good reason to start. Belmont wanted to bar Arnold from the track, but the politics were thorny. He feared Arnold's power, knowing that Arnold could use his political connections to plug up the legal-betting loophole as easily as he had helped create it back in 1913.

When Arnold heard the news that Belmont wanted to boot him, he rushed to Wall Street to see Belmont in his office. Belmont said it hurt the sport to have such a conspicuous figure around. "You know what people are saying, Arnold. Half the country believes you were the man who fixed the World Series." Arnold was indignant. The stories about him, he said, were exaggerated. After he threatened to spend a million dollars to shut down New York racetracks, they compromised: Arnold promised to go to the track only on Saturdays and holidays.

One non-Saturday, Belmont was strolling in the paddock when he spotted Arnold and asked what he was doing there. Arnold said it was a holiday. A holiday? "Why yes, you ought to know, Mr. Belmont. It's Rosh Hashanah."

From his early days as a gambler, when the Hart-Agnew legislation gave him his first shot at handling a legal gray area, Arnold symbolized the blurry schism between the truth of America and its longing for purity and legitimacy, a national passion that was sharpened by the Great War.

To justify America's entry into the war, George Creel, of the Committee on Public Information, advertised America and its values to the world. In *How We Advertised America,* Creel writes that until the war, the little American news that reached foreign lands tended to concern "murder cases, graft prosecutions, sensational divorces, the bizarre extravagance of 'sudden millionaires.' Naturally enough, we were looked upon as a race of dollar-mad materialists, a land of cruel monopolists, our real rulers the corporations and our democracy a 'fake.'" Creel adds, referring to the Rosenthal Affair: "When the 'gunmen' were executed in New York, papers in South America actually printed accounts that told of an admission fee being charged, with Governor Whitman taking tickets at the door."

The war and its aftermath — a new world order with the United States on top — required a wholesome America, a place of irrefutable ideals. Clear-cut moral reform, it was thought, would replace nebulous morality with the universal good of "set truth." Instead, absolute vice repression carved a pattern of lies into American life. Corruption was no longer a local matter for neighborhood machine bosses, but a big federal game run from the top. In Philadelphia, a federal prosecutor wrote that the legal system there became demoralized in the first year of Prohibition, as politicians fought to be the state director of Prohibition so they could trade legal protection for campaign donations. It was the same in Washington, DC. When Ohio's Warren Harding, who won the presidency by supporting Prohibition, made his campaign manager, Harry Daugherty, the US attorney general, Daugherty used the office to sell protection to bootleggers.

In this new age of corporatized vice, when a sharper line was drawn between the underworld and the overworld, between Arnold and Belmont Jr., Arnold once again flowed with the times. He decided to imitate the Belmonts of the world and join them where they lived. In the fall of 1921, weeks after his confrontation with Belmont, he launched Redstone Holding Company and leased three buildings on West Fifty-Seventh Street, annexing much of the block between Fifth and Sixth Avenues for office space and apartments, stores and loft showrooms. He became the force behind a sprawling empire that would include Pan-Continental Film, Texas Oil, Rothmere Realty, and Redstone Material & Supply, twenty-six companies in all. Redstone headquarters didn't resemble a Wall Street banking firm — it was more exposed brick than austere mahogany — but it employed secretaries, accountants, and lawyers.

After work, Arnold walked to his new haunt, Lindy's, a Broadway deli known for its cheesecake and smoked-tongue sandwiches. The prewar lobster palaces like Jack's were disappearing, another casualty of Prohibition. Lindy's, with its window display of gift baskets and takeout items, represented the scaled-down dining scene of the postwar city. One regular, Harpo Marx, categorized the Lindy's crowd as "cardplayers, horse-players, bookies, song pluggers, agents, actors out of work and actors playing the Palace, Al Jolson with his mob of fans, and Arnold Rothstein with his mob of runners and flunkies."

Arnold once said that he would rather be a king of rats than a rat of kings, and at Lindy's he was king. Of his status there one writer recalled, "They always knew that in case of serious argument the person opposed to Rothstein would get the worst of it, and without Rothstein raising a hand"—meaning that no one challenged Arnold, because other patrons, eager to do him a favor, would eliminate a problematic person without being asked. "His vanity was overwhelming, but since he had real abilities upon which to rest it, his outward aspect merely was that of a man entirely sure of himself."

Arnold sat down, and the proprietor delivered a stack of messages. He read the notes, then tore them up, placed the shreds in an ashtray, and lit them on fire. The fire was the sign that he was ready to see those waiting for him, who, armed with an idea, approached his table one by one. To each he said, "Tell me the story."

Some wanted to carry out a heist, fence stolen jewelry, run bootleg liquor, or bet on a sure thing. Other investments were legitimate. His friends the Selwyn brothers, who cofounded Goldwyn Pictures, the future MGM, borrowed $56,348.10 for a movie theater in Times Square. For $25,000 he underwrote a play called *Abie's Irish Rose,* about a Jewish boy who defies his father by marrying an Irish girl. The play turned out to be the biggest Broadway hit of the so-called Theatrical Twenties, earning its author millions.

Other deals were attractive for their synergies. When Arnold's brother-in-law pitched him on a restaurant chain, he agreed to fund the venture, provided that the first restaurant be located in the lobby of his Fifty-Seventh Street building. Similarly, when a favorite tailor faced bankruptcy, Arnold spent $40,000 to install a tailoring shop at Fifty-Seventh Street, then made everyone who owed him money go there to buy a new suit. He often requested that loan seekers become his tenants, and when he saw someone on the street who was under obligation to him, he might ask, "Where are you living these days?" "The hotel so-and-so," might be the reply. "Why, you must be mad," Arnold would say. "You move right over to my place." After he filled the residential space on Fifty-Seventh Street, he purchased the Fairfield Hotel on Seventy-Second Street and converted it into apartments.

To guarantee the loans he made, Arnold partnered with a legitimate businessman named A. L. Libman. He set Libman up as the president of a life insurance company and took out policies on his borrowers. That way, if the borrower got killed, the debt would be paid. If a borrower didn't pay, the insurance payout would cover the price on their head—the cost of having the debtor knocked off, and in such a way that made the death appear accidental. Taking out life insurance on third parties, which was legal at the time, protected investments that involved large capital and high risk, such as bootlegging and drug smuggling. To Arnold, the drug trade was just another business, and many criminals he worked with, such as Charlie Lucania, were involved.

His heirs, Lucania and Lansky, called Arnold "the Ph.D.," an abbreviation of the Yiddish expression *Papa hat gelt*—Father has money, or dough—and hung on his every word. He urged them to look at the way big business was run and copy those methods. They set up a corporate office and organized their bootlegging business, with departments for logistics, bribery, intelligence, and defense. Arnold took Lucania shopping and made over the thug with oxford gray suits, white silk shirts, and dark-blue ties.

"Arnold give me a whole new image," Lucania later recalled, "and it had a lotta influence on me. He taught me how to dress, how not to wear loud things but to have good taste. He taught me how to use knives and forks and things at the dinner table, taught me about holdin' a door open for a girl or helpin' her sit down by holdin' the chair. He was the best etiquette teacher a guy could ever have—real smooth."

If these criminals believed they would merge seamlessly into corporate America, it was because their elite clientele treated them as Arnold predicted, not as corruptors of public morals but as stewards of the public interest. The elites wanted their liquor, and they didn't care what chance the other fellow took to get it, so long as it wasn't their risk.

Lansky preferred to hang back, but Lucania enjoyed mixing with their rich and powerful customers. He developed a passion for golf and earned a low handicap at the country clubs where his liquor stocked the bars. One customer, a member of the Whitney family, invited Lucania to his Long Island estate to watch him play polo and supply the party afterward. At the party, young women gathered around Lucania and asked him about being a bootlegger. What was it like to hijack shipments? To shoot it out with rivals?

One admirer asked him to drive her home, Lucania recalled. "When we got to her old man's estate, we drove through the gates and there was about a mile of grass on both sides of the driveway. She reaches over and turns off the ignition, pulls me outta the car and practically made me screw her right there on the grass. All the time we're doin' it, she's yellin', 'Hijack me! Hijack me!'"

At Arnold's Fifty-Seventh Street office there was one employee, a "hunchback" known as Moe Tear (as in rip), who sat behind three desks stacked high with newspapers, kept his boss apprised of events, and helped spot opportunities. Arnold enjoyed certain kinds of news, such as stories about bankers loaning money to revolutionaries and financing foreign wars. He both envied and resented the persnickety bankers, who waded through blood for a score and then, on the way home to their estates, convinced themselves of their honesty and prudence.

The equivocations of corporate America intrigued Arnold, and he felt at home in its murky reflection. Like the businessmen, he could theorize and analyze, attack and withdraw, joke and smile and run away. In the end, though, the bankers were bankers, and no fidelity to conservative elegance could obscure the fact that Arnold, in this new era, was something else. Banished to the netherworld, he could no longer be a big man among big men, and this ate at him.

The big men treated him with disdain. When Harry Daugherty, the US attorney general who sold protection to bootleggers, learned that his son, a troubled war veteran, was working for Arnold Rothstein's insurance company, Daugherty called and asked what his son was doing in such pernicious surroundings. "Arnold was annoyed by the lad's father," Carolyn recalled. He thought that by giving the son a job he was doing a favor for Daugherty, an old friend.

Even as Arnold's empire grew, he nursed a sense of grievance, a conviction that he was unfairly maligned and that everyone turned their back on him when they got what they wanted or when his friendship became inconvenient. It wasn't just Belmont and Daugherty who blew him off. Often, an aspiring judge and his wife would dine with Arnold and Carolyn until the hoped-for judicial post was attained, then pretend not to know the Rothsteins.

If his exposure for his role in the Series hurt him, a greater embarrassment came in the fall of 1923, when he was forced to testify in the bankruptcy of a bucket shop called E. M. Fuller, whose demise was the biggest brokerage-house failure of the postwar era, leaving 1,600 duped clients wanting to know what had happened to their $5 million in investments.

During the years of E. M. Fuller's operation, Arnold collected $366,768 from checks drawn on E. M. Fuller's account. These checks created the appearance that Arnold was financing Fuller's scheme, that they were repayments on his investment. But Arnold claimed the checks were payments for gambling debts, including bets that Eddie Fuller placed with Arnold on the 1919 World Series. The attorney for the creditors decided to accept this narrative, and see if he could use it to his

Equine tragedy and "horse removal" (above) were common features of prewar city life. The horse poisoners impressed the underworld by exacting large sums from Adams Express (below), the toughest trucking company in Manhattan. *(Author's collection)*

Meanwhile, other gangsters worked for the Jewish garment unions, as labor sluggers, or *shtarker*s. During strikes, *shtarker*s assaulted and murdered scab workers and the garment manufacturers who employed them. Here, a maker of men's shirts resisted union demands, and paid the ultimate price. *(New York City Municipal Archives)*

The *shtarker*s were supported by the *Forward* newspaper. In 1912, editor Abraham Cahan (right) built the ten-story Forward Building at 175 East Broadway. The beaux arts masterpiece was the East Side's tallest structure. *(Author's collection)*

LOUIS ROSENBERG

After their convictions in the Rosenthal case, Charles Becker and Louie Rosenberg were put to death in the electric chair at Sing Sing (below). Becker was the first American cop to receive the death penalty. *(Author's collection)*

By 1915, it was said that there was a new East Side. Above, girls walk to school unmolested. Below, youngsters clean the streets. *(Author's collection)*

East Siders shopped and played ball in pickpocket-free streets. *(Author's collection)*

The Orchard Street market (above), once considered repellent, became an attraction for non-locals and tourists. Below, Cherry Street scrapped its rough-and-tumble image from the horse-poisoner days. *(Author's collection)*

On October 1, 1919, fans pack Times Square to watch the first game of the World Series broadcast on the side of the Times Building. The outfielder "Shoeless Joe" Jackson, batting fourth for the Chicago White Sox, later confessed to throwing the Series, which Arnold Rothstein was accused of fixing. *(Author's collection)*

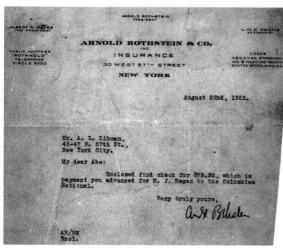

In the twenties, Arnold's many businesses encompassed a life insurance company, A. L. Libman, which issued its own stock. Above, forty-six-year-old Arnold in 1928, the year of his death. *(Author's collection)*

Arnold's empire mimicked corporate America, but his multifarious enterprise meant
that his name was known to stock brokers (above) and drug cops alike. In the NYPD
narcotics room (opposite page, above), a rogue's gallery of drug dealers sits atop a glass case
containing samples of opium, morphine, heroin, cannabis, hash, cocaine, and other drugs.
(Author's collection)

Arnold's wife, Carolyn (below right, at fifty, ten years after Arnold's death) and his girlfriend, Inez Norton (below left, at thirty, five years after Arnold's death) published memoirs of their experiences with him. *(Author's collection)*

When Abe Shoenfeld wrote about the underworld, a ban of his novel earned the book a place in his favorite institution. Above, the New York Public Library's Rose Main Reading Room in 1911, the year it opened. Below, Abe in 1968, at seventy-seven, with his wife, Annie Evans. *(Author's collection)*

advantage. If the creditors could prove that Arnold had cheated Fuller in gambling, taking bets on a Series he fixed, then maybe they could claw back the money. This strategy was a long shot, given that Arnold had never been convicted of fixing the Series, but four years had passed and new evidence of his role in the fix had come to light.

On the witness stand, he remained bland and serene, appearing compliant while avoiding direct answers — until the attorney asked him if he knew William Kelly. "What's that got to do with this case?" Arnold snapped.

"He's a lawyer, isn't he?"

"I know him as something else," Arnold said. "I think he's a blackmailer, to tell you the facts."

In fact, Kelly had come into possession of the "lost" affidavits implicating Arnold in the Series fix, and he blackmailed Arnold for $53,000. When the attorney asked Arnold if the $53,000 paid to Kelly represented legal fees, Arnold lashed out: "This is no place to ask that kind of question. You ought to be ashamed. Before I'd be a tool like you are I'd jump in the Hudson River." The attorney bore down. Arnold's hostility grew.

> *I'd like to know who's paying you to ask me these questions.*
> *The next thing you'll be blaming the Japanese earthquake on me.*
> *There must be something the matter with these cough drops you're eating.*

In public Arnold rarely revealed an emotion he didn't wish to, but now he cracked. That unruffled repartee, famous of Broadway nights, became, in the cold light of day, the badinage of a wounded boy. The creditors failed to claw back their money, but the Fuller case touched off a crisis in Arnold. Unlike his staged and controlled testimony in Chicago regarding the Series fix, his raw response to this grilling betrayed fear and vulnerability.

One night after testifying, he was unwinding with a game of high-stakes poker and won a huge hand on a bluff. There was a time when such a betting coup would've gotten him high as a junkie, but now he felt nothing save the compulsion to keep betting. Returning home, he told Carolyn there was something inside him that kept driving him but he didn't know what it was, and that was a terrible feeling, he realized, because if you didn't know what you wanted then how did you know when you got it?

In late 1923, after Arnold's first round of testimony in the Fuller case was concluded (the case would tie him up for years), his younger brother, Jack, came to the Fifty-Seventh Street office with information regarding the Rothstein family that helped draw Arnold out of his funk. Jack said that their father, Abe the Just, had lost everything in the 1922 collapse of the cotton-goods market and needed a quarter of a million dollars to avoid bankruptcy.

Ever since Arnold's marriage to Carolyn, he and his father had seen each other occasionally, usually when Arnold came to the family house on Eighty-Fourth Street, near where he and Carolyn now lived, to lavish Jack and his sister, Edith, with gifts. But for Arnold these visits never really felt like coming home, since he communicated with Abe the Just through a chilly fog of suspicion and resentment. Now, the idea that he, Arnold, could help his father — his immaculate father, whom US Supreme Court justice Louis Brandeis had extolled at a 1919 testimonial dinner in honor of Abe's selfless work as a mediator in garment-industry disputes — well ... the idea was irresistible. "Tell him to go to the U.S. Bank tomorrow and ask for the loan," he told Jack.

"But if Papa knows it's your money, he won't take it," Jack said.

"He won't know whose money it is unless you tell him," Arnold said.

Still, it didn't take long for Abe the Just to figure out what had happened, and the incident brought about a rapprochement. The experience of falling on hard times had humbled Abraham Rothstein, while, for Arnold, helping his father made him feel like an equal.

"Now, when Arnold wanted to escape the noisy street life he'd come home and eat something at his mother's table," Abe the Just recalled of their new dynamic. "And then he'd become like a baby. He'd fool around, call me Pop. He'd tell me interesting facts he picked up in life, something that happened somewhere, or some illuminating encounter. And then, in the middle of a warm and hearty conversation, he would suddenly run to the telephone to call this one and that one: ten, fifteen calls, one after another."

Reuniting with his father gave Arnold new ideas about reclaiming the respectability of prior days. Sitting in his office one day, flipping through news clippings, he read that the prestigious Arbitration Society of America was searching for a new home. Arnold decided to submit an offer of free space on Fifty-Seventh Street, and for good measure he enclosed a $500 contribution to the ASA. He even suggested renaming the place the Arbitration Society Building, or perhaps the Hall of Justice, but no response came back.

25

It's a Racket!

IN EARLY 1924, WHEN THE LAWYER LOUIS MARSHALL went to Washington to make his case for open borders, the preponderance of Jewish bootleggers was a concern for Marshall and others in his uptown circle. Later, history would place Italians at the center of bootlegging, but more than half of America's major bootleggers were Eastern European Jews. In Boston, bootlegging was dominated by Charles "King" Solomon. Waxey Gordon covered Philadelphia. In Detroit, booze was supplied by the all-Jewish Purple Gang. Solly Weissman controlled bootlegging in Kansas City. A syndicate run by Moe Dalitz, Morris Kleinman, and Louis Rathkopf distributed liquor across Ohio and Pennsylvania. From Canada, the Russian-Jewish Sam Bronfman exported upward of fifty thousand gallons of whiskey per month to the States.

"Every Jewish bootlegger does more harm to the Jews as a body than all the [Henry] Fords could possibly inflict with their falsehoods, libels and slanders," Marshall wrote. In general, as Jewish-Americans became successful during the twenties, Marshall was more inclined to criticize them.* For instance, when universities instituted quotas to keep their Jewish populations down, Marshall, who fielded endless requests to intervene in battles between school administrations and Jewish students, believed the students should cool their heels. "They are always looking for grievances and seem to relish the idea of being martyrized," he wrote. "There is nothing more unfortunate than to acquire the persecution complex."

The reputational damage caused by Jewish bootleggers, on the other hand, was serious. As one German Jew wrote to Marshall, it was a *shande,* an embarrassment that "lent itself to willful misrepresentation on the part of our enemies." And it did. In Washington, when Marshall urged the House Immigration Committee to consider the effects of immigration restriction on Eastern European refugees, a congressman reminded Marshall that Jews were among the nation's foremost violators of Prohibition.

The snake had returned. Marshall was in Washington because Congress was voting on the Immigration Restriction Act, which was an update to the Emergency Quota Act of 1921, which was itself an update to the Literacy Act of 1917. These laws trended toward total restriction, and now, in testimony to the immigration committee about the new proposed act, Americanization and purity were the explicit themes.

We must strive for homogeneity among the citizenship. Therein lies the strength of a republic.

America cannot exist with a large number of communities where a foreign language is spoken and where foreign ideas prevail.

---

* The country's population of Russian Jews now dwarfed that of the German Jews. As those successful Russian Jews moved uptown, the elite congregation at Temple Emanu-El prepared to move its house of worship twenty blocks north. The ostensible reason for the move was Midtown noise, but it was also an attempt to dissociate from the uptown flow of former East Siders. Ironically, the new temple's first service would be for Marshall's funeral, and the eulogy would be delivered by Emanu-El's first Russian-Jewish head rabbi.

The aim of immigration policy should be to eliminate mongrel communities with discordant views and aspirations.

To achieve homogeneity, the new act had a twist, a cynical ploy at the heart of it: to calculate annual quotas for each immigrating nationality, the Immigration Restriction Act called for using 1890 census numbers. By design, this measure eliminated from the quota calculations the 2 million Eastern European Jews and 4 million Italians who had arrived after 1890. Lawmakers believed that this measure would "freeze" America's pre-1890 ethnic composition.

Marshall, who had fought against restriction for three decades, was on the ropes. His former partners in that fight, Jacob Schiff and Judah Magnes, were gone, and Marshall soldiered on in a different era. The KKK had spread across the country, with headquarters in Washington, DC, and a bipartisan membership of 4 million, including sixteen senators, dozens of congressmen, and eleven governors. Many joined the Klan because it was willing to take action against, as one Klansman put it, "the homebrew and the Hebrew."

As policies, immigration restriction and Prohibition were part of the same package. The fear of immigrants, one historian observed, "was the most powerful ideological club of the drys [Prohibition supporters]." Both policies started out with strong Southern support in Congress, gained Western support, and finally pulled the North along. Eighty percent of Eastern congressmen who voted for Prohibition also voted for immigration restriction. In each instance, Yankee Protestants, not big business, took the lead. If the corporate lobbies had been left to decide, they would have opted to regulate the flow of immigrant labor according to their needs, preferring to keep the billion-dollar liquor industry rather than hand it over to the criminal class.

Addressing the politicians, Marshall attacked immigration restriction as self-contradictory. This contradiction, he said, stood out in a committee report that defended the shift to the more restrictive 1890 census base: "It is used in an effort to preserve, as nearly as possible, the racial status quo in the U.S.," the report said. But to preserve the racial status quo, Marshall argued, was to preserve the country's present *heterogeneity*.

"When I hear reference to the census of 1890," Marshall said, "the first thing that comes to my mind is why not make it 1790? Or 1492? It is ridiculous." But he couldn't sway the politicians. Only six senators voted against the Immigration Restriction Act.

In the years between 1881 and 1924, 24 million immigrants had come to America, a rate of immigration that would now be reduced by 97 percent, prompting one commentator to remark, "One of the great folk movements in the history of man has come to an end."

There were opportunities to take stock of the turmoil created by Prohibition and compromise, to find some regulation to help ameliorate the genuine social ills of alcohol while modifying the most egregious problems created by Prohibition, such as violence, corruption, and death from tainted liquor. But the passing of immigration restriction emboldened the drys, and in 1924 the nation doubled down on Prohibition.

Congress added four thousand new agents to the Prohibition Bureau, expanded the mandate of the newly created Border Patrol, and gave the Coast Guard naval destroyers and small craft mounted with machine guns. As violence on the seas and highways proliferated, the price of liquor soared and criminals of Lucania and Lansky's kind entered yet another phase in the evolution of the American gangster. With armies and wealth, they now had the resources to "muscle in" on any legitimate trade — dentists and grocers, florists and bakers, truckers and garment manufacturers — that would pay them for protection against themselves.

The word "racket," which once denoted a dance or a vacation or simply a good time, was now used to describe a gangster who had a good time extorting American business. On Broadway, where the "racket guys" used their wealth to turn speakeasies into cabarets, Billy Rose, the Jewish lyricist who produced cabaret shows, hated his bosses. "These trigger-happy slobs were vainer than any woman I ever met," Rose recalled of the racketeers. "As soon as one of them assault-and-battered his way into a bankroll, he would preen himself like a king's mistress. Togged out in his new duds, the gangster was no longer satisfied to pitch pennies in a garage. All dressed up, he needed a place to glow. And the only place where he was welcome was Broadway."

Creative types who worked in the cabarets were traumatized by the violence they witnessed. Rose recalled "crying like a baby" when the bootlegger Waxey Gordon, angered by a drunk's wisecrack, beat the offender "until there was no face left." Another cabaret entertainer, the Jewish jazz musician Mezz Mezzrow, wrote of the twenties, "I was surrounded by a race of gangsters running amuck, a hundred million blowtops born with ice cubes for hearts and the appetites of a cannibal."

The gangsters devoured one another, and rarely lasted long. "Someone stronger always muscled in," write the authors of *It's a Racket!*, "like rats fighting and killing each other: The king is murdered so that another may become king."

But if the gangsters died as brutally as they lived, they would also be glorified in a way that actual business titans never were. Papers reported on the colorful lifestyles of gangsters, and many crime journalists transitioned to screenwriting, where their subjects made ideal movie characters. Romantic figures whose lives were dense with dramatic action, beautiful women, and riches beyond dreaming, gangsters offered moviegoers the vicarious thrill of resisting the corporate and legal domination that controlled their own lives. In turn, this habit of glorification gave license to underworld figures to self-righteously maintain that they were misunderstood. "I only want to do business with my own class," said Al Capone. "Why can't they let me alone? I don't interfere with their racket. Get me? They should let my racket be."

It's a Racket!

Prohibition changed New York City, observed author F. Scott Fitzgerald: "Many people who were not natural alcoholics were lit up four days out of seven, and frayed nerves were strewn everywhere; groups were held together by a generic nervousness and the hangover became a part of the day as well allowed-for as the Spanish siesta. Most of my friends drank too much — the more they were in tune to the times, the more they drank. And so effort *per se* had no dignity against the mere bounty of those days in New York, a depreciatory word was found for it: a successful programme became a 'racket' — I was in the 'literary racket.'"

In 1922, Fitzgerald, whose drunken antics helped make him the era's literary poster boy, moved his wife, Zelda, and their daughter, Scottie, to Great Neck, on Long Island, where they lived between two of Arnold Rothstein's associates: Eddie Fuller, the bucketeer whose bankruptcy had put Arnold in the hot seat, and Arnold's old journalist pal Herbert Bayard Swope, now the mysteriously rich editor of the *World*. There, on a spit of land called King's Point, Swope's Victorian mansion, a twenty-thousand-square-foot Colonial Revival lit from cellar to tower, was a scene of around-the-clock revelry.

While Arnold came up in the world during the 1910s, so did Swope. His coverage of the Great War won him the first Pulitzer Prize for reporting, in 1917, and the editorship of the *World*. Some said Swope used his position at the paper to gather insider stock information and trade on it. Whatever the source of his wealth, he and his wife, Pearl, moved to an apartment at 135 West Fifty-Eighth Street in 1921, at the same time Arnold purchased the buildings on West Fifty-Seventh Street. Like Arnold, Swope expanded, acquiring the apartment above his and making a twenty-eight-room spread with eight baths and twelve telephones. As one frequent guest there observed, a bit malevolently, Swope "reminisced about all sorts of things, especially police court days, and paying loving attention to Gyp the Blood [Harry Horowitz], Lefty Louie, Whitey Lewis, Dago Frank [Cirofici], Jack Rose, Lieutenant Becker, Governor Whitman, and other dignitaries of 1912, with particulars about Swope's behavior in connection with them."

Another guest, James M. Cain, the future dean of American crime fiction, noted that the self-regarding Swope took these roastings with "the utmost good humor." And during those first party-hearty years of Prohibition, in what many claimed was the "wettest" city in America, he and Pearl were grouped among the best hosts in Manhattan. Writes his biographer:

> Swope's guests, an endless stream, were often on the scene before he was, since he rarely got home from the paper before midnight. He would usually arrive bursting with some tidbit of late news that it pleased him to be able to divulge a few hours before it would reach the newsstands and become public knowledge. In some respects the 58th Street menage was less like a private home than a public establishment.

The Swopes' place in Great Neck was a different scene. "It was an absolutely seething bordello of interesting people," recalled Pearl. She had boxers and poets, polo players and professional gamblers, senators and Supreme Court justices. She had Dorothy Parker and the Fitzgeralds. Swope's biographer called the house "a decompression chamber between social extremes." One night, in the spirit of decompression, Zelda Fitzgerald stripped off her clothes and tried to seduce Pearl's adolescent brother, until Pearl ran Zelda out of the house, yelling, "Not with my brother, sister! Not in my house, Mrs. F!"

In Great Neck, the Fitzgeralds were surrounded by crime and booze. "I have unearthed some of the choicest bootleggers!" Zelda wrote to a friend. A bootlegger named Max Gerlach sent Fitzgerald a letter: "En route from the coast — Here for a few days on business — How are you and the family old Sport? Gerlach."

Of this period Fitzgerald wrote, "The whole golden boom was in the air — its splendid generosities, its outrageous corruptions and the tortuous death struggle of the old America in Prohibition." The alcohol ban plunged Fitzgerald into his own death struggle, as he progressed from a party drinker to a steady drinker. In a 1923 diary entry, he wrote: "Intermittent work on novel. Constant drinking. . . . I drive into a lake."

After *The Great Gatsby* was published, in the spring of 1925, Fitzgerald received a fan letter from an older novelist, Edith Wharton, who congratulated him on creating "the perfect Jew." Wharton was referring to the gangster Meyer Wolfsheim, based on Arnold Rothstein, whom Fitzgerald met, at least once, and later credited with inspiring *Gatsby*. The nature of that meeting, and the extent of their acquaintance, was unknown. They could have met as early as 1914, when Fitzgerald, then a Princeton freshman, would visit what he called "the New York of undergraduate dissipation, of Bustanoby's, Shanley's, Jack's" — all Arnold's haunts. But they almost surely would have met at Swope's parties, in Manhattan or on Long Island or both.

As a literary character, Wolfsheim provided what Fitzgerald called the book's crucial source of "hauntedness," the big revelation being that Wolfsheim is the dark force behind the success of bootlegger Jay Gatsby. Gatsby's fall is foreshadowed when he fires his servants and replaces them with Wolfsheim's "sisters and brothers," who "used to run a small hotel."

On the surface, Fitzgerald's cartoonish depiction of Wolfsheim bore little resemblance to the real Arnold Rothstein. Arnold didn't have hairy nostrils or tiny eyes. He certainly didn't wear "human molars" for cufflinks, but neither would he have joked that he did. He might have been impressed by an associate's having gone to "Oggsford College," as Wolfsheim said of Gatsby, but Arnold probably wouldn't have bragged about it.

At the same time, certain details of Wolfsheim reflect a keen understanding of Arnold. Take his telling of the Rosenthal murder. When Gatsby and the novel's narrator, Nick Carraway, meet Wolfsheim in a "Forty-Second Street cellar," he says: "I can't forget as long as I live the night they shot Rosy Rosenthal." In recalling that 1912 event, Wolfsheim places himself at Rosenthal's table at the Metropole, depicting himself as having tried to stop Rosenthal from going outside when summoned by his murderers. This wasn't true: Arnold hadn't been there. But one could see Arnold, in the role of this character, spinning just such a self-exculpatory yarn. And also perhaps nodding along when Nick Carraway thinks: "I remembered, of course, that the World's Series had been fixed in 1919, but if I had thought of it at all I would have thought of it as a thing that merely *happened,* the end of some inevitable chain."

In the twenties, another writer, Abe Shoenfeld, crossed paths with Arnold a couple of times, but in the thousands of pages he produced for the Kehillah between 1912 and 1917, the name Arnold Rothstein appeared nowhere. For all that Abe discovered and brought to light, he never realized that Hirsch Investments, the firm that had tried to lure him away from the vice crusade, was a Rothstein affiliate.

But now, as Abe watched the puritanical reform of the twenties turn the street thugs of his youth into what he called "high-riding corporate gangsters," he knew all about the significance of Rothstein, whom Abe referred to, in later writings, as the Wolf of Broadway.

Looking back, prewar reform seemed like a period of true progressive ascendancy, when a substantial cross section of Americans — bigoted and self-interested as they might have been — at least believed in the potential of a rational citizenry to seek out information about problems and test solutions. The reformers of Abe's day didn't know what would come of their neighborhood cleanups, but they could at least *see* what they wanted to clean: the local pimp, the sweatshop boss, the pawnshop that fenced stolen goods. During the twenties, reform changed from pragmatic activism whose success or failure could be observed locally, to a federal abstraction that was measured in dollars and prison time, a story no one believed.

In 1915, "reformer" was a complimentary term. By the twenties, it was a term of contempt. In an article called "The Irritating Qualities of Reformers," the *Atlantic* magazine described the new reformer as someone who "must conduct himself as solemnly as John Sumner, who once confessed that he never assumed in his own study a posture which he would not have taken in the Senate of the United States." As head of the New York Society for the Suppression of Vice, John Sumner spent the twenties banning literature. Abe detested Sumner so much that he set to work on a novel maligning the new reformers, a group he no longer recognized.*

The interwar years marked Abe's literary period. He kept the office on Rector Street and earned a living as a private investigator in order to finance his reading and writing habits. His novel-in-progress, *The Joy Peddler,* imitated James Joyce's stream-of-consciousness style. It referenced "lesbic brothels," "anal conjunctivitis," and reformers whose "olfactories are easily offended." There was a prostitute whose "hard tipped breasts" touched off "an avalanche of hearts," a corporation of syphilitic pimps, a district attorney who "is pompous, cruel, venomous, revengeful, and unethical," and a journalist who wonders: "It took nature a million years to make the man you see today and now these $1,200 a year clerks who connect with one of those reform institutions think they can change the bodies and minds of human beings by passing laws."

---

* Even Natalie Sonnichsen, Abe's first partner in the vice investigations, had become foreign to him. It was Natalie, coincidentally, who translated and helped disseminate *The Protocols of the Learned Elders of Zion*, which was published as *The Jewish Peril* in early 1920 and later spread around the world via Ford's *Dearborn Independent*.

As Abe worked on the novel, he hung out in the city's blue-chip bookshops, like Brentano's and Dauber & Pine, befriended wealthy men in the rare book trade, and saw Enrico Caruso and Rosa Poncelle perform dozens of times. Ever since Abe was thirteen, when his father brought home a phonograph record of the opera *L'Elisir d'amore, The Elixir of Love,* Caruso's "Una furtiva lagrima" had "haunted" him. Of seeing Caruso live, he recalled, "Liquid gold poured from his throat, and whenever he stood in front of the old Met I touched my hat. When he died in August, 1921, I wept like a stricken child."

He ran with editors and writers, political radicals and gray-area types. In his apartment on Riverside Drive he kept a barrel of Chianti and a cabinet full of Canadian rye. As for the past, he didn't possess a single page he wrote for the Kehillah. Every report and letter had gone to Jerusalem with Magnes. But he did keep one memento of the vice crusade. Fixed to the wall of his apartment was the rusty bayonet, the weapon that might have killed him in 1913, had the cop Moe Stein not jumped in with his weighted umbrella. What strange conversations that bayonet must have inspired over the years.

"My friends were all unique," Abe recalled of the twenties. "They laughingly defied Prohibition, that 'noble experiment' that corrupted American society and pointed up a system of corruption that would endure for years."

The federal government doubled down on drug enforcement, just as it did with Prohibition. In 1926, drug agents raided a downtown loft where they discovered heroin, morphine, and cocaine packaged in crates shipped from Germany, a major exporter of narcotics in the early years of the American drug trade. Of this period, one East Side addict recalled: "We bought an ounce of H—and this is H that's a hundred percent, that came from Germany in a little square box with gold rims. Jack Diamond [an associate of

Arnold's] had gone to Germany, and they had made a big connection with a drug firm. [A dealer] gave me this square tin box wrapped in cellophane . . . it had German lettering — 'Drogen: Morphium.'"

At the downtown drug bust, the agents arrested two of Arnold's associates, one a retired cop. Arnold provided bail, but he couldn't fix the federal case, and the judge meted out a combined twenty years in prison, which newspapers called "a record dope sentence."

The judge hoped the stiff sentences would force the defendants to implicate their financier, but they stuck, and the federal prosecutor in New York set his sights on Arnold. "It became obvious to us that the dope traffic in the United States was being directed from one source," recalled the prosecutor. "More and more, our information convinced us that Arnold Rothstein was that source." The prosecutor didn't trust the agents assigned to the Narcotic Division's New York office, so he imported three undercover agents from Washington to follow Arnold.

26

Don't Write Good Things about Me

I N THE MIDDLE OF A MANHATTAN NIGHT IN THE FALL
of 1927, Arnold hurried back to the brownstone on West Eighty-
Fourth Street where he and Carolyn lived. She had called him at Lindy's
and said that two men were knocking on the door and making demands.
By the time Arnold arrived, the men had disappeared. But this wasn't the
first sign of danger, and Carolyn was rattled. He tried to placate her, purchasing a palatial duplex at 912 Fifth Avenue, which he outfitted with
steel doors and a fancy air-purification system, but the menace continued.
A man who looked like Arnold was kidnapped coming out of the Fifty-
Seventh Street building, and a car that resembled his was riddled with
machine-gun fire as it stood outside the Fairfield Hotel. Carolyn asked
him, for the last time, to stop the life he was living.

"They'd think I was afraid," he said, but Carolyn could see he *was*
afraid.

He was funding so many criminals that warfare among his associates, with Arnold in the middle, was common, and many resented him
for it. One Broadway producer recalled that many gangsters hated

Arnold, but because he had cash to loan and police and judges in his pocket, they needed him. But now they needed him less and less as the mobster class transcended party politics. "I made it a policy that we wouldn't just line up with Tammany and the Democrats," recalled Charlie Lucania. "We went with the Republicans, too. In my book, it was a three-party system — them two and us."

Carolyn said she wanted a divorce. She'd stuck with him for twenty years, resigning herself to a childless and often lonely marriage. He had wanted a mother figure and she gave him that — keeping his secrets, advancing his agendas, even defending him against critics and opportunists. But the twenties had changed him. He could no longer claim, as he had in the 1910s, that he remained above the criminal fray by not taking part in the conspiracies he financed. His role in the drug trade was more direct — he met with European suppliers and arranged deals. His partners in that business were the stone-cold Diamond brothers, Jack and Eddie, who had once been his bodyguards but now figured more and more conspicuously in his affairs. Carolyn recalled: "It was not until Arnold became associated with the Diamonds, and ceased for the most part mingling with men of good reputation in sports and betting, that he lost his perspective, and started to drift downwards. My husband, as is true of so many other persons who are well acquainted with him, had not much respect for the criminal law as it is administered. But even his close friends, who weren't the sort to be annoyed by a violation of the gambling laws, or liquor laws, or even of the Bucket Shop laws, considered that he went too far when he began to associate exclusively with folk like the Diamond brothers, and to harbor public enemies in his hotel and his apartments."

Arnold pleaded with her to stay. "You're the one thing I can be sure of every minute of every day," he said. "You're part of me."

Carolyn insisted on the split. She said she wanted to move to London, where she was seeing a younger man. Arnold hedged. He told her to go and test out the relationship. If, after six months, she was of the same frame of mind, he promised to give her a divorce and a thousand dollars a month for the rest of her life.

As Arnold contemplated this loss, another family member drew away. "During the separation he came to see me and began to weep," Carolyn wrote. "He told me that his brother Jack had eloped with Miss Fay Lewisohn and had changed his name from Rothstein to Rothstone. I am sure that this was by far the worst blow Arnold ever suffered in his life. He was as fond of his brother Jack as of any other human being, and had done him many services."*

But Carolyn put her pity for Arnold aside. She sailed for Europe on Christmas Eve, and it felt wonderful to finally be away.

A month after Carolyn left, Arnold was walking through a restaurant when a female friend called him over and introduced him to Inez Norton, without mentioning Arnold's last name. He later sent Inez flowers and invited her to the Colony Club, a smart and clandestine underworld destination, where he told her that he was in real estate and insurance. When Inez went to the powder room, he slipped a scrap of paper beneath her plate that said, "the most beautiful & sweetest girl in the world." They were smitten with one another, but Inez hadn't the remotest idea who Arnold was until the third outing, when she introduced her date as "Mr. Arnold," and he blew up.

"I'm not in disguise!" he said. "Nor am I hiding anything! My name is Arnold Rothstein. If you're ashamed to say it, you shouldn't introduce me to your friends!"

---

* Fay Lewisohn, a socialite and fashionista, was the striking granddaughter of Sam Lewisohn, the German-Jewish cosponsor of the Kehillah vice crusade. Fay would have known Arnold, or known about him. In 1922, at twenty, she opened a high-end dress store at 8 West Fifty-Seventh Street, next to Arnold's buildings.

This episode left Inez with an impression of Arnold's sensitivity, but she fell for his gentler side and his nonstop lifestyle. At forty-six, Arnold was nearly twice her age, but the twenty-five-year-old Inez, an athletic blonde with cheery energy, had already lived several lives. Back in Georgia, she had been a Sunday school teacher until fifteen, when she married an army captain and did Red Cross work during the war. At sixteen she had a son, then got divorced. When she returned home after the war, she discovered that her family fortune had been wiped out, so she came to New York, found work as a chorus girl in the Ziegfeld Follies, and married the son of a Jewish family. But the family's refusal to accept Inez, she claimed, drove a wedge between them, and that's when Mr. Arnold, who was also technically still married, came along.

Inez couldn't believe how much Arnold did in a day. He might spend three hours in the Fifty-Seventh Street office, interviewing architects and attorneys, then make calls regarding building plans and sewer permits. Then stop at Lindy's, where underworld types reported to him. Then slip over to the theater to check on a play he was financing. Then visit a nightclub, of which he owned a piece. Then go to his apartment to read documents and count money. Then go out again just to "see what's doing." She was enamored of the pride she felt as "Rothstein's girl," and the respect she got on the street, where she was no longer catcalled.

And of course she liked the gifts — the jewelry, the stocks and bonds, a horse to ride in Central Park, and a suite in the Fairfield, where he built her a rooftop tennis court. She appreciated his inconspicuousness, how he'd wait until she was seeing him to the door, then lean in and whisper, "Goldilocks, slip your hand in that pocket, that one there, maybe you'll find something, oh, some candy or some chewing gum," and she'd reach in and pull out a diamond or a brooch. Inez, not unlike Carolyn twenty years earlier, came from a culture of chorus girls who often hooked up with so-called Broadway sports for the familiar transaction. But Inez said she wasn't in it for the money alone. "Had I been a gold digger I could have taken him for a fortune," she later wrote. "I know a few girls, who, with my chances, would have."

Even so, freeloaders surrounded him. By 1928, the Fairfield was a colony of Arnold's criminal associates, plus a random assortment of hangers-on and dependents who tended to be, as Inez characterized them, "actresses out of work, his personal cronies who had 'gone wrong' in the market, a bookie or two who had been slapped by the tails of a few long shots, an indigent playwright against whom 'the producers had a conspiracy,' and hopped-up widows who made bootleggers rich for synthetic stuff that would take the polish off the furniture where it slopped over the glass."

Arnold often loaned money to people he knew couldn't pay it back. The Fairfield, where many lived without paying rent, bespoke that compassionate side, his father's side. Abe the Just had Beth Israel Hospital, where the poor were treated for free. Arnold had the Fairfield. But Inez wanted to be more than another of Arnold's dependents. All that stood in the way was her second husband, who refused to divorce her. Since adultery was the only ground for divorce in New York, Arnold arranged for the husband to be "discovered" in a hotel room with what the *Sun* called "a woman, not his wife." Now Inez was free to marry Arnold, so long as he followed through with his own divorce when Carolyn returned from Europe.

That summer, Inez stayed on Long Island, near Long Beach, with her ten-year-old son, and Arnold visited them on weekends and evenings. The three of them swam and played on the beach. Arnold was besotted with the boy, whose love of sweet potatoes inspired Arnold to nickname him the Sweet Potato Kid. Here Arnold was the fun-loving family man, the doting father. He lay in the sand, next to a beaming Inez, and smiled at the sky.

Back in the city, on Broadway, there was talk about Arnold and his debts. He had a considerable amount of "paper" floating around, the kind of

IOUs that he himself would never accept from a debtor. Arnold's closest associates urged him to take it easy, but he shrugged, said he couldn't help it, couldn't stop, didn't know why but it was part of him. He said he'd gamble till the day he died. "The gambling fever that was always part of Arnie's make-up appeared to have gone to his brain," Meyer Lansky recalled of 1928. "It was like a disease, and he was now in its last stages. He gambled wildly.... He started to look like a man suffering from some terrible sickness, as if some great disaster had torn his life to pieces."

Addictively, he played his no-limit game in the big world even as troubling signs emerged. There were the legal problems. He'd managed to make an indictment against him for tax-evasion disappear, but the creditors in the Fuller bankruptcy still hounded him for that $366,768. And then there were the drug agents. In July, Arnold narrowly escaped a drug sting, but three of his associates were arrested. When he bailed them out, one of the narcotics investigators imported from Washington, James Kerrigan, confronted Arnold, saying, "One day you're going to die with your shoes on if you keep this up."

"None of us knows how we're going to die," Arnold said, "but if I'm ever knocked off there'll be a terrible record left in New York."

He knew he was treading a dangerous path, but, as Carolyn suggested, his vanity had developed into a kind of megalomania, a sense that he was too smart and important to come to grief. His ties to officials would protect him, he believed, as would his new role as a developer. He spent thousands a week on a seventy-four-acre housing development in Maspeth, Queens. He envisioned selling insurance and mortgages to home buyers, then adding a golf course, a greyhound track, and a motor speedway. It would, he thought, be an undeniable emblem of legitimacy, until he discovered that his construction manager had botched the project, and all 143 homes had been built on swampland, without cellars or foundations.

The development, Inez — these were all just stories, impulses generated by his multiplicity, the vast compilation of personas that Inez taxonomized, writing: "Picture in one individual a sentimental and tender lover, a genial and humorous companion, a charitable giver, a loyal friend — and — a wholesale drug dealer, a crooked sports fixer, a welching gambler, a stolen securities fence, a rum-ring mastermind, a corrupter of police, a grafter through politics, a gunman, a judge-briber, a jury-tamperer, a blackmailer, a pool shark, a swindler."

His gambling losses piled up. On Labor Day he blew $130,000 at Belmont Racetrack. A month later, in early October, he joined a high-stakes poker game at the Park Central Hotel on Seventh Avenue, a happening place where gamblers rented rooms for marathon card games while the clarinetist Benny Goodman, King of Swing, played on the balcony. The game didn't go well. Arnold felt it was fixed. So, when he won a hand, he took cash out of the game, but upon losing a hand, he put up an IOU. Some thirty hours later, daylight flooding through the windows, the green felt was littered with $360,000 of Arnold's IOUs. He rose and said, "All right, I made a note on how much I owe. Now just give me the IOUs back so I don't have them floating around for somebody to look at." The players protested. Arnold said they had nothing to worry about.

But he didn't want to pay, and confided to the con man Nicky Arnstein his suspicions of having been cheated. Nicky sympathized but reminded Arnold that cheating was part of their business: "Arnold, rigged or not, you have to pay off," Nicky said. "Even if it was crooked, no point in advertising you were a sucker." But before Arnold could advertise anything, the debt became a public matter, with headlines reading: ARNOLD ROTHSTEIN HIT FOR $360,000.

In late October, when Carolyn returned from Europe, Arnold went to see her and confessed that his "affairs were heavily involved," then asked if she had changed her mind about the divorce.

"No. And from what I heard I thought you reached the same decision."

"She's a nice woman," Arnold said of Inez, "but she isn't you. If you wanted it over, I could end it in two minutes."

Carolyn said she thought a divorce was best, so on November 2 they signed the papers, and that night Arnold proposed to Inez.

Two days later, on November 4, a Sunday, Arnold went to the office on Fifty-Seventh Street, where he finished placing his election-day bets. He was betting a parlay on Herbert Hoover to win the presidency and Franklin D. Roosevelt to win the gubernatorial election. If both Hoover and FDR lost, he would lose $1,250,000, but if both won he would make $570,000. He met Inez for dinner and they talked about buying a house in the country — Westchester or Long Island, they were undecided. Then he dropped her at a movie theater to see *The Wedding March*.

That night, at Lindy's, he got a call from one of the gamblers he owed money to for the poker loss, asking for a meeting at the Park Central Hotel. Before leaving for the hotel, Arnold borrowed a .38 Smith & Wesson from a fellow Lindy's regular, then thought better of it and gave the gun back. The Broadway reporter Damon Runyon followed Arnold to the hotel. In the lobby, Arnold told Runyon, "I'll be down in a couple minutes if you want to wait. I just got to calm these guys down a little."

In room 349, Arnold argued with the gamblers, both of whom had been drinking, and a gun went off. The bullet entered Arnold's lower right abdomen, ruptured his bladder, and cut through his intestines. The gamblers fled and came pounding through the lobby, where they saw Runyon. One, as he ran by, yelled, "I am not here!" The other said, "It wasn't supposed to come to this!"

On the third floor, Arnold stumbled down the corridor, clutching his side. He navigated two flights of stairs and pushed open a pair of heavy fire doors, where he saw the elevator operator and said, "Get me a taxi, I've been shot."

*   *   *

After the movie, Inez returned to the Fairfield Hotel, where an agitated crowd filled the spacious lobby. When she entered, there was a dramatic hush and the elevator boy, normally obsequious to a fault, stared at her open-mouthed. In her rooms she found the wife of one of Arnold's attorneys, who asked, "Have you heard?"

"Heard what?"

"Arnold has had...an accident. He's been...it wasn't serious...he was shot."

At 912 Fifth Avenue, Carolyn lay in bed and smoked a cigarette to calm her nerves. During the marriage she had struggled with anxiety, and when Arnold was in trouble she often became acutely anxious. Now she felt that gnawing premonition.

On West Eighty-Fourth Street, Arnold's parents knew something terrible would happen to him eventually. Every time they heard a newsboy shout "Extra!" their hearts would sink and they would think: *Arnold!* And it was indeed an "extra" that told them Arnold had been shot.

On Monday morning, in a private three-room suite at the Polyclinic Hospital on Second Avenue, Arnold's family and ex-wife gathered around him. After a blood transfusion kept him alive, Arnold opened his eyes and saw Carolyn. Even now, after the divorce papers had been signed, there was a bond between them. "I knew you'd be here," he said. "When will they operate?"

Carolyn said the doctor didn't think an operation was necessary. Arnold asked, "Will I pull through?"

"Sure you will," she lied. "And I'll take care of the banks in the morning," she added, knowing without being told that his chief worry would be those bank balances.

But he didn't seem to hear this. "Well, if I don't need an operation then we'll go home," he said, and with those words, his last, he tried to get up but couldn't. The next morning, on November 6, 1928, Arnold Rothstein died at 10:17 a.m., hours before Herbert Hoover and FDR won their elections.

Earlier that year, when confronted by the federal drug agent James Kerrigan, Arnold had said that if he was killed, "a terrible record" would be left behind. Now Kerrigan worried about the local New York officials who wished to see that evidence disappear, so he and his team raided Arnold's Fifty-Seventh Street office and broke into the safe at his Fifth Avenue apartment, where they confiscated a reported "56,000 scraps of paper" that chronicled, among other things, a drug network that reached Belgium, China, and Germany. ROTHSTEIN BARED AS BACKER OF BIGGEST DRUG RING, read a headline from the *Brooklyn Daily Eagle*. Based on information from the safe, the US attorney ordered the arrest of six of Arnold's smuggling associates, who were found with a combined $10 million worth of heroin, opium, morphine, and cocaine.

Arnold's associates pleaded guilty and refused to cooperate, but before they went to trial, a leading source of information in their cases, the drug agent Kerrigan, himself died, following an operation to relieve stomach pain. The government claimed Kerrigan's pain was due to internal injuries sustained during the raid of an opium den, but the surgeon reported finding a condition "as if Kerrigan had been kicked in the abdomen, a symptom often connected to poisoning."

The smugglers walked free, and so did Arnold's killer. There were arrests and witness testimonies. There was little doubt about who pulled the trigger. But the question of what corruption might be revealed by further investigation into Arnold's life and death concerned a multitude of the powerful, and the murder case was managed out of existence. As for the 56,000 scraps of paper taken from his safe, the district attorney said they were "too dreary" to waste time over, and they disappeared.

In President Hoover's inaugural address, he said that "disobedience to law" was the "most malign danger facing the nation," and that pervasive criminality was too big a problem to be left to local authorities. Hoover envisioned a sprawling federal law-enforcement complex that would expand on what had been built during Prohibition. To implement his vision, Hoover needed to show that Prohibition enforcement could be improved upon, so he ordered a nationwide study, known as the Wickersham Commission, but the results were not what he hoped for.

In its multivolume report, the Wickersham Commission unpacked the injustices of a coercive nation-state: overzealous agents, corruption, and "lawlessness" at all levels of government. Police practice was "shocking in its character and extent," the commission found, and reported that "widespread species of torture" — beatings and floggings, sleep and food deprivation, the "water cure," and "threats of bodily injury or death" — were "well known to the bench and bar." State-run asylums reported that the number of "demented persons due to alcoholism" had increased tenfold since 1920, when Prohibition began. The commission linked crime to poverty, unemployment, and "race prejudice," and concluded that the best way to reduce the costs of crime was "limiting the extent to which social controls by means of criminal law is attempted."

Hoover declared the Wickersham Commission "rotten," but there was one finding he approved of, a glimmer of support for his worldview. One problem with Prohibition, the Commission said, was that "respectable citizens" didn't believe in banning alcohol. Their feelings about banning narcotics, however, were different. There was enormous profit in breaking drug laws, and enforcement of those laws was in many ways more challenging than in the case of alcohol: "Yet there are no difficulties in the case of narcotics, beyond those involved in the nature of the traffic, because the laws against them are supported everywhere by a general determined public sentiment."

Even as the Wickersham findings arrived, a year after Arnold's death, the papers were continuing to report new revelations about those who had been tainted by Arnold, including the chief of the narcotics division, whose son and son-in-law had once worked for Arnold, as lawyer and accountant, to make a tax case disappear in Washington. DOPE UNIT IS IN FOR SHAKE-UP, headlines blared, and Hoover cited the Rothstein scandal as another reason to consolidate federal policing power.

He announced that he would uncouple the drug war from the alcohol war, taking the narcotics division out of the fast-sinking Prohibition Bureau and establishing the Federal Bureau of Narcotics. To head the new bureau, Hoover installed Harry Anslinger, a former stalwart of the anti-liquor crusade, whose proposals for draconian penalties had made little headway. But now, in the drug context, Anslinger's call "to jail offenders, then throw away the keys" would find amazing success.

The English-language press pursued Abraham Rothstein, but he declined comment until one day in the spring of 1929, eighteen months after Arnold's death. A reporter for the Yiddish *Forward* knocked at the door of A. E. Rothstein, the cotton goods company on Eleventh Street, seeking clarity on a matter of family history.

Forward editor Abraham Cahan had asked the reporter to find out whether Arnold Rothstein was the grandson of Yehoshua Rothstein, a long-dead rabbi and businessman who was also known as Harris Rothstein. Cahan recalled that this man, in addition to running a hat company, had founded the first free religious school on the East Side, during the initial years of Russian-Jewish immigration in the 1880s. Yehoshua was the rabbi. Harris was the hatmaker. "It would be interesting to know whether Arnold Rothstein came from his family," Cahan said. "If he did, we'll have a remarkable piece of history on Jewish families in America. The grandfather and the rabbi! The grandson and the underworld!" Yes, Abe the Just confirmed: Harris Rothstein was his father, Arnold's grandfather.*

The *Forward* reporter described Abe the Just, now seventy-one, as tall and slim, silver-haired yet youthful, and well read. He was impressed by how many writers Abe the Just quoted as he spoke. "And not in an affected way—it came naturally to him," the reporter noted. "When he wanted to characterize certain people, he compared them to character types from works of literature or famous artists. 'He had a face that Rembrandt himself wouldn't say no to painting.'" The reporter added: "There were times when his eyes sharpened, becoming prickly and set, and a look of bitter, bilious resentment came into them: why does everyone want to paint his son in such disreputable colors? And then there were times when his gaze became soft, helpless, melted by hot sobs inside his heart."

As the interview turned to Arnold, Abe the Just vacillated between grief and resentment. "The papers, day in and day out, run stories about my Arnold. All the troubles of big-city life in America are pinned on him. And don't think that I speak blindly because I am his father. I understand how it came to that. When someone becomes popular in a field, everything that takes place around that field is attributed to the person who has risen to fame....The popular person becomes like a splinter carried away by the current, like a straw blown away by the wind. He is no longer his own person." Abe the Just extolled Arnold's virtuous side and minimized the rest, adding, "I only want to ask you this: If you write bad things about my son, don't write good things about me."

---

* While his sons grew the business he started and moved uptown, Harris himself never left the East Side. He remained in the original family home on Henry Street, where Arnold was born. Harris died there in a 1903 fire, at the age of eighty-two.

Others knew the true extent of Arnold's influence, had experienced it firsthand, and still remembered him fondly. Decades later, for a book called *Addicts Who Survived: An Oral History of Narcotic Use in America, 1923–1965,* elderly New York drug addicts recalled that Jews had dominated the drug trade in the twenties, importing pure narcotics and selling them uncut. "The Jews were businessmen," said one East Side addict. "They gave it to you the way they got it. They knew you were going to hit it"—cut it and resell it for profit—"but they figured that you'll be in business...and you'll come back tomorrow, and he'll make another dollar on you, and another dollar, and another dollar."

But addicts said they experienced a marked shift in the underworld in 1929: "The allegation that the Jewish dealers had been driven out of business by the Italians, who then adulterated drugs to unheard-of levels, surfaced repeatedly in our interviews." After Arnold's death, one addict recalled, "The fucking wops took over and they started to knock off the Jews. First it was the Italian guys with the handlebars: Don Pepe, all the mustache guys, you know, Don Pasquale, Francesco. Then the Americanized guys came in, the mafia guys. Charlie Lucky [Charlie Lucania, a.k.a Lucky Luciano] got in it.... The Italians were selling shit, chemical acid. These sons of bitches were so hungry for money that they cut it half a dozen times—then he sold it to his brother-in-law, and his nephew, and by the time you got it, it was ruined." Another addict said: "After Rothstein died, the Italians infiltrated. Because Rothstein really had them bulldozed—listen, them Jews were tough bastards. And them Italians, they stayed in their place as long as he ruled the roost."

Abe Shoenfeld had only wanted to clean up his neighborhood. In 1913, when he broke into the offices of defense attorneys, ordered pretextual arrests, or paid telephone operators for information, he didn't foresee the consequences of expanding police power. He never imagined that the same censorship apparatus he and Harry Newburger invoked to shut down plays and movies about Jewish prostitution would be used, years later, by John Sumner, head of the New York Society for the Suppression of Vice, to ban both Abe's literary inspiration, Joyce's *Ulysses,* and Abe's own novel, *The Joy Peddler*—which he wrote, ironically, to skewer Sumner.

"I cannot understand why my works were seized," Abe told a reporter. "There is nothing indecent in *The Joy Peddler.* Unless Mr. Sumner takes exception to the way I denounce professional social reformers. My book has been lauded by prominent clergymen and laymen. Only recently Dr. Magnes praised my work and urged me to continue. It touches upon nightlife and a harlot and the city fathers."

Bans have unpredictable consequences, and this one brought press attention to the book, including a solid review: "Although Mr. Shoenfeld suffers from an ineffectual desire to imitate the James Joyceian style, the book is an interesting and worthwhile purchase, and should not be missed by anyone who has ever sensed the real New York." Consigned to the black market, the novel shot up in price to $25 and the New York Public Library wrote to the author to request a copy.

EPILOGUE

I N THE EARLY 1960S, ARTHUR GOREN, A BUDDING ACADEMIC, was doing graduate work at Columbia University, pioneering a new field of study, Jewish-American history. Goren, who in the fifties had used America's GI Bill to get his bachelor's degree at Hebrew University in Jerusalem, traveled back to his alma mater to research the life of Judah Magnes. In 1918, Magnes had cofounded the university with Albert Einstein and the Russian-born biochemist Chaim Weizmann, who became Israel's first president in 1949. Goren wanted to do his dissertation on the rabbi, who'd once been the controversial leader of New York's Jewish community but was now pretty much forgotten.

In Jerusalem, as Goren dug through the "Kehillah" portion of the Magnes archive, a fascinating story unfolded about the contentious process by which the German-Jewish uptowners sought to assimilate the new arrivals from Eastern Europe. He read about the Kehillah's public initiatives entailing education and health care, and its battles against anti-Semitism and immigration restriction. Then he stumbled on something unexpected. A section of the archive, labeled "Vigilance Committee," dealt with crime—thousands of pages chronicling a prodigious East Side underworld and the Kehillah's nonpublic efforts to eliminate it. The writing was rich. There were tales of gamblers and horse poisoners. There were pimps who ran a cooperative, madams and thieves who attended synagogue, and prostitutes who became crusaders. Goren had gone to Israel to research a forgotten rabbi, and discovered a lost world.

When he interviewed Magnes's widow, Beatrice, at her home in Jerusalem, he asked if she remembered anything about "vice work on the East Side." Beatrice recalled that her husband was "very indignant" about downtown crime, and she remembered that Mayor Gaynor appointed a young Jewish lawyer as third deputy police commissioner.

"Yes," Goren said, "and there's a fellow who kind of gathers the information?"

"Abe Shoenfeld," Beatrice said. "He could get in anywhere and everywhere." For years Abe would call late at night, after her children were asleep, she remembered, and Magnes would run to the phone as if the fate of the world depended on what Abe had to say.

Back in New York, in 1965, Goren went to Abe's apartment on Central Park South and knocked on the door. He was in luck. Abe had recently retired from his last and longest crusade. In 1938, the American Jewish Committee had hired Abe to investigate stateside Nazis. Five years later, on behalf of the AJC, Morris Ernst — the ACLU attorney who challenged the *Ulysses* ban and represented scores of authors — wrote a letter to the assistant secretary of the interior. Ernst began, "Dear Oscar, I have been keeping my eyes open for tough guys with our prejudices," and continued:

> I have located a man with unique background and training. His name is Abe Shoenfeld, and he has worked over the years on intimate matters with [former Kehillah lawyer] Eddie Greenbaum, now General. I told Abe to drop in to see you, calling up in advance to make an appointment. He will tell you his own story, and together with what Eddie will sing in the way of Abe's praises, I think I have got a find for you.

He is the opposite of a Harvard graduate, having picked up his learning and culture in odd moments of life, and having specialized in more valuable aspects of what in general terms is called policing. The only public job he ever had was secretary to the deputy police commissioner under the Gaynor administration.

For the next twenty-two years, Abe and his spies infiltrated white supremacist organizations and befriended their leaders. He also ran spies in the Middle East and reported his intelligence to an AJC handler, a former US attorney who passed his information to the FBI.

But now, at seventy-four, Abe considered the Kehillah vice crusade to have been the most important episode of his life.

"These things are as fresh and vivid with me as if they happened this morning," he told Goren. Abe, who was married but childless, had become the kind of man who spoke *at* you rather than *with* you, and Goren could hardly finish a question before Abe unspooled another memory, often without context, saying, for instance: "It was Dollar John who bought the pistol and gave it to Red Phil Davidson and told him, 'That'll make you the big man if you'll knock off Jack Zelig.'" During the two-day-long interview, Abe told quite a story. "I'm not taking my light from under a bushel now," he said, "but a book written on this period would never be believed, impossible."*

In 1970, Goren published *New York Jews and the Quest for Community: The Kehillah Experiment.* The book covered all aspects of the Kehillah's activities, and included two chapters on Jewish crime and the vice crusade, but concluded that the crusade didn't achieve its goals. Goren might

---

* This phrase originates in Matthew 5:15–16: "Neither do men light a candle, and put it under a bushel.... Let your light so shine before men" (KJV). One's "light"—one's talents and abilities—should not be concealed, or hidden under a bushel, but shared with the world. Accordingly, Abe *should* take his light from under a bushel.

have been swayed by another interview he did with a retired judge, Jonah Goldstein, who was still bitter about his exclusion. Goldstein told Goren, "Magnes tried to sell me a bill to keep ours up, so as to take the spotlight off Shoenfeld." It was an old-timey way of saying that Magnes bullshitted Jonah and strung him along as a decoy. Goldstein laid out his grievances, which found credence in Goren's book.

Unsurprisingly, Abe took issue with Goren's telling, and penciled one "No" after another in the margins of his copy of the book. He didn't approve of much that was written about the prewar period, including E. L. Doctorow's novel *Ragtime*. It was the kind of sentimental claptrap that the hippie generation enjoyed, the same people who thought dissidence boiled down to not cutting your hair. So, in the final years of his life he returned to a writing project that he had started decades earlier, during his interwar literary period, called *Crime Buster: My Memoirs to 1921.* He worked on the unpublished book until his death in September 1977, a month before I was born.

During my younger years, growing up in Minnesota, I discovered three books that expanded my understanding of Jewish-American history and my own heritage.

The first was *Low Life: Lures and Snares of Old New York,* by Luc Sante, who lived on the Lower East Side in the late seventies and early eighties, "in dumps where the floors slanted and the walls were held together with duct tape and the window frames had last been caulked in 1912."* The East Siders who came of age in the 1910s were, like Abe, dying off. Landlords, instead of spending money on removal vans, would drag the belongings of the deceased down to the sidewalk, where Sante helped

---

* Since publishing *Low Life,* Luc Sante has become Lucy Sante.

himself, he wrote, to "photographs and books and curiosities" that became the source material for "a mythology of New York, a pool of tales" about "the sporting life of temptation" and "the forces of order, repression, and profit." *Low Life,* published in 1991, was a revelation to me. Having been born in the long shadow of the Holocaust, and enrolled in a grinding course of genocide studies, I'd hardly imagined there was a Jewish-American community prior to World War II. Sante's book, with references to Yiddish theater and Jewish crime, was my first inkling of such a community, and the East Side ghetto became an abiding interest.

Three years later, in 1994, Nicholas Dawidoff published his excellent biography of Moe Berg, *The Catcher Was a Spy.* An Ivy League graduate and polymath who appeared on quiz shows, Berg played fifteen seasons of Major League Baseball while practicing law in the off-season, and worked as an American spy during World War II. Here, in the intrepid Berg, was another Jewish subject who lay outside my blinkered perspective. Perhaps, I thought, there were others like him. It was around then that I told my mother that if I ever became a writer I wanted to tell the story of the "Jewish Rambo" — some story, not just of resistance, but of victory, some antidote to the legacy of horror that often left me ashamed of who I was and afraid to know too much about where I came from. Jewish Rambo? Mom was dubious. She said our culture didn't have those types.

Lastly, my mother's mother self-published a memoir in 1998 that traced her German-Jewish lineage to the 1700s. From her book, *A Charmed Life: My Footprint in Time,* I learned that my triple-great-grandfather, Jacob Klee, my first American ancestor, had emigrated from a village in Germany to the city of Pittsburgh in 1846. It was a decade in which forty thousand German Jews came to the New World, having read Gottfried Duden's *Report on a Journey to the Western States of North America,* and other US travel guides then being published in Germany. Upon reaching Pittsburgh, the twenty-three-year-old Jacob was delighted: the junction of the three rivers reminded him of his boyhood military service in Coblenz, where the Rhine River met the Moselle.

Jacob had no money, but in the next seven years he became wealthy by doing what many German-Jewish immigrants did in those pre–Civil War years. He hoofed around one-hundred-pound sacks of secondhand clothing and sold it door-to-door. In 1854, he traveled back to his village, where he asked the rabbi for the hand of his nineteen-year-old daughter, and gave his older brother money for passage to America.

With his brother as a partner, Jacob established Klee & Co., manufacturing men's clothes, and became, according to a book on the history of Pittsburgh, "the first to produce ready-made rather than custom-tailored clothing for gentlemen." The Klee brothers expanded by investing in cattle and oil. They established the city's first Reform synagogue, and their growing families spread out across the homes of Sheffield Street, known as Klee Row. And then there was the ultimate proof of assimilation: When Jacob's eldest daughter reached courting age, the *Pittsburgh Social Mirror* announced that she was ready "to be seen."

As a well-known figure in town, he might have become a target. While walking home from work one winter night, Jacob, whom newspapers described as "a large and powerful man" and "rather muscular," was assailed by highway robbers, one of whom choked him while the other struck him on the head with a handy-billy, a lead-filled leather ball. As Jacob's head poured blood, reported the *Pittsburgh Weekly Gazette,* "he set up a loud call for help, meantime keeping the villains at bay with his fists." He recovered, but passed Klee & Co. to his son, Benjamin, my double-great-grandfather, who moved the business to New York in the 1880s and established his own new business model, making custom suits at readymade prices.

The lures and snares of the old East Side, the intriguing model of Moe Berg, my roots in the prewar city — these were distinct histories, until they merged.

Epilogue

*   *   *

Years later, as a writer, I was working on a contemporary story about a gang of Orthodox rabbis who assaulted husbands for refusing to give their wives a *get*, the biblically mandated bill of divorce required to unchain a woman from the bonds of religious matrimony. In search of context, I read up on the history of Jewish crime, and returned often to the New York of the early 1900s, having found Arthur Goren's Kehillah chronicle and other books on the subject.

In the background of these works was a shadowy figure — a writer, or an investigator, seemingly a young man, who produced reams of reportage and intelligence about the Jewish underworld of pre–World War I New York. One historian referred to Abe as "a private detective." Another called him "a keen student of the underworld whose first-hand accounts of Jewish crime on the Lower East Side are an unparalleled source of crime history." But it was a third characterization of Abe — as "a knowledgeable vigilante" — that made me sit upright. He was more than a mere observer of his world, it turned out. He'd been enlisted in some kind of war on crime. Enlisted by whom? And to what end?

I discovered that Abe's grandniece, Ellen James, had recently donated his papers to the American Jewish Historical Society, and that the archive contained more of Abe's writing about the East Side underworld, plus multiple drafts of *Crime Buster*. I also traveled to Hebrew University — atop Jerusalem's Mount Scopus, overlooking the Old City — to search through the Magnes archive. I found other relevant archives, such as the records of eminent families and the files of other reform committees that Abe worked for prior to joining the Kehillah. I interviewed an eighty-nine-year-old man named Harold Eriv, who had worked as Abe's typist from the late 1950s to the 1970s. Eriv, who later became a publisher of law textbooks, recalled the Kehillah stories Abe had told him during the nights they spent working together in Abe's apartment.

The underworld that provoked the crusade was documented gener-
ously in newspaper and magazine coverage, indictment records and affidavits at the New York City Municipal Archives, oral histories at the
New York Public Library, and hundreds of trial transcripts preserved at
the John Jay College of Criminal Justice.

For five years I read and cross-referenced these trials with the characters and crimes described in Kehillah documents. Raw and vivid, the
trials were like time machines to a forgotten demimonde, the hidden side
of New York during one of the city's most interesting periods. Immigrant
witnesses escorted me through the streets, and took me into tenements
and cafés, saloons and casinos, brothels and dance halls, opium dens and
black-market abortion providers. I read about criminal collectives and
gangs of all kinds, from horse poisoners to *Forward*-financed labor
sluggers.

Here, in the archives, were the *real* people, the *real* lives. Aside from
my German-Jewish heritage, via my maternal grandmother, I knew that
the other three branches of my family had been Russian Jews, tailors and
ragpickers who fled the Pale of Settlement around 1900 and came to Boston and Baltimore. But despite years of Jewish education, I'd never read
accounts like those related in the trials — the unmediated narratives of
the great majority.

From case records and Abe's writings, an important new character
surfaced. As I compiled the episodes of Antonia Rolnick's life, it became
clear that, even if her story was extreme, her struggles with exploitation
and marginalization, as well as her mettle, reflected common themes
among young Russian-Jewish women, mostly teenagers, whose role in
the community's eventual uplift was no less central than Abe's. These
were some of New York's most powerless citizens. As garment workers
they waged pitched battles in the streets, went to prison, died in factory
fires, and inspired reforms that changed American labor law and planted
the seed of the nation's social welfare system. Tony's saga, from refugee to

child laborer to prostitute to vigilante to labor thug, was a harrowing journey out of a brutal past, a sweep of immigrant experience that revealed a vanished time and place with shocking intimacy.

Her childhood friend, Lily, may not have been a central player in events — more like a straw carried on the wind — but she lived through it all, survived like Rambo, and then sat down and recorded her story in a four-part newspaper series, with a sensitivity and wit far beyond her nineteen years.

The ultimate shocker was the discovery that the Shoenfeld family knew the German-Jewish branch of my family, the Klee ancestors whose company became collateral damage during the Kehillah vice crusade, and the reason for Abe and Mayer's coming to blows. In fact, the information was right there on page one of Goren's interview with Abe: "You see, my father complained that bombs were going to be thrown at Lafayette and Fourth Street when I was in the P.D., and he wanted me to assign men, and I said, 'I'm not assigning men for the manufacturers.'" Abe references the story again, citing "that business of my father demanding that I send cops over to the Klee factory on Fourth Street."

I chalked it up to coincidence. There were countless tailors named Goldstein and Rosenberg. Surely, I figured, there were at least a few Klee factories, until I picked up my grandmother's memoir and read the bit about Klee *not* being a common Jewish name. Still, she never mentioned anything about bombings. I went back to the John Jay archive and discovered two trials concerning the bombing gang — one for the 1913 bombings of the Klee factory and dozens of others that year, and a second for the murder of a Chinese laundry owner. It turned out that the gang, a mix of Jewish and Italian teens, purchased explosives at a Bowery saloon called the Tub of Blood, where laborers working on the Lexington Avenue subway excavation came at the end of a day to trade their pilfered dynamite for after-work drinks. The prosecutor asked the gang leader, Alfred Lehman, known as the Boy Bomb King: "Do you know that every bomb you shot off is a crime punishable by fifteen years in state's prison in each instance?"

"Yes, sir."

"And you shot off thirty-three bombs?"

"Yes, sir."

"And killed a Chinaman besides?"

"I didn't kill any Chinaman."

"You were the one that struck the final blow with the billy?"

"Yes, I struck the blow with the billy."

"Well, what did you intend to hit him with, a sausage?"

Like Bastian in *The Neverending Story,* the boy who becomes a character in the book he's reading, I felt as though I'd stepped into the book I was writing. Although my personal connection to *The Incorruptibles* was tangential and didn't change anything about the story, it was one more surprise in a project that kept twisting in new directions.

The story of Arnold Rothstein took many turns, and several firsthand sources helped me through the maze, particularly Carolyn Rothstein's scarcely available memoir, *Now I'll Tell,* and two previously undiscovered documents, both published in 1929, the year after his death — the *Forward* interview with Abe the Just, and an eight-part newspaper series by Inez Norton.

Inez said she wasn't interested in Arnold for his money. Nevertheless, she did sue his estate for a $20,000 life insurance policy that he allegedly signed over to her on his deathbed. In those proceedings, she claimed that Arnold had proposed to her on three occasions. When the court declined to believe her, she said she was his kept woman. Eventually an appeals court ruled in her favor, but depression and financial troubles followed Inez and she attempted suicide. When she resurfaced in head-lines, at thirty-two, it was for her plans to marry a twenty-four-year-old who stood to inherit a million dollars. He and Inez encountered opposi-tion from his father, the young man said, "but we brought him around to our point of view."

In 2018, I traveled to the home of Abe's grandniece, Ellen James, in Mar-tinez, California, outside San Francisco. As a child growing up in New Jersey during the forties and fifties, Ellen would visit Abe and his brother, Dudley, a pioneering psychologist, in Manhattan. As a college student, she would sit on Abe's couch and listen to him talk about whatever he was reading at the time. Later, after graduating from law school at Berke-ley and becoming a judge, Ellen inherited Abe's papers, which she later donated, and his library, which she kept, allotting most of her shelf space to Uncle Abe's books.

I pulled down a bound anthology of Mayor William Gaynor's letters and speeches. In one speech, he wrote of his reverence for Jewish history, what he called "that lone unbroken lineage, down from twilight . . . those early centuries before medieval kings took the Jewish son and made a servant of him." As I flipped through the book, out of its pages fell an actual 1913 letter that Gaynor wrote to a Kehillah lawyer. The lawyer, apparently, had passed on to Gaynor a plan written by Abe, entitled "Legalized Prostitution," that called for a formal red-light district that would include two buildings, a staff of doctors, and free drugs used to treat syphilis and gonorrhea. Gaynor had heard such ideas before and didn't think much of them. "The natural tendency of these women is to congregate in districts, and no law is needed for that," he once said. "I would rather we see that they are not driven out of their natural congre-gations and scattered all over into thousands of flats." Now, in his amused reply, Gaynor wrote:

The document submitted by Mr. Shoenfeld (Prettyfield) is one of the most extraordinary that has ever come to my attention. It seems to be based on the notion that all that is necessary to do a thing is to pass a law for it to be done. Will he catch all the women and put them in these places? And will he then stand guard and keep them there? And how strong a guard would you need? Or does he think they will go there and stay there voluntarily? Ask him what he thinks of segregating virtue instead of vice. Would it not be an easier job? But we must not poke too much fun at him.

Sincerely,
William Gaynor

Since the age of fifteen, when he read William Sanger's *The History of Prostitution* ("Chapter 1: The Jews"), Abe had known that vice was an ineradicable fact of life, but the anti-prostitution drive of his youth came out of a profound prewar faith in social progress, and in making order out of the chaotic conditions that arose from galloping urbanization, industrialization, population explosion from immigration, ethnic diversity, and the independence of women. That spirit of reform, initially intended to clean up cities, took a sharp turn when it encountered the belief that coercive legislation could annihilate social ills and engineer universal human goodness. Gaynor predicted this inevitable chain, knowing that once you started cleaning, it was hard to stop, and so it went for Abe, whose final Kehillah report argued:

We must get away from this one pipe, one room, one man idea. The fact that a man may have one opium pipe in his room for private use should not save him. Inspectors can say they cannot arrest him. But the fact is that they can hold him on Section 1752. Or take 218 East 9th Street. Sure, the street is quiet at night, but pipe fiends live upstairs and half of the flats are being used for disorderly purposes. Never mind the lack of evidence. The flats should be raided and smashed to pieces. Break their furniture. Throw it out through a back window. That is the only way to deal with a house of this kind.

Prohibition began a couple years later, and soon thereafter Abe became dismayed by a world that he, as a tool of reform, had helped bring about. He fought to sever the connection between crime and politics, but the weapon in that fight, vice repression, created a more formidable and enduring connection. "What political power meant for the defense of all those people," he said, referring to the old East Side criminals, "Prohibition meant years later." By midcentury he called for the decriminalization of gambling, drugs, and prostitution, and felt that corporate control of elections was the biggest threat facing the country. And still, on the communal scale of uplift, particularly the plight of Jewish women, the cause that drew him into reform, he could see a line of progress from his first days to his last.

Back in 1913, when one of Abe's sisters gave birth to a daughter, a baby who later became the mother of Abe's grandniece, Ellen James, the experience of becoming an uncle renewed Abe's sense of purpose, and in a Kehillah report he wrote: "My dear Magnes, we may not be able to drive out prostitution entirely, for it may exist even in the Palace of the King, but we can lessen it, and a great aid toward this result is the fact that more and more women are coming into their own, leaving the fields of dependence and becoming independent." Six decades later, his greatest joy of old age was seeing Ellen, at thirty-two, become one of the first female judges in California.

In his final years, at the apartment on Central Park South, he also entertained a grandnephew, Steven Mandel, a cop for the NYPD. While working night shifts, Steven often dropped in and usually found Abe, who suffered from a bad back and had trouble sleeping, in the lobby of his building with a pot of coffee that he shared with the doorman and the prostitutes outside who roamed Fifty-Ninth Street. One night, as they walked back from a late meal, a panhandler reached across Steven and asked Abe for change. When Steven, irritated, swatted the panhandler's arm away and made a rude comment, Abe elbowed his grandnephew in the side hard enough that Steven doubled over. "Don't ever push away a man who is so troubled that he has to lower himself to beg," Abe said. "Give him something."

GLOSSARY OF THE EAST SIDE UNDERWORLD

Alphonse. A pimp; *also* cadet, mack, *schimcha* (Yiddish).

Bad fall. An arrest in which the fix does not hold; *compare* right fall.

Bail sticker. One who ropes in a landlord or property owner on a jump-bond.

Banker. A man who takes money at racetracks and casinos.

Battleship. A sturdy woman.

Begroben (Yiddish). In hiding; (literally) buried. "He'll remain *begroben* until the investigation is over."

Betsy. A revolver; *also* gat, git, iron, rod, smoke wagon.

Blow. To run away; the passage of semen.

Bolawala. Bullshit; *also* soft music.

Booster. A thief who steals from the counter of a retail store; a shoplifter.

Bridge. A pocket.

Bull-slinger. A bluffer or bullshitter; *also* fourflusher.

Butter factory. A brothel; *also* disorderly house, fish market, natch.

Can. A prostitute who offers anal sex; *also* red-bow. "That one-dollar house is running full force with thirty girls, three of them cans"; *compare* middle-bridger.

Cashier. One who pays out in a gambling parlor.

Chinning. Making casual conversation, or joking.

Coffee-and-cake mack. A cheap pimp; also *pezevenk* (Yiddish).

Coke fiend. One who sniffs cocaine; *also* sniffer.

Come across. To inform, squeal; *also* throw up.

Complaint detective. A dishonest cop who obtains warrants of arrest only so that he can make money by steering cases to defense lawyers.

Defi. An act of defiance.

Dropper. A killer.

Fade away. To get away.

Fall. An arrest; *see also* right fall, bad fall.

Fall dough. A fund of money to use when arrested.

Fan. To frisk another's pockets.

Fence. One who receives and sells stolen goods.

Firebug. An arsonist.

French. Oral sex; *see* snake-charmer.

Frisch' schore (Yiddish). Prospective prostitutes; (literally) fresh goods; *also* chicken.

Gazlunim (Yiddish). Criminals.

Geelik. A fool; gee.

Goo-goo boy. A good-government activist, often used pejoratively to describe a fake reformer.

Gun. A pickpocket; *also* cannon, dip, instrument, stall, tool, wire.

Gun-moll. A woman who steals from a man; *compare* moll-buzzer.

Gut. The red-light district of a city.

Harness copper. A rookie cop.

Heeled. Armed. "I had my back to the wall and was well-heeled, a betsy in my belt holster."

Heylik zakh (Yiddish). A holy thing. "The true identity of the bagman is a *heylik zakh*."

Hoggish. Greedy.

Hop. Opium; *also* oatmeal.

Hophead. Opium user.

Hunk. To get even, to settle a score. "I don't squeal. I'll get hunk in my own way."

Hustler. A streetwalker, or independent prostitute; *also* cruiser, tot, trotter.

IBA (Independent Benevolent Association). Union of Jewish pimps.

Jump-bond. A bail secured so that a prisoner can jump it.

Just pimp. A low-level pimp who aspires to own a brothel and secure membership in the IBA.

Lady dick. Woman detective.

Lammister. A bail skipper or fugitive; one who owes another money and does not pay.

Lighthouse. A watchboy who looks out for cops and solicits trade to a brothel.

Mazuma (Yiddish, slang). Money; *also* gelt, kale, sugar.

Meckler (Yiddish). A middleman; someone with no criminal record who leases real estate on behalf of agents, who in turn sublease the property to pimps and madams.

Middle-bridger. A prostitute who sells her "middle pocket"; *compare* can.

Mockey. An immigrant Jew (pejorative).

Mockey mob. A gang of Jewish pickpockets, often made up of immigrants.

Moll-buzzer. One who steals from a woman, i.e., who buzzes the molls; *compare* gun-moll.

Moos. Measure, i.e., an amount of money, as in graft or protection money. "Whenever he came for the *moos,* I gave, and I didn't want to know where it went."

Moozle. A kiss.

Mouthpiece. A lawyer; *also* rat.

Nafke (Yiddish). Prostitute; *also* fish, gash.

Ongegreyt (Yiddish). Savings (saved money).

On the chalk. On account; used of a debt that will never be recovered. "Mark it on the chalk." *Also* on the ice.

Peruvnik (Yiddish). A double-crosser.

Pipe. A certainty, or sure thing.

Platte schoire (Yiddish). Stolen goods.

Poke. A pocketbook.

Punching gun. Talking of thievery.

Queter. A quarter.

Quimbo. A young prostitute; *compare* star.

Racket. A ball with dancing and booze, usually given by criminals in order to raise money; a criminal endeavor, often involving extortion by intimidation.

Racket-runner. One who runs balls.

Rall. Syphilis.

Red flag. Period of menstruation. "Her red flag is out."

Right fall. An arrest made only for show; the arrestee is released; *compare* bad fall.

Romance. To exaggerate or lie; *also* vapor.

Rubber-neck car. A wagon that takes tourists to the ghettos of the East Side and Chinatown.

Settled. Convicted of a crime.

Shaft. Thighs and legs of a woman.

Sheet-writer. One who writes bets down.

Shomis (Yiddish; plural *schamussin*; also *shamus* or *shammes,* from the Hebrew *shamash,* a helper, servant, or functionary; and the ninth candle on a menorah). A detective. Yinglish: *"Schick aweg* the *schamussin,* and I will give you *fimf hundert shtanges."* Translation: "Send away the detectives and I will give you five hundred dollars."

Shtanges (Yiddish). Dollars; *also* beans.

Shtumi (Yiddish). A dumb person.

Sixer. A six-month jail sentence.

Skeemio. A pedophile; pimp who lures children into prostitution.

Snake-charmer. A prostitute who offers oral sex; *see* french.

Spieler. A good dancer.

Squealer. An informer; *also* stool, stool pigeon.

Star. A well-known prostitute; *compare* quimbo.

Steerer. One who gets cases for a lawyer, or customers for a casino.

Stick. To demonstrate loyalty to a cause, to not inform or squeal; *also*
halt den pisk (Yiddish).

Stock exchange. A hangout where pimps and prostitutes gather.

Stone getter. One who steals stickpins and other jewelry.

Sucker. One who blows his money.

Swim. Business, or good business, usually criminal in nature. "When
this investigation is over we'll be back in the swim."

Switcher. One who sells fake jewels.

Trombanik (Yiddish). A person who hangs around; *also* bumbatch,
lobbygow, lobby guy.

Trotter. A streetwalker, or independent prostitute; *also* cruiser,
hustler, tot.

Vag. The catchall crime of vagrancy, often used as a verb. "If you can't
get charges on him, vag the punk."

Velvet. Easy money; *also* soft dough.

Venire-men. Jurors.

Verdiner (Yiddish). A male who makes a living by stealing.

Verdiniker (Yiddish). A female who makes a living by stealing.

Yard. A hundred dollars. "The mouthpiece got five yards to appear for us."

Yegg. A safecracker.

Yelapa. A foreign place a pimp receives money from. "He gets his
money from Yelapa." Likely originates from Yelapa, Mexico.

Yenhawk. An opium pipe.

Yenshee. Ashes of smoked opium, often used to adulterate pills for hopheads who can't pay full price.

Yot. A child.

Zhit. A nickel.

ACKNOWLEDGMENTS

Back in the day, in the garment-inflected lingo of bygone New York, if a person was unusually genuine and dependable, it was said of them that they were all wool and a yard wide. The book in your hands was made with the assistance of many such folks.

My literary agent, Farley Chase, supplied essential feedback during the germination phase. Vanessa Mobley gave *The Incorruptibles* a welcome home at Little, Brown. When Vanessa left the book business to pursue a new path, Asya Muchnick stepped in and assumed editorship as if the project had been hers from the start: as a Russian-Jewish immigrant herself, it sort of *was*. Asya's moxie and zeal for the work, her censure of the semicolon and all needless complications — these attributes are like jet fuel for an author.

From dependable to dependable, my book and I were ferried along by an excellent squad that included Maya Guthrie, Katharine Myers, Anna Brill, Marieska Luzada, Pat Jalbert-Levine, Albert LaFarge, Allan Fallow, Sarah Russo, Laura Di Giovine, Laci Durham, and Peter Dyer. Shulem Deen, my Yiddish translator and researcher, found loads of important articles in the archives of Yiddish newspapers. Many Yiddish words and phrases from the old days are no longer in use, or now mean something else entirely. When language enigmas came up, Shulem decoded them quickly, and his etymology lessons were one of my favorite parts of working on the book.

I owe unpayable debts to the staffs of the archives I consulted, and to Rob Cavaleri, who took the author photo and edited a killer book trailer, all the while pouring one masterful latte after another.

Given such partners, I often sensed some higher power watching out, guiding the project to completion. That feeling of fate was confirmed in 2020, when Andrea Evans Young, of Lelands auction house, began the yearslong process of selling off—week by week, image by image—the archive of Brown Brothers, a news photography service that operated in New York during the early 1900s. Each week, like a fossil record shouldering its way to the surface, another batch of stunning photos appeared: hopheads and horse poisoners, breadlines and labor sluggers, the six-day bicycle race and Arnold Rothstein's Broadway. Of the sixty-plus images that illustrate these pages, most came from the Brown Brothers archive, a mix of original prints and glass negatives that had been stored away for a century.

Though my sons can't yet view the photos or read the book, *The Incorruptibles* is dedicated to them. Six years ago, Silas was two when I began sifting through Kehillah reports. A year later, I was surrounded by stacks of trial transcripts when it was time to go to the hospital to welcome Felix into the world. My dear boys: If you've grown up with the impression that "the Jewish underworld" is some enchanted destination, please know that the truly magical place, ever and always, is the joyful life that you, by existing, have given me.

I've learned this craft from innumerable storytellers—writers and editors, filmmakers and performers. But, these days, my life-and-death mentors are the people in our family and community who surround me with their support and friendship: the Rady-Kemerys, Pacheco-Hills, Tucker-Eikenberrys, Barr-Nguyens, Chaix-Weavers, Pollard-Bernsteins, Hoverman-Laceys, Nicholson-Callanans, Speerts and Millners, Herberts and Plimptons, Renners and Ryders, Palumbos and Popps, Toths and Dorfmans, Soupons and Luards, Farmers and Thomases — without you, I wouldn't necessarily know what it looks like to be an amazing neighbor, or a devoted parent. My family wouldn't have local food without Sport Hill Farm, or a cozy café without Greiser's Market, or books galore without the Easton Public Library. I couldn't renovate a forest without Jeremy Carlson, build a bridge without Jim Marshall, or raise my children properly without Carrie Reilly and Elisa Lennox. I wouldn't be healthy without the therapy of Nancy Vernooy, Taylor Ashton, and Cynthia Quintanal, or the yoga of Lisa Giordano, Holly Arcadi, and Nicole Kim.

It's impossible to summarize my gratitude for the three women in my life. Nancy Speert Slater gives me love and education, a model of decency and resilience. Martha Stewart shows me what it means to be fearless and forgiving, faithful and true, and she entrusts me with that singular gift, her niece, Sophie Martha Herbert Slater, whose love and light are the hinge upon which all good things have swung my way.

NOTES

PART ONE: NOBILITY IN DOLLAR LAND

CHAPTER ONE: BETWEEN WORLDS

Details of Arnold's boyhood, in school and the streets, can be found in a ten-part newspaper series by Joseph Lily, published in the *New York Telegram* in November and December of 1929; Michael Alexander, *Jazz Age Jews* (Princeton, NJ: Princeton University Press, 2001), 19–23; and Leo Katcher, *The Big Bankroll: The Life and Times of Arnold Rothstein* (New York: Harper & Brothers, 1958), 18–24. The many Rothstein residences and business addresses, going back to the arrival of Arnold's grandfather in the mid-1800s, are catalogued in Nick Tosches, *King of the Jews* (New York: Ecco, 2005).

Arnold's older brother is identified as "Harry" in Katcher, *Big Bankroll,* and as "Bertram," or "Bertie," in Tosches, *King of the Jews*. I've gone with Bertie because Tosches, though much of the material in his book is uncited, delivers the most extensive chronicle of the Rothstein family history. The background of Abraham Rothstein appears in Katcher, *Big Bankroll,* 11–15; Tosches, *King of the Jews,* 134–140; Benjamin Stolberg, *A Tailor's Progress* (New York: Doubleday, 1944), 139–40; and the 1929 *New York Telegram* series by Joseph Lily. The fullest portrait emerges in an interview with Abraham Rothstein himself—"Arnold Rothstein's Father Pours His Heart Out to Forward Correspondent," *Forward,* April 3, 1929—in which the reporter verifies the subject's reputation as "Abe the Just."

The notorious labor conditions of the time can be found in Stolberg, *Tailor's Progress*; Joel Seidman, *The Needle Trades* (New York: Farrar & Rinehart, 1942); Louis Levine,

Notes

The Women's Garment Workers: A History of the International Ladies' Garment Workers' Union (New York: B. W. Huebsch, 1924); J. M. Budish and George Soule, The New Unionism (New York: Harcourt, Brace & Howe, 1920); Bernard Weinstein, The Jewish Unions in America: Pages of History and Memories (Cambridge, UK: Open Book Publishers, 2018); Sam Liptzin, Tales of a Tailor: Humor and Tragedy in the Struggles of the Early Immigrants Against the Sweatshop (New York: Prompt Press, 1965); Elias Tcherikower, The Early Jewish Labor Movement in the U.S. (New York: YIVO Institute for Jewish Research, 1961); David Von Drehle, Triangle: The Fire That Changed America (New York: Grove Press, 2003); Richard A. Greenwald, The Triangle Fire, the Protocols of Peace, and Industrial Democracy in Progressive Era New York (Philadelphia: Temple University Press, 2005); Mike Wallace, Greater Gotham: A History of New York City from 1898 to 1919 (New York: Oxford University Press, 2017); Graham Adams Jr., Age of Industrial Violence, 1910–1915 (New York: Columbia University Press, 1966); Leon Stein, ed., Out of the Sweatshop: The Struggle for Industrial Democracy (New York: Quadrangle, 1977); and Susan A. Glenn, Daughters of the Shtetl: Life and Labor in the Immigrant Generation (Ithaca, NY: Cornell University Press, 1990).

The plight of young immigrants is explored in Elizabeth Ewen, Immigrant Women in the Land of Dollars: Life and Culture on the Lower East Side, 1890–1925 (New York: Monthly Review Press, 1985); and Glenn, Daughters of the Shtetl.

Arnold's early gambling career can be found in Alexander, Jazz Age Jews, 28–30; and Katcher, Big Bankroll, 31–40.

It was said of Big Tim Sullivan that there was never a greater admixture of good and evil in one human character. Big Tim's background and the unique position he held in East Side life can be found in Andy Logan, Against the Evidence: The Becker-Rosenthal Affair (New York: McCall Publishing, 1970), 55–59.

In the early 1880s, when Big Tim was nineteen and the East Side was still mostly Irish, he opened his own saloon at 71 Chrystie Street. This was a time, according to a report by the state legislature in Albany, when one square East Side block might contain as many as thirty-five saloons. Big Tim's saloon became a hangout for the Whyos, known as the worst of the Irish street gangs that sprang up in the years after the Civil War. The Whyos took their name from the cry they gave when they were about to attack such rival gangs as the Rags and the Boodles. When these gangs weren't fighting each other, they made beer money by robbing, burgling, and hiring out as thugs. But the gangs' biggest earning season came at election time, when Tammany Hall leaders "booked" them—hired them to serve as "repeaters" who voted several times apiece, and as terrorists who intimidated voters, dragging reluctant Democrats to the polls and suppressing the Republican vote. Logan explains the origins of Tammany's tie-up with gamblers: "To keep gang members in funds between elections, the politicians found jobs for them in the off-season months. Gambling houses, with their need for resident thugs, offered the ideal solution. Gambling houses all over town found they had a far better chance of staying in business if they enlarged their overhead with retainers to these friends of local democracy, many of whom were no-shows except on payday."

This system is elaborated on in Harold Zink, *City Bosses in the United States* (Durham, NC: Duke University Press, 1930). By 1901, Zink writes, "Practically every saloon, poolroom, and gambling house in the district served as an active center for vote-getting and afterwards payrolls were opened to reward faithful political workers. The Comanche Club [a casino owned by the Jewish gambler Dollar John Langer], the Association headquarters, and numerous lodging houses and saloons of the Bowery registered hundreds of 'mattress' voters at every election and thus helped to swell the Sullivan vote."

For more on Big Tim, see M. R. Werner, *Tammany Hall* (New York: Doubleday, 1928), 438; Alvin F. Harlow, *Old Bowery Days* (New York: D. Appleton, 1931), 489; Stephen Paul DeVillo, *The Bowery: The Strange History of New York's Oldest Street* (New York: Skyhorse Publishing, 2019), 157–160; Alexander, *Jazz Age Jews,* 19; and Katcher, *Big Bankroll,* 23–29. Clearing up confusion around the term "poolroom," or "pool room," Katcher writes: "Lottery, because of the manner in which winnings were paid off, was called 'pool.' Since lottery tickets were sold all day and the drawings were not held until late in the evening, proprietors of poolrooms installed billiard tables to occupy their customers during the long waiting periods. The game of billiards was either too slow or too difficult. . . . They devised a game of their own, first called 'pocket billiards' and later 'pool.'"

Big Tim's prophecy for Arnold and Herman appears in Katcher, *Big Bankroll,* 28. The role Canfield played in Arnold's imagination can be found in Carolyn Rothstein, *Now I'll Tell* (New York: Vanguard Press, 1934), 26. Canfield's life is chronicled in Alexander Garfield, *Canfield: The True Story of the Greatest Gambler* (New York: Doubleday & Doran, 1930); Herbert Asbury, *Sucker's Progress: An Informal History of Gambling in America* (New York: Dodd, Mead, 1938; reprint, New York: Thunder's Mouth, 2003); and Richard O'Connor, *Courtroom Warrior: The Combative Career of William Travers Jerome* (Boston: Little, Brown, 1963), 94–109.

The gambling scene at Saratoga is covered in Alexander, *Jazz Age Jews,* 28–30; Rothstein, *Now I'll Tell,* 25–27; Katcher, *Big Bankroll,* 48–49; and Hugh Bradley, *Such Was Saratoga* (New York: Doubleday & Doran, 1940). Bradley writes that the early patrician bookmakers "presumed, reasonably enough, that their functions were similar to those of Wall Street brokers. They advertised in leading newspapers, sometimes on the front page and next to the advertisements of famous banking houses, as Turf Exchanges. . . . Those with the strongest financial and political backing formed the Metropolitan Turf Association, which preempted the best places in the betting ring and practically controlled horse-race wagering in New York State" (282).

The betting-parlor raid occasioned Arnold's first appearance in the news: "'Bachelor Apartment' Raided," *Sun,* January 1, 1907. But this raid didn't deter him. In Rothstein, *Now I'll Tell,* Carolyn reflects that when she first met Arnold, in September of 1908, he was, unbeknownst to her, "operating what might be termed a poolroom, and living modestly in an apartment, in West Fifty-First Street, with [gambler] Felix Duffy. They had a room with two or three telephones, and handled bets" (21–22).

CHAPTER TWO: THE CRUSADING PATH

The strikers' march on the Shoenfeld home is chronicled in "New York's Big Strike," *Wilkes-Barre (PA) Times Leader,* May 18, 1997; and Abraham Shoenfeld, *Crime Buster: My Memoirs to 1921* (unpublished). Abe worked on *Crime Buster* for roughly fifty years and turned out at least nine drafts, seven of which are archived in the Abraham Shoenfeld Papers at the American Jewish Historical Society (hereinafter: ASP-AJHS), Series 1. I gathered another two drafts, plus associated notes and marginalia, from private sources, as well as additional biographical material from Harold Eriv, who worked as Abe's typist for fifteen years, from the late 1950s to the 1970s. Since these materials are either unnumbered, unpaginated, unarchived, or all three, I will refer generally to *Crime Buster* when citing details of Abe's personal story.

The rise of labor leader Mayer Shoenfeld—also called "Meyer" and "Schoenfeld" in newspaper coverage—during the mid-1890s is chronicled in "Meyer Schoenfeld: The Leader of the Great Coatmakers' Strike in New York City," *Garret Clipper,* October 4, 1894; "Out on Strike: Twelve Thousand New York Tailors Fighting Sweat Shops," *Democrat and Chronicle,* July 29, 1895 ("He has the same influence over the tailors that Joseph Barondess formerly had over the cloakmakers. The audience shouted and yelled with delight when he approached"); "Many Tailors on Strike: 25,000 Workers May Be Involved," *New York Times,* July 29, 1895 ("Shoenfeld told the people: 'We will down the sweating system if it takes six months!'"); "Labor's Latest and Best Leader and Friend: Meyer Shoenfeld, Who Is Not an Agitator, But Has Good Sense," *Chattanooga Daily Times,* August 18, 1985 ("At sixteen years of age he came to this country. For twelve years he worked in the sweatshops and tenements.... Shoenfeld's moderation, his marked ability to control men—these overworked, hysterical, excited products of the sweatshop, and an inbred race—placed him at the head of the union"); "Shoenfeld Takes Hold: Decides to Lead the Striking Brotherhood of Tailors," *Sun,* December 19, 1895 ("The girls flung flowers at him, and then clambering to the platform fought for the possession of the flowers that touched him").

By 1896, Mayer Shoenfeld was struggling to mollify the Brotherhood of Tailors and contain their aggression. At mass meetings, he often locked the doors to prevent irate mobs of strikers from attacking factories and the scab workers who filled their positions during strikes. "Strikers Begin Rioting," *Sun,* August 3, 1896; and "Frenzied New York Strikers: Numerous Fights between Pickets and Non-Union Tailors," *Brooklyn Daily Eagle,* August 3, 1896 (Mayer: "We are now winning, and we do not want to play into the hands of the law, as that is just what the contractors want").

The meaning of "slack season" is described by a Russian-Jewish immigrant named Maurice Hindus, who emigrated from the Pale of Settlement in 1905, when he was fourteen. Hindus, born the same year as Abe Shoenfeld, lived in typical ghetto fashion, working as an errand boy for a sweatshop boss. In *Green Worlds* (New York: Doubleday & Doran, 1938), he recalled the period known simply as "slack":

> Though it was a new word to me, it did not take me long to
> learn its harrowing meaning. Girl after girl was laid off.
> Expressmen ceased coming up with cases and rolls of
> cloth. Fewer and fewer messenger boys called with packages.
> Finally, all the "operators" were told not to come any more.
> The engine was at a standstill, and so were the machines, and
> the quiet was at first deafening. Lina [a girl whom Hindus
> had a crush on] and her mother were still needed to sew
> buttons on the heaps of remaining garments. I too was
> needed to sweep the floor, fold the garments, pack them into
> boxes, and carry them to the express office. With Lina and her
> mother around, the shop still had glamor. But soon there
> were no more garments on which to sew buttons, and Lina
> and her mother were laid off until the "new season," which
> might begin in two months and might not start in less than
> four.... Soon I too was needed no longer and was dismissed.

Mayer Shoenfeld's decision to return to union leadership in 1897 inspired the tailors: "Strike Spreading: Meyer Schoenfeld Agrees to Lead Movement," *Boston Globe,* May 18, 1897 ("The news that he had taken up the management of the strike caused the tailors to become demonstrative in the streets, and imbued them with more confidence than would have the news that every garment worker in the city had struck"). The victory party was reported in "Strikers Hold a Picnic: Five Thousand in Attendance," *Brooklyn Daily Eagle,* June 16, 1897; Mayer's health problems were reported in "Schoenfeld Breaks Down," *World,* June 17, 1897.

When Schiff visited the Shoenfeld home, he and Mayer had a preexisting relationship, Schiff having served as a mediator in the recent strike: "Tailors Returning to Work: Efforts of Jacob Schiff to End the Strike," *New-York Tribune,* June 4, 1897. Mayer's agreement to establish a New Jersey Colony, financed by Schiff and the Baron de

Hirsch Fund, is reported in "Schoenfeld to Colonize Tailors and Cloakmakers," *Baltimore Sun,* December 29, 1897; and "Schoenfeld to Colonize Poor Tailors," *New York Times,* January 4, 1898. The Kenilworth colony is described in Shoenfeld, *Crime Buster,* and documented in AJHS, Records of the Industrial Removal Office.

The German-Jewish experience in America is documented in Stephen Birmingham, *Our Crowd: The Great Jewish Families of New York* (New York: Harper & Row, 1967). The Germany they left behind, and their history there, can be found in Ruth Gay, *The Jews of Germany: A Historical Portrait* (New Haven, CT: Yale University Press, 1992); and Amos Elon, *The Pity of It All: A Portrait of the German-Jewish Epoch, 1743–1933* (New York: Metropolitan Books, 2002). German-Jewish Wall Street, reform, and the merger movement are chronicled in Wallace, *Greater Gotham*; Carey Goodman, *Choosing Sides: Playground and Street Life on the Lower East Side* (New York: Schocken, 1979); Naomi W. Cohen, *Jacob H. Schiff: A Study in American Jewish Leadership* (Hanover, NH: Brandeis University Press, 1999); Ron Chernow, *The Warburgs: The Twentieth-Century Odyssey of a Remarkable Jewish Family* (New York: Random House, 1993); Irving Howe, *World of Our Fathers: The Journey of the East European Jews to America and the Life They Found and Made* (New York: Schocken, 1976); and Birmingham, *Our Crowd.*

The threat that Eastern European Jews posed for German Jews is addressed in Sven Beckert, *The Monied Metropolis: New York City and the Consolidation of the Bourgeoisie, 1850–1896* (New York: Cambridge University Press, 2001), 265–66. Beckert explains why, in the late 1800s, anti-Semitism spread among Wasps: "For one, economic competition, especially in the world of investment banking, gave Protestants a strong incentive to isolate their Jewish competitors from some of the social networks that were the lifeblood of that business. Moreover, the influx of thousands of unskilled workers from the ghettos of Eastern Europe . . . helped link the bourgeois fear of workers [generally] to the [specific] fear of Jews, especially because Jewish workers showed an exceptional tendency to embrace trade unions and socialism."

The East Side's pecking order and intra-ethnic resentments are explained in Stephen Birmingham, *The Rest of Us: The Rise of America's Eastern European Jews* (Boston: Little, Brown, 1984), 31. East Side green spaces and the organized play movement are covered in Goodman, *Choosing Sides.*

Firsthand accounts of the early years of Jewish vice on the East Side can be found in Shoenfeld, *Crime Buster*; the Judah L. Magnes Archives (hereinafter: MA), 1779–93; and Maude E. Miner, *Slavery of Prostitution: A Plea for Emancipation* (New York: Macmillan, 1916). In his autobiography, *The Education of Abraham Cahan*, vol. 3 (unpublished), the writer and Yiddish newspaper editor Abraham Cahan, who emigrated from Eastern Europe in 1882, recalls Allen Street as "the most disgusting section of the city." Cahan writes:

At night the windows in the houses of prostitution were illuminated by red lamps, and the expression "red light district" derives from that time. Allen Street was the center of this shameful district, and the owners of the houses of prostitution and procurers, or Alfonsos, as the disgusting creatures were called... ruled there with unlimited power. It was literally a danger to walk through that street. Men were actually grabbed and dragged into the "red light" little houses, and sometimes they were also robbed and beaten. To yell for the police was senseless. Even if a policeman were standing nearby, he did not interfere, unless he helped to beat the victim, or he dragged him to the station house on false charges.

Of Cahan's five-volume autobiography, written in Yiddish, the Jewish Publication Society of America published English translations of volumes 1 and 2 before interest, or funding, expired. However, one of the translators on that project, Leon Stein, left an unpublished translation of vol. 3 in his papers at Cornell University's Kheel Center for Labor Management, the Leon Stein Collection.

Like Cahan, Michael Gold was also marked by red-light memories. Gold, whose birthname was Itzok Isaac Granich, was born on the East Side in 1894, three years after Abe Shoenfeld. "The East Side of New York was then the city's red light district, a vast 606 playground under the business management of Tammany Hall," Gold begins his fictionalized autobiography, *Jews Without Money* (New York: Horace Liveright, 1930).* "There were hundreds of prostitutes on my street," Gold continues. "They occupied vacant stores, they crowded into flats and apartments in all the tenements.... The girls were naked under flowery kimonos. Chunks of breast and belly occasionally flashed.... Earth's trees, grass, flowers could not grow on my street; but the rose of syphilis bloomed by night and by day." In *Crime Buster,* Abe writes, "We were in a period of growing apprehension regarding venereal disease. The city was doing nothing about it."

Historical chronicles of Jewish vice include Jenna Weissman Joselit, *Our Gang: Jewish Crime and the New York Jewish Community, 1900–1940* (Bloomington: Indiana University Press, 1983); Albert Fried, *The Rise and Fall of the Jewish Gangster in America* (New York: Columbia University Press, 1980); Rose Keefe, *The Starker: Big Jack Zelig, the Becker-Rosenthal Case, and the Advent of the Jewish Gangster* (Nashville: Cumberland House, 2008); Edward K. Bristow, *Prostitution and Prejudice: The Jewish Fight*

---

* The phrase "606 playground" refers to Salvarsan 606, a syphilis treatment — efficacious but costly at six dollars a vial.

against White Slavery, 1870–1939 (New York: Schocken, 1983); Arthur A. Goren, *New York Jews and the Quest for Community: The Kehillah Experiment* (New York: Columbia University Press, 1970); and Jean Ulitz Mensch, "Social Pathology in Urban America: Desertion, Prostitution, Gambling, Drugs, and Crime among Eastern European Jews in New York City between 1881 and World War I" (PhD diss., Columbia University, 1983). In *Greater Gotham,* 584–87, Wallace explains the difference between the Irish and Jewish underworld.

Documentation of the Committee of Fifteen's activities in 1901, including the evidence gathered, can be found at the New York Public Library Committee of Fifteen Records (hereinafter: NYPLCOF). (That same year, Schiff wrote that it was "horrifying" to discover that 23 percent of delinquents in New York reformatories were Jewish, given that Jews then constituted only 14 percent of the city's population.) The Committee of Fifteen vice crusade is described in Wallace, *Greater Gotham,* 109; and O'Connor, *Courtroom Warrior,* 70–72. A first-person account of Jerome's crusade can be found in Alfred Hodder, *A Fight for the City* (New York: Macmillan, 1903). Jerome's campaign for DA is chronicled in O'Connor, *Courtroom Warrior,* 77.

Abe's homelife and experience in school are described in *Crime Buster,* and his school records are archived at ASP-AJHS, Series 1. Louie's childhood travails and juvenile criminal record are laid out in an interview with his father in *The Survey,* April 4, 1914, 14. A description of Roosevelt's Valentine's Day visit to Little Hungary can be found in Michael Lesy and Lisa Stoffer, *Repast: Dining Out in the New American Century, 1900–1910* (New York: W. W. Norton, 2013), 131–38.

Horrific first-person accounts of the early-1900s pogroms can be found in two contemporaneously published books. The first is Michael Davitt, *Within the Pale: The True Story of Anti-Semitic Persecution in Russia* (New York: A. S. Barnes, 1903). Davitt, an Irish republican activist who served two prison terms before being elected to Parliament, based *Within the Pale* on his travels through Russia. Because of Davitt's credentials back home, he was able to access Russian officials, many of whom made comparisons between Russia and America. One official tells Davitt: "These people [Russian Jews] are not of us, any more than the Chinese of San Francisco, or the ten millions of emancipated Negroes, are free citizens in the United States Republic. They are a danger to the Empire from within." Another official says: "We never will admit a people [Russian Jews] so foreign in every respect to the Russians in racial traits and character, in faith and in general reputation, to an equality of citizenship. You might as well ask the American people to permit Chinamen to become Mayors of San Francisco or members of Congress." Another says: "What can we do with them? They are the racial antithesis of our nation.... We cannot admit them to equal rights of citizenship for these reasons and, let me add, because their intellectual superiority would enable them in a few years' time to gain possession of most of the posts of our civil administration." Another contemporaneous account of the pogroms and Jewish life in the Pale can be found in Henry W. Nevinson, *The Dawn in Russia, or Scenes in the Russian Revolution* (London: Harper & Brothers, 1906). More recent works include John D. Klier and Shlomo Lambroza, eds., *Pogroms: Anti-Jewish Violence in Modern Russian History* (Cambridge: Cambridge University Press, 1992); and Steven J. Zipperstein, *Pogrom: Kishinev and the Tilt of History* (New York: Liveright, 2018). After Kishinev, the word *pogrom*—meaning "devastation" in Russian—entered the international lexicon to describe a violent outrage against a particular ethnic group.

As early as 1903, the East Side was thought to be the most densely populated ghetto in the world: "To Improve East Side, Public Playgrounds and Widening of Allen St. Strongly Urged," *New-York Tribune,* April 26, 1903; and by 1910, it had become an accepted fact: "The Old East Side Gives Way to the New," *New York Times,* April 3, 1910. In June of 1906, as Abe pondered his academic future, the dislocation that attended the influx of immigrants seemed to climax with the so-called Adenoidal Riots. On a June morning, mobs of Jewish mothers descended on schools throughout the East Side, shrieking in Yiddish. They were responding to rumors that the Board of Health planned to cut their children's throats. In an effort to rescue their kids, the Jewish mothers threw bricks through windows, smashed doors, and assaulted teachers who got in the way.

In the end, it took seventy-five cops, dispatched from eleven precincts, to quell the riot and resolve the confusion. One school, it turned out, had detected children who suffered from adenoidal growths, a common ghetto affliction. The principal sent home a letter asking parents for permission to remove the troublesome tissue, which, if unremoved, caused respiratory and speech problems. Unable to read English, but doing their best to comply with American customs, the parents signed the forms. When I first read about this episode, I laughed, then cried when I realized that, to these immigrants, the subsequent rumor of throat-slashing was perfectly plausible, given the massacres from which they had fled. "East Side Schools Mobbed by Hordes of Parents: Aroused by False Rumor of Children Being Slaughtered," *World,* June 27, 1906; and "East Side Parents Storm the Schools: Cheap Doctors Told Them Their Children Were Being Killed," *New York Times,* June 28, 1906.

The Shoenfelds' involvement with the 1906 Hughes campaign is chronicled in Shoenfeld, *Crime Buster*; "East Side Hughes Campaign: Mayer Shoenfeld Organizing It in the Jewish Quarter," *Sun,* October 9, 1906; " 'Spellbinding by Phono': Instruments Will Resound for Hughes on East Side Streets," *Baltimore Sun,* October 23, 1906; "Phonograph Talks Hughes: Mayer Shoenfeld Makes an Experiment on the East Side," *New York Times,* October 24, 1906; and "Attack on Hughes Man: Roughs Throw Rocks and Bricks at Carriage of Mayer Shoenfeld, No Arrests Made," *Buffalo Morning Express,* November 7, 1906.

CHAPTER THREE: MAKING YOUR MARK

The corporate, financial, and physical transformations of New York are captured in Wallace, *Greater Gotham*. The battle over regulation of racetrack gambling and the Hart-Agnew law can be found in Merlo J. Pusey, *Charles Evans Hughes* (New York: Macmillan, 1951), vol. 1, 225–32. The law's significance for Jewish bookmakers is covered in Wallace, *Greater Gotham*, 620–21; and Alexander, *Jazz Age Jews*, 29–30.

Jewish involvement in the liquor trade is chronicled in Simon Dubnow, *History of the Jews in Russia and Poland* (Philadelphia: Jewish Publication Society of America, 1920), vols. 1–3; and Glenn Dynner, *Yankel's Tavern: Jews, Liquor, and Life in the Kingdom of Poland* (New York: Oxford University Press, 2014). The modern history of Jewish prostitution can be found in Laurie Bernstein, *Sonia's Daughters: Prostitutes and Their Regulation in Imperial Russia* (Berkeley: University of California Press, 1995); Laura Engelstein, *The Keys to Happiness: Sex and the Search for Modernity in Fin-de-Siècle Russia* (Ithaca, NY: Cornell University Press, 1992); and Bristow, *Prostitution and Prejudice*. Jewish involvement in the original vice, moneylending, can be found in Jerry Z. Muller, *Capitalism and the Jews* (Princeton, NJ: Princeton University Press, 2010); Werner Sombart, *The Jews and Modern Capitalism* (London: T. F. Unwin, 1913); Marvin Lowenthal, *The Jews of Germany: A Story of Sixteen Centuries* (Philadelphia: Jewish Publication Society of America, 1936); Barbara W. Tuchman, *A Distant Mirror: The Calamitous Fourteenth Century* (New York: Alfred A. Knopf, 1978); and Rebecca Rist, *Popes and Jews, 1095–1291* (New York: Oxford University Press, 2016).

Carolyn describes meeting Arnold, their engagement and wedding, and Arnold's opening of the Forty-Sixth Street casino, in the first and second chapters of Rothstein, *Now I'll Tell*. The scene at Jack's is memorialized in Edwin C. Hill, "Ghosts of a Gayer Broadway," *North American Review*, May 1930, 551, as cited in William Grimes, *Appetite City: A Culinary History of New York* (New York: North Point Press, 2009), 141–42. Although Carolyn felt lonely in the relationship, she notes that before Arnold embarked on his all-night routine, the couple would dine early at "Rector's, Churchill's, the Beaux Arts, or the Cadillac"—the so-called lobster palaces of Times Square's early years. If Arnold ordered lightly at these places, he was perhaps attempting to spare his already shaky digestion, for a full meal at Rector's, the original lobster palace, might have included oysters and clams, foie gras and braised sweetbreads, lamb chops and squab, deviled veal kidney and lobster thermidor, plus a dessert platter of éclairs, assorted ices, and savarin with cream and maraschino jelly. The extravagant menus can be found in Grimes, *Appetite City*. The phantasmagorical illumination of Broadway's "sky signs" can be found in Wallace, *Greater Gotham*, 429–430; and James Traub, *The Devil's Playground: A Century of Pleasure and Profit in Times Square* (New York: Random House, 2004), 43–52. Arnold "ate cakes and drank milk continually" (Rothstein, *Now I'll Tell*, 31).

A writer who hung out with Rothstein at Jack's recalled, "It was at this time that he formed the habit of walking home by devious routes in the gray dawns after hot gambling nights, and of buying a box of figs from an all-night street stand on the way. He never gave up his fondness for figs, nor his belief that they were about the only medicine that a man who watched his diet, and was fairly successful in getting his sleep, even if by daylight, really required" (Donald Henderson Clarke, *In the Reign of Rothstein,* New York: Vanguard Press, 1929).

Theatrical life inside the Hippodrome must have been crazy. That world is illuminated in the transcript of a 1911 trial, in which a Hippodrome electrician is charged with attempted murder for stalking a chorus girl, a coworker who rejected him. As the electrician explained, the relationship was risky from the start: "In August of 1910, when she started to rehearse there, we put on a specialty of chorus girls going down in the water, with electrical suits on. When they came up out of the water, they were all lit up." John Jay College, Trial Transcripts of the County of New York, 1883–1927 (hereinafter: JJC), 1389.

The friendship between the Rothsteins and the Swopes is described in E. J. Kahn Jr., *The World of Swope* (New York: Simon & Schuster, 1965); and Rothstein, *Now I'll Tell.*

An account of Carolyn's introduction to Arnold's parents, and Sullivan's granting of the Tenderloin concession, can be found in Katcher, *Big Bankroll.* (In that book's acknowledgments, Katcher notes, "I had a long series of interviews with Carolyn Rothstein.") Unlike in Big Tim Sullivan's heyday, when dozens of saloons occupied a single square block of the East Side, a 1913 survey—cited in Ewen, *Immigrant Women,* 167—showed that in fifty-seven East Side blocks occupied by the Jewish community, there were 112 candy stores and ice cream parlors, 93 butcher shops, 43 bakeries, 78 barbers, and only 70 saloons. Notably, Big Tim was focused on all immigrant communities. In 1909, two years after Colorado became the first state to make Columbus Day a state holiday, Big Tim followed suit, introducing a successful bill in the New York state legislature, a move that New York's Italian-Americans never forgot. Other politicians took note, such that by 1910, fifteen states had officially adopted the holiday.

CHAPTER FOUR: TONY THE TOUGH

The culture of Grand Street is described in "Keeping in Style," *New-York Tribune,* August 26, 1900. Lily's friendship with Tony, and their subsequent estrangement, can be found in Lily's four-part series for the *Washington Post,* published in June and July of 1914: "The Story of an Underworld Wife." In newspapers and archival materials, Tony was also known as Tona and sometimes her last name was written as Rollick. An account of life in Bialystok, including the 1906 pogrom and the resulting emigration, can be found in Charles Zachariah Goldberg, *Tales of Bialystok: A Jewish Journey from Czarist Russia to America* (Montpelier, VT: Rootstock Publishing, 2017).

The era's lady reformers, mostly non-Jews, churned out a wealth of reporting about the experience of East Side Jewish girls. The "danger of corruption" comes from "A New Social Adjustment," a report by the pioneering reformer Mary Kingsbury Simkhovitch, which is anthologized in "The Economic Position of Women," *Proceedings of the Academy of Political Science in the City of New York,* Columbia University, vol. 1, no. 1 (October 1910), 81–89. "The great bulk of girls in industry in New York are not American, but Irish, Jewish, and last of all Italian," Simkhovitch writes. Regarding prostitution, she draws a fascinating distinction between Irish and Jewish girls:

> Whatever the reason—Catholic training, native chastity, an
> inborn sense of restraint and good taste—Irish girls form a
> small element of women workers in danger of corruption....
> The Jewish girl comes from a protected and highly developed
> family life. But the Jewish ideas of family and religion are so
> intimately connected that the child who is not held by one
> will not be held by the other. In this respect there is a great
> difference between Catholic and Jew. The Catholic girl thinks
> of her religion as greater than anything else, including the
> family. The Jewish girl thinks of her religion as part of her
> family life, to stand or fall together with it. In the Jewish
> religion there is nothing corresponding to that devotion to
> the Virgin Mary which naïvely, almost hypnotically, involves
> an idealism of womanhood.

Another veteran reformer noted an upside to not being naïve. When Mary Van Kleeck interviewed girls in the millinery trade, she observed a difference between Italian and Jewish workers. Italians, she wrote, tended to view their work solely as a means of supplying money for their families.

> The Jewish girl, on the other hand, will plunge at once into a
> discussion of her trade, its advantages and disadvantages,
> wages, hours of work, and instances of shabby treatment in
> the shops, or of unsanitary conditions in the workrooms. Her
> attitude is likely to be that of an agitator. Nevertheless, she
> has the foundation of that admirable trait, "public spirit,"
> and a sense of relationship to a community larger than herself.
> It follows that the Italian girl is more willing than the Jewish

girl to accept conditions as she finds them. The owner of a large factory says that he prefers to employ Italians because they "are more tractable." (Van Kleeck, *Artificial Flower Makers* [New York: Russell Sage Foundation, 1913])

Simkhovitch, who learned Yiddish and lived in the settlement houses, echoed Van Kleeck, writing: "The Jewish mind is centripetal; everything it discovers it appropriates, and in that way becomes richer and more fertile, like an old garden plot well cultivated. But it cultivates only what comes within its grasp. And America felt little responsibility for offering to its newcomers all its possibilities" (Mary Kingsbury Simkhovitch, *Neighborhood* [New York: W. W. Norton, 1938], excerpted in Milton Hindus, ed., *The Old East Side: An Anthology* [Philadelphia: Jewish Publication Society of America, 1969], 261).

In *Working Girls in Evening Schools* (New York: Russell Sage Foundation, 1914), Van Kleeck writes that many of the Russian-Jewish garment workers she interviewed said they had tried to unionize their shops but gave it up as a hopeless task. "It took time that we might spend on a book, or studying, or going to the theater," one Russian-Jewish milliner told Van Kleeck. "And besides, it's no use trying to organize the American women. They don't care about anything but making dates. It's all men and dances.... When you begin on unions, they call you a socialist, and that ends it; or if you talk about women's suffrage, they laugh at you." Details about day-to-day financial realities can be found in Sue Ainslie Clark and Edith Wyatt, *Making Both Ends Meet: The Income and Outlay of New York Working Girls* (New York: Macmillan, 1911).

The physical and emotional disadvantages of Eastern European Jewish immigrants are catalogued in Deborah Dwork, "Health Conditions of Immigrant Jews on the Lower East Side of New York: 1880–1914," *Medical History,* vol. 25, 1–40. Dwork cites a series of 1902 articles by Maurice Fishberg, MD, entitled "Health and Sanitation among the Immigrant Jewish Population of New York." Fishberg found that East Siders wrestled with above-normal rates of mental illness. "Neurasthenia and hysteria are more frequent among them than among any other race," he wrote.

He noted that alcohol consumption was relatively low among East Side Jews, while tea was their big vice: "Having their nervous system often fatigued and exhausted from worry, care and anxiety, they require some agreeable stimulant which will remove, at least temporarily, the sense of fatigue, and give a feeling of wellbeing. Other nations use alcohol for such purposes, but the Jews prefer tea, and a depression is the result, which requires larger doses of tea to overcome it. A vicious cycle is thereby established, which by no means contributes to the health and wellbeing of the Russian Jew." Of East Side café culture and the tea habit, one paper wrote, "They drink their tea slowly, biting off bits of the sugar, in true Russian style, instead of dropping it into the glass. It is not the most healthful occupation in the world, after a long day's work to sit and sip tea until long after midnight, but it makes an interesting sight for spectators. These people do not give their overwrought brains much time to rest" ("In the East Side Cafés," *New-York Tribune,* September 30, 1900).

Decades later, the comedic actor George Burns, born Nathan Birnbaum, looked back on the health hazards of his impoverished East Side childhood with a sense of humor. The morning meal for Burns and his eleven siblings consisted of large stale rolls and canned herring. The food wasn't tasty, but it was inexpensive and substantial. "You couldn't lift those sandwiches," he remembered. "You had to wear a jockstrap to be able to eat breakfast." Like many ghetto kids, Burns often took his ablutions in the East River's "floating baths," which were "full of garbage, full of manure and everything else.... You'd pull your hand out of the water and slap the garbage, and it would spread, and you'd swim through it, and then you'd pull out your left hand and slap it again" (George Burns Interview, American Jewish Committee, Oral History Library (hereinafter: AJCOHL)).

Among East Siders, the phrase "Dollar Land" seems to have been in common usage. In Samuel Ornitz's comic novel about East Side corruption, *Haunch, Paunch, and Jowl: The Making of a Professional Jew* (New York: Boni & Liveright, 1923), the main character remarks, "Father had a dread of the shop sickness, the plague of Dollar Land" (43).

Details of the dance-hall culture, its customs and dangers, can be found in the Research Committee of the Committee of Fourteen, *The Social Evil in New York City: A Study of Law Enforcement* (New York: Andrew H. Kellogg, 1910), 54–57: "One of the favorite dances in halls of this type is the spiel, which requires much twirling and twisting, and is an objectionable dance.... [The spieler] usually belongs to a gang or immoral class of young men, and his influence for the most part is bad." The immoral influence of female spielers, it's noted, "is also bad." Another investigation of dance halls can be found in George J. Kneeland, *Commercialized Prostitution in New York City* (New York: The Century Co., 1913), 67–73: "No places of amusement are so filled with moral dangers to boys and girls.... Young girls have been seen to yield themselves in wild abandon to their influence, and have been carried half fainting to dark corners of the hall and there, almost helpless, have been subjected to the most indecent advances."

More about working girls during this era can be found in Alan Dawley, *Struggles for Justice: Social Responsibility and the Liberal State* (Cambridge, MA: Harvard University Press, 1991); Kathy Peis, *Cheap Amusements: Working Women and Leisure in Turn-of-the-Century New York* (Philadelphia: Temple University Press, 1986); Ewen, *Immigrant Women*; and Glenn, *Daughters of the Shtetl*.

The S-curve silhouette's place in fashion history is explained in Caroline Reynolds Milbank, *New York Fashion: The Evolution of American Style* (New York: Harry N. Abrams, 1989), 50. The relationship between Tony and Motche, which is sometimes written as Mortche or Mordka, is described in Kehillah letters; Rosenberg, "Underworld Wife"; Shoenfeld, *Crime Buster*; and affidavits in NYCMA 105054. Motche's background in Eastern Europe, and the global migrations of Jewish pimps, are chronicled in Bristow, *Prostitution and Prejudice*; as well as Engelstein, *The Keys to Happiness*; Bernstein, *Sonia's Daughters*; and Jarrod Tanney, *City of Rogues and Schnorrers: Russia's Jews and the Myth of Old Odessa* (Bloomington: Indiana University Press, 2011). The history of the IBA is covered in Bristow, *Prostitution and Prejudice*; Ernest A. Bell, ed., *War on the White Slave Trade* (Chicago: Charles C. Thompson, 1909); Kneeland, *Commercialized Prostitution*; and Rockefeller Archives Center, Bureau of Social Hygiene (hereinafter: RACBOSH).

CHAPTER FIVE: NIGHT OF RUIN

The *Forward* reported in "Eighteen Hundred Girls Gone Missing Last Year in New York" (March 20, 1913) that in addition to the 1,800 cases reported to police, an estimated additional two thousand had disappeared, and that such annual numbers were typical of the era.

In *Crime Buster,* Abe addresses his early days as a student of moral reform. The movement's origins and development are documented in Paul Boyer, *Urban Masses and Moral Order in America, 1820–1920* (Cambridge, MA: Harvard University Press, 1978); Michael McGregor, *A Fierce Discontent: The Rise and Fall of the Progressive Movement in America* (New York: Free Press, 2003); and James A. Morone, *Hellfire Nation: The Politics of Sin in American History* (New Haven, CT: Yale University Press, 2003). The undercover methods of reform committees are explored in Jennifer Fronc, *New York Undercover: Private Surveillance in the Progressive Era* (Chicago: University of Chicago Press, 2009).

I stumbled on the anonymous letter, purportedly written by a Jewish detective, in the Lillian D. Wald Papers at Columbia University. The 1908 letter is likely authentic because the writer alleges that Bingham's primary goal "is getting material from the records for a book [he wants to write]." Three years later, that book appeared as Theodore A. Bingham, *The Girl That Disappears: The Real Facts about the White Slave Traffic* (Boston: Gorham Press, 1911).

The influence of George Kibbe Turner's articles in *McClure's,* and the response to them from German-Jewish uptowners as well as downtown Yiddish newspapers, are described in Goren, *New York Jews*, 138–44.

Notes

The evolution of the Mann Act and its role in the beginnings of moral legislation can be found in Jessica R. Pliley, *Policing Sexuality: The Mann Act and the Making of the FBI* (Cambridge, MA: Harvard University Press, 2014); and *Crossing Over the Line: Legislating Morality and the Mann Act* (Chicago: University of Chicago Press, 1994). Tony's relationship with Abe can be found in Shoenfeld, *Crime Buster*.

Judah Magnes's experience at Emanu-El, and his clash with its congregation, can be found in Norman Bentwich, *For Zion's Sake: A Biography of Judah L. Magnes* (Philadelphia: Jewish Publication Society of America, 1954); and Arthur A. Goren, ed., *Dissenter in Zion: From the Writings of Judah L. Magnes* (Cambridge, MA: Harvard University Press, 1982). The origins of the Kehillah as a spinoff of the American Jewish Committee are chronicled in Naomi W. Cohen, *Not Free to Desist: The American Jewish Committee, 1906–1966* (Philadelphia: Jewish Publication Society of America, 1972). In the conclusion to his 1910 Passover sermon, Magnes issued a directive: "Look into your hearts and ask yourselves, do you or do you not wish to remain Jews? The way of life and the way of death is before you. Choose." Two weeks later, when Magnes learned that the sermon had, as he wrote to Emanu-El's board, "encountered the hostility of a majority of your honorable body," he redoubled his position, writing: "If I should remain with Temple Emanu-El, I would expect to amplify my views as stated in my Passover sermon.... If you are not ready for this, I beg leave herewith to tender my resignation."

As an outspoken Zionist, Magnes was controversial upon arrival at Temple Emanu-El, wrote the *New York Times*. The bulk of Emanu-El members were not Zionists, and many looked on Zionism as a "religious fad." "Dr Magnes a Rabbi of Emanu-El at 29: He Is an Earnest Zionist," *New York Times,* May 9, 1906. In coming years, Zionism would grow more divisive, both within the Jewish-American community and in the country at large.

On the subject of Magnes, Schiff had always been torn, but his decision to stay for the Passover sermon illustrated his affection for Magnes despite their disagreements. Among his own crowd of uptown German Jews, Schiff was known to be imperious — "rule or ruin," as one uptowner said of him — but with Magnes he often found himself submitting. In 1908, when Schiff asked Magnes to temper his Zionism, Magnes refused. Magnes told Schiff that if his American citizenship ever conflicted with his Zionism, "I am free to say that I should, without hesitation, cast my lot with Zionism or Judaism." In 1909, when Magnes used his position at Emanu-El to endorse a political appointment in Washington, Schiff again objected and Magnes stood his ground.

These episodes and others also demonstrated Schiff's obsession with assimilation, a sort of Americanization that he called "patriotism." This didn't mean conformity. It meant melding the notions of charity and justice, *tzedakah,* with the American ideals of refuge and opportunity. It meant keeping religion but avoiding separatism. *I am not a race Jew but a faith Jew,* he often said. Even as he promoted Judaism and an observant lifestyle, he insisted that Jewish-Americans must put America first, lest they be seen as nominal citizens or worse, smeared as opportunistic globetrotters.

A dramatic and entertaining account of Gaynor's mayoral campaign can be found in Lately Thomas, *The Mayor Who Mastered New York: The Life and Opinions of William J. Gaynor* (New York: William Morrow, 1969). Prime selections from Gaynor's letters and speeches can be found in *Some of Mayor Gaynor's Letters and Speeches* (New York: Greaves Publishing, 1913). The East Side loved Gaynor, and the feeling was mutual. When a street preacher, the president of the New York Evangelical Society, applied for a permit to preach on the East Side, Gaynor replied: "It seems to me that this work of proselytizing from other religions and sects is very often carried too far. Do you not think the Jews have a good religion? Have not the Christians appropriated the entire Jewish sacred scriptures? Was not the New Testament also written entirely by Jews?" He concluded: "I do not think I should give you a license to preach for the conversion of the Jews. . . . Would you not annoy them and do more harm than good? How many Jews have you converted so far?" At a dinner of the Council of American Hebrew Congregations, presided over by Jacob Schiff, Gaynor praised the "adaptability" of the Jewish people. Throughout their long history, he reflected, Jews hadn't hesitated to modify or abandon "nonessential regulations . . . in order to keep pace with the teachings of experience, even as they held fast to the fundamental tenets of their faith."

As for the reformers of his own era, Gaynor called them "bone hunters" and "hypocrites." Of vice laws generally, he told the Lutheran Ministers Association: "You may pass all the laws you please, but they will become a dead letter if they are not backed up by the will of the community. This has been true ever since the beginning of law and will continue to the end of the world." Of Wasp hypocrisy, he told another audience: "Why, these clubs up on Fifth Avenue, or Eighth Avenue where I live in Brooklyn, why, dear me, they sit in their common rooms and drink all day on Sunday. And I suppose that those people think they have as much right to do that as others. And they are absolutely right. They have as much right!" Gaynor mocked calls by moralists to pass anti-prostitution laws. He saw no solution to the ancient problem so long as the moral standards of a community condoned it. And morals, he stressed, were the province of church and school, not the police. He cracked down on the practice of undercover cops posing as johns to ensnare what he called "wayward women."

Following the shooting, Gaynor fought fatigue, as well as spasms of coughing and retching. "The neuralgic pains are now setting in," he wrote. "The ball entered just behind my right ear, and seems to have followed at least three courses, and in some way went through my throat, cutting cords which control my tongue, so that my tongue is still crooked and I am able to speak only with much difficulty" (Thomas, *Mayor Who Mastered New York,* 314–16). Gaynor's mission to stanch police corruption can be found in Thomas, *Mayor Who Mastered New York,* 411–35.

CHAPTER SIX: THE GIRL WHO EARNS HER OWN LIVING

The story of Percy Hill's losing night, and its significance for Arnold's career, can be found in Katcher, *Big Bankroll,* 64–70; and Rothstein, *Now I'll Tell,* 30. A definition of the "sporting man" can be found in Rothstein, 220–21.

A fascinating history of the "crooked work" in early baseball can be found in Eliot Asinof, *Eight Men Out: The Black Sox and the 1919 World Series* (New York: Henry Holt, 1963), 10–15; and the fix behind the 1912 Series between the Giants and Red Sox is explained in Asinof, 46. Carolyn describes going to that Series in Rothstein, *Now I'll Tell,* 41: "He got no pleasure...from watching Christy Mathewson strike out a batter at a critical moment. All he cared for then, as always, was the betting percentage."

Details regarding the new Jewish gangster can be found in Logan, *Against the Evidence,* 73. Jack Zelig's family background can be found in Keefe, *Starker.* Abe's description of Zelig appears in MA 1779, St. 14: "He is about 26 years of age; 5 ft 11 in; somewhat bandy legged and raw boned; broken nose; clean shaven; healthful, dark, fearless eyes; splendid disposition and a very good conversationalist.... I wish to state that if ever a man has done real good work for the East Side, unknowingly, it was he." The favor Zelig enjoyed had something to do with his independence. Though he was the East Side's most visible underworld character, he *rejected* Tammany affiliation, and was once seen kicking a cousin of Big Tim Sullivan down the street.

As stated above, Tammany had a custom of keeping their election-day thugs in funds by forcing gambling houses to hire those thugs for "protection." Among gambling-house owners, the Tammany-assigned thugs were known as "C.O.D. men" because they appeared for work only on payday. Zelig, on the other hand, took the job seriously, and at a time when East Side gamblers needed help fighting off the Italian gangs who, supported by the same Tammany Hall that Zelig defied, were trying to push past Mott Street and encroach on their territory. The details of all this, along with Louie Rosenberg's role in it, can be found in MA 1779, St. 14.

The activities of philanthropists and reformers can be found in Wallace, *Greater Gotham.* The yearslong milk pasteurization project to stem the spread of tuberculosis is documented in the Nathan Straus Papers, NYPL. Straus, an uptown German Jew, used the fortune he made from his family's business, Macy's department store, to finance an array of philanthropic and political endeavors. Abe's early days in the movement are described in Shoenfeld, *Crime Buster.* The settlement house culture is explored in Allen F. Davis, *The Social Settlements and the Progressive Movement, 1890–1914* (Brunswick, NJ: Rutgers University Press). An excellent explanation of reform's shift from the "social purity enthusiasts" of the early Gilded Age to the "coercive moral reformers" of Abe's generation can be found in Boyer, *Urban Masses.* I've stolen Boyer's phrase "a fragile but authentic intimacy" to describe Abe's relationship to prostitutes.

More advice for ladies seeking financial independence in the prewar era can be found in Anna Steese Richardson, *The Girl Who Earns Her Own Living* (New York: B. W. Dodge, 1909). "Dress to suit your position," Richardson advises. "If you work in a dirty office, such as a printing concern, wholesale grocery or a hardware shop, wear skirts that clear the ground by at least three inches; but if you are employed in the private office which has been well furnished and nicely carpeted, wear longer skirts, not trains, but cut to escape the ground. Your employer will want you, like furniture and pictures, to dress in harmony with the furnishings of his office. Avoid garish colors."

Abe's research tactics can be found in Shoenfeld, *Crime Buster*; and his early vice reports can be found in RACBOSH and in the New York Public Library, Committee of Fourteen Records (hereinafter: NYPLCOFR). Objecting to the prison rabbis who earned money on the side by steering divorce cases to lawyers, Abe wrote that legal practice "is a work, a profession, it is true enough, but not for interpreters of the laws of God to make a living thereby — men who are supposed to advise people in their matrimonial troubles, and not make money by them in this manner" (MA 1791, St. 918).

Mayer Shoenfeld took control of the *Kibitzer* in the summer of 1911. Abe's scathing piece about police corruption, entitled "Oh, the Sins," was signed *Der Lebediger,* the Lively One. His dustup with the cops appears in Shoenfeld, *Crime Buster*; and in Shoenfeld Interview, AJCOHL, 173.

CHAPTER SEVEN: VENGEANCE

The beautification of New York City is chronicled in Wallace, *Greater Gotham*. One can imagine how tantalizing the new NYPL would have been to a library rat like Abe. Wallace describes how call slips traveled down through a system of brass pneumatic tubes to a multitiered storage area of steel racks. A page read the call slip, retrieved the book, and, by a system of lifts and conveyors, shot it up to the reading room in seven minutes flat. With 8 million volumes borrowed annually, circulation figures at the NYPL were the highest in the world.

To their credit, Jacob Schiff, Felix Warburg, and Lillian Wald helped launch the National Child Labor Committee, which was chartered by an act of Congress in 1907, but the new child labor laws, the first of which were passed in 1902, weren't effectively enforced. The most extensive treatment of the Triangle fire and its aftermath, as well as the changing composition of factory ownership, can be found in Von Drehle, *Triangle*. During the first decade of the nineteenth century, women's clothing became the third-largest consumer-goods industry in America. In 1900, the number of its factories totaled 1,224; by 1910, the number had grown to 21,701 (Howard M. Sachar, *A History of the Jews in the Modern World* [New York: Alfred A. Knopf, 2005], 372).

The study regarding the impact of charity—the "Thirtieth Annual Report of United Hebrew Charities 1904," 34—is cited in Mensch, "Social Pathology in Urban America."

The father-son estrangement—addressed in Shoenfeld, *Crime Buster*; and Shoenfeld Interview, AJCOHL—would drag on for years, as suggested by a 1916 letter from Abe to Magnes: "I haven't had business dealings with my father, political or otherwise, in any shape, form or manner, since the time when I commenced to do Kehillah work. Because of some domestic misunderstandings, I am rather ashamed to confess that the relations between my father and myself have been somewhat strained and to such an extent that we have not been on speaking terms" (MA 1768).

Tony's background and experience as a prostitute can be found in Rosenberg, "Underworld Wife"; Shoenfeld, *Crime Buster*; NYCMA 105054; and MA 1779–93. For further context about Tony's world, I turned to Kneeland, *Commercialized Prostitution in New York City*; and I. L. Nascher, *The Wretches of Povertyville: A Sociological Study of the Bowery* (Chicago: Jos. J. Lanzit, 1909).

CHAPTER EIGHT: THE KILLING OF A JEWISH GAMBLER

Lily lays out her relationship with Louie in Rosenberg, "Underworld Wife." The migration of East Siders up to the Bronx is addressed in Cahan, *Education of Abraham Cahan,* vol. 3.

In early June, when Lily was at home in the Bronx, Louie was back down in the old neighborhood, with Zelig and Whitey Lewis, getting in a saloon brawl with their Italian enemies, the Five Pointers. By the time the police arrived, Zelig was astride one Italian, banging his head on the floor, while Louie leaned against a wall. He'd been shot in the foot. The battle wasn't over. Later, in the early morning hours, after the Avenue Boys were charged with disorderly conduct, they descended the stairs of Essex Market Court and walked across the street. As Zelig led them through the doorway of his lawyer's building, a bullet tore through the back of his head and lodged behind his ear. Louie wadded up his coat and pressed it to Zelig's head while Whitey hustled Zelig up to the lawyer's office, where Zelig collapsed on the couch. When a cop questioned him about the shooter, Zelig said, *"Freg mir b'acharayim"*—"Ask my behind" (Keefe, *Starker,* 142–47). Abe's biographies of Bald Jack Rose and Bridgey Webber can be found in MA 1785, St. 122.

The meeting between Arnold and Herman is described in Rothstein, *Now I'll Tell*; and Katcher, *Big Bankroll*. Herman's struggle to make good in the Tenderloin, as well as the internecine spats among East Side gamblers, appear in Logan, *Against the Evidence*.

There are many good books about the Rosenthal case, including Jonathan Root's *One Night in July* (New York: Coward-McCann, 1961) and Mike Dash's *Satan's Circus* (New York: Three Rivers Press, 2007). The closest look at Rosenthal himself—and a view somewhat at odds with his one-dimensional reputation as a brash dunderhead—appears in a unique memoir by Viña Delmar, *The Becker Scandal: A Time Remembered* (New York: Harcourt, Brace & World, 1968).

Delmar, born Alvina Croter in 1903, was the daughter of Yiddish theater actors. Her father, though not involved in the underworld, grew up with Herman Rosenthal in the early years of the Jewish East Side, and they remained lifelong friends. Delmar and her father visited Herman's place the day before he was murdered. As a little girl, Delmar, over her mother's objections, would tag along with her father on fancy outings with Herman, always on Herman's dime, the kind of evenings that her workaday parents couldn't afford. She was treated to taxi rides and restaurant meals. Herman and his gambler pals doted on her, and the heavily powdered ladies of their entourage—all childless, some former prostitutes—treated Delmar like their daughter. "I was hugged and complimented and allowed to be thoroughly obnoxious," she recalled.

The story of Eddie Gallagher's crusade to become a witness to the murder appears in Root, *One Night in July*, 21–23. Rosenthal's posthumous affidavit appeared as "Rosenthal's Own Story of His Rise and Fall in Favor of the System," *World*, July 17, 1912. My account of the murder at the Metropole is cobbled together from all the above sources, plus the subsequent trials, JJC nos. 3198 and 3200.

In the wake of the Rosenthal murder, the Sam Paul Association received quite a bit of coverage. "Paul Men Hated Rosenthal," *New York Times*, July 22, 1912.

PART TWO: MISTER PRETTYFIELD

CHAPTER NINE: WAKING UP

Schiff's devotion to his morning routine, and all routines, can be found in his daughter's self-published memoir, Frieda Schiff Warburg, *Reminiscences of a Long Life* (1956); *Jacob H. Schiff, His Life and Letters,* ed. Cyrus Adler (2 vols.; New York: Doubleday & Doran, 1928), vols. 1–2; and Cohen, *Jacob H. Schiff*. Of her father, Frieda recalls, "He was extremely punctual, and the clerks who knew him in the shops along Fifth Avenue used to say that they could set their clocks by the time of his daily passing by their doors on his three-mile walk toward his office in the morning. When he came to the end of his walk, he was either met by Neville, the chauffeur, or took a trolley car on the Elevated the rest of the way. Louis Marshall and other friends frequently accompanied him."

Notes

The German-Jewish epoch that produced Schiff is explored in Elon, *The Pity of It All*.

The significance of the Rosenthal murder for the Kehillah, and how it instigated the vice crusade and Abe's hiring, is described in Goren, *New York Jews,* 134–69; Shoenfeld, *Crime Buster*; Shoenfeld Interview, AJCOHL; Beatrice Magnes Interview, AJCOHL; and Jonah Goldstein Interview, Columbia University Oral History Project (hereinafter: CUOHP). The minutes of the July 28 meeting can be found in MA 1753–54.

The idea of a small group of wealthy men making major decisions on behalf of an entire community, such as the decision to wage a war on crime among their co-religionists, was—although normalized by the times—as controversial then as it might be now. Fascinating context for privately funded law-enforcement posses can be found in Beckert, *Monied Metropolis,* 293–322.

Views of Magnes can be found in the following AJCOHL interviews: I. B. Berkson, Alexander Dushkin, J. B. S. Hardman, Benjamin Koenigsberg, Beatrice Magnes, Samuel Margoshes, Bernard Richards, and Harry Sackler. "Magnes was important no matter where he went, even if by accident he got in the wrong door," said Hardman. "It was Magnes that made the Kehillah, not the Kehillah that made Magnes."

Schiff's countless endeavors on behalf of Russian Jews in the Pale of Settlement, and Eastern European immigrants in the US, are laid out in Cohen, *Jacob H. Schiff*. His attempts to defeat czarism, such as financing Japan in the Russo-Japanese War, are covered in Cohen, *Jacob H. Schiff*; and G. Edward Griffin, *The Creature from Jekyll Island: A Second Look at the Federal Reserve* (self-pub, 2010).

"Benefactors of the East Side" is described in Beth Kaplan, *Finding the Jewish Shakespeare: The Life and Legacy of Jacob Gordin* (Syracuse, NY: Syracuse University Press, 2007), 113.

The coda to the scandal when Jesse Lewisohn and Mortimer Schiff were found gambling in Richard Canfield's casino—an unexpected result of the Committee of Fifteen's vice crusade—highlighted the hypocrisy of moral reform. When they tapped William Travers Jerome to lead the crusade, Schiff and the other honchos who headed up the Committee of Fifteen figured that Jerome would confine his crime-fighting to the ghetto. When Jerome worked his way uptown, raided Canfield's palace, and then demanded that Mortimer Schiff and Jesse Lewisohn testify against Canfield, both young men, on the strength of their families' legal resources and political pull, refused. When Jerome tried to get a subpoena from a judge, he was denied.

This was a major reason why, when Jerome later ran for district attorney, he ridiculed uptowners to their faces. During a campaign rally at Carnegie Hall, he told the city's wealthiest citizens: "Morally, you are as bad as the people I am fighting in the lowest dive. Morally, you are not worth the powder to blow you out of existence. . . .

Every dollar you have laid by, every step you have climbed in the social scale, has laid upon you an obligation of civic leadership, and you have failed."

The private funding provided to Whitman for the Rosenthal case was public knowledge at the time, and is reported in Logan, *Against the Evidence*, 94. Decades later, a former member of DA Whitman's staff, recalling the case, told Logan: "Whenever we had any problems, Whitman would just pick up the phone and make a call and a couple of hours later Schieffelin [the leader of the Citizens Union, and head of his family's legacy drug firm] would come in with a bundle of money. Those Simon Pure fellows [Waspy reformers] were really generous. They were so grateful to have someone working hard to clean up the city." When certain Kehillah members decided to throw their financial backing behind the Cits, Magnes resented the loss of funding. "Our best men have again been led off by the goyim," he wrote on August 22, 1912. "They are contributing to the fund of the Citizens Committee... so that it is impossible to approach them now for the large sums needed in order to make such an investigation" (MA 1749).

An account of the first meeting between Abe and Magnes can be found in Shoenfeld, *Crime Buster*; and Shoenfeld Interview, AJCOHL. Magnes's letter regarding Abe's hiring can be found in MA 1757.

Arnold's maneuvering in the wake of the Rosenthal case can be found in Logan, *Against the Evidence*; Rothstein, *Now I'll Tell*; and Kahn, *World of Swope*. When Swope joined the *World* in 1909, Kahn writes, reporters had no telephones at their desks. At the *World*, when reporters wanted to make a call, they used one of three phone booths at one end of the city room. Swope would arrive early in the morning, direct three copy boys to occupy all three booths, and give each of them a number to call. While a Tammany leader or bank president or bookmaker waited impatiently on two of the lines, Swope could move from one source to another without losing time. The paper's city editor later recalled, "Swope was probably the best reporter not only on the *World* but in the whole wide world. His personality could break down almost any barrier. He had a tremendous fund of background information for any story that came along and could see further ahead in the development of a story than any newspaperman I ever met" (Allen Churchill, *Park Row* [New York: Rinehart, 1973], 316).

CHAPTER TEN: TO THE WALL

For Whitman's background, I turned to Logan, *Against the Evidence*; Root, *One Night in July*; Kahn, *World of Swope*; Shoenfeld, *Crime Buster*; and Shoenfeld Interview, AJCOHL. A detailed chronicle of the Triangle fire appears in Von Drehle, *Triangle*. Whitman's early moves in the Rosenthal case can be found in Root, *One Night in July*.

The Rothstein-Swope-Whitman meet is alluded to in Swope's own coverage: "Mysterious Caller Tells Graft Secrets," *World,* July 19, 1912; and expanded on in Logan, *Against the Evidence.* While Whitman may have been led astray by Swope in the Triangle case of 1911, he now had reason to see Swope as friendly to his cause. Immediately following the Rosenthal murder, Swope began hammering the police department, once again laying out Whitman's case for him. POLICE MUST EXPLAIN THESE STRANGE THINGS IN KILLING OF ROSENTHAL, read one headline, such as the fact that five uniformed cops had been within three hundred feet of the murder. Two days later: WHAT POLICE LEFT UNDONE, AIDING SLAYERS' ESCAPE. Other newspapers, meanwhile, took Rosenthal's allegations less seriously. In "Bankroll for Rosenthal," July 23, 1912, the *New York Times* wrote:

> Whether through the enmity of the big west side gamblers,
> who did not wish to see one of the small fry from the East
> Side breaking in on their preserves, or whether the police
> were not willing to give Rosenthal as much scope as others...
> he found it impossible to conduct a decent, quiet little house,
> where a few congenial spirits might lose money for his
> benefit, and he considered that he was being hardly used. He
> expected a certain amount of interference, for that was all in
> the game, but the persistence of the police of the West Forty-
> Seventh Street Station annoyed him greatly.

Whitman's announcement regarding his prerogative appears in "Big Tim's Name in the Case," *New York Times,* July 23, 1912.

Lily writes about her escapades in the wake of the murder in Rosenberg, "Underworld Wife"; and further details about their time on the run appear in "'Gyp' and 'Lefty' Taken in Queens," the *Brooklyn Daily Eagle,* September 15, 1912; "'Gyp' and 'Lefty' Caught at Last, Here in Town," *New York Times,* September 15, 1912; and "Suspects' Wives Had Fun Dodging Sleuths," *Sun,* September 16, 1912. A history of Coney Island can be found in *Sodom by the Sea: An Affectionate History of Coney Island* (New York: Doubleday & Doran, 1941).

The backstory regarding Zelig, Bald Jack Rose, and the Rosenthal murder is explained in Keefe, *Starker,* 228–34. Zelig said that compared to Bald Jack, who "would hang his own brother to clear his skirts," the fellows mixed up in the Rosenthal case were decent chaps, including Rosenthal himself (Henry H. Klein, *Sacrificed: The Story of Police Lieut. Charles Becker* [New York: Isaac Goldman, 1927], 83).

Abe's meeting with Zelig on the trolley appears in Shoenfeld, *Crime Buster.* In those years, trolleys operated along an underground cable that ran through a slot between the tracks. When the motorman turned the wheel, a clip beneath the trolley grabbed the cable and pulled the trolley forward. The trolleys could be dangerous, particularly when men jumped off to retrieve their windblown hats and tried to get back on.

In the interviews archived in the AJCOHL, many East Siders recounted being bullied as "Christ killers." Mordecai Gorelick, who later became an admired theatrical designer, was a Russian Jew who emigrated to the East Side after many of his family members were killed in pogroms. Gorelick remembered an Irish kid telling him that he was going to beat Gorelick up because "your people killed Christ." When Gorelick pointed out that Christ died two thousand years ago, the Irish kid replied, "Yeah, well I just found out about it." Abe's history of Zelig's gang can be found as a stand-alone document in ASP-AJHS, Series 1.

Abe and Zelig may have been on opposite sides of the fence legally, but perhaps they shared a philosophy of upright living, even if that philosophy remained mostly aspirational for Zelig. Around the time of the trolley meeting, a reporter had asked Zelig about his views on fatherhood, and Zelig laid out a set of principles: "Make an athlete of your boy, keep him off the streets. Never let him play marbles for keeps. Keep him away from the small dice and pool rooms. Make a companion and chum of him" ("Gunman Gives Some Advice," *Guthrie Daily Leader,* August 23, 1912).

CHAPTER ELEVEN: PAL ZEL

An overview of the six-day bicycle race can be found in "Behind the Scenes with the Long-Distance Bikers," the *Buffalo Sunday Morning News,* January 12, 1913.

Of the general scene at Siegel's Café, Abe writes, "This place is patronized principally by pickpockets, con men, gamblers, pimps, owners of disorderly houses; also their women and their kept women. . . . Prostitutes hanging out in 76 Second Avenue very often insult each other, have windy arguments, and it is not an uncommon thing to see a salt measure or a sugar bowl being throw into someone's face" (MA 1779, St. 6). An account of Zelig's death at the hands of Red Phil Davidson can be found in MA 1780, St. 16; Root, *One Night in July,* 133–34; and Keefe, *Starker,* 239–44. Keefe's account contains original reporting from her interview with an eyewitness, a man who had been a small boy on the trolley when Zelig was shot. Dollar John's ecstatic reaction to the news of Zelig's death comes from Shoenfeld Interview, AJCOHL. Zelig's note is described in Shoenfeld, *Crime Buster.* Louie's note to Zelig, as well as notes from the other three gunmen, were found on Zelig's person when he died. They are reprinted in full in Keefe, *Starker,* 241–46.

Also found among Zelig's effects was a letter he had written to Harry Horowitz, or Gyp the Blood, but never sent. Later, during the gunmen's case, Harry, like Louie, would protest when he was referred to by his nickname, but even Zelig used it. "Dear

Pal Gyp," Zelig's letter begins: "Yours received and it was more than pleasant to hear from you.... Gyp, keep cheered up and keep cheering one another up. Your innocence will be proved and what a grand time we will have on that day." In conclusion, Zelig speaks of Harry's wife, Lily Horowitz, who, at the time, was still being held in the Tombs: "It seems to be the hardest thing in the world to get your wife out. No one wants to go on the bonds. But cheer up, old boy, everything will turn out the best in the end. Jack."

Zelig's comment about no one wanting "to go on the bonds" to get Gyp's wife out of prison shows how, in order to maintain the system, the East Side underworld had collectively decided to sacrifice Becker and the gunmen. Zelig and the Avenue Boys, once the toast of the East Side, were personae non gratae.

By the time of Zelig's murder, in early October, the prior three months had given Mayor Gaynor a hell of a time. He was accustomed to attacks, but after the Rosenthal murder he was embattled like never before. DA Whitman wanted his job. Gaynor's deputy mayor wanted his job. And the reform crowd wanted him to join the growing chorus of police critics, which he was unwilling to do.

In September, Gaynor agreed, grudgingly, to testify in DA Whitman's parallel investigation into police corruption. Immediately the exchange grew heated.

The questioner asked: "We are anxious to know how the mayor keeps in touch with conditions in the police department."

"Mainly by letters from the police commissioner," Gaynor said. "Sometimes he talks with me."

"You have no way of learning about conditions except through the commissioner?"

"Oh, take it that way if you want to."

"What way would you like me to take it?"

"Let me put it this way," Gaynor said. "Every time a policeman stops a runaway horse or assists in a rescue at a fire, that policeman is praised but no credit is given to the organized force. Yet, let one or two policemen out of 10,000 wearing the uniform be remotely implicated in a case, and everyone yells that the police department is crooked. Meanwhile, if a bad priest is defrocked, whoever heard of the press standing up on its hind feet and bawling out madly to the mob that the entire church is crooked, or that Christianity is on the wane?"

The skirmish continued. Gaynor shouted, "You cannot scandalize me! I have a reputation that cannot be scandalized! I was engaged in purifying the government here long before you ever came on earth!"

"Grilling Gaynor Thankless Job for Committee: New York's Mayor Proves Artful Dodger in Aldermanic Probe," *Williamsport Sun-Gazette,* September 11, 1912; "Ruffles His Honor: Mayor Gaynor Proves Himself a Testy Witness," *Nebraska State Journal,* September 11, 1912; and "Mayor Gaynor in Fine Fettle," *Boston Globe,* September 11, 1912. Gaynor's muted response to the news of Zelig's death is reported in

"Whitman Loses by Zelig Killing: Admits Gang Leader Was Important Witness against Becker," *Sun,* October 7, 1912. In that same article, Louie, his trial approaching, unloads his feelings about his friend's slayer, saying of Red Phil Davidson: "He's a bum. Jack used to give him quarters and halves so he could feed.... I know him four years now and he's very low. Awful low. He's always run messages for girls, that's all he is. He never was anything but a cadet, and when he says he ever had trouble with a prince like Jack Zelig, he's a liar.... [Red Phil] wouldn't have the head to shoot Jack alone. It was somebody else's head. He was forced to do it."

Abe and Magnes's first meeting with Gaynor is described in Shoenfeld, *Crime Buster;* and Shoenfeld Interview, AJCOHL. Each source describes the meeting a bit differently. In the latter, Magnes is calling the police department. In the former, Gaynor makes the call—I chose this version because it makes more sense. Abe describes Cahalane's raids of Dollar John's gambling houses in Shoenfeld Interview, AJCOHL.

An account of Zelig's funeral can be found in Logan, *Against the Evidence,* 170–171; Arthur A. Goren, *Saints and Sinners: The Underside of American Jewish History* (Cincinnati: Brochure Series of the American Jewish Archives, 1988); and Keefe, *Starker,* 232–53. The latter provides views on Zelig from various Yiddish newspapers. The exchange between prostitutes appears in MA 1788; and Shoenfeld, *Crime Buster.* Abe's account of the charity ball for Zelig's wife can be found in MA 1789, St. 272.

After the capture of Louie and Harry, their wives, Lily and Lily, were detained in the Tombs as witnesses. The Tombs, built on the old Collect Pond of New York's colonial days, dripped with moisture, and the lower tiers flooded in heavy rains. The tiny cells had no sanitation except for a tin pail, and no ventilation save a few small chutes. It was the kind of place a person might say anything to get out of. Lily Rosenberg was no squealer, but she knew that DA Whitman wanted her to be, so she wrote Whitman a letter, hinting that she was pregnant. In her "condition," she said, she could not stand the Tombs any longer (Rosenberg, "Underworld Wife"). Whitman released her, and she gave interviews to the press, boasting of Louie's and her exploits on the lam and how they evaded capture. "Evidence Hidden in Suspects' Flat," *Sun,* September 16, 1912; "Suspects' Wives Had Fun Dodging Sleuths," *Sun,* September 17, 1912.

Accounts of the trials of Becker and the gunmen can be found in Logan, *Against the Evidence*; Root, *One Night in July*; "Heard Becker Make Threat to Kill Rosenthal," *New York Times,* October 12, 1912; "Webber Supports Rose's Testimony," the *Dispatch,* October 14, 1912; and "Severe Test for Webber on the Cross-Examination," *World,* October 14, 1912. The trials themselves are archived as JJC nos. 3198 and 3200. Lily's meeting with Louie in the Tombs is described in Rosenberg, "Underworld Wife."

The doctored quote from Becker in the *World* stemmed from a short exchange Becker had with reporters as he left the courtroom one day during his trial. All major papers except the *World* quoted Becker as saying, "How could any juror vote to convict on the testimony of known criminals like that?"

Bald Jack was equipped to capitalize on the literary and dramatic opportunities afforded by his role in the Rosenthal Affair—even Herman Rosenthal himself said so in his posthumous affidavit: "This fellow Rose had a fair education and was a little better versed in the use of words than most of the boys on the East Side, and they looked up to him as a wise fellow—a sort of mouthpiece" ("Rosenthal's Own Story of His Rise and Fall in Favor of the System," *World,* July 17, 1912). A month later, Bald Jack was quoted as saying, "Believe me, this writin' stuff is a pipe [a sure thing]....I hate to talk about meself, but that stuff I wrote that was printed in the papers [his confession] made some hit" ("Informers Busy as Real Authors of 'Literature,'" *World,* August 17, 1912).

Accounts of the witnesses' exit from the West Side prison appear in "Informers Make Ready to Get Out of Gotham," *Lincoln Journal Star,* November 20, 1912; "Waiting for Rose, Vallon and Webber," *World,* November 21, 1912; "Informers Disappear Soon after Release," the *Courier-Journal,* November 22, 1912; and "Informers in Rosenthal Case Exhibit Fear when Emerging from Prison," the *Inquirer,* November 22, 1912.

The *Collier's* piece, "The Defeat of the Underworld," November 9, 1912, was written by the veteran journalist Richard Harding Davis, who had covered crime in the late 1800s. Comparing the eras, he wrote:

> In the old-fashioned days, murder was an adventure that was
> not entered into without precaution and hesitancy. Then the
> man who contemplated murder, and the hanging to which in
> those days it frequently led, went about it only after some
> thought and preparation.... Those were the days that made
> Sherlock Holmes necessary. The "gunmen" have changed all
> that. Of murder they made a sport like the potting of rabbits,
> a profession, which, with a slight profit, combines just
> enough of danger to make it exciting.... The New York
> gunman is a dandy, an exquisite, scented, wearing silk socks,
> silk ties to his tan shoes, with rings on his well-kept fingers
> and a gold watch in his well-pressed clothes. Jack Zelig was a
> daily patron of a manicure parlor; "Gyp the Blood," "Lefty
> Louie"—all of the gangsters—were regular members of the
> Order of the Turkish Bath. If the murder of Herman Rosen-
> thal brought about no other good, it served to force into the

limelight these Morlocks of the lower world. It convinced an incredulous public of the real existence of these armed degenerates. It established the fact that in New York City the price of the life of any man, at union rates, is two-hundred dollars.

CHAPTER TWELVE: BRIDGING THE WIRES

The scene at Rebelle's is assembled from MA 1779, St. 6; MA 1783, St. 30; MA 1785, St. 197; and MA 1788, St. 231; and a remarkable twenty-eight-page report from one of Abe's undercover informants, Marcus Braun, who posed as an IBA pimp. I found Braun's report filed, or perhaps misfiled, in NYPLCOFR, Series 1.

Tony's experience as a prostitute can be found in Rosenberg, "Underworld Wife"; and Shoenfeld, *Crime Buster*. The scene at Barth's Salon is described in MA 1782, St. nos. 21, 24, and 28.

Abe's introduction to Magnes appears in Shoenfeld Interview, AJCOHL; and Shoenfeld, *Crime Buster*. Gramercy Park as a neighborhood for reform-minded professionals such as Magnes and Newburger is described in Wallace, *Greater Gotham,* 308–10. The wire-bridging operation with Faurot comes from Shoenfeld, *Crime Buster*. Faurot's movie cameo is described in Kevin Brownlow, *Behind the Mask of Innocence: Sex, Violence, Prejudice, Crime: Films of Social Conscience in the Silent Era* (Berkeley: University of California Press, 1990), 160–61. Dollar John Langer went under several aliases, including Matthew Coyle. Talks between Gaynor, Newburger, and Magnes regarding law-enforcement policy and appropriate methods for investigating and suppressing crime are memorialized in a series of late-1912 letters, archived in MA 1758–62. Abe's thinking about whether to accept the position in the police department, and the conditions he makes on his acceptance, appear in Shoenfeld Interview, AJCOHL; and Shoenfeld, *Crime Buster*. The conflict between Jonah Goldstein and Magnes is laid out in MA 1770; Goldstein Interview, CUOHP; and Shoenfeld Interview, AJCOHL.

Abe's recruitment of the "hello girls" calls for further explanation. Why would telephone operators in places like hotels be useful to a vice crusade? Pimps and gamblers would often leave business cards, bearing the address of a brothel or casino, with hotel clerks. The clerk, or "capper," would, in exchange for a commission from the underworld figure, hand the card to hotel guests who inquired about such activities. In the course of making these arrangements, there was a lot of phone activity at the hotels. Abe's recruitment of Tony can be found in Shoenfeld, *Crime Buster*.

CHAPTER THIRTEEN: EVERYMAN'S FRIEND

The German-Jewish uptowners' yearslong battle against immigration restriction is chronicled in Cohen, *Not Free to Desist,* 37–53; and Morton Rosenstock, *Louis Marshall, Defender of Jewish Rights* (Detroit: Wayne State University Press, 1965), 79–89. The Warburg family history in Germany and America, the Warburg mansion of Felix and Frieda, Felix and his philanthropic endeavors—they are all covered in Chernow, *Warburgs*; Birmingham, *Our Crowd*; and Schiff Warburg, *Reminiscences*.

Of Felix's many pleasures, Frieda writes: "He enjoyed soft, smooth materials, such as cashmere or vicuna for outerwear and woven silk for underwear." He loved toys, and always walked quickly past Abercrombie & Fitch, lest he buy every double-purpose gadget in the place. Frieda's comment about Felix's generosity appears in Schiff Warburg, *Reminiscences*. Felix was the leading contributor to the American Association for Labor Legislation, the organization of social scientists that lobbied for a system of state-run health insurance (Wallace, *Greater Gotham,* 557–60).

The two-way road of resentment, from Upper Fifth Avenue down to Division Street, is captured throughout Howe, *World of Our Fathers*. The two cases referred to, in which that resentment turned to violence, are documented in trial transcripts: JJC nos. 1657 and 624. Of course these cases were rare. Most episodes of uptown-downtown social friction didn't end with one party dead or maimed. But many East Siders had stories to tell of times they'd been made to feel less-than. The Russian-Jewish immigrant Maurice Hindus, for example, recalled his boyhood experience at the Educational Alliance on East Broadway, which the German Jews founded to assimilate and Americanize the downtowners. In *Green Worlds,* Hindus recalled going to the Alliance's reading room and suffering harassment at the hands of a librarian, who repeatedly demanded that Hindus sit upright while reading. "Incensed with her arbitrariness, I shoved the books off the table to the floor and dashed out of the room. Now I knew that the things I had heard about people uptown were true. Haughty and domineering, they didn't like the poor people downtown."

Columbia's effort to limit Jewish enrollment didn't work, and by 1918 roughly 25 percent of its entering class was Russian Jewish. At NYU, Russian Jews would constitute about half of the student body by 1917 (Wallace, *Greater Gotham,* 371).

An account of life in the Warburg household can be found in Edward M. M. Warburg Interview, AJCOHL. Edward, the youngest of Felix and Frieda's five children, recalled that the walls of the mansion were hung with "all these sacred pictures of the Christian faith, but nothing of the Jewish thing at all." He continues: "But pop [Felix] liked this. He had a Stradivarius quartet and he was very much sort of a duke of one of the Rhineland duchies. He had a court." Looking back on his childhood, Edward resented his cosseting: "I mean, you weren't allowed out in the street, you weren't allowed to go to the theater. We didn't go to the movies together. There wasn't anything like that. There wasn't any sport. You couldn't go out and play football in the park, because some of those kids from the West Side might rough you up. And so I was brought up like one of the princelings. Awful!" A more detailed (and fonder) remembrance of life in the Warburg mansion, with its mix of "solemn grandeur" and "madcap comedy," can be found in a richly illustrated pamphlet, *"1109" The Warburg House: An Informal Guided Tour by Edward M. M. Warburg* (New York: The Jewish Museum, 1996).

Abe's exchange with Mayer and his subsequent speech to the underworld appear in Shoenfeld, *Crime Buster*.

CHAPTER FOURTEEN: MISFITS

The amazing adventures of Tourbillon are chronicled in "Almost Fell into Lion's Den: Bicyclist's Peril Stampedes Crowd," *San Francisco Examiner*, June 1, 1904; "Lioness Ran through Crowd Causing Panic: Five Thousand People Witnessed Dangerous Beast Escape from Cage," *Fairmont West Virginian*, August 23, 1905; "Tourbillon in Trouble," *Holyoke Daily Transcript*, March 26, 1906; Rothstein, *Now I'll Tell*, 209–19; "Raffles Demands New Trial," *Sun*, November 18, 1911; "Polished Burglar Guilty," *New-York Tribune*, November 18, 1911; and "Evidence Disappears," *New York Times*, January 24, 1913. Tourbillon often went by the alias Dan Collins, aka Dapper Dan.

E. W. Hornung, *The Complete Short Stories of Raffles: The Amateur Cracksman* (London: Souvenir Press, 1984) contains, by way of introduction, an excellent essay by George Orwell, which I quote from later in these notes.

The Rothstein biographies—one a book, the other a newspaper series—are Clarke, *In the Reign of Rothstein*; and "Murder of Arnold Rothstein, New York's Biggest Gambler, Is Still Mystery After a Year," *St. Louis Star and Times*, November 25, 1929.

The fullest portrait of Nicky Arnstein appears in Herbert G. Goldman, *Fanny Brice: The Original Funny Girl* (New York: Oxford University Press, 1992). Despite his connections at Jack's, Nicky spent plenty of time in prison. In New York, he began his first period of incarceration in 1915, for working the "sick engineer swindle." In this scheme, the con man "ropes the mark" and takes him to an office near Wall Street, where he introduces the mark to a confederate posing as a stockbroker. The broker expresses eagerness to buy a certain mining stock that has suddenly become valuable. Then, before the mark can verify any of this, the con man takes him to an apartment to visit a second confederate, who poses as an engineer for the mining company. The engineer is not in good health, he says, and needs to raise money for his medical care. Moreover, the "sick engineer" knows nothing about the rise in value of his stock, and offers to sell it to the mark for a nominal value. This transaction is timed to take place on a Friday afternoon, after the "broker" has left for the day. When the mark presents himself at the broker's office on Monday, to resell his newly acquired stock for a big profit, he learns that the man he's looking for had rented the office for a short time only, and departed without leaving an address. Returning to the apartment of the "sick engineer," the mark discovers that he, too, has left for parts unknown.

Charles Gondorff, King of the Wiretappers, also went to prison in 1915, when a wire went sideways. If the name Gondorff sounds familiar to film lovers, it's because it was given to the veteran con man Henry Gondorff, the character played by Paul Newman in the 1973 movie *The Sting*. In that film, Newman's Gondorff trains Robert Redford's character, the big-con tenderfoot Johnny Hooker, to run a wire on the underworld kingpin Doyle Lonnegan (played by Robert Shaw). *The Sting* is a great movie, but now, after working on *The Incorruptibles,* I see one problem. The movie is set in 1936, more than a decade after wiretapping cons were killed off by the advent of radio and other forms of mass communication.

The book that informed *The Sting* is David Maurer, *The Big Con: The Story of the Confidence Man and the Confidence Game* (New York: Bobbs-Merrill, 1940; reprinted as *The Big Con: The Story of the Confidence Man,* New York: Anchor Books, 1999).

A history of how the Mann Act helped create the FBI can be found in Pliley, *Policing Sexuality.*

Notably, the badger game, though supercharged by the Mann Act, predated it. Prior to the Mann Act, the "badger" was a prostitute who, working with a pimp, frequented department stores and restaurants. She didn't openly solicit johns, but conducted mild flirtations, enough to start a conversation. She confided to the mark that she was married to a traveling salesman, or some such, and that they were quarrelling over another woman. She suggested that they retire to her apartment, which the mark found furnished in a manner consistent with the badger's story. A conspicuously placed photo, he was told, depicted the husband, to whom she gave a name such as John Henry Jones. As soon as the mark was in a compromising position, the pimp rushed in, carrying a suitcase initialed JHJ. The alleged husband pulled out a revolver and threatened to kill the badger and the mark. The badger pleaded for the life of the mark, who in turn tried to settle, offering to leave everything of value behind. If the mark was married and had disclosed his identity, he could be further blackmailed.

The lawyer's quote about Arnold appears in Gene Fowler, *The Great Mouthpiece: The Life of William J. Fallon* (New York: Blue Ribbon Books, 1938). Carolyn had a different opinion: "Arnold said he'd do anything for a friend. But he didn't want friends, not really. They were a luxury. Like a wife." Zoe Beckley's interview with Arnold appears in "Dubs Who Can't Rich Call Him Crooked, but It's Brains, Says Rothstein," *Brooklyn Daily Eagle,* November 27, 1928.

The Shoenfeld family's reaction to Abe's new public status in the vice crusade and his defiance of the Sam Paul Association appears in Shoenfeld, *Crime Buster*. Of his mother, Dora, who doesn't appear often in his writings, Abe recalled, "My mother's favorite was the Book of Ruth, read to me over and again during my youth. She instilled in me a love for the Bible, and all through my life I have studied it and its mysteries. Her father, Yusel Bruder, was a leading rabbi in Hungary, and was honored with four audiences with Kaiser Franz Joseph, consulting on Jewish affairs." Abe mentioned that his father's two brothers were also prominent rabbis in Hungary. He said his father was "Sephardic-Hungarian" and his mother "Ashkenazi-Hungarian."

PART THREE: THE INCORRUPTIBLES

CHAPTER FIFTEEN: WHACKED UNMERCIFULLY

Abe's assembly of the squad, which was known officially as Special Squad No. 4, can be found in Shoenfeld Interview, AJCOHL; and Shoenfeld, *Crime Buster*.

Inspector Cahalane's experience with Abe and the vice crusade might have set his career on a new path. Cahalane became a model cop, and published a well-received policing manual: Cornelius F. Cahalane, *Police Practice and Procedure* (New York: NYPD, 1914).

The crusade against gamblers, which began in September 1912, can be found in MA 1779–1793, St. nos. 11–12, 39, 51, 53–59, 82, 87, 180, 200, 203–4, 206, 237, 263, 266, 268–9, 279, 443, 475, 692, 748, 788, 874, 938, 1057, 1301, and 1303. At this point, the Kehillah had not yet been named as the force behind the vice crusade, but the crusade's progress was tracked in news coverage: "No More Steel Bars for Gambling Places: Drastic Treatment of Fine Mahogany Stirs 'Gambling Belt' — Tables 'Marked for Identification,'" *New-York Tribune*, February 7, 1913; and "Gamblers' Tools Seized in Raids 'Marked' to Bits," *World*, February 7, 1913. But hints of Jewish involvement creep into news coverage. In "Gaynor for Ten Heads of Police: More Deputies Would Soon End Graft, the Mayor Thinks," *Sun*, February 27, 1913, the paper quotes Gaynor: "Recently, the Mayor said, Rabbi Magnes and Mr. Newburger, with the cooperation of the police, have suppressed twenty-three gambling houses of the East Side." In the *Sun* piece, Gaynor refers obliquely to the pre-NYPD phase of the Kehillah crusade, a remark that must have confused readers: "Did any newspaper in this town acquaint Albany with what Rabbi Magnes and Mr. Newburger did? . . . Those two men are entitled to the thanks of the entire city. I tried to reward one of them by making him a deputy police commissioner."

Notes

The gambling raids are tallied in a five-page Kehillah report, written by Abe and titled "Gambling," which can be found in MA 1771. The surveillance and raids of poolrooms and hangouts are chronicled in MA, St. nos. 98, 176–77, 196, 232, 241, 244, 248, 250, 252, 283–84, 461, 468, 473–74, 484–86, 490, and 680. He chronicles and complains about other types of hangouts, such as saloons, in MA 1779–1793, St. nos. 183, 229–30, 242–43, 254 ("Many a 'French' stunt is pulled in the private rooms"), 264, 273–74, 481, 494–96, 499, 633, 635, 690, 693, 696, 704, 706–7, 736, and 821. Regarding the origins of a phrase later associated with the Italian mob, Abe writes in St. 635: "This saloon is a hangout for Warshover men [criminals from Warsaw] who are known as 'wise guys.'" But it seems the phrase wasn't specific to Warsaw crooks. In a 1912 report, he refers to an East Side casino owner nicknamed Shomis (literally: Detective) as "one of these so-called wise guys. You can't tell him a thing, he knows it all. Incidentally, he is considered to be worth lots of money." In a 1914 report about a group of gamblers whose wives are all thieves, he writes that one "used to be a Houston Street 'Punk.' Today he is a big Second Avenue Man. 'A wise guy' — he can play pinochle for $500 a game." The quotation marks he uses in these reports — for "punk" and "wise guy" — perhaps indicate that they were new additions to underworld argot. In a 1915 letter to Magnes, about vice in Broadway hotels, Abe writes: "Here it is where hundreds of sharks, thieves, scoundrels and 'wise guys' are located . . ."

Kehillah drug reports can be found in MA 1779–93, St. nos. 25, 29, 155, 192, 783, 822, 838, 896, 904, 910, 914–17, and 919. As drugs such as cocaine and opium went from being legal to illegal, a process that unfolded roughly between 1907 and 1912, there was a period in which pharmacies continued to sell them, illegally, and became enmeshed with the underworld. See the above Kehillah reports, plus "Police Blind to Cocaine Selling: With Drug Store as Headquarters Sidewalk Dealers Reap Rich Harvest from Victims, Gunmen Gangs Protect Them," *New-York Tribune,* December 2, 1912. The article notes: "Another term used to describe [a "coke sniffer"] is 'leaper,' and this is derived from the fact that the nervous twitching grows upon them, so that eventually they become unable to control their movements and will, after a dose of the 'dope,' jump about as if in sheer boyish exhilaration."

The best — and perhaps only — nonfiction book about the first years of drug prohibition is the gritty and intimate memoir by Leroy Street, *I Was a Drug Addict* (New York: Arlington House, 1953). Leroy Street was a pen name, but there are hints in the book that he was either Jewish or Italian. His drug use began in the fall of 1910, when one could still buy pure heroin, regarded chiefly as a cough medicine, from pharmacies. Street's habit became problematic in 1911, after he witnessed the horrors of the Triangle fire. Of the drug vocabulary, he writes that "heroin was called 'junk' and its addicts 'junkies.' Opium was called 'hop' and its devotees 'hopheads.' Cocaine was 'snow' and those who used it 'snowbirds' until they reached an advanced stage when they were called 'leapers' because of their jerky movements, almost like St. Vitus dance" (19–20).

Abe wasn't all that interested in due process. "You must recall that I was only twenty-one years of age and youth probably outweighs the more careful deliberations of maturity," he wrote later in *Crime Buster*. "I knew all about those arguments, about seizure, 'every man's home is his castle,' the need for warrants. Of the hundreds of raids I made in 1913, the year I spent in the Department, until after Mayor Gaynor died, I don't remember using more than a few dozen warrants, plus. I raided *only* when I was certain I would find a felony case or even a case of lesser violation."

Further tales of East Side thieves and "fences" — including fish thieves and chicken fences, fake watch and cologne vendors, and fake money-machine vendors — and their fate at the hands of the Incorruptibles can be found in MA 1779–93, St. nos. 51, 61, 107, 109–10, 144, 149, 185, 209, 270, 442, 443, 614, 640, 738, 742, 800, 846, 870, 924, 1004, and 1320. The untouchability of Frank Cassassa and other squad members is described in MA 1784, St. nos. 258 and 270.

When Simons Pawn Shop staged a burglary and then closed, the ensuing chaos was chronicled in "$10,000 Reward in Pawn Theft: Mob Packs Hester Street," *Sun,* March 18, 1913; "Angry Crowd at Looted Pawnshop," *New-York Tribune,* March 18, 1913; and "Rush to Redeem Gems from Simons," *New York Times,* March 22, 1913.

In court proceedings, the vernacular that "Max Prettyfield, sociology student" helped translate was described by the *World* as "the lingo of the East Side crook — half Yiddish, half English." Here's an example of such lingo, from the mouth of a teenage thief: "The dick flagged me and frisked me. I had no front [story, or alibi], and when he said I would get it all [a full prison sentence] for being a gun [a thief] I made up my mind not to do any hop-scotching [bullshitting]. I saw it was a case of John O'Brien [fleeing on a freight train] for mine, but only if I could get to be a lammister [a fugitive]. I knew I was a lobster [cooked, caught] and, not having any *mazuma* [cash], I had to come across [squeal]" ("Boy Crook Tells How Fagin Trained 'Pupils' in Crime: Samuel Fattman, Seventeen Years Old, Uses Weird Vocabulary in Story," *World,* May 2, 1913).

The naming of a cop who conspired with thieves didn't lead to a public prosecution but there was news coverage, such as "Tells How Police Tore Up Evidence to Save 'Fence': Isidor Rader Continues Confession, Implicating Detectives as Bribe Takers," *World,* June 23, 1913. Attempts to bribe Abe and Newburger are explained in Shoenfeld Interview, AJCOHL; and Shoenfeld, *Crime Buster.*

Of Marcus Braun, Abe recalled, "This man wormed his way in nicely." Braun was an old hand at such investigations. Back in 1908, when American reformers were participating in international vice investigations, the Yiddish-speaking Braun "studied and surveyed" Warsaw's Jewish brothels. Back home the following year, Braun took a nationwide tour of the American brothel scene and estimated that there were "50,000 alien prostitutes" in the country (Bristow, *Prostitution and Prejudice,* 62–66, 156–57). East Side prostitution, including the full history thereof; the IBA and pimp life; the dangers of movie theaters; a rundown of sexually transmitted diseases; and the Kehillah's crusade against all of it are covered in MA 1779–93, St. nos. 6, 13, 18–24, 27, 30, 32–33, 35–36, 43–44, 48, 61, 71, 73–77, 89, 92–93, 108, 113, 135, 145–46, 150, 157–58, 160–61, 163–64, 169, 171, 173, 191, 197, 215, 218, 224, 237, 240, 251, 259, 262, 275, 277, 288, 444–45, 448, 610, 674, 736, 771, 773, 781, 802, 804, 807, 820, 823, 835, 856, 864, 880, 888, 905–6, 935–37, 963–64, 978–80, 1015, 1019–20, 1023, 1038, and 1052–54; Shoenfeld Interview, AJCOHL; and Shoenfeld, *Crime Buster.* Natalie Sonnichsen's reports are filed in NYPLCOFR, Series 5: Investigations.

Barth's Hair Salon is castigated in MA 1782, St. 179 ("[Barth's] lease on life has been too long…he should be blacklisted as a bondsman in the various courts"). Courthouse graft is covered in MA 1779–87, St. nos. 5, 80, 138 ("Magistrate Frederick B. House, commonly known as Frederick B. Louse in the underworld"), 225–26, 666, 668, 691–92, 716, and 870A.

The reading habits, or "intellectual mania," of young East Siders during the time of Abe's youth is featured in "Jew Babes at the Library," *Evening Post,* October 3, 1903. East Siders withdrew English-language books from the Chatham Square branch of the public library at the rate of a thousand per day. Popular selections were the Bible, Helen Guerber's *The Story of the Chosen People,* Eugène Sue's *The Wandering Jew,* and Shakespeare's *The Merchant of Venice.* "Excuses for maltreated books give glimpses of home life," wrote the *Evening Post.* " 'The baby dropped it in the herring' is the favorite explanation of a soiled cover."

Lily's post-trial life and her fight to free Louie can be found in Rosenberg, "Underworld Wife."

CHAPTER SIXTEEN: YEAR OF THE RED-LIGHT DRAMA

The new industry paper, *Variety,* referred to red-light dramas as "patchouli and kimono pictures," and warned that they could lower the esteem in which film was held.

The best source on red-light dramas in film, and the silent-film era generally, is Brownlow, *Behind the Mask of Innocence.* Many of the silent films Brownlow discusses are lost; thus, the only record of their content exists in news coverage.

Notes

Abe's concern about prostitutes moving into tenements and husbands taking their heavenly joys down the hall was depicted in a red-light drama called *Who's Your Neighbor?* The 1917 film — lost, but described by Brownlow — is about a prostitute. Following the raid of her brothel, she moves into an apartment house and causes havoc in the lives of a young boy and his father. *Moving Picture World* called it "one of the most insidious, moral-destroying" films ever produced: "It will lower to the level of a bawdy house any theater in which it is shown. It reeks with a filthy sex element that struts across the screen in the sheep's clothing of alleged propaganda advocating the segregation of vice." And yet, *Moving Picture World* admitted that the story was "original and strong," so much so that "people of refinement" might turn away.

For more on the situation for East Side girls, see Sydney Stahl Weinberg, *The World of Our Mothers* (New York: Schocken, 1988); and Sydelle Kramer and Jenny Masur, eds., *Jewish Grandmothers* (Boston: Beacon Press, 1976).

The first newspaper mention of Mother Rosie Hertz that I could find pertains to an early arrest of Mother in "Drugged and Robbed in New York Hotel: Barnard Rice, of Buffalo, Has Painful Experience in Metropolis — Forced Entertainment," *Buffalo Courier,* September 21, 1904. Tony's interaction with Mother Hertz can be found in NYCMA 105290; and Shoenfeld, *Crime Buster.* Mother's background, including a rundown of her criminal family, can be found in MA 1780, St. 13. The manner in which detectives gathered evidence for brothel cases can be found in Cahalane, *Police Practice and Procedure,* 182–83: "To establish that the premises are disorderly it is only necessary to prove that women were there for the purpose of prostitution. To do this, bargain with a woman on the price, and question her as to where the act can be committed.... Have this conversation in the presence of the proprietor, if possible, and pay the woman the amount she finally settles on."

Abe's comment about Winnie's grafting appears in Shoenfeld Interview, AJCOHL, 21: "All the money he got went to Fox, who invested it in his movie houses and later established Twentieth-Century Fox with Winnie Sheehan's money, the graft that he got," Abe said. Ironically, the first person to name Winnie publicly was Herman Rosenthal, in the affidavit published after his murder:

> Becker was able to work as he wished because he was satisfied
> that the newspapers were "fixed." He believed that this had
> been done by Winnie Sheehan, the private secretary to
> Commissioner Waldo, who was a newspaper reporter before
> he received his appointment in the Police Department.
> Sheehan often boasted of his "pull" with the newspapers and
> of his friendship with men high in editorial positions on the

daily press. He frequently mentioned their names as among
his friends and men who would do anything for him and
would suppress or print news at his wish.... This gave Becker
his great drag.

Becker never squealed on Winnie, but other cops did, and his name soon hit the headlines: "Find Money Link between a Man Close to Waldo and Inspector under Suspicion," *World,* August 23, 1912; "Captain's $15,000 Graft Story Out: Former Under Sheriff Accuses Waldo and Sheehan of Inspiring It," *Sun,* September 18, 1912; "Waldo Aide Named in Graft Inquiry," *Daily Free Press,* September 20, 1912; "Winnie Sheehan Knew the Gangs," *Brooklyn Daily Eagle,* September 20, 1912; and finally, "Sheehan Joins William Fox: Waldo's Secretary Becomes Associated with Theatrical Enterprises," *Sun,* January 3, 1914.

In Vanda Krefft's biography of Fox—*The Man Who Made the Movies: The Meteoric Rise and Tragic Fall of William Fox* (New York: Harper, 2017)—we learn that Fox claimed he went into business with Winnie because they'd become "close and fast friends." But Krefft points out that it was a curious friendship: "They had almost nothing in common, especially not personal values." But even though Winnie, by his own admission, knew nothing about the film industry, it's easy to see why Fox considered him indispensable. For one thing, Winnie knew something about scouting talent and promoting events, having once managed the amateur careers of NYPD cops who moonlighted as boxers. Also, Fox, a scrappy businessman who was often engaged in legal battles, knew he needed a shrewd political ally. See Krefft, *Man Who Made the Movies,* 118–20; and "Buffalo Man Boosts New York Police Athletes: Winfield Sheehan, Ex-Enquirer Reporter, Said to Be the Best Friend to the Husky Coppers on the Metropolitan Force Who Want to Go to the Olympic Games," *Buffalo Enquirer,* June 4, 1912.

Fifteen years after joining Fox in the movie business, when Winnie froze Fox out of his own company, Fox vented about it in a self-published biography by Upton Sinclair: *Upton Sinclair Presents William Fox* (1933). Further biographical material of Winnie can be found in "Films' Future Is in Talkies, Says Sheehan," *New York Telegram,* March 27, 1929; "'Winnie' Sheehan, Hollywood Dynamo, Ex-World Reporter," *World,* October 5, 1929; and "Winfield Sheehan, Film Pioneer, Dies after Devoting 31 Years to Industry," *Variety,* August 1, 1945.

A search turned up no transcript of the Hertz trial, but it is covered in "Two More Inspectors May Be Indicted on Wrenn's Confession: Rosie Hertz Weakens and Gives Whitman Amazing Story of East Side Extortion," *World,* March 10, 1913. A year later, when the grafting cop named by Mother filed a libel suit against a newspaper, Mother became emotional when she testified. Fed up, the judge told Mother, "I can see no occasion for this outburst. It is unfortunate enough that I should have to listen to your story" ("Rose Hertz Cries and Almost Stops Wasserman Suit," *World,* May 11, 1914).

The seduction of girls at Seward Park and the Dorman assault are chronicled in MA 1789, St. nos. 443 and 446; Shoenfeld, *Crime Buster*; and Shoenfeld Interview, AJCOHL, in which Abe discusses having worked with an East Side educator, Miss Robbins, to revive Seward Park and provide a hundred pairs of roller skates to be used in the park. The episode led to Abe and Newburger forming the League of East Side Parents, which was covered by Yiddish papers later in 1913: "A Meeting of East Side Mothers," *Varheit,* November 6, 1913 ("The league is half a year old and already accomplished much regarding child prostitution"); and "Parents War against Hoodlums," *Varheit,* November 28, 1913, which states: "Mr. Abe Shoenfeld, who as secretary to deputy police commissioner Newburger had investigated all instances of assault on Jewish children reported to the police, said yesterday that he expects the League of East Side Parents...to be ready to take action within several weeks."

The movie theater as a place of iniquity is explained in, among others, MA 1785–90, St. nos. 280, 603, 606–07, 622–32, 702, 778, 780, and 805.

Abe's belief that the means justify the ends, and his ideas for more aggressive strategies, appear in MA 1780–89, St. nos. 22, 261, 624, and 912; and Shoenfeld, *Crime Buster*. In St. 624, Abe writes of throwing his weight around in the dance halls, which he'd always railed against:

> On May 21st, at 9:20 p.m., I entered 106 Forsyth St. I had
> been attracted here by the sweet strains of ragtime being
> played by four real "tough guys." Another tough stood at the
> door and held up all who entered for 15 cents admission. On
> entering I found a fairly jammed hall. Most of the men were
> gentile and many of them Italian. Most of the girls were
> Jewish. Somewhat of an invasion!!
>
> The dancing here was the real sort. You could not "do it"
> any tougher. When they "got wise" to me, the special officer
> on the floor stopped two couples and asked them to be careful
> in dancing. They looked at him, thinking he had gone
> crazy....I will see that this place gets immediate attention.

Abe's reports on "professional panhandlers" can be found in MA 1774, St. nos. 166, 187–90, and 198–99. We are told, for example, that Pekin Eddey rubs salve on his arm, in a circle, then cuts around the circle with a knife. "In two or three days," Abe explains, "this piece of meat which has been outlined by the knife scratch, due to the workings of the salve, loosens and comes off, leaving a raw wound...When he goes up to a person to beg alms, the smell of the raw wound is enough to knock anyone dead." Abe describes other notable panhandlers and their methods. In *Police Practice and Procedure,* Cahalane writes that professional "fit-throwers" worked in gangs of two or three: "If no policeman is in sight, one of the gang will put into his mouth a powder which the saliva will cause to effervesce, making him appear as though foaming at the mouth, and will fall to the street.... The confederate then makes a little speech calling attention to 'this terrible condition in a city of wealth' and when he has sympathy well aroused takes off his hat and passes it around, starting the collection by dropping into it a fair-sized bill" (116).

Prostituted children, polluted minds, and poor ventilation were not the only hazards associated with the early years of the movies. Fires were a constant concern. For instance, when a film machine at the Houston Street Hippodrome malfunctioned and began to spew smoke, a boy's cry of "fire" created a stampede that resulted in two fatalities: "Two Dead, 20 Hurt in Theater Panic," *New York Times,* February 3, 1913. The East Side's Houston Street Hippodrome is not to be confused with the live theatrical space up on Sixth Avenue. The East Side Hippodrome was less distinguished than the uptown landmark. The building, originally constructed by Catholic priests as a mission hall, was sold to Bald Jack Rose in 1911. Bald Jack painted over the religious murals with blue, white, and gold, and relaunched the space as the Houston Athletic Club, a boxing venue, then resold it to theater people when he got caught up in the Rosenthal Affair. At the new venue, a music hall that combined Yiddish and English vaudeville with movies, patrons used Yonah Schimmel's famous knish shop as a snack bar.

Newburger's ad hoc internal-affairs department played a significant role in the Kehillah vice crusade. It is not clear how many cops he investigated and/or disciplined, but many cases were covered in the news. "Policemen Shoot Craps in Station? No, Sirree! Never!," *World,* July 10, 1913; "Policemen Deny Crap Game: Trial Commissioner Gets Angry and Will Bring Graver Charges," *Sun,* July 11, 1913; and "Rain Drove Us Indoors, Defense of Detectives," *World,* August 27, 1913. Newburger gained a reputation as fair and impartial. Soon he was inspecting precincts all over the city. "Patrolman Is Exonerated: Commissioner Newburger Shows Prisoner's Charge of Violence False," *New York Times,* April 27, 1913.

While monitoring his own staff, he also found the time to chase criminals. An unyielding crusader, Newburger would time raids to occur simultaneously, so that word of a single raid couldn't spread to others and give them time to shut down their operations and flee. "Raids on Seven Houses," *New York Times,* April 13, 1913. Newburger so frustrated Dollar John Langer's attempts to reopen a casino that the gambler asked a magistrate to issue a summons against Newburger on the grounds of police oppression. "Asks Summons for Newburger: Deputy Police Commissioner on Bench when Magistrate Refuses," *Sun,* April 15, 1913. Newburger's interview appears in "How Deputy Police Commissioner Newburger Put the East Side's House in Order," *Sun,* May 4, 1913. Abe chronicled police corruption in MA 1780–82, St. nos. 41, 201, 227, and 258.

CHAPTER SEVENTEEN: *IL NOSTRO GET*

Accounts of Magnes's 1913 address to the underworld, a version of which apparently took place again the following spring, can be found in Shoenfeld, *Crime Buster*.

The origins of "ghetto" are described in Mitchell Duneier, *Ghetto: The Invention of a Place, the History of an Idea* (New York: Farrar, Straus & Giroux, 2016), 4–11. My understanding of Jewish history in Western Europe, from the end of classical antiquity to the High Middle Ages, is informed by many wonderful books, including Duneier, *Ghetto*; Muller, *Capitalism and the Jews*; Sombart, *Jews and Modern Capitalism*; Lowenthal, *Jews of Germany*; Gay, *The Jews of Germany*; Robert S. Lopez, *The Commercial Revolution of the Middle Ages, 950–1350* (Cambridge: Cambridge University Press, 1976); Ferdinand Gregorovius, *The Ghetto and the Jews of Rome* (New York: Schocken, 1948); Rist, *Popes and Jews, 1095–1291*; and Tuchman, *Distant Mirror*. Tuchman notes that the law against simony — the Tammany-esque buying and selling of ecclesiastical offices, privileges, and pardons — was violated about as routinely as the usury law. Tuchman writes: "Money could buy any kind of dispensation: to legitimize children, of which the majority were those of priests and prelates; to divide a corpse for the favorite custom of burial in two or more places; to permit nuns to keep two maids; to permit a converted Jew to visit his unconverted parents; to marry within the prohibited degree of consanguinity (with a sliding scale of fees for the second, third, and fourth degrees)..." (28). Jonathan I. Israel, *European Jewry in the Age of Mercantilism, 1550–1750* (London: Littman Library of Jewish Civilization, 1998) takes the story into the early modern era.

A full chronicle of the Crusades can be found in Steven Runciman's three-volume *A History of the Crusades* (New York: Penguin Classics, 2016), published originally in the 1950s. *Chronicles of the First Crusade,* ed. Christopher Tyerman (New York: Penguin Classics, 2012), is an incredible collection of contemporary accounts.

What is a crusade? And what relationship did the early-twentieth-century "vice crusades" have to Christianity's big-C Crusades? In his foreword to *Chronicles of the First Crusade,* Tyerman writes that "crusading has always lacked objective precision in definition, practice, perception or approval." The term, Tyerman writes, "has been understood as warfare to defend a beleaguered faith;...an agent as well as symbol of religious, cultural, and ethnic identity, even superiority; a vehicle for personal self-aggrandisement; commercial expansion and political conquest;...an example of recrudescent western racism; an excuse and incentive for religious persecution, ethnic cleansing and acts of barbarism; a noble cause; or...'one long act of intolerance in the name of God.'" There are a lot of possibilities. But, of the big-C Crusades, Tyerman proposes a unifying theme, which I found helpful for thinking about crusading in general: "The sense of embattlement upon which the ideology of crusading rested ensured that the wars of the Cross persisted so long as the religious assumptions that had given rise to and sustained them remained intact: the authority of the pope and Church to mediate penance and redemption" (viii–x).

The essential work on Eastern European Jewish history is Dubnow's three-volume *History of the Jews in Russia and Poland,* which explains how liquor laws operated with respect to Jews. See also Dynner, *Yankel's Tavern.* In *Within the Pale,* the Irishman Michael Davitt writes, "Unnatural social and economic conditions necessarily engender correlative abuses and evils. Poverty, illegal pursuits, the smuggling and sale of liquor, evasion of coercive law, bribery and corruption protested against the causes which begot them, until finally an Imperial Commission had to be appointed" (12–16).

Paraphrasing the commission's findings, Davitt explains how anti-Semitic legislation, including vice legislation, turned the Russian peasant class against Jews (just as it had with Polish peasants in the previous era): "With the expulsion from villages of the Jews, the retail sale of spirits [sale of corn to a distiller] would be carried on by tapsters of the native rural class, so that drunkenness would not diminish [among the native peasants], but only a decrease would take place in the number of agriculturists [growers of corn]. A peasant had previously been in the habit of selling his corn on the spot to a Jew, but now he was obliged to proceed to the nearest town, at a loss in time and labour, to sell his produce to a Jew, and the money realised he would still spend on brandy, bought from the same Jew."

When a czar prohibited occupations for Jews, thereby turning the masses into paupers, many Jewish shopkeepers in the Pale *depended* on bribery, and hoped for police who were "takers" (Goldberg, *Tales of Bialystok,* 59).

In 1908, New York's 120,000 horses deposited about 60,000 gallons of urine and 2.5 million pounds of manure on the city streets each day. "When steamy fresh, the dung attracted flies, which carried communicable diseases. When dry, it got pulverized by traffic, then floated up and hung in the air, ready for ingestion" (Wallace, *Greater Gotham,* 245). Wallace notes that roughly fifteen thousand dead horses needed to be removed from the streets each year, or about forty-one per day. Many sick or injured horses were simply abandoned by their owners, in which case the duty of disposal fell to cops. A police manual instructed: "In shooting a horse, try first to get it close to the curb so that it will not interfere with traffic. Place the muzzle of the gun at a point four or five inches above a line drawn across the eyes and about half an inch to the left of center" (Cahalane, *Police Practice and Procedure,* 97). If this seemed brutal, the older method, used by stableman until the early 1900s, "profoundly disturbed" East Side children, as Peter Casill recalled in *New York Memories of Yesteryear,* 88: "The animal was taken out of the stable into the street, a thick dark cloth was placed over his head, completely covering his eyes. The stableman would then raise a long-handled ax and bring it down with full force on the skull of the beast. The animal would let out a groan, then fall on his side, with blood spouting from the deep hole in his head."

In 1910, the city's horse population peaked at 250,000, then began a rapid decline, such that by 1912 autos outnumbered horses ("Hosed: Is There a Quick Fix for the Climate?" *The New Yorker,* November 8, 2009).

In addition to *When I Was Last on Cherry Street* (New York: Stein and Day, 1965), Harry Roskolenko published another memoir, *The Time That Was Then: The Lower East Side, 1900–1913* (New York: Dial Press, 1971). The social divisions among Jewish, Irish, and Italian kids were recalled by Sam Jaffe, a Russian Jew who grew up at 97 Orchard Street, present site of the Lower East Side Tenement Museum: "When you went to the Jackson Street baths, that was the Irish section, and they'd see you in the nude and they knew what you were and you'd have a fight," said Jaffe, who became an Oscar-nominated Hollywood actor. "We called the Irish, the Christians, 'Mickey bottles,' because their penises weren't cut." On Ridge Street, Jaffe continued, "there was the St. Mary's Church, with two huge steeples and crosses, and the [Irish] would all come dressed up with their Bibles, and we'd wait for them to come down out of church, those fellows who beat us up, and we'd get our revenge. Now, with the Italians, they had pushcarts with fruit. And the Italians ate a lot of vegetables, so we called them *gruz*-eaters, grass-eaters" (Sam Jaffe Interview, AJCOHL).

Terrifying tales of spooked horses can be found in "Pitfalls in Fifth Avenue: Horse Falls into One of Them and a Man at Work Has a Narrow Escape," *Sun,* September 22, 1909; "Horse's Hoofs Spared Baby: They Wrecked Perambulator, but the Bundled Infant Was Unhurt," *Sun,* April 27, 1911; "Woman Badly Hurt as Scared Horse Overturns Wagon: Plucky Policeman Stops Runaway in Which Teacher and Sister Are Injured," *World,* July 2, 1912; "Scared Horse Bolts; Grocer's Neck Broken; Two Others Are Hurt," *World,* June 17, 1913; "Scared Horse Kills Boy: Firecracker Causes Animal to Run, Throwing Out Little Driver," *Sun,* July 5, 1914; and "Six Run Down by Horse Scared in Thunderstorm," *World,* August 21, 1914. In the case of runaway horses, the police manual instructed cops to "judge his speed; run in the same direction and cut diagonally across. . . . If you have confidence in yourself, it takes very little effort to vault to a running horse's back after once securing a grip on his mane, for the reason that the forward pull assists you into place" (Cahalane, *Police Practice and Procedure,* 102).

The meeting of the stablemen and the crusade of the farrier Louis Blumenthal are chronicled in "Witness in Blackmail Case Is Shot Dead: Slayer Quickly Escapes," *New-York Tribune,* January 29, 1912. A week later, the police claimed that Blumenthal's killer was "the head of the horse poisoners of the East Side" ("May Get Gang's Chief: Head of Horse Poisoners Killed L. Blumenthal, Police Say," *New-York Tribune,* February 6, 1912). Whoever he was, he also shot a barber who got in his way during his escape, shattering the barber's elbow. The trial in which Blumenthal was to have testified, *People of the State of New York v. Charles Vitusky,* is archived as JJC 1607. Although Blumenthal paid with his life, his crusade bore fruit: "A Voice from the Grave: Testimony Given by Man Now Dead Convicts an Extortioner," *New York Times,* February 20, 1912.

The quote about "Mr. L." comes from another horse-poisoner trial, *People of the State of New York v. Samuel Levine, John Levinson,* archived as JJC 1648. In that case, the terror spread by the gang is apparent in one testimony, when a barely coherent witness for the prosecution finally confesses that, yes, he knows John L. "Everyone says, 'This is John L. He is a good fellow.'"

"A good fellow?" the prosecutor asks.

"Yes, sir," the witness says. "He poisons horses."

"A good fellow *and* a horse poisoner?"

"Yes, sir."

The history of horse-poisoning in New York can be tracked in "Poison for Horses: A Veterinary Surgeon Recalls Thirty Cases of This Kind," *World,* May 1, 1894; "Two Horses Poisoned: Alleged Cruel Crime of Blackmailers Who Had Been Refused," *New York Times,* July 6, 1897; "Horses Killed by Poison: Sixty Animals, Owned by East Side Fruit Dealers, Lost — A Rival Suspected," *New-York Tribune,* July 14, 1900; "Accused of Giving Poison to Horses: Russian Peddler Dropped It in Feed Bag," *New-York Tribune,* August 4, 1903; and "Latest Gang of Blackmailers Poison Horses: Band Known as the 'Yiddisher Black Hand' Spreads Terror on East Side," *World,* February 18, 1909. Poisoners targeted businesses that dealt in perishable goods, such as produce or ice cream, since they relied on prompt delivery. Joseph Toblinsky, then twenty-eight, begins making headlines in 1910: "Three Men Held on Extortion Charge," *Standard Union,* April 13, 1910; "Pay $500 Dues or Lose Your Horses, Is Threat," *Brooklyn Daily Eagle,* April 13, 1910; and "Poisoned Over 1,000 Horses," *Brooklyn Daily Eagle,* April 22, 1910. Toblinsky's escape and capture are tracked in: "Alleged Members of 'Arsenic Club' Flee," *Brooklyn Times Union,* May 26, 1910; "Alleged Poisoner Caught in 'Frisco," *Brooklyn Daily Eagle,* January 9, 1911; and "Toblinsky Back; Fled 4,000 Miles," *Brooklyn Times Union,* January 30, 1911. Abe's thoroughgoing account of the gang, titled "Horse Poisoners, Also Known as the Yiddish Black Hand," appears in MA 1782, St. 40. The Kehillah vice crusade's pursuit of Toblinsky and his crew is chronicled in Shoenfeld Interview, AJCOHL; and Shoenfeld, *Crime Buster.*

A postlude: For his testimony against the ice cream dealers, Toblinsky was paroled in 1916, seven years short of his ten-year sentence. "Sixteen Paroled from Sing Sing," *Asbury Park Press,* December 22, 1916. By then, workhorses had been mostly phased out of city life, and Toblinsky moved on. In 1919, he was pinched for ripping off foodstuffs: "Thief Gets Four Years for Stealing 100 Bags of Beans," *Brooklyn Times Union,* December 27, 1919. In the twenties, he tried his hand at bootlegging, and managed to stay out of prison until 1931, when he reappeared in headlines — writers only vaguely remembering his old street handle — for knocking over a truckload of woolens: "'Yeska N****r' Held in Hold-Up," *Brooklyn Times Union,* January 30, 1931. Two years later, Toblinsky, now fifty, was arrested with his teenage son for the same crime: "'Horse' Racketeer of Earlier Day Seized with Son: Joseph Toblinsky Accused of $12,000 Woolen Theft," *Brooklyn Times Union,* July 11, 1933.

In 1935, when he was nabbed again, this time for robbing a pharmaceutical truck, an East Side police captain pointed out that Toblinsky had been arrested twenty-one times since 1902. "There is no use wasting time on this fellow," the captain told detectives. "Toblinsky, I want to tell you that you are through." And he was: a new state statute, the Baumes law, mandated a life term for anyone convicted of three separate felonies. In covering Toblinsky's life sentence, a veteran newspaper reporter noted that citizens in 1935 thought erroneously of racketeering as a modern development, but Joseph Toblinsky had plied his "despicable trade in the pre-automobile era, when legitimate business, then as now, was the target of extortioners" ("Hijack Traps 'Horse Poison King' of 1900," *New York Daily News,* July 18, 1935).

CHAPTER EIGHTEEN: YOUR CITY

For Abe, the revelation that some East Side business owners resented the vice crusade took him by surprise. "Let me make this clear," he says in Shoenfeld Interview, AJCOHL. "We made enemies of the underworld and, believe it or not, we made enemies of the upperworld. Despite the fact that people had to pay tribute to the gangsters and lesser notables who ran these dances and ballrooms to collect funds, . . . despite all that, merchants felt that we were taking money out of circulation. They wanted a more or less wide open system where money circulated, where men gambled that income, spent it. That might sound peculiar to you."

Simons Pawn Shop, on the corner of Hester and Chrystie Streets, is mentioned in MA 1789, St. 270. The closing of Simons, and the alleged tomfoolery surrounding it, is chronicled in "10,000 Reward in Pawn Theft: Mob Packs Hester St.," *Sun,* March 18, 1913; "Angry Crowd at Looted Pawnshop: Fact That All Wires Which Might Have Sounded Alarm Were Avoided Leads Police to Believe It an 'Inside Job,'" *New-York Tribune,* March 18, 1912; and "Rush to Redeem Gems from Simons: Patrons Mostly of Poorer Class and Weep when Told Treasures Are Gone — Child Is Injured," *New York Times,* March 22, 1913.

In addition to profits lost, East Siders resented the involvement of uptowners in their business. An article in a Yiddish newspaper argued, "We don't need German Jews and their hired reformers. If the East Side needs to be cleaned, we can do the job ourselves" ("War against East Side Gangsters Begins," *Varheit,* August 12, 1913). Mayor Gaynor tried to counter this view. In an interview that he, Abe, and Newburger gave to the same paper, Gaynor said, "The East Side has always taken care of itself. With this battle against the gangs, you show once again how vibrant the East Side is and how little she needs outside instructors and lecturers" ("Vigilance League Already Founded," *Varheit,* August 5, 1913).

The Kehillah's ongoing problems with Jonah Goldstein are documented in Shoenfeld Interview, AJCOHL; Goldstein Interview, CUOHP; Goren, *New York Jews*; and MA 1757; MA 1770; and MA 1788, St. 772. It's hard to tell where Goldstein actually fit in. Was he a genuine reformer? Well intended? Or was he as subversive as Abe alleges?

    Goldstein's bid for attention as a vice crusader began back in February 1913, after he learned that his function had been usurped ("Gambling in Pool Parlors: Social Betterment Workers Agree New Ordinance Is Needed," *New York Times,* February 28, 1913). His establishment of the ESNA is chronicled in "War Begun to Wipe Out the Gangsters," *New York Times,* August 12, 1913; and "Fight on Gangsters Urged: Neighborhood Association Wants Residents to Defy Them," *Sun,* September 1, 1913.

The ultimate horse-poisoner trial, *People of the State of New York v. Max Swersky and David Kalhofer,* is archived as JJC 3226.

The formation of the Bund and shifting alliances in the Pale of Settlement — between factory owners and laborers, police and criminals — are described in Ezra Mendelsohn, *Class Struggle in the Pale: The Formative Years of the Jewish Workers' Movement in Tsarist Russia* (Cambridge: Cambridge University Press, 1970). The power of Jewish gangsters in the Pale is depicted vividly in the fiction of Isaac Babel's *Odessa Stories.* The underworld gangsters in Babel's fiction were supported by police *and* employers, so that all three groups were aligned against the workers' movement. In *Class Struggle in the Pale,* Mendelsohn describes how the police and factory owners turned to the Jewish underworld to fight off the Bund. The criminals, who regarded the workers' movement as a threat to their own underworld authority, were happy to oblige, and this led to an intra-ethnic war that peaked in Russia between 1900 and 1905, a period in which, on average, there was one labor strike per day in the Pale. During this time, the Jewish working class came to hate the underworld, and vice versa. At a 1905 wedding in Warsaw, a fight between a pimp and a member of the Bund spilled into the streets, where Jewish workers launched a three-day-long riot known as the *alphonsepogrom* — literally, the pimp massacre (see Bristow, *Prostitution and Prejudice,* 58–60; and Mendelsohn, *Class Struggle in the Pale,* 85).

An eye-opening book about the corporatization of labor violence is Edward Levinson, *I Break Strikes!* (New York: Arno, 1969).

Notes

Benjamin Fein's background and his tie-up with the garment unions are documented in *People of the State of New York v. John Doe* (1915); and *People of the State of New York v. Morris Stupnicker, Max (Morris) Sigman, Julius Wolf, Solomon Metz, John Auspitz, John Wedinger, and Max Singer* (1915). Both trial transcripts are archived at Cornell University's Kheel Center for Labor Management. An absorbing and terrifying chronicle of how UHT bosses and their thugs intimidated scabs can be found in a series of interviews conducted by the Kehillah's Bureau of Industry, archived in MA 1763.

The details surrounding Morris Sigman's recruitment of the Dope illustrate how the labor wars worked. To "take down a shop" — invade a factory and remove scabbing workers — the UHT paid the Dope half of what it believed the shop to be worth in membership dues. His first job, in early 1913, was at a cloak factory. Sigman told the Dope that he wanted the scabs there beaten with clubs or pipes, and badly enough that they couldn't return to work. After doing the job, the Dope collected $600 from Sigman at a saloon on Fourth Street. Leaving that meeting, the Dope was shot three times, probably by the hired hands of the factory owners. Five days later, he met Sigman at the same saloon and said he needed money to see the doctor. Sigman promised the Dope that he'd get plenty more money if he could settle the strike in the white-goods industry, ladies undergarments. The Dope and his crew hit three white-goods factories, in the course of which the Dope was stabbed, arrested, and sentenced to thirty days in the workhouse. But the UHT got its result: ten thousand girls now paid $3 each to join the union. Word spread among the union bosses that the Dope could settle any strike in any industry. He was put on the UHT's payroll at $25 a week, with a guarantee of $15 a day for each day he sat in jail.

Now, for once, the battle seemed evenhanded, and both sides fought ruthlessly. When a crowd of angry strikers amassed outside a raincoat factory and chased the factory's scab workers down the street, one scab ran into a nearby tailoring shop, grabbed a long-knife cutter, and "whipped it across [a striker's] throat from ear to ear" ("Striker's Throat Cut as Mob Traps Non-Union Tailor," *World*, January 22, 1913). In early February, union thugs used blackjacks and hatchets to beat out the brains of two brothers who were walking to work ("Two Brothers Beaten by Band of Strikers on Way to Work," *World*, February 5, 1913). Two weeks later, six gunmen broke into a union meeting, hurled paving stones and bricks, waited for the stampede to begin, and opened fire into the crowd ("Girls in Panic as Man Is Shot in Raid on Strikers: Strike Breakers Attack Meeting with Guns and Missiles — Riot in Hall Follows," *World*, February 21, 1913). One factory came out ahead in the battle by hiring lady scabs from the West Indies. When union thugs invaded, the Black women cried "Throw them out!" and charged them with scissors and the sticks on which muslin was rolled ("100 Girls Beat Gunmen Who Shoot Up a Factory: Scissors and Sticks Win," *World*, April 14, 1913).

By then, however, the unions had commenced bomb attacks. One bomb shook nearby homes, shattered windows, and would have blown up hundreds of sleeping girls in a factory dorm had the bomb's fuse not been severed when it sailed through a broken window ("Bomb from Auto Hits Girl Asleep with 24 Others: Second of Three Missiles Flung Aimed at Murder of 300 Strikebreakers," *World,* February 27, 1913; and "Strike Bomb Shakes the Police Building," *New York Times,* March 2, 1913). The bombings were effective, resulting in thousands of new union members, and the UHT felt itself to be on the winning side. At one point, the *Forward* even advocated peace in its pages, but discovered that the mob, once incited, was not easily brought to heel: strikers, disagreeing with the paper, stormed the Forward Building, in effect turning on their own government. "Many of the strikers were armed with bricks and other missiles, and their charge was followed by the sound of breaking glass. The strikers struggled madly in the vestibule, and threw themselves against the window of the cashier's department" ("Garment Strikers Storm the Forward: First Seeks a Retraction," *New York Times,* March 2, 1913).

Abe's initial position on the labor wars is established in an early 1913 Kehillah report—MA 1789, St. 282. He may have supported the union cause but he regarded labor thugs with the same contempt he reserved for any criminal. In thinking about how to tackle the problem of the thugs, Abe's first idea was to target their habitats. In MA 1790, St. 852, he argues for raiding a hangout located in the square blocks that the Dope controlled—around Forsyth, Broome, Eldridge, Grand, and Chrystie Streets:

> The F&E Bakery at 264 Grand St. has become the official
> hangout for Dopey Benny and his mob of blackguards, men
> who are of no earthly use, and who retard the progress of the
> youthful element, corrupting the morals by their actions,
> manners, deeds, and everything else. Confound them! The
> automobiles used for shady jobs are seen standing in front of
> the [bakery]. Very often the mob sits in the rear of an auto
> unseen to passersby but having a full view of all pedestrians.
> Pistols are also hidden in the automobiles.

The events surrounding the rough treatment of the Dope are chronicled in " 'Dopey Benny,' Boss Gunman, Is Jailed," *New York Times,* August 10, 1913; and MA 1788, St. 719. Decades later, Abe described the episode in *Crime Buster,* acknowledging that such police tactics might be objectionable in postwar America and writing, "Where were you, ACLU? Benny could have used you."

CHAPTER NINETEEN: SCARLET ROOM

The fluid boundaries Carolyn refers to are echoed in Maurer, *Big Con*. One of Maurer's many insider sources, a con man, says: "You'd be surprised at the number of good businessmen who make friends with con men, loan them bank rolls, and entertain them at home. All con men have good legitimate friends in the cities where they live. They always play square with these friends, as they consider them 'folks.'" Maurer adds: "Some [con men] enjoy friendship with celebrities, sportsmen and socially prominent persons from legitimate society who may consider it 'smart' to be seen in the company of a confidence man" (171).

Carolyn notes how Arnold relished such associations. One of his happiest moments, she recalled, was when Babe Ruth, a big gambler himself, sent Arnold a box of autographed baseballs. "He couldn't have shown more joy over this gift if he had been a small boy," Carolyn recalled. "The great Babe Ruth had shown him a special courtesy. He was a Big Shot!" On another occasion, Arnold dropped in on a "testimonial dinner" to honor a judge, and stood in the back of the banquet hall. He later described the evening to Carolyn: "The Mayor [Jimmy Walker] was just coming down from the speaker's platform to go the men's room. His eyes happened to catch mine, and he turned and came right across the hall in front of everybody there and shook hands. We had a pleasant, and rather lengthy chat before he went away. I call that pretty fine of Jimmy. A lot of them, you know, aren't like that when they are up there on top" (Rothstein, *Now I'll Tell,* 144–45).

The history of the Belmont dynasty can be found in David Black, *The King of Fifth Avenue: The Fortunes of August Belmont* (New York: Dial Press, 1981). The Belmont Jr.–Murphy–Arnold relationship is chronicled in Rothstein, *Now I'll Tell*; Katcher, *Big Bankroll*; David Pietrusza, *Rothstein: The Life, Times, and Murder of the Criminal Genius Who Fixed the 1919 World Series* (New York: Basic Books, 2003); and Kahn, *World of Swope*.

Tammany's political battles of the early 1910s are explained in Jack O'Donnell, *Bitten by the Tiger: The True Story of Impeachment, the Governor, and Tammany Hall* (Chapel Hill, NC: Chapel Hill Press, 2013). The garment unions' push for a universal closed shop can be found in Stolberg, *Tailor's Progress*; Seidman, *Needle Trades*; Levine, *Women's Garment Workers*; Budish and Soule, *New Unionism*; Greenwald, *Triangle Fire*; Stein, ed., *Out of the Sweatshop*; and Julius Henry Cohen, *Law and Order in Industry* (New York: Macmillan, 1916). The ways in which union bosses strong-armed workers into joining the union are captured in MA 1775, St. nos. 443, 613, 700, and 778.

The progressive Republicans, or Waspy reformers, protested Whitman's decision to accept Tammany's backing: "Mr. Whitman cannot, must not accept this offer. He stultifies himself by it.... Instead of defeating Tammany, he enters the race to elect Tammany. He makes himself Murphy's candidate." The headline of the piece in which this quote appears—"Whitman to Decline Murphy's Support for Mayor," *World,* August 26, 1913—was upended two days later, when Whitman accepted Tammany's backing. Whitman said the quiet part out loud: since the Wasps had not chosen him to be their mayoral candidate, he had no obligations to them ("Whitman Says Designation by Tammany Proves That Entire Voting Body Is Back of Him," *World,* August 28, 1913).

The Healy's episode is chronicled in "Police Ordered to Defy Decision; Will Out Diners," *World,* August 9, 1913; "Healy Gets Warrants Charging Oppression against the Police," *World,* August 12, 1913; "Police Hurl Women in Street for Merely Eating Supper," *World,* August 13, 1913; "District Attorney Promises Aid in Getting Warrants against Patrolmen," *World,* August 14, 1913; "Clubs in Healy's; Whitman Put Out," *New York Times,* August 14, 1913; and, finally, "Healy's Wins Fight, But Closes at 1 A.M.: Gaynor Calls Police Off, Saying Raids Are Useless as Whitman's against Them," *New York Times,* August 15, 1913. Newburger's own account of the event is archived in MA 1774.

Sigman's tactics in his so-called Court of Special Sessions, and the *Forward*'s financing of union violence, can be found in *People of the State of New York v. John Doe* (1915); *People of the State of New York v. Morris Stupnicker, Max (Morris) Sigman, Julius Wolf, Solomon Metz, John Auspitz, John Wedinger, and Max Singer* (1915); *Education of Abraham Cahan,* vol. 3; and MA 1790, St. 871, in which Abe writes: "The Jewish newspaper known as the *Vorwartz* or *Forward,* is also mixed up in this war, supporting these scoundrels Liebowitz and Kasimirsky [union bosses],... the ugliest scoundrels that ever took a hand in labor matters." Referring to union members, Abe writes, "These men were robbed, fooled, bluffed, sold out and bossed any which way by Liebowitz and Kasimirsky."

The connection between the Yiddish newspaper and the labor thugs is also underscored in the 1915 trial of a Russian-Jewish immigrant named Sam Dudek, a *shtarker* who terrorized the East Side baking industry. In that trial, a bakeshop owner testified: "I got 120 people, and not one of them stopped working—that is until Mr. Dudek and all like him [union thugs] said there was a strike. They have it in the *Forward,* that is their paper. [When the *Forward*] says there is a strike, [the union thugs] go to the groceries and break the windows" (JJC 2073A). The recollection of "shocking violence" appears in Ida Klaus Interview, AJCOHL.

CHAPTER TWENTY: DON'T TELL LIES FOR ME

Klee's face-off with the garment unions, including the bombings, is described in "Bomb Explodes under Stairs of Tailor Shop, 450 Employees Scared: Panic Is Averted by

Presence of Mind of Superintendent—Trouble Due to Strike," *World,* September 16, 1913; "Strikers Wreck a Factory: Explode Bomb under Clothing Plant in Lindhurst, N.J.," *New York Times,* September 25, 1913; "Lyndhurst Shop Is Wrecked by Bomb: Striking Tailors Blamed for Explosion in Place of Klee & Co.," *Morning Call,* September 25, 1913; and JJC nos. 1823 and 1903. Abe's argument with Mayer over what to do with respect to Klee can be found in Shoenfeld Interview, AJCOHL; and Shoenfeld, *Crime Buster.* The incident Abe refers to, in which two Klee guards clubbed a striking worker who later died from his injuries, is chronicled in "Striker's Head Is Fractured: Two Strikebreakers' Guards Suspected of the Crime," *Boston Globe,* February 24, 1913.

The seemingly fixed trial and exoneration of the Klee guards is covered in "Confesses Guilt after Acquittal: Milo, Discharged by Court, Takes Stand and Admits Assault to Clear Another," *New York Times,* May 24, 1913. Prior to the trial, one guard was acquitted on the grounds of insufficient evidence. Then, in the trial, the acquitted party testified that his codefendant could not have committed the assault, because he himself had done it.

The Kehillah's efforts to cut off the *shtarkers'* ball fundraising appears in MA 1788, St. nos. 719 and 744.

The campaign event at City Hall Park is described in "5,000 Nominate Gaynor, Who Is Near Collapse, Before City Hall Crowd: City's Chief Executive Pale and Trembling as Great Throng Cheers," *World,* September 3, 1913. Gaynor's funeral is reported in "Gaynor Buried as City Mourns: Outpouring to Honor Late Mayor Greatest of Kind in History of New York," *Sun,* September 23, 1913. The Kehillah's struggle with DA Whitman, including the German-Jewish uptowners' attempts to oust him from office, are covered in a series of letters, and other documents, such as anti-Whitman fliers, archived in MA 1771–76. The death of the bystander in the shootout was eventually the subject of a 1916 murder trial, *People of New York v. Irving Wexler* [aka Waxey Gordon], archived as JJC 2253. In this trial, we get testimony from Joe Rosenzweig, alias Joe the Greaser, who by then had been in prison for two years. Joe, we learn, was married when he took up with Tony, for whom he still, apparently, had feelings. When a lawyer asks if Joe knows "Tony Rollich, known as Tough Tony," the reference triggers Joe and he becomes reactive: "I beg your pardon?" Joe says. "You know that ain't so."

"I know what ain't so?" the lawyer asks.

"That they call her Tough Tony. She is known as Tona, not Tough Tony."

Prior to the Anti-Defamation League's 1913 campaign against portrayals of Jewish crime in popular culture, general concerns about how the depiction of violence and crime in film influenced American youth dated to at least 1907. In 1909, ten civic organizations in New York—most of them composed of Wasps and German Jews—formed the National Board of Censorship. But many in the country complained that the Gotham-based censors were too lax, too influenced by the "complicated, liberal and abnormal life" of the city (Wallace, *Greater Gotham,* 419). See also "Bloodcurdling 'Movies' in the Cheaper Resorts Show Need of Regulation: Films Depicting Scenes of Carnage, Murder, Theft and Gambling a Menace to Children Who Flock to Them," *Sun,* December 2, 1912.

The concerns of ethnic groups, specifically, related to prejudice in American entertainment. For years, minorities in America had watched the vaudeville industry reduce them to Jewish cheapskates, drunken Irishmen, knife-wielding Italians, and Black chicken thieves. Money-mad stage Hebrews, with names like Isidore Nosenstein, wore prosthetic hook noses, oversized shoes, grungy black coats, and hats pulled down over their ears as they went about defrauding insurance companies. In one popular routine, the character of Jacob Schiff sends newsboys out to Coney Island on the train each summer for a swim. At the beach, Schiff tells a newsboy named Ikey Epstein that he looks pretty dirty, to which Ikey replies, "I know it. I missed the train last year."

By 1913, when the ADL started up, Jews and other minorities had learned that if they summoned enough outrage and influence, they could eliminate derogatory portrayals (Wallace, *Greater Gotham,* 448–50). The role that representations of Jewish crime in film, theater, and print played in the creation of the ADL is evident in the League's initial announcement: "To Stop Defamation of Jews: National Society Formed to Prevent Stage Caricatures," *Intelligencer Journal,* September 18, 1913. The ADL's smut crackdown was nationwide: "Jews Here to Help Put Ban on Ridicule," *St. Louis Star and Times,* September 18, 1913.

The Inside of the White Slave Traffic is summarized in Brownlow, *Behind the Mask of Innocence,* 80–84; and the 1914 trial regarding its censorship, *People of the State of New York v. Harry C. Bohn and Samuel A. London,* is archived as JJC 2234. Later, the defendants Bohn and London were sued for libel by Solomon Hechter, proprietor of Hechter's Oriental Restaurant, at 76 Second Avenue, formerly Siegel's Café, where Big Jack Zelig drank his last seltzer in 1912. Hechter was angry because the filmmakers used an exterior shot of his restaurant to represent White Slave Headquarters. "Says Film Libeled Them: Solomon Hechter and Wife Object to White Slave View of Their Hotel," *New York Times,* December 24, 1913.

The ADL's smut crackdown, via the instrument of the Kehillah vice crusade, is chronicled in "Warrants Asked to Stop the Two 'Red Light' Plays: Planned to Close Indecent Dramas at Once as Public Nuisances," *World,* September 6, 1913; "Arrest of Actress Stops a Vice Play: Cecil Spooner Rides to Night Court in Patrol Wagon — Manager a Prisoner, Too," *World,* December 10, 1913; "Newburger Forbids Miss Spooner's Play: Sees 'The House of Bondage' and Condemns It as Unfit," *World,* December 11, 1913; "Police Confiscate White Slave Films: Raid Park Theatre and Arrest Attendants when They Persist in Showing Pictures," *New York Times,* December

21, 1913; "White Slave Films Cause Fresh Raid," *New York Times,* December 24, 1913; and "White Slave Movie Men Found Guilty: But Jury Recommends Bohn and London to Court's Mercy," *Sun,* March 6, 1914.

The alleged cop assault was tried as *People of the State of New York v. Benjamin Fein.* The trial transcript is archived at JJC 1817. Coverage of the trial appears in "Jury Names Hidden at Gunman's Trial: 'Dopey Benny' Put in Cell," *New York Times,* January 20, 1914; "Dopey Benny's Gang Driven from Court: Swaggering Gunmen Cowed by Old Attendant's Slaps and Jabs," *Sun,* January 20, 1914; "'Dopey Benny' Found Guilty; Gangsters Rage: Police at Judge's Order Escort Jurors Home after Verdict Is Given," *World,* January 21, 1914; and "5-Year Sentence for 'Dopey Benny,' Gangster's Head," *World,* January 23, 1914.

Surely many East Siders felt it necessary to kowtow to the gangsters, but some citizens stood up to them. When Jacob Kalich, a young Yiddish stage actor and art designer, felt that his theater catered too much to the underworld element, he took action. In Jacob Kalich Interview, AJCOHL, he recalled: "[Gangsters] used to buy up the first four rows and they used to sit down with those girls who were dressed, you know, *exaggerated.* And they made noise and of course decent people [stayed away]. So I made a speech to them. I said, 'Look, I know what you are. I can't stop you from going to the theater. You can come in individually, not as a group. If you come in as a group, I'll call the police and they'll take you out. And there is no such thing as the first row for you.' Somehow I made an impression on them. They kept away from the theater and that's how we got the decent class of people back."

Lily describes her last visit to Louie in Rosenberg, "Underworld Wife." The doomed couple's feeling that Becker had played them was reinforced by the publicizing of Becker's assurances: "Becker Braces Up the Four Gunmen in Death House: Has Never Lost Hope," *World,* January 10, 1913. The details surrounding Becker's appeal, his grant of a retrial, and his treatment at the hands of his former Tammany allies are covered in Logan, *Against the Evidence.* The gunmen's final hours are covered in "Electric Chair in Readiness: Father of 'Lefty Louie' Meets State Executioner," *Los Angeles Times,* April 12, 1914; and "How Four Gunmen Died Told in Full Detail; 'Dago Frank' Went First," *World,* April 13, 1914; and "East Side Hushed as 'Boys' Return, Dead: Throngs in Front of Undertaking Houses Are Difficult to Control," *Sun,* April 14, 1914.

Becker's retrial is recounted in "Rose's Story Is Unshaken under Fierce Grilling," the *Philadelphia Inquirer,* May 14, 1914; "Says She Lied at First Becker Trial to Save Lefty Louie," *Boston Globe,* May 16, 1914; "Witness against Becker: Mrs. Lillian Rosenberg's Testimony Created a Sensation," *Garrett Clipper,* June 11, 1914; "Dead Gunman's Wife Admits His Crime to Strike at Becker: Swears Rose Told 'Lefty Louie' Killing Rosenthal Was Only Way to Thwart 'Frame-Up' by Ex-Lieutenant," *New-York Tribune,* May 16, 1914; "Gunman's Wife Deals Blow to Becker," *Binghamton*

Press and Sun-Bulletin, May 16, 1914; and "'French Doll' Tells Why She Told Story That Will Send Becker to the Death Chair," *Seattle Star,* May 25, 1914.

Bald Jack Rose's own story of his life as a gambler can be found in "World Famous Criminals, Herded in One District, Gamble Away Blood Money at 'Stuss' and Steal Again to Gratify Passion for Game," *Indianapolis Star,* January 19, 1913; and "Sons of Rich and New Kings of Finance Lured to Run by Old Tricks of Underworld," *Muncie (IN) Star Press,* January 26, 1913. Later that year, Bald Jack hit the speaking circuit and got into the movie business, endeavors that are covered in "New York Gunmen in Film Picture: Rose and Vallon Act in *Wages of Sin,*" *Washington Times,* June 8, 1913; "Another Example of Amazing Popularity," *Camden (NJ) Courier-Post,* September 22, 1913; "Public Popularity Is Now Bestowed upon Queer Performers: All Roads of Crime, Misfortune and Adventure Lead to Vaudeville These Days," *Oregon Daily Journal,* November 9, 1913; "Jack Rose Bald from His Schooldays: Was Beginning of His Troubles — Playmates' Jeers Drove Him into Truant School," *Norwich Bulletin,* September 24, 1913; "Blames His Bald Head: Witness in Rosenthal Murder Case Lectures on Downfall, Speaks in Brooklyn Church," *Baltimore Sun,* September 22, 1913; "Jack Rose Is Preacher Now: 'Humanology' His Theme," *Berkshire Eagle,* December 19, 1913; "Criminals Are Made, Not Born: Jack Rose Declares in Address Here," *Boston Globe,* May 18, 1914; and "'Bald Jack' Rose Now 'Movie' Man: Rosenthal Murder Witness Talks Sociology and Dramatizes His Life," *Oakland Tribune,* July 26, 1914. Lily's rejection of Bald Jack's offer to star in one of his films appears in "Gunmen's Widows Spurn Rose Offer," *Waterloo (IA) Courier,* June 25, 1914.

CHAPTER TWENTY-ONE: THE TOUGHEST MONEY IN THE WORLD

Abe's remark, in early 1914, that this year all gang conditions will be written up with the operations of the unions, appears in MA 1790, St. 871, a multipage report that covers the garment unions the *shtarkers* they hire, the battles among *shtarkers* to get the union work, and private conversations among *shtarkers,* such as the one that took place at the opium den. More about the *shtarkers* appears in St. nos. 177, 230, 870, 999, 1009, and 1035. In another Kehillah report about "Joe Abrams alias Joe the Greaser," Abe wrote that Joe, at thirteen, came to New York from Romania with his parents: "Joe is a mack, a sneak thief, a guerilla and a strikebreaker. For assault in cutting a man with a knife he served one year on Blackwell's Island. About two years ago he was selling raffle tickets on Eldridge Street. He asked a man to buy five tickets from him. The man answered that he was out of work — that he had nothing to eat and no place to sleep. Joe simply said, 'You either buy these tickets, or I will cut your head off.' The man again remonstrated when Joe pulled out the knife and cut his face. For this Joe was never arrested." Abe's discovery that Tony had taken up with Joe appears in MA 1791, St. 1000. We'll never know if Tony's love for Joe was real, but when Joe was sentenced to ten years, one paper noted: "His sweetheart, Tona Rollick, became so hysterical that she had to be removed from the courtroom." "Ten Years for Gangster: Rosenzweig Pleads Guilty in East Side Labor Trouble Plot," *New York Times,* December 24, 1915.

The friction among Joe, Pinchey Paul, and Benny Snyder was the subject of a late-1914 trial, described in "City Shown to Be at Mercy of Gangsters: Benny Snyder Refers to Stabbing and Slugging as Mere Incidents," *Sun,* December 21, 1914; "Gangsters Tell of Many Crimes to Save Selves: Followers of 'Joe the Greaser' Will Try to Send Him to the Chair," *World,* December 22, 1914; and "Hired Gunmen End Puzzle in Many Attacks: Confessions Clear Mystery in More than 25 Murders and Assaults," *Sun,* December 22, 1914. Benny explained on the witness stand, "Me—I was always a fellow that had been knocking around. So one time, when them union men was supposed to take a shop from the bakers, they took me along, and they got a liking to me when they seen that I was good for it, that I stick."

The sting at Salmoniwitz's place appears in MA 1790, St. 871; the resulting indict-ment, *People of the State of New York v. Benjamin Fein and William Siegel,* with accompanying affidavits, is archived as NYCMA 101799. Coverage of the case, men-tioning only Costigan's role, appears in "Fein and Siegel Held: Magistrate Fixes $7,500 Bail Each on Extortion Charge," *New-York Tribune,* September 24, 1914; and "'Dopey Benny' Held on Extortion Charge: Gangster and Companion Said to Have Threatened Kosher Butchers' Agent," *World,* September 23, 1914.

Further details about the operations of the UHT bosses, such as Sigman, Liebowitz, and Kasimirsky, can be found in NYCMA nos. 105804–11, 105834–37, 105839, and 105894; as well as "Thugs Hired in East Side Strikes: Twenty-Two Others Charged with Minor Crimes—Four Arrests at Prince George," *New-York Tribune,* May 12, 1915; "Hope Now to Rid New York of Gangsters: Authorities Pierce to Vitals of System through Dopey Benny," *Sun,* May 13, 1915; "Had Fixed Rates for Gang Raids: Leader Charged $150 for Wrecking Small Shops, While 'Knockouts' Cost $200," *New York Times,* May 13, 1915; "Dopey Benny's Amazing Tale of Crimes for Hire: Women Thugs Supplied, Loaded Umbrellas Used," *World,* May 13, 1915; "Big Unions Levy $250,000 to Aid Indicted Chiefs: More Indictments Expected Soon," *New-York Tribune,* May 13, 1995.

As the union bosses went to trial, the separate trial of the *shtarker* Sam Dudek, ar-chived as JJC 2073A, shed more light on the Forsyth Bath House.

Everything anyone wanted to know about prewar bathhouses—their origins in an-tiquity; their construction and health benefits; the difference between a caldarium and a vapor room, a plunge bath and a douche — is covered in J. J. Cosgrove, *Design of the Turkish Bath* (Pittsburgh: Standard Sanitary Mfg. Co., 1913). In addition to manicures and pedicures, a typical Turkish bath might offer "an electric vibratory department where vibratory massage, faradic, galvanic and sinusoidal electric treatments are administered by electro therapeutic specialists; and electric light cabinets. There are one hundred 16-candle power incandescent electric lights in each bath cabinet, and the numerous rays from these lights are multiplied and focused on the occupant of the cabinet by mirrors and reflectors . . . thereby stimulating vital forces." (For comparison, streetlamps had 400 candlepower.)

CHAPTER TWENTY-TWO: TAILOR'S PROGRESS

The military despotism of Nicholas I is chronicled in vol. 2 of Dubnow, *History of the Jews in Russia and Poland*; and Michael Stanislawski, *Tsar Nicholas and the Jews: The Transformation of Jewish Society in Russia, 1825–1855* (Philadelphia: Jewish Publication Society of America, 1983). A vivid and gut-wrenching description of Jewish children in the Russian army appears in the memoir of Alexander Herzen. In 1835, while exiled in Kirov, Herzen encountered a group of children being herded through the country by a convoy officer. The officer told Herzen: "Oh, don't ask; it'd even break your heart. Well, I suppose my superiors know all about it; it is our duty to carry out orders and we are not responsible, but looking at it as a man, it is an ugly business." Herzen pressed the convoy officer for more info. "You see, they have collected a crowd of cursed little Jew boys of eight or nine years old. Whether they are taking them for the navy or what, I can't say. At first the orders were to drive them to Perm; then there was a change, and we are driving them to Kazan. I took [possession of] them over a hundred versts [about sixty-six miles] farther back. The officer who handed them over said, 'It's dreadful, and that's all about it; a third were left on the way.' [The officer pointed to the earth.] 'Not half will reach their destinations.'" When Herzen asked if epidemics killed off the children, the officer said, "No, not epidemics, but they just die off like flies. A Jew boy, you know, is such a frail, weakly creature, like a skinned cat; he is not used to tramping in the mud for ten hours a day and eating biscuits — then again, being among strangers, no father nor mother nor petting; well, they cough and cough until they cough themselves into their graves. And I ask you, what use is it to them? What can they do with little boys?" (Alexander Herzen, *My Past and Thoughts,* trans. Constance Garnett [New York: Vintage, 1974], 169). The quote from Ben-Ami comes from Jacob Ben-Ami Interview, AJCOHL.

In *Tales of Bialystok,* the author writes, "In those days there were people called *makhers*. For the right price, they would cause an appropriate injury. Sometimes the *makhers* would cause deafness or would pour drops in the eyes. Sometimes, they would even chop off a finger" (15).

Notes

The story of Cahan's youth in Russia, his "conversion" to socialism, his first years in New York, and his tie-up with the Bund, are covered in vols. 1 and 2 of Cahan, *Education of Abraham Cahan*; Tony Michels, *A Fire in Their Hearts: Yiddish Socialists in New York* (Cambridge, MA: Harvard University Press, 2005); Ronald Sanders, *The Downtown Jews: Portraits of an Immigrant Generation* (New York: Signet, 1976); and Stolberg, *Tailor's Progress*. Cahan's view on the murder case of the union bosses appears in vol. 5 of his autobiography (untranslated). Cahan claimed Herman Liebowitz died by accident when he tripped down stairs.

Harry Newburger's run for a senate seat, Abe's showdown with the Dope, and the job-offer-cum-death-threat from Charlie Murphy are chronicled in Shoenfeld Interview, AJCOHL; and Shoenfeld, *Crime Buster*.

The story of how Abe got the photo of Magistrate John Campbell and defense lawyer Nathan "Nattie" Tolk is told in Shoenfeld Interview, AJCOHL; and Shoenfeld, *Crime Buster*. Abe first wrote about the Tolk-Campbell grafting scheme in 1913, in MA 1790, St. 870A. Three years later, in 1916, Tolk went to trial for the very court corruption Abe described, the "bondsman's graft." *People of New York v. Nathan Tolk* is archived as JJC 2182. In the trial, the "bondman's graft" is broken down. In any graft, someone must get screwed. Here, the Tammany lawyer Tolk forced legitimate business owners to "go the bond" when a *shtarker* like the Dope was arrested. That meant that the business owner—a tailor, say—would put up the deed to his tailoring shop to cover the bond. Some business owners—such as Barth, who ran the hair parlor for prostitutes—took this "bonding business" voluntarily. But Barth was dealing with a population, prostitutes, who could always come up with the money to buy their case: they could just go out and make it. However, thugs arrested for violent crime were a trickier population to bond out, because they were unreliable. Thus Tolk often bankrupted business owners, such as one Essex Street tailor, in order to keep the Dope on the streets.

In Tolk's trial, that tailor's wife testified: "I said, 'Mr. Tolk, look what you have made of us. I have pawned everything. My baby is sick and I have not even a dollar for a doctor. Look what you have made out of my husband. Look how your wife lives. Now look how I live.' He said, 'Your husband is a tailor, and I am a lawyer.' That is what Mr. Tolk answered me." The trial is a marvel of moral relativism. On the witness stand, the defendant Tolk explained:

> And this Benjamin Fein became a client of mine. His work
> was for a labor union. If they had a strike and there were scabs
> he was supposed to go out and break a couple of scabs' necks.
> That was his business. But when a man comes to you and
> wants you to take care of his interests, well, as a lawyer it is
> your duty to do the best that you can for him. If a man comes

to me to defend him for murder, that is my business. So
Benjamin Fein came to me and gave me a good deal of work.
I gradually gained confidence and faith in Benjamin Fein. I
would not say that his moral reputation or his legal reputation was so good, but I knew he was a man of his word. I
knew that if I bailed him out or any of his friends recommended by him, I knew those men and women would be in
court at the proper time to respond.

The last utterance I found from the Dope himself appears in one of his many indictment files, archived as NYCMA 113061. It's a 1917 letter to an unnamed addressee,
apparently written from prison and unsent. "My Dear Senator," the letter begins, and
continues (with scant punctuation):

A few lines to you to ask you for a favor for a good personal
friend of mine as he is the same kind of a man like me just
got out of trouble and is all in and wants to get to work. He
is a useful man at that work for what he will tell you in
person. Hopefully you will grant me this favor and do what
you can for him as I will never forget you for same. As I know
it is in your power to do it at Haskell New Jersey Plant or
somewhere else. With best regards to you and luck and also
Mr. Ward the same regards and luck. I Remain Your True
Friend, Benie Fein

Symbols of the crusade's success are related in "Boy Police Busy Reforming East Side:
Girls Will Join Them in Spring Cleanup Next Week," *World,* March 31, 1914;
"Shopkeepers Obey Boy Police Orders: One Hundred Cigarette and Ice Cream Sellers
Responded to Their Summonses," *World,* June 1, 1914; "Juvenile Police Active: Pro-
prietors of 76 'Hangouts' on East Side Warned," *New York Times,* June 29, 1914;
"Juvenile Police Aid the Big Cops in Running the City: There are 5,000 of Them on
East Side, and They Wear Uniforms and Drill," *World,* February 26, 1915; and *Com-
mercialized Prostitution in New York City: A Comparison between 1912, 1915, 1916, and
1917* (New York: Bureau of Social Hygiene, 1917).

New developments for East Siders were everywhere evident, but at least one thing never
changed: their appetite for books. In 1914, the annual report of the New York Public
Library, whose main building was now three years old, reported that patronage and circulation numbers continued to skyrocket. "The East Side held its leadership as the district hungriest for knowledge, the Seward Park branch reporting the heaviest circulation

for the year" ("More Read Books; More Books Read: The East Side Leads," *Sun,* March 12, 1914). Mayer Shoenfeld's remarks appear in "Girl Mother Feeds Six on $1 a Week: 15-Year-Old Child Wife Arouses Sympathy for East Side Toilers," *Sun,* June 6, 1914.

Charles Becker's execution, Murphy and Arnold's reactions to it, and the media commentary that followed appear in Logan, *Against the Evidence*; and Root, *One Night in July.*

PART FOUR: INEVITABLE CHAIN

CHAPTER TWENTY-THREE: SUBVERSIVE MIGHT

The significance of Schiff "breaking into" the great Wasp redoubt of Mount Desert Isle and his relationship with Harvard's Eliot are covered in Birmingham, *Our Crowd*; and Judith S. Goldstein, *Crossing Lines: Histories of Jews and Gentiles in Three Communities* (New York: William Morrow, 1992). The trips to Maine were "formidable undertakings," Frieda recalls in *Reminiscences of a Long Life.* Part of the difficulty had to do with the number of vacation homes the Schiff-Warburgs owned between them: a five-hundred-acre estate in White Plains, an estate on the Jersey Shore, and the place in Maine. Frieda explains:

> On the last Thursday in July, the children had early supper at the old Belmont Hotel in time to board a private car, usually Mr. Harriman's of the Union Pacific Railroad. Felix and I generally followed a week later. They traveled in luxury with their grandparents, a nurse, governess, valet, maid and some 60 pieces of luggage, including several large trunks. Their car was presided over by Madison, the chef, and a helper. The family group was so large that another car was often needed to accommodate the overflow. The task of moving our horses from White Plains to New Jersey and then to Maine was equally complicated. Much packing and planning went on, the carriages were loaded with tack and equipment, the stable was in a whirl of excitement. As the horses had to be driven, ridden or led from White Plains to New York and then taken by boat to the Jersey coast, men and animals were rested for several days before and after the trip.

Schiff's handling of the loan request is chronicled in Birmingham, *Our Crowd*; and Cohen, *Jacob H. Schiff.* The Morgans' opinions on Schiff, Warburg, and Kuhn Loeb appear throughout Jean Strouse, *Morgan: American Financier* (New York: Random House, 1999). Madison Grant and his cohort get the full biographical treatment in Daniel Okrent's magisterial *The Guarded Gate: Bigotry, Eugenics, and the Law That Kept Two Generations of Jews, Italians, and Other European Immigrants Out of America* (New York: Scribner, 2019). I also turned to John Higham, *Strangers in the Land: Patterns of American Nativism, 1860–1925* (New Brunswick, NJ: Rutgers University Press, 1988); and the 2018 PBS documentary *The Eugenics Crusade*.

Abe's January 5, 1915, report to Magnes—urging a continuation of the vice crusade and touching on his racial paranoia—appears in MA 1768. Until now, Black people had showed up in four Kehillah reports and were mostly identified as "colored people." Abe used the N-word twice in relation to Black johns, and referred to Black prostitutes as "wenches." This language is certainly derogatory, but it's hard to tell if it's any more so than the words he used to describe underworld figures of his own ethnicity, who are also called N-words, whores, etc. The racist remarks appear in MA 1789–90, St. nos. 755, 934, 935, and 973.

Even as Newburger worried that *any* level of Jewish crime would be used by their "Christian neighbors" and others to restrict immigration (MA F-47), he was also becoming disenchanted with his anti-vice work. Referring to his sullied reputation, based on rumors that he had been a grafter in the NYPD, he wrote to Magnes: "It is the penalty one is bound to pay for having been identified with the kind of work I have been engaged in for the past two and a half years."

For Abe, an opportunity for another crusade arrived in 1915. That spring, a federal drug investigator—one of the many tax collectors who'd been assigned the job of regulating and taxing narcotics, per the Harrison Act—wrote to Newburger: "It has occurred to me that you, as counsel of the Kehillah, might be in a position to render effective assistance in cooperation in our work of uncovering violations of the Harrison Drug Act. A great many of these violations occur on the East Side and must surely come to your attention." Newburger connected the feds with Abe, who showed them around the city's drug dens and helped make a few busts, which he addresses in Shoenfeld Interview, AJCOHL. Later, in 1917, with one last drip of Kehillah funding, Abe wrote a 102-page drug report, archived in MA 1793.

The immigration restriction movement, twenty years in the making, scored its first victory with the literacy test: "Senate Overrides President's Veto: Immigration Bill, Containing Literacy Test, Becomes Law of the Land," *Moline (IL) Dispatch,* February 6, 1917. The racial hysteria, xenophobic zeal, and nativist crusades that ripened during the war years are chronicled in Adam Hochschild, *American Midnight: The Great War, a Violent Peace, and Democracy's Forgotten Crisis* (New York: Mariner, 2022); David H. Bennett, *The Party of Fear: The American Far Right from Nativism to the*

Militia Movement (New York: Vintage, 1995); Nancy MacLean, *Behind the Mask of Chivalry: The Making of the Second Ku Klux Klan* (Oxford: Oxford University Press, 1994); Kenneth T. Jackson, *The Ku Klux Klan in the City, 1915–1930* (Oxford: Oxford University Press, 1967); Eliot Asinof, *1919: America's Loss of Innocence* (New York: Donald I. Fine, 1990); and Dawley, *Struggles for Justice.* In *The Perils of Prosperity: 1914–1932* (Chicago: University of Chicago Press, 1958), William E. Leuchtenburg writes:

> Political fundamentalism was an attempt to deny real
> divisions in American society by imposing a patriotic cult
> and coercing a sense of oneness. Admiration for the Constitu-
> tion became a tribal rite....Constitution-worship was a kind
> of magical nativism, a form of activity in which, as the
> anthropologist Ralph Linton writes, "the society's members
> feel that by behaving as the ancestors did they will, in some
> usually undefined way, help to recreate the total situation in
> which the ancestors lived."

Later, in the political battle over the 1924 Immigration Restriction Act, a congressman from Kansas said, "On the one side is beer, bolshevism, un-assimilating settlements and perhaps many flags — on the other is constitutional government; one flag, stars and stripes."

The letters between the brothers-in-law Magnes and Marshall, written with rising hostility, are archived in MA F-28. Schiff's refusal to back Newburger for a judgeship is in MA F-70. Newburger's auto accident is reported in "Lawyer Hurt in Auto Crash: Former Police Commissioner in Hospital Suffering from Concussion," *Hackensack (NJ) Record,* June 4, 1917.

The episode of the Liberty Bond thefts is described in Katcher, *Big Bankroll,* 174–78; and "Accuse 15 More as Plotters in Bond Robberies: Surety Officials Get Amazing Tales of Disposal of Stolen Millions," *Sun,* May 3, 1920.

The cop-shooting incident played out for a year, beginning with "Gambler Shoots Three in Craps Raid: Two Policemen Wounded," *New-York Tribune,* January 20, 1919, and ending with "Grand Jury Postpones Rothstein Inquiry," *New-York Tribune,* January 10, 1920. The backlash against the accusing cop, Dominick Henry, was the subject of two trials, archived as JJC nos. 2823 and 3261.

There are many theories about Arnold's alleged fixing of the 1919 World Series. The most learned and persuasive account I've seen appears in Asinof, *Eight Men Out.* The chain of events in the fall of 1920 can be followed in: "Rothstein Quits as

King of Gamblers: Coupling His Name with Baseball Scandal Is Too Much of a Shock," *New York Herald,* October 2, 1920; "Arnold Rothstein and St. Louis Player Are Exonerated from Complicity after Testimony before Chicago Grand Jury," *El Paso Herald,* October 27, 1920; and "Comiskey Knew Players Were Crooked, Grand Jury Is Told: Arnold Rothstein Puts Blame on Attell," *Buffalo Times,* October 27, 1920.

Arnold did blame the fix on Abe Attell, the former Jewish boxing champ. Carolyn wrote that of all the men linked with Arnold's name, "My husband really knew and was fond, in his own way, of Abe Attell for all of the years I knew him. In his prime, when Attell was featherweight champion, he and Arnold were close friends. And when Attell won a fight my husband won money on bets. Later, when Attell was older and slipping, and Attell lost fights, my husband won on those. Arnold told me that he never lost when Attell was fighting" (Rothstein, *Now I'll Tell,* 207).

Thus, Attell was understandably angry about being fingered by Arnold, to whom Attell had been loyal for years. In the fall of 1920, during the grand jury proceedings in Chicago, a reporter caught up with Attell in Times Square. Attell, the reporter noted, flew into a rage and accused Arnold of scapegoating him. "You know the Rothstein millions have bought up everyone in sight," Attell said. "The buck is being passed at my expense. Rothstein is in back of the whole affair." ("Won't Let Rothstein Make Him Baseball 'Goat,' Says Attell: Will 'Shoot Scandal Lid to the Sky in a Few Days,' Says Fighter," *Brooklyn Daily Eagle,* September 29, 1920). Attell reflected on the early 1900s, when Attell was a boxing champ and Arnold was an upstart bookie. "I have done many things for Rothstein," Attell said. "When he didn't have a cent I fed him and boarded him and even suffered a busted nose defending him from a bootblack in Saratoga. We've not been on the best of terms for the last year, but I didn't think it would end up this way" (Asinof, *Eight Men Out,* 183).

Carolyn's coy remarks regarding the Series fix chime, in part, with Asinof's theory of the fix in *Eight Men Out.* She wrote: "If, however, it were charged that Arnold had been sounded out on the subject of bribing baseball players, that he had declined, but had used his inside knowledge of the bribes to make winning bets on a World Series, I would believe it. I might go further and say I *know* it, except that I was not present at any such meetings, of course" (Rothstein, *Now I'll Tell,* 170).

The battle between the German-Jewish uptowners and Henry Ford is chronicled in Neil Baldwin, *Henry Ford and the Jews: The Mass Production of Hate* (New York: Public Affairs, 2001) and Rosenstock, *Louis Marshall.* The "International Jew" series, collected in four volumes, is widely available online. The classic work on the *Protocols* is a graphic novel: Will Eisner, *The Plot: The Secret Story of the Protocols of the Elders of Zion* (New York: W. W. Norton, 2005).

What motivated Ford to launch his viral attack upon Jews was never clear. Biographers have established no single conversion moment for Henry Ford, raving anti-Semite — just a series of potential stimuli. Ford grew up in Michigan during the

1870s, where he was educated with the popular *McGuffey's* readers. These texts taught generations of American children a version of history that featured Jews as greedy shylocks and Christian boys as loyal sons who would not wake father from his nap for all the gold in the world. Decades later, he blamed the Great War on German-Jewish bankers (Baldwin, *Henry Ford and the Jews,* 59–60). Then, in 1918, when Ford ran for the US Senate and lost, he attributed the failure of that campaign to Jews and Jewish capitalism. This last incident was a likely precursor to what he did with the *Dearborn Independent*. Ford wanted a platform at a time when the advent of radio and mass communication was creating a phenomenon known as "pseudo environments," a splintering of information channels that would boost demagogues by thwarting the ability of citizens to make judgments based on facts.

By the summer of 1920, Schiff's breathing was difficult and he couldn't sleep. Auto trips helped relieve his airways, and he often went out as late as eleven at night, in the hope that sleep might come. Most nights he sat up, reading and writing letters, because he was more comfortable sitting up than in a reclining position. In May, he wrote to an acquaintance in Europe, "The conditions which this horrible war brought about everywhere, and the increased labors—not in business but for altruistic work—which have been heaped upon everyone who has a heart, have apparently been a little more for me than I could bear at my age." In August he felt as though he was improving, but in late September he died in his bed, on a Saturday evening, just as the Sabbath ended. President Wilson said, "By his death, the nation has lost one of its most useful citizens."

Three invaluable books about the court Jew and Jewish life in Germany during the period of absolutism are Selma Stern, *The Court Jew: A Contribution to the History of the Period of Absolutism in Central Europe,* trans. Ralph Weiman (Philadelphia: Jewish Publication Society of America, 1950); Lowenthal, *Jews of Germany*; and R. Po-chia Hsia and Hartmut Lehmann, eds., *In and Out of the Ghetto: Jewish-Gentile Relations in Late Medieval and Early Modern Germany* (Cambridge: Cambridge University Press, 1995). One of the original court Jews, Samuel Oppenheimer, was born in 1630, in the middle of the Thirty Years' War, and got his start by rounding up and reselling battlefield debris from that war. Later, Oppenheimer supplied munitions to the entire Austrian army during the Habsburg Empire's series of wars with France (Sachar, *History of the Jews,* 22–24). The trial of Jud Suess, including original court documents, is chronicled in Yair Mintzker, *The Many Deaths of Jew Süss: The Notorious Trial and Execution of an Eighteenth-Century Court Jew* (Princeton, NJ: Princeton University Press, 2017).

CHAPTER TWENTY-FOUR: A TOOL LIKE YOU

The meeting between Arnold and Meyer Lansky, the subsequent introduction of Charlie Lucania, and their partnership during the twenties are related in Dennis

Eisenberg, Uri Dan, and Elie Landau, *Meyer Lansky: Mogul of the Mob* (New York: Paddington Press, 1979); Martin A. Gosch and Richard Hammer, *The Last Testament of Lucky Luciano* (Boston: Little, Brown, 1974); and George Wolf with Joseph DiMona, *Frank Costello: Prime Minister of the Underworld* (New York: William Morrow, 1974). More details, and more versions of the story, can be found in Robert Lacey, *Little Man: Meyer Lansky and the Gangster Life* (Boston: Little, Brown, 1991); Stephen Fox, *Blood and Power: Organized Crime in Twentieth-Century America* (New York: William Morrow, 1989); and Richard Hammer, *Playboy's Illustrated History of Organized Crime* (Chicago: Playboy Press, 1975).

In early 1920, when Prohibition became law, it was supported by many Americans. Now drinkers could finally break that habit, and children could grow up without the horrors of alcohol. It didn't work out that way, of course. People drank just as much, except that now they went to the black market, or got prescriptions for booze from their doctors, or joined a synagogue in order to capitalize on the "sacramental wine" exception. "Rabbis" sprang up everywhere, Irish and Jew, inflating the sizes of their congregations in order to get more wine.

The generations-old temperance crusade had culminated in a legislative victory, but what about enforcement? The Republican Party, ascendant in the twenties, was in favor of Prohibition but also of small government—a knotty contradiction—which was why Congress allocated a mere $4.75 million to fund the Prohibition Bureau, and assigned enforcement duties to 1,500 agents.

Prohibition advocates knew that if the law was going to work, it had to work in New York, arguably the "wettest" city in the country. Indeed, as soon as the city's saloons and nightclubs shut down, thousands of speakeasies opened—and widespread corruption began. Agents robbed liquor from bootleggers, and arrived for work in new cars and sporting jewelry. One year into Prohibition, the federal government brainstormed new methods. What about the states? States, the feds said, should have their own anti-liquor laws, and should requisition local police to enforce them. New York passed its Mullan-Gage Enforcement Law, which made carrying a liquor flask the legal equivalent of carrying an unlicensed handgun. Now the NYPD made thousands of arrests, seized millions in liquor, and, like the federal agents, grew fat on bribes.

Arnold, too, found a new sideline in the Mullan-Gage law. The law permitted cops to use padlocks to close speakeasies. But there was a loophole: If challenged by the owner of the closed premises, the cops had to prove that the place had in fact been a speakeasy. If the cops failed to prove it, the owner could seek an injunction against further raids: a veritable license to run a speakeasy. So Arnold's lawyers would search for premises that had been raided. Then he would lease the real estate, seek an injunction against raids, and sublease the place for use as a speakeasy. Since there could be no injunction granted if there hadn't first been a raid, Arnold went a step further, arranging for the NYPD to raid places that had never even been speakeasies. Usually these schemes went off without a hitch, but occasionally an honest cop protested. One complaining cop, when asked by a judge if he knew who was behind this scheme, replied, "Everybody figured that Arnold Rothstein had something to do with it." For his incorruptibility, that cop was soon reassigned to Staten Island, the ultimate punishment (Katcher, *Big Bankroll*, 25–56).

In *The 3rd Degree: A Detailed Account of Police Brutality* (New York: Vanguard Press, 1930), a police reporter named Emanuel Lavine observed: "As a cop, it didn't pay to fight Tammany Hall. He may make an arrest and have the prisoner turned out by the desk lieutenant or captain. If he insists on going through with the arrest, he would incur the enmity of his superiors, and receive numerous 'sees' or visits from the sergeant, who would be out to get him for some dereliction of duty."

This was what happened to Honest Dan Costigan, whose 1921 retirement was another casualty of Prohibition-era corruption. Costigan claimed that the police commissioner had instructed a detective to follow him, looking for charges they could use to oust the old Incorruptible. But Costigan wasn't bitter about it. In his exit interview, he told reporters, "Tonight I'm going home, and I'm going with the knowledge that I can face my family as clean as I was thirty-two years ago, when I dropped my carpenter's tools to carry a nightstick" ("Costigan Quits; Says Enright Has Revived 'System': Dogged Four Years," *New York Times,* January 17, 1921).

Belmont's effort to banish Arnold from the racetrack is covered in Rothstein, *Now I'll Tell*; Pietrusza, *Rothstein*; Kahn, *World of Swope*; and Toney Betts, *Across the Board: Behind the Scenes of Racing Life* (New York: Citadel Press, 1958).

In *How We Advertised America* (New York: Harper & Brothers, 1920), George Creel invokes the Rosenthal Affair again when describing the use of film in the US propaganda campaign. "What we wanted to get into foreign countries were pictures that presented the wholesome life of America, giving fair ideas of our people and our institutions," Creel writes. "What we wanted to keep out of world circulation were the 'thrillers' that gave entirely false impressions of American life and morals. Film dramas portraying the exploits of 'Gyp the Blood' [Harry Horowitz, partner of "Lefty Louie" Rosenberg], or 'Jesse James,' were bound to prejudice our fight for the good opinion of neutral nations" (281).

The literature on Prohibition and the corruption it unleashed is vast and rich. I turned to Daniel Okrent, *Last Call: The Rise and Fall of Prohibition* (New York: Scribner, 2010); Lisa McGirr, *The War on Alcohol: Prohibition and the Rise of the American State* (New York: W. W. Norton, 2016); Michael A. Lerner, *Dry Manhattan: Prohibition in New York City*, (Cambridge, MA: Harvard University Press, 2007); and David E. Kyvig, ed., *Law, Alcohol, and Order: Perspectives on National Prohibition* (Westport, CT: Greenwood Press, 1985). In *Era of Excess: A Social History of the Prohibition Movement*

(Boston: Little, Brown, 1962), Andrew Sinclair suggests that the century's earlier vice laws, such as bans on prostitution and abortion, hadn't provided Wasps with a strong enough scythe. Prohibition, Sinclair writes, was the final assertion of the rural Protestant mind against the new urban polyglot culture.

The Lindy's writer quoted is Henderson Clarke, *In the Reign of Rothstein*. Carolyn wrote that Archibald Selwyn and his wife, Brownie, were lifelong friends. I discovered the $56,348.10 loan to the Selwyn brothers thanks to an ephemera collector who showed me an extraordinary document—a single piece of paper, dated January 29, 1924, on which Arnold, or a secretary, typed a list of ten loans he made in 1923 and the dates they were due for repayment. The loan to "Selwyn & Co." was the largest, while the smallest loan was $150 to "JW Arnold," which surely referred to Julius Wilford Arnstein, alias Nicky Arnstein. It would be a while before Arnold saw repayment of that debt, however. In 1924, Nicky was convicted for carrying stolen securities into Washington, DC, and spent the next three years in Leavenworth prison. Arnold's method of moving debtors into his apartments is described in Rothstein, *Now I'll Tell*.

By November 1921, the United Electric Service was taking out advertisements boasting that it supplied electricity to 28–30 West Fifty-Seventh Street, described as a seven-story building, incorporating all the latest improvements for well-lighted showrooms and lofts. The ad said: "The owners and builders are the 28–30 West 57th Street Corporation, Arnold Rothstein, President."

The insurance scheme, convenient for protecting large and risky loans, helped facilitate Arnold's narcotics investments, but there is a larger context to his foray into drugs.

Federal narcotics regulation predated the national alcohol ban, but it started more slowly and uncertainly. Back in 1914, the Harrison Act merely required anyone dispensing cocaine, opium, morphine, or heroin to register and pay tax. It didn't specifically criminalize nonmedical users, and for the next five years most courts refused to go along with efforts to prosecute users. Judges interpreted criminalization as going beyond the intent of Congress. But when a 1919 Supreme Court decision forbade nonmedical addiction maintenance, maintenance clinics across the country began shutting down. On April 8, 1919, federal drug agents raided physicians and druggists who were prescribing opium, cocaine, and heroin. That weekend, in New York, some two thousand addicts walked into Bellevue Hospital begging for a fix. Arnold went to check it out. He observed the addicts writhing in the hallway outside the emergency room and said, "Nobody here wants to be treated. They just want some drugs" (Jimmy Breslin, *A Life of Damon Runyon* [New York: Ticknor & Fields, 1991], 186–88).

Addicts—who for generations had been viewed as morally weak, more pathetic than dangerous—were now criminals. This was very different from Prohibition, wherein drinkers who defied the law were revolutionaries.

Notes

In 1922, when the last of New York's maintenance clinics closed, Congress established the Federal Narcotics Control Board, outlawing the import and export of opium and heroin. Now there was no choice for addicts but the underworld. In this new marketplace, dealers and smugglers would need funding and protection, and there was Arnold, who took out life insurance on his first drug smuggler in 1923. To Arnold, drugs were just another business, and a lot of people he knew were involved in the traffic.

In fact, that September, Charlie Lucania came to Arnold with a drug-related problem. As a youngster, Lucania had peddled heroin on the East Side and landed in juvenile prison, where he was helped out by his Jewish employer. Years later, in the summer of 1923, when Lucania took another drug rap, he found that his law-enforcement contacts vis-à-vis bootlegging were useless in the drug context. Illegal liquor was one thing, but drugs had carried a whiff of shame even before their criminalization. He did walk away from the charge, but only after trading information he had about a heroin stash. This episode, which received some publicity, created embarrassment for Lucania. "I got tabbed as the big guy in the junk business," he recalled. "I was really ashamed to face all the friends I made in society, guys I played golf with."

The story of early narcotics legislation is told in David F. Musto, *The American Disease: Origins of Narcotic Control* (New York: Oxford University Press, 1973); and Richard J. Bonnie and Charles H. Whitebread II, *The Marijuana Conviction: A History of Marijuana Prohibition in the United States* (New York: Lindesmith Center, 1999).

Arnold's testimony in the Fuller bankruptcy case is reprinted in Pietrusza, *Rothstein,* 244–59. The exchange Arnold had with Carolyn regarding his existential crisis and the loan to his father are covered in Katcher, *Big Bankroll,* 221–22.

Even before the humbling collapse of the cotton-goods industry, it seems that Abe the Just's orthodoxy had begun to soften. In business he'd always been a mediator, but now, in his early sixties, he sought compromise elsewhere too, even in religion. At the Jewish Center, a new Orthodox seminary on the Upper West Side, the board of trustees wanted to expel the center's progressive rabbi, Mordecai Kaplan. Abe the Just was one of Kaplan's only defenders. "My principle is that when a man meets you more than halfway you must not repel him," he told the traditionalists in 1921. "Dr. Kaplan has done his utmost to accede to your wishes.... He wants peace. Then why refuse to accept his proposal?" (Jeffrey S. Gurock and Jacob J. Schacter, *A Modern Heretic and a Traditional Community: Mordecai M. Kaplan, Orthodoxy, and American Judaism* [New York: Columbia University Press, 1997], 121).

The quote about his renewed relationship with Arnold comes from Abe the Just's 1929 interview with the *Forward,* "Arnold Rothstein's Father Pours His Heart Out to Forward Correspondent." He said: "Arnold was always on the go. He was always in a hurry. He could not talk to anyone for more than five minutes." Zoe Beckley, the journalist who scored an on-record interview with Arnold at his West Fifty-Seventh Street office, also noted the freneticism: "Arnold is always engaged, always busy with this endless torrent of callers who want God-knows-what of him. Pretty much everything, is our guess" ("Dubs Who Can't Rich Call Him Crooked, but It's Brains, Says Rothstein," *Brooklyn Daily Eagle,* November 27, 1928).

CHAPTER TWENTY-FIVE: IT'S A RACKET!

The Jewish presence among bootleggers is chronicled in Marni Davis, *Jews and Booze: Becoming American in the Age of Prohibition* (New York: New York University Press, 2012); Okrent, *Last Call*; Lerner, *Dry Manhattan*; and Rosenstock, *Louis Marshall,* which also describes Marshall's fight against the anti-immigration law and his criticism of Jewish students who protested university quotas. Of those students, Marshall wrote: "They are always looking for grievances and seem to relish the idea of being martyrized....A little more of the American spirit of give and take and a little less politics and chutzpah would be my prescription for the epidemic from which they are suffering" (243).

An illuminating thread in the larger saga of Prohibition concerns rumrunners, seagoing smugglers, and the evolution the US Coast Guard.

The first few years of Prohibition comprised the golden era of rum-running. There were "rum rows" all along the Atlantic seaboard, from the Chesapeake Bay up to Montauk Point. Rumrunners, boats loaded down with imported booze, anchored just outside the US territorial limit, the three-mile line, where they did around-the-clock business. The daily quotes on cases of Scotch, rum, champagne, and brandy were chalked on blackboards displayed in the rigging. The larger rumrunners featured happy hours, concerts, dancing, and call girls who got double their shoreside price.

The founder of Rum Row, Bill McCoy, was the sort of "gentleman bootlegger" who dominated the trade in the golden years. McCoy captained shiploads of liquor from the Bahamas up to Montauk. During those early years, small smugglers and rumrunners competed for business, and violence among them was limited. But that began to change in 1923, McCoy recalled: "Most of the vessels on Rum Row were now armed, for New York gangs were learning that there were softer pickings out to sea than they could find even along Broadway."

After the 1924 expansion of Prohibition policing, the rum-running business became too dicey for the gentlemen bootleggers. They retired, clearing the way for gangsters to inherit the seas.

Tales of rum-running can be found in Frederic F. Van de Water, *The Real McCoy* (Mystic, CT: Flat Hammock Press, 2007); Harold Waters, *Smugglers of Spirits: Prohibition and the Coast Guard Patrol* (New York: Hastings House, 1971); Robert Carse, *Rum Row* (New York: Rinehart, 1959); Everett S. Allen, *The Black Ships: Rumrunners of Prohibition* (Boston: Little, Brown, 1965); Alastair Moray, *The Diary of a Rum-Runner: A Crazy Ship, a Mutinous Crew, Lurking Hijackers, and the Inquisitive Federal Authorities* (Mystic, CT: Flat Hammock Press, 2007); Eric Sherbrooke Walker, *The Confessions of a Rum-Runner* (New York: Ives Washburn, 1928); and Malcolm F. Willoughby, *Rum War at Sea* (Washington, DC: U.S. Government Printing Office, 1964).

The takeover of Broadway by the "racket guys" can be found in Fred D. Pasley, *Muscling In* (New York: Ives Washburn, 1931); John O'Connor, *Broadway Racketeers* (New York: Horace Liveright, 1928); and Debby Applegate, *Madam: The Biography of Polly Adler, Icon of the Jazz Age* (New York: Doubleday, 2021). Broadway Billy Rose chronicles his experience with the racketeers in *Wine, Women and Words* (New York: Simon & Schuster, 1948).

In *It's a Racket!* (Chicago: Les Quin Books, 1929), the authors Gordon L. Hostetter and Thomas Quinn Beesley write, "Jews are unquestionably the most racketeered element in any city where rackets operate." They relate the story of Chicago's Maxie Eisen, who "yearned for a Cadillac as the final symbol that he had put the push-cart days behind him." For his Cadillac fund, Eisen demanded $25 from every fishmonger. Like Billy Rose, Hostetter and Beesley document that Lucania-like evolution: "In the early stages of the racketeer's social development he is apt to betray himself by some uncertainty as to accessories of dress and combination of colors, but this mellows into a greater assurance and a more harmonious ensemble. When his swagger has modulated into a brisk aggressiveness, and his 'hardness' developed toward a cool reserve, he has become the ideal racketeer. He resembles perfectly the successful executive of a large American business enterprise."

The racket guys were something quite different from Arnold Rothstein's old circle at Jack's, those con men and gentlemen thieves, like Ratsy Tourbillon, whom a judge once compared to the literary character Raffles. Later, in an essay about Raffles, George Orwell looked back on this period and noted the interplay between gangsterism, media violence, and political extremism. After 1918, Orwell observed, a detective story not containing a murder became a rarity: "In the old style crime story, one escaped from dull reality into an imaginary world of action. Now one's escape was into cruelty and sexual perversion . . . the means justify themselves, provided they are dirty enough. This idea colors the outlook of all sympathizers with totalitarianism in any of its forms." The gangster theme, Orwell wrote, was the triumph of the strong over the weak. "If ultimately one sides with the police against the gangsters, it is merely because they are better organized and more powerful, because, in fact, the law is a bigger racket than crime" (Orwell's essay was later used as the introduction to Hornung, *Complete Short Stories of Raffles*).

The dirty tactics of cops are documented in Lavine, *3rd Degree*. A kick in the shins, a poke in the ribs with a blackjack, a lighted cigar pushed against the neck — such moves, Lavine writes, "were usually sufficient to convince a prisoner that it is useless to protest about bruised constitutional rights." But sometimes it wasn't sufficient. Lavine describes one case he observed in which an Italian thief refused to name his partners: "Next, the detective pulled out his blackjack and struck Rumore across the Adam's apple with all his strength. I thought the lad would have an apoplectic attack. He shuddered and shook.... Blood spurted across the room. What seemed like minutes elapsed before he was able to get some air flowing.... The detective motioned to have the head pulled back again....It was repeated a third time" (80–84). Of a Bronx detective, Lavine wrote, "He would wait until his subordinates became exhausted practicing calisthenics on the prisoner. He would then back the man against the wall and question him again. If the prisoner persisted in proclaiming his innocence or refused to answer, the police official would place his fists against the rear of either jaw and press in and down until he succeeded in dislocating the jaw. In a few instances he caused the bone to snap" (49–50).

Two excellent books about gangsterism and mass culture are David E. Ruth, *Inventing the Public Enemy: The Gangster in American Culture, 1918–1934* (Chicago: University of Chicago Press, 1996); and Claire Bond Potter, *War on Crime: Bandits, G-Men, and the Politics of Mass Culture* (New Brunswick, NJ: Rutgers University Press, 1998).

The Fitzgerald essay quoted from is "My Lost City." My brief bio of Scott and Zelda, through the lens of booze and Prohibition, is gathered from two Fitzgerald essays, "Early Success" and "How to Live on $36,000 a Year"; as well as Nancy Milford, *Zelda* (New York: Harper Perennial, 1992); Matthew J. Bruccoli, *Some Sort of Epic Grandeur: The Life of F. Scott Fitzgerald* (New York: Harcourt Brace Jovanovich, 1981); Jonathan Yardley, *Ring: A Biography of Ring Lardner* (New York: Random House, 1977); and Kahn, *World of Swope.*

Out on King's Point, not everyone loved the Swope parties. The sportswriter Ring Lardner lived a hundred yards away, across a grassy expanse. Lardner found it impossible to work or even sleep, he wrote, because the Swopes conducted "an almost continuous house party." Fitzgerald wasn't as party-averse as Lardner, but both writers were big drinkers, and they admired each other's work. Often, at night, they sat outside Lardner's home, drinking bootleg liquor while watching the goings-on at the Swope mansion.

During those boozy nights, Fitzgerald and Lardner covered many subjects, including baseball. Fitzgerald was a fan, and Lardner, who began covering the sport in the 1890s, had been one of baseball's most outspoken early boosters. Then came the Black Sox Scandal, which Lardner seemed to take personally. Eddie Cicotte, the pitcher who confessed to throwing the Series, was Lardner's favorite player. After 1919, Lardner moved away from baseball as a central preoccupation, and had few good things to say about Arnold Rothstein.

But for Fitzgerald, who wanted to break new creative ground for his next novel, to move on from the autobiographical material of his early work and imagine, as he told his editor, "a sincere and yet radiant world," what he found on King's Point inspired him. So much material — if only he could capture it! But Fitzgerald had a plan for the book. He would reject, as he later recalled, "all of the ordinary material for Long Island, big crooks, adultery theme and always starting from the small focal point that impressed — my own meeting with Arnold Rothstein for instance" (Larry W. Phillips, ed., *F. Scott Fitzgerald on Writing* [New York: Scribner, 1986], 573). The "inevitable chain" passage appears on page 73 of F. Scott Fitzgerald, *The Great Gatsby* (New York: Scribner, 1925).

Abe's interwar years are addressed in Shoenfeld, *Crime Buster*. "At a Wooster Street saloon, frequented by police officials and others in the so-called know, I purchased my Penn Rye and Frontenac Ale from Canada. A truck unloaded the stuff. Uniformed cops stood guard until the finish." Of the bayonet, he wrote, "It had a fancy and thick bone end, grooved to fit the end of a gun. It was an ugly weapon." John Sumner's anti-literature crusade appears in Paul S. Boyer, *Purity in Print: Book Censorship in America* (New York: Charles Scribner's, 1968).

The 1926 drug bust and subsequent 1927 trial can be found in "$500,000 Narcotics Held in New York," *Fort Worth Star-Telegram,* July 14, 1926; "Vachuda Jurors Declare 3 Guilty," *Brooklyn Daily Eagle,* February 23, 1927; and "Record Dope Sentence: Webber Gets 14 Years for $400,000 Smuggling Operation," *Brooklyn Times Union,* February 24, 1927. In what was later known as the "ten pin" drug case, William Vachuda, a former NYPD detective, was sentenced to seven years and his partner Charles Webber got fourteen years. While awaiting trial, they were held on $15,000 bail each, the bond being provided by the Detroit Fidelity and Surety Company, with Arnold's name written as guarantor across the back of the bond. The first federal drug agent in New York, Max Roder, often said that the biggest name he had on his list of dealers was Arnold Rothstein. "Every time you mentioned his name in the office," Roder said, "five people on his payroll went to the phone to call him up" (Breslin, *Life of Damon Runyon,* 188). The quote from the heroin user appears in David Courtwright, Herman Joseph, and Don Des Jarlais, *Addicts Who Survived: An Oral History of Narcotic Use in America, 1923–1965* (Knoxville: University of Tennessee Press, 1989).

After the Vachuda-Webber trial, Arnold's life became more and more precarious. A few months later, on June 1, 1927, a *New York Times* headline read: "Silent on Kidnapping: Arnold Rothstein Reported Attacked Here by Chicago Gangsters." He declined to discuss reports "that four men tried to force Rothstein into a taxicab as he was leaving his office. Rothstein broke away and ran back into the building. It was said that since the kidnapping attempt Rothstein had surrounded himself with guards. However, he left his offices yesterday unguarded."

It's interesting to consider that while all of this was going on — Arnold's drug associates getting record prison sentences, death threats coming his way — his father was being sanctified. In honor of Abe the Just's seventieth birthday, Beth Israel Hospital, where he had been vice president since 1904, announced that November 7, 1927, would be a holiday. In honor of his philanthropy, visitors were admitted to visit family at the hospital outside of regular visiting days, and special meals were prepared for doctors, patients, and nurses ("Hospital Honors A. E. Rothstein," *Standard Union,* November 10, 1927). A few months later, in March 1928, Abe the Just attended a speaking event about "fostering goodwill and better understanding between Jew and Gentile," attended by fellow Jewish luminaries — judges and rabbis, bankers and givers ("Noted Jewish Publisher to Speak in City," *Bridgewater (NJ) Courier-News,* March 26, 1928). These were the people, Abe the Just later said, who approached him in the street following Arnold's death and shook their heads pitifully, telling him that he was a fine person, and that it was too bad he'd been "punished" with a son like Arnold. "They want to comfort me," Abe the Just said. "I don't want such comforting. Why do they stick their noses into my soul?" ("Arnold Rothstein's Father Pours His Heart Out to Forward Correspondent," *Forward,* April 3, 1929.)

Meanwhile, Arnold was appearing in *New York Daily News* coverage as "Arnold Rothstein, gambler," alongside the likes of "convicted bucket shop operators." Still in court for the Fuller bankruptcy, Arnold now identified as an insurance broker, though he admitted that he had once been a gambler. Of gambling, he told the court, it was "no gold mine." He discussed the ethics of his former profession. He said he never bet on a fighter who was his friend, never cashed checks for patrons, and never kept books. Arnold's longtime Black butler, Thomas Farley, was now testifying on Arnold's behalf in the Fuller proceedings, the papers reporting: "Thomas A. Farley, colored, Rothstein's confidential man, also swore the gambler had been merely a go-between for Fuller and the bookies" ("Rothstein Case to Wasservogel," *New York Daily News,* March 8, 1928; "Suit for $366,768 Arouses Rothstein: Fuller-McGee Gambling Debt Claim Hotly Denied," *New York Daily News,* June 22, 1928; "Rothstein Betting Agent for Fuller, Witnesses Swear: Tell of Payments Made on Behalf of Bankrupt by Well-Known Gambler," *Brooklyn Daily Eagle,* June 22, 1928; and "Pity Poor Gambler! Rothstein Tells Court It's 'No Gold Mine'! But He Gave Brokers Aid of Thousands," *New York Daily News,* June 23, 1928).

CHAPTER TWENTY-SIX: DON'T WRITE GOOD THINGS ABOUT ME

Carolyn writes about her scare at the brownstone, and other paranoia-inducing events in 1927 and 1928, in Rothstein, *Now I'll Tell.* Lucania speaks of his new political approach in Gosch and Hammer, *Last Testament of Lucky Luciano.*

There could have been any number of "public enemies" living in Arnold's hotel and apartments, but Carolyn cites one, an Italian gangster named Ciro Terranova, known as the Artichoke King because he racketed that corner of the produce business. "In its galaxy of leaders the racket boasted no more singular figure than Ciro Terranova, who had exploited the meek and lowly artichoke, lifting it from humble membership in the vegetable family to the rank of beer and booze as a gun-controlled commodity," writes Pasley in *Muscling In,* 138–43. Ciro was a classic Mustache Pete—having lost both his father and stepfather to vendettas—but Arnold didn't mind him, and even Lucania, who tended to hate all Mustache Petes, later allied himself with Ciro in the Italian mafia wars of the late twenties and early thirties.

The list of foodstuffs upon which tribute was levied included flour, milk, syrup, fish, grapes, and spinach.

John "Jack" Rothstein's name change to Rothstone, and his marriage to Fay Lewisohn, made headlines: "Rothstein's Brother Married to Heiress: Society Due for Surprise on Mystery Mate," *New York Daily News,* February 6, 1928; as did their split: "Divorces J. P. Rothstone: Former Fay Lewisohn Receives a Divorce Decree at Reno," *New York Times,* October 12, 1934. So did Jack's second marriage: "Levy Daughter and Rothstein Brother Elope," *New York Daily News,* March 14, 1936; and their split: "Jack Rothstone Sued for Divorce: Wife Charges Spouse Gambled Her Money," *Miami News,* February 7, 1946. The second wife, like the first, came from status and money. Bernice Levy's father was the Manhattan borough president. Bernice married Jack when she was twenty-one and he was forty-one. In the suit for divorce, she claimed that she borrowed $43,500 from her mother so that Jack could purchase a seat on the New York Stock Exchange. When his application to the NYSE was rejected, he never returned the money. She alleged that she then obtained more money from her parents for Jack to open a jewelry store that went bust. In 1943, the couple moved to Miami for Jack's health, but his gambling and alcohol addictions worsened. When a court granted their divorce, papers referred to Jack as owner of a Miami Beach nightclub called Club 22 ("Night Club Owner's Wife Gets Divorce," *Miami Herald,* August 17, 1946). Bernice was awarded custody of their eight-year-old son.

I imagine Jack Rothstein/Rothstone as having been a complicated figure, maybe a mix of his brother and father. On one hand, Carolyn wrote that Arnold was as fond of Jack "as any other human being," which suggests that Jack evinced some magnanimous or generous spirit, or that he was loyal or enterprising in ways that appealed to Arnold. On the other hand, Carolyn wrote that Arnold did Jack "many services." If so, it may've been the case that Jack, despite his virtues, often needed help. On one spring evening in 1920, Jack was driving through Midtown Manhattan when he struck two pedestrians, a woman and her husband. The woman was uninjured, but her husband had a broken hip. Jack placed the couple in his auto and headed for the hospital. But ten blocks later, he hit a *third* party, a young man who suffered facial lacerations. Jack proceeded to drive all three victims to the hospital, where he was promptly arrested.

According to one report, "He was released when Arnold Rothstein appeared before Magistrate Francis X. McQuade in the Night Court and gave a $1,000 bill as bail" ("Two Hurt in Auto; Runs Down Another: Jack Rothstein, Brother of Arnold, Finally Gets His Victims to the Hospital," *New-York Tribune*, May 24, 1920).

Inez Norton wrote about her whirlwind year with Arnold in an eight-part newspaper series published in late 1929: "Secrets of Arnold Rothstein: Intimate Revelations of the Private Affairs of New York 'Master Mind,' Picturing Him in Phases Never Yet Disclosed, Shedding Light on Many Mysterious Workings of Gangsters, Gamblers, Stars, Millionaires, and Politicians." Ahead of publication, the *New York Evening Journal* ran teasers: "At night, in the silken intimacy of the apartment he gave her, Arnold Rothstein dropped his cold eyed gambler's mask and became the *lover* of beautiful Inez Norton."

Arnold's drug activities in 1928 and his pursuit by undercover drug agents are chronicled in Pietrusza, *Rothstein*, 317–29.

Lansky's quote about Arnold's gambling addiction appears in Eisenberg, Dan, and Landau, *Meyer Lansky*, 105. Incidentally, Arnold's losses in the poker game at the Park Central Hotel ($360,000) were close to what the creditors wanted from him in the Fuller bankruptcy ($366,768).

The housing development in Maspeth, the so-called Phantom Village, appears in Rothstein, *Now I'll Tell*; "Rothstein 'Phantom Village' Being Razed: Wreckers Attack 143 Dwellings Built by Slain Gambler at Juniper Valley—Charge Buildings Flimsy," *Brooklyn Daily Eagle*, March 21, 1930; and "A 71-Acre Park for Middle Village," *Brooklyn Daily Eagle*, October 9, 1931 ("The plot isn't 'tainted land' just because Rothstein owned it"). Three years later, the Rothstein estate still owned the land, and Park Commissioner Robert Moses was trying to buy it ("Study Rothstein Phantom Village for Park Site," *New York Daily News*, September 28, 1934). The sale of the land to the city was authorized in 1935, and three years later: "Big Recreation Field to Cover Rothstein Site: Children to Play on Site of Gambler's Dream," *Brooklyn Daily Eagle*, June 12, 1938.

The fifty-six thousand scraps of paper found in Arnold's safe disappeared, but somehow many of them made their way into Craig Thompson and Allen Raymond's *Gang Rule in New York: The Story of a Lawless Era* (New York: Dial Press, 1940), 59–79. They concerned litigations and loans, mortgages and insurance, the fencing of stolen jewelry and letters of introduction, and recommendations for lawyers and private detectives.

Kerrigan died two weeks after he was part of a law-enforcement team that seized the contents of Arnold's safe ("Agent Kerrigan, Hurt in Drug Raid, Dies in Hospital," *Brooklyn Daily Eagle*, December 27, 1928; and "Kerrigan, Prominent Narcotics Agent,

Dies," *Asbury Park Press,* December 28, 1928). Still, the reach of Arnold's drug empire and his corruption of federal drug cops were mainstays of headlines for the next two years: "Grand Jury Raps Narcotic Bureau: Says Gotham Agent Committed 'Indiscretions,' Son and Son-in-Law of Nutt [deputy commissioner of prohibition in charge of narcotics] Found to Have Served Rothstein," *Chattanooga Daily Times,* February 20, 1930; "'Dope' Unit Is In for Shake-Up: Ax Is About to Descend upon High Officials," *Cincinnati Enquirer,* February 23, 1930; and "New U.S. Dope Bureau Starts," *San Francisco Examiner,* July 2, 1930. An incisive analysis of the Wickersham Commission's voluminous reports can be found in the excellent McGirr, *War on Alcohol,* 222–29.

Arnold's death made many New York officials want to hide, but it also brought some out of the woodwork, such as the former district attorney and ex-governor, Charles Whitman, who hadn't drawn a sober breath in years. In 1929, while campaigning on behalf of a DA candidate, Whitman bashed the present DA for his "half-hearted method of prosecution" in the Rothstein murder. "Whatever the reason," Whitman told crowds, "this is neglect the public should take thought of in this election" ("Whitman Aids Coudert," *New York Times,* October 18, 1929).

Exactly when Lucania became Charlie Lucky, or Lucky Lucania, and later Lucky Luciano, is a matter of dispute. Some have said he acquired the nickname Lucky at age thirty-three, after he was found unconscious by the side of a Staten Island road, having survived a grisly assault at the hands of Salvatore Maranzano, one of the covetous Mustache Petes who for years had been trying to muscle in on the younger gangster's empire. But contemporaneous news coverage of that assault indicates that Lucania had already been known as Lucky ("Ride Victim Who Escaped Locked Up to Save Life," *New York Daily News,* October 18, 1929). The elderly drug addict interviewed for *Addicts Who Survived* referred to having bought drugs from "Charlie Lucky," which suggests he might have acquired the name as early as his teenage years, in the 1910s, when he was an East Side street dealer.

Of the allegations that Italians ruined the drug trade, post–Arnold Rothstein, Lucky didn't comment directly, but he did say: "So what if I used to muscle some guy because he didn't pay up? What does the stockbroker do when his customers can't meet an overcall? He just sells the guy out, and then the poor bastard goes up to the top of some buildin' and jumps off" (Gosch and Hammer, *Last Testament of Lucky Luciano,* 78).

EPILOGUE

Abe's archives at the American Jewish Historical Society (ASJH) contain reports from the long years he spent as an investigator for the AJC, but I found them to be too impenetrable and diffuse to make much sense of: the reports cover mid-century geopolitics and the personalities of obscure diplomats; the League of Arab Nations and the United Nations; Black-Jewish relations; Communism and anti-Semitism, etc. His investigators seem to have been working undercover among such organizations as the American Nazi Party, the Christian Educational Association, the John Birch Society, and the National Renaissance Party. The fascist landscape that prompted Abe's hiring is described in John Roy Carlson, *Under Cover: My Four Years in the Nazi Underworld of America* (New York: E. P. Dutton, 1943); Steven J. Ross, *Hitler in Los Angeles: How Jews Foiled Nazi Plots against Hollywood and America* (New York: Bloomsbury, 2017); and Donald Warren, *Radio Priest: Charles Coughlin, the Father of Hate Radio* (New York: Free Press, 1996).

In the late 1890s, Benjamin Klee tried his new idea, offering custom suits at readymade prices. In 1899, Klee & Co. ran a half-page job ad in *Clothiers' and Haberdashers' Weekly,* aimed at traveling salesmen who could pitch the concept to men's clothing stores around the country: "If you are the right kind of a man, here is your opportunity! We want live, ambitious agents, to whom we can offer a splendid line of samples for custom tailoring orders. Suits and overcoats from $9.50 up. Trousers from $2.50 up."

The venture paid off, and Klee grew by bounds. In 1906, an exultant full-page ad in *Men's Wear,* headlined THE MARCH OF PROGRESS, boasted:

> "Once upon a time" — as our mothers used to say — we
> launched our barque upon the commercial sea, with this flag
> nailed to our mast: "Klee & Company, Who Tailor Best in
> New York." Despite storms and buffetings our flag flew high,
> and passing vessels dipped their colors in respectful salute.
> From a mere barque the ship has grown to be an ocean
> greyhound, but the flag that first flew, still streams proudly in
> the breeze. On January 1st, we will drop anchor into far more
> commodious quarters, corner of Lafayette and Fourth Streets,
> where 60,000 square feet of floor space, equipped with every
> latter-day appliance and convenience known to the craft of
> tailoring, will be at our command — and yours.

Five years later, in late 1911, six months after the Triangle fire, Benjamin Klee died, likely of a heart attack. "Mr. Klee was fifty-two years of age and was one of the most popular and highly respected men in the clothing trade," wrote *Clothier and Furnisher.* "He was a straightforward, forceful character; aggressive when he felt that he was right, bold in maintaining a position once taken, resourceful and untiring. He had a warm heart, quickly responsive to the needs of those less fortunate than himself."

Benjamin's successor was his twenty-six-year-old son, Walter, my granduncle. Raised in luxury on the Upper West Side, Walter was perhaps ill-equipped to captain the company. A year after Benjamin's death, when the labor wars began to turn violent, with the unions deploying bombing gangs and the Dope's *shtarker* army, Walter tried to hold his ground, to stick by his father's commitment to running an "open shop," rather than agree to turn hiring decisions over to the union. Walter hired a detective agency to shuttle his employees from the Astor Place subway station to the factory across the street. This led to an affray with striking tailors, and the death of one tailor named Israel Frank in early 1913 — at the same time Abe and Newburger were moving the vice crusade into the NYPD ("Striker's Head Is Fractured: Picket for New York Tailors Is Dying, Two Strike-Breaker's Guards Suspected of the Crime," *Boston Globe,* February 24, 1913). That death haunted Walter, and he subsequently disavowed detective agencies, a move that apparently caught the attention of Mayer Shoenfeld, who'd always pushed for peaceful labor strikes. But when Mayer asked Abe to have the police guard the Klee factory, Abe refused, and the company was blown out of existence.

After the bombers were arrested, following the second Klee bombing at the pop-up factory in New Jersey, the Boy Bomb King and his associates confessed to dozens of other bombings. They related what newspapers called "the most astounding narrative of wholesale crime ever told on the witness stand in New York...a story not equaled even in the 'blood and thunder' yarns of the penny novelettes" ("Bomb Thrower's Amazing Story: Had No More Regard for Human Beings Than for Annoying Insects, He Says," *Burlington Daily News,* January 28, 1914; JJC nos. 1823 and 1903). During the trials, in early 1914, Klee was liquidated, roughly fifty years after Jacob Klee and his brother founded the company in Pittsburgh. Walter went to Wall Street, lost his shirt in the Depression, and took his life by poisoning, leaving behind a wife and their two adopted children ("Walter S. Klee a Suicide, Business Worry Blamed," *New York Daily News,* May 12, 1932).

My article about the gang of rabbis, "Undercover in the Orthodox Underworld," November 4, 2019, appeared in *Medium,* the online magazine.

As I read the trials archived at John Jay, I noted how the era's tightening of laws affected not only the underworld but legitimate business too. New antitrust laws, for instance, resulted in thirteen members of the East Side's "Chicken Trust" going to prison for three months for conspiring to fix the price of kosher poultry. In another case, a ship captain was on trial for the atrocious mistreatment of the sixty-five turtles he was hired to bring up from Cuba. Deckhands, incredibly, had secured the turtles in the ship's hold by cutting holes in their flippers, running a cable through the holes, and lining the turtles up on their backs. Three days later, when the ship arrived in the East River, officers from the American Society for the Prevention of Cruelty to Animals came aboard to inspect the cargo, and screamed bloody murder. But the judge struggled with the idea of prosecuting the ship captain, since, prior to the new animal cruelty laws, men had been at liberty to do as they pleased with their property. The prosecutor had to thread the needle: "The purpose of this prosecution is not to humiliate or punish the defendant," he told the jury. "He is a man, I assume, of the highest character. But it is started for the purpose of stopping an inhuman and cruel practice."

Moral quandaries were everywhere. One judge puzzled over the implications of a new policing tactic—what would later be called "reverse stings"—in which cops fished for arrests by posing as criminal entrepreneurs, such as sex traffickers and drug dealers. Were our police becoming criminals, the judge asked, in order to catch people who may or may not be inclined to criminality?

Another judge was confused by the sentencing guidelines for the crime of "attempted conspiracy." He quipped: "It was said long ago that of the making of books there is no end. I think the distinguished author of that saying, were he alive today, would strike the word 'book' and insert the word 'law'—of the making of laws there is no end. It sometimes seems almost to be an actuating principle that whatever is, is wrong, and therefore we must change the law. Reformers have changed our law until now it is in such condition that even lawyers and judges oftentimes do not understand it, and are nonplussed at the questions that arise."

During the summer of 1913, when Abe was pushing the law to its limit and telling the Incorruptibles to arrest every panhandler, the police commissioner called him to NYPD headquarters, pointed to a stack of summonses that had been filed against Abe for police oppression, and threatened to take his badge away: "I don't give a Knox hat who put you here. You're not a policeman. You're a secretary, a civilian employee, and you're breaking the law. If you raid without a warrant again I will dismiss you!"

The next day—as Abe recalled in *Crime Buster* and Shoenfeld Interview, AJCOHL—he hopped a train to the North Shore of Long Island, where the Gaynor family spent weekends at their farm, and found Mayor Gaynor in the fields tending lettuce. "The commissioner wants to shut us down because there are summonses against us," Abe complained.

Gaynor, days away from death, righted himself with a grunt. His raspy voice was barely audible when he said, "Well, are you getting warrants or not?"

"I raid only on good information," Abe said. "The only way to clean properly is to allow police to use such force as they deem necessary."

Gaynor shook his head. "The law presumes that if no evidence can be got against a place, or a person, then they are harmless," he said. "This country has more to fear from the encroachment of arbitrary power than from all the vices combined." He believed in the Fourth Amendment's bar against unreasonable searches and seizures, the guarantee of privacy that would be gutted in order to accommodate the policing exigencies of vice prohibition. In the end, Abe got his way, but Gaynor's last words, a kind of prophecy, lived on in his head.

INDEX

ABOUT THE AUTHOR

Dan Slater is the author of *Wolf Boys,* which was a Chicago Public Library best book of the year, and *Love in the Time of Algorithms.* A graduate of Colgate University, New York Film Academy, and Brooklyn Law School, he has written for more than a dozen publications, including the *Wall Street Journal,* the *Washington Post,* the *New York Times,* the *Boston Globe, The Atlantic, The New Yorker* online, *GQ,* and *Texas Monthly.* Raised in Minnesota, Slater lives in New England with his wife and their two sons.